DEVELOPMENT POLICY — THEORY AND PRACTICE

Studies based on the work of the Development Advisory Service, and written under the auspices of the Center for International Affairs, Harvard University

DEVELOPMENT POLICY— THEORY AND PRACTICE

EDITED BY GUSTAV F. PAPANEK

Harvard University Press • Cambridge, Massachusetts

1968

To

Edward S. Mason

Respected Revolutionary

More often than advocates of rapid change would like to think, the most effective innovator is one respected by the established order. If his intellect, character, and style are respected, he may be able to introduce drastic changes that would otherwise be long delayed. To those who know him, Edward S. Mason is such a revolutionary.

In 1953 few faculty members could have convinced Harvard University to undertake a project calling for the university to provide a group of advisors to a foreign government. Why should the university, whose traditional functions are teaching and research, undertake any responsibility toward a government — and a foreign one at that? If it did, why begin with the government of Pakistan, whose viability, competence, and receptivity to foreign advice were regarded in some quarters as at best uncertain? Why furnish advice for economic "planning," a word that was then distasteful in many influential quarters? Under ordinary sponsorship any of these issues might have been enough to abort the enterprise. But when the innovation was proposed by Edward S. Mason, it was accepted.

The establishment of a Development Advisory Service at Harvard some ten years later was a step with even less precedent. The questions that first needed resolution were legion, ranging from the uncertainty of international politics to the difficulty of fixing salary scales. Without Edward S. Mason's sponsorship there would have been no Development Advisory Service.

Those who have worked with Ed Mason know why his opinions are accepted, even by notoriously unrevolutionary institutions, and why he is consulted by governments with differing ideologies as well as by universities, banks, and foundations. Although many economists share his high professional standards, few possess his unerring judgment on the politically possible or the persons who can make it possible. Few people continue to be so open as he to new ideas, regardless of the eminence or age they have attained. And even fewer are the intellectual fathers who encourage their extensive progeny to evolve naturally, risking unforeseen and perhaps not entirely welcome results. Those who combine all these attributes are the scarcest breed of all.

This volume, which stems from one organization that is his creation, is a small way of expressing its members' appreciation, respect, and affection for Edward S. Mason.

Preface

The essays in this book cover a variety of economic subjects but have a common genesis — they are based on the experience of advisors sent to less developed countries by the Development Advisory Service (DAS) of Harvard University. A major objective of the DAS is to forge generalizations about the growth process by participating in the work of government agencies concerned with economic policies and plans.

To achieve its objectives, the DAS, acting only at the invitation of foreign governments and other institutions, organizes international teams composed mostly of economists to provide advice on, and engage in analysis of, problems of economic development. Although the teams are normally attached to planning agencies, and much of what they do is commonly regarded as planning, the service neither espouses a particular planning methodology nor is otherwise intoxicated with the term. It prefers to think of planning as a process that begins with analysis of the long-range or structural problems of an economy and ends with the implementation of specific projects, programs, and policies. It is prepared to participate in any stage of this process to which an economist can make a contribution based on his professional skills. The normal result of this orientation is that the service's advisors engage in what might be described as "policy analysis."

Advisors associated with the DAS were asked to prepare papers dealing with planning, program, or policy issues of concern in their work but relevant beyond the country of their service. The unifying theme of the papers was to be the actual application of economic theory and analytical techniques to important government policy issues, showing the lessons learned as a result of that application.

Twenty-three DAS advisors or former advisors submitted papers; seventeen of their papers were selected for discussion at a conference. Included among the participants at the conference were not only the authors but also commentators from the Harvard faculty and experts from the countries under discussion. The presence of economists who were outsiders to the DAS but familiar with the countries involved proved particularly valuable. The participants included the Honorable Cyril Bright, Office of National Planning, Liberia; John Delaplaine, Inter-American Development Bank; David Felix, Washington University; Francisco Garcia Olano, Catholic University, Argentina; Alvaro Lopez Toro, Princeton University and Junta Monetaria, Colombia; Geoffrey Maynard, University of Reading; John Sheahan, Williams College; Willy van Rijckeghem, University of Ghent; R. S. Weckstein, Brandeis University; and Stanislaw Wellisz, Columbia University. The following participants came from Harvard University: Richard M. Bird, Hollis B. Chenery, Alfred H. Conrad, Harold B. Dunkerley, Walter P. Falcon, Richard V. Gilbert, Lester E. Gordon, William C. Hollinger, Richard D. Mallon, Robert Pogson, Wouter Tims, Raymond Vernon, and myself.

DAS advisory groups, and therefore the particular advisors whose experience provided the conference raw material, are financed by the Ford Foundation, the World Bank (IBRD), the United Nations, and the governments concerned. One Argentine project was entirely financed by the Argentine government, drawing on an Inter-American Development Bank loan, while other governments generally met local costs, sometimes by drawing on counterpart funds accumulated under the U.S. aid program. A grant from the Ford Foundation to support the establishment of the DAS provided the financing necessary for the travel of some participants to the conference. The facilities of the Villa Serbelloni, made available by the Rockerfeller Foundation, helped to create a calm and scholarly atmosphere, rather different from the supercharged environment in which most of the essays were conceived.

The number and quality of papers submitted for the conference exceeded expectations. Ten outstanding contributions, revised to benefit from the discussion, appear here. The procedure proved such an excellent means for recording the experience gained by the advisors that it was decided to repeat such publications at irregular intervals in a *Development Policy* series, of which this is the first volume. Succeeding volumes will appear often enough to make the experience of DAS advisors more generally available, not so often that the quality of papers suffers.

GUSTAV F. PAPANEK

Cambridge, Massachusetts
December 1967

Contents

Tables

Figures

Part I

PLANNING, MACRO-MODELS,
AND DEVELOPMENT STRATEGY

1

A Growth Model and Its Application — Pakistan

A fruit knife is an excellent instrument for peeling a pear. He who uses it in order to attack a steak has only himself to blame for unsatisfactory results.
— *Joseph Schumpeter*

The preparation of a Five Year Plan is a time-consuming process, which imposes a heavy burden on a small number of planners. In Pakistan it took two and a half years to construct the Third Five Year Plan (1965–70). Although there were ups and downs in the level of activity during this period, roughly half the staff of the Planning Commission and the provincial Planning and Development Departments was almost continuously involved in the process. At the four or five culminating stages, where major policy decisions had to be prepared and taken, substantial portions of the staff of other government agencies were also involved.

The nature of the process makes it rather difficult to find out at any one moment where such a plan stands. The composition is continuously changing, because of new information that compels the planners to revise earlier decisions or because of pressures by strong executing agencies. The prospects for raising resources, both domestic and external, are fluid most of the time; and the decision to include or exclude a relatively large project may have profound effects on the requirements or possibilities in other parts of the economy. Even in the Planning Commission, where most of the lines converge, the picture may at times be very diffuse or even confused.

The preparation of a development plan is necessarily decentralized if the objective is to benefit from specialized and expert knowledge available from the executing agencies entrusted with specific sectoral responsibilities. Although this decentralized approach implies a need for coordination, it would be unrealistic to insist on full and continuous coordination between the efforts at the "lower" (project) level and the activities of the macro-planners. It suffices to create "coordinating points" in the process when the results of decentralized activity are brought together and merged into a reasonably coherent and balanced plan-frame. In the case of Pakistan's Third Five Year Plan, four of these points can be distinguished, about half a year apart, culminating in the formulation of the final document.

THE PROCESS OF PLAN FORMULATION

In the early stages of plan preparation in Pakistan, when the first set of targets was formulated in the Planning Commission, there was only limited use for econometric techniques or models. It was much more important at that point to obtain a clear picture of actual progress in the Pakistan economy. Were the targets of the Second Plan within reach? How was the sectoral balance maintained? What was happening with regard to the utilization of external assistance? These and many other questions had to be answered before projections for the next five years could be attempted.

Only in the next phase did it become important to have a comprehensive description of the economy and of the interrelations between macro-variables and sectoral activities. More detailed information about past progress became available, and tentative sectoral programs started to flow back to the Planning Commission. One major problem then encountered was the reconciliation of the resources and balance-of-payments gaps. Different assumptions about the future rate of growth, the marginal rate of savings, and investment requirements as related to growth rates of the economy would give alternative estimates of external resource requirements. A balance-of-payments deficit on current account could also be derived so as to compare export targets to import requirements, which of course had to equal the resources gap.

Although it was possible to solve this and a number of other

problems by trial and error techniques — selecting values for some
of the variables and then calculating the values of the others in
each alternative — such techniques became more and more cumbersome as the number of variables on which information was required
rapidly increased and as the number of interrelations to be taken
into account multiplied even faster. It also became clear that increasing difficulties were being met in coordinating the work on the
Third Plan within the Planning Commission itself. The International Economics Section would make certain changes in its balance-
of-payments projections; the estimates of domestic resources would
be revised in the Fiscal and Monetary Section; and at the same
time, some of the sectoral growth targets and investment requirements would be altered in discussions with the Provincial Governments. As a result, the plan would suddenly become distressingly
inconsistent. Some means for keeping track of these changes and
their consequences was a necessity, and therefore the Perspective
Planning Section developed a set of interrelated tables in which
the consequences of changes at any place in the plan could be traced
throughout. With the exception of a small set of equations, relating
the balance of payments to the domestic resources, this group of
tables in fact represented the recursive solution of a macro-economic model. At the midpoint of plan preparation this approach
made it possible to have a continuous record of all important
changes made in different parts of the plan and of their consequences elsewhere. By providing a full picture at regular intervals
for the different sections of the Planning Commission, the necessary coordination in the preparation of the plan could be achieved
quite well.

   Many of the planners nevertheless continued to feel that this
approach was like tackling steak with a fruit knife. The absence
of sectoral detail was disquieting, especially with regard to imports
and the composition of investment. Considerable uncertainty existed regarding the required and feasible levels of import substitution — a matter almost completely untouched in the macro-ap-
proach. Finally, the consequences of higher rates of growth in the
agricultural sector became one of the most important unanswered
questions.

   In addition to the need for some means of tracing the consequence of changes in one part of the plan, it was also necessary,

especially at the later stages of plan preparation, to find some way of projecting the consequences of alternative policies. For instance, should the planners strive to raise the rate of growth in agriculture in order to affect the balance of payments, given a set of assumed values of other variables? The most efficient way to chart out a full set of alternatives quickly and in sufficient detail was the use of an econometric model.

THE FUNCTION OF A GROWTH MODEL

There are many different types of models, and it would be wasted effort to construct an econometric model that gave only a quantitative description of an economy. A model should rather be formulated in a way that makes it a useful tool in the process of decision-making. It must therefore specify the major problem areas as well as the policy instruments used to tackle them. In addition, the model must contain all of the variables representing constraints on the development program, either of an economic or a political nature.

In the case of Pakistan, the ultimate goal was the selection of a feasible growth target for the economy, both in overall terms and in more specific detail. With regard to sectoral growth, a careful study of the relations between the agricultural and nonagricultural sectors was extremely important. It was necessary to determine the level of investment associated with different rates of growth and its distribution between sectors. Then, given a specific effort to generate domestic savings, one could estimate the order of magnitude of the resource gap and of the gap in the current account of the balance of payments. Given estimates of domestic resource and investment requirements, as well as an independent estimate of exports, one could determine the permissible level of imports and compare it with the projected demand for imports.

Each of these magnitudes could have been estimated in fair detail by simple and straightforward calculations, making assumptions about the values of variables and the interrelations in the economy at every step. Moreover, the calculations might have been extended over a great range of alternative estimates and different assumptions. Within the actual time available and constraints on manpower, however, such a procedure would not have been wise.

In this respect, an econometric model had great value, for alternative assumptions could be inserted and projections generated in a very short time.

An added attraction to the use of a model was that all assumptions could be made explicit, and the user as well as the onlooker could find out what they were. Models are often criticized for their assumptions, and validly so, but in too many cases the criticism is presented as though only model-builders make assumptions. Projections made without a model are necessarily based on at least the same number of assumptions as model-based projections, but the user — perhaps even the maker — may not always be aware of them all.

A second, fairly common criticism pertains to the statistical basis of models. It is true that statistics in developing countries are generally unreliable, although not as unreliable as some people tend to believe. The doubts about econometric models based on unreliable data ignore the fact that plans are always based on the same data whether a model is used or not. The construction of a model can actually be quite helpful in suggesting the kind of data needed in the planning process, thus giving some direction to the statistical work.

Finally, a model can be used, as it was in Pakistan, to alert policy-makers to the implications of their suggestions or decisions. As Mahbub ul Haq of Pakistan's Planning Commission stated in discussing the use of analytical techniques in development planning: "Policy makers would pick up one or two elements and say: 'Well, we'll buy a taxation of about 600 million dollars, but we will not buy a 10 percent rate of growth of exports; we'd like to see it as 6 percent, and we'll have a little less import substitution if that's possible.' And we would have to point out to them that these choices are not quite consistent . . . There is always a tendency to pick out various elements in the alternatives which are not consistent, and the use of analytical techniques again was to make them consistent, translate them, and present them again." [1] In a slightly different sense the model in Pakistan also indicated limits to feasible policies. Given the constraints on domestic savings rates, exports, foreign assistance, and import substitution, the model could

1. Organisation for Economic Cooperation and Development (OECD), Secretariat Internal Working Document DD/AT (66)1, April 12, 1966, p. 16.

easily be used to find the range within which overall growth and sectoral growth were confined for the next five years.

THE STRUCTURE OF THE MODEL

Only a summary description of the model will be given here, since a full description is given in the background documentation of the Third Plan.[2] The model used during the final stage of the preparation of the Third Five Year Plan is of the linear inter-industry type. It differs from most other models of this type in that it is based not on a single year's input-output table but on two — one for the beginning and one for the end of the preceding plan period. The tables were aggregated to seven producing sectors, and a large part of the equation system is based on marginal coefficients derived from comparisons between the two tables. This had the advantage that some effects of structural changes in the economy which would otherwise have been obscured by the level of aggregation could now be represented by changes in technical coefficients and other propensities. The use of marginal coefficients had the disadvantage of implying changing elasticities over time, all tending in the direction of unity, which confined the use of the model to medium-term projections. The model can also be described as of the two-gap type with an internal adjustment mechanism. One part of the model generates estimates of investment requirements and domestic savings, which together determine the resources or financing gap. The second part generates an estimate of import requirements and an export estimate — the latter partly determined outside the model — which together determine the balance-of-payments gap. Ex post these two gaps will be equal by definition, but there is no specific reason that they should be so ex ante. The way in which a country adjusts to one or both of these gaps in order to equalize them is a matter of conscious policy. The model uses import substitution as the main instrument, changing first the balance-of-payments gap, but assuming that it will also change the resources gap as a consequence of relatively costly investment in import-substituting industries. The adjustment mechanism of the model is designed to esti-

2. A number of background studies have been published by the Planning Commission in a volume entitled *Report of the Consistency Committee on the Third Five Year Plan* (Karachi, 1965). This volume also contains a complete description of the model.

mate the amount of import substitution that will be required to equalize the two gaps under alternative growth assumptions.

Another property of the model relates to the treatment of the agricultural sector. Whereas production in all other sectors depends on values assumed for other exogenous variables and the endogenous model relations, such is not the case with agriculture. This sector does not integrate very well with the rest of the economy, because the production function is of a special composition, and it would be unwise to estimate the growth of the sector on the basis of intermediate and final demand projections for agricultural products. Given the importance of agriculture in Pakistan's economy, it makes more sense to start from independent estimates of the agricultural growth potential under conditions of specific input availability. The estimate is then introduced into the model as an exogenous factor, leaving to the model to determine the absorptive capacity for agricultural products under different assumptions for overall economic growth. In order to provide a balancing item between the supply of, and domestic demand for, agricultural products, agricultural exports are determined as a residual in the model. This procedure is quite realistic in that all major agricultural products of Pakistan have a market at prevailing international prices.

The growth of the national product is kept exogenous to the model in order to produce a series of projections based on different growth alternatives. Finally, the exports from nonagricultural sectors and the marginal rate of savings are exogenous, the first because special studies on exports are a better guide than model projections, the second because it depends on resource mobilization policies.

The "sequence of events" can now be described as follows. Given an overall rate of growth and a growth rate in the agricultural sector of the economy, the model generates growth in other model sectors and therefore indicates the demand for inputs and intermediate imports. Given the rate of saving, the model also produces a set of consumption estimates and, through the use of capital coefficients, investment requirements. Investment minus savings gives the resource gap, which must be equal to the balance-of-payments (current account) gap. The latter gap, however, is separately determined, partly by exogenous exports and partly by import requirements. If the import requirements turn out to be higher than the permissible import level, the composition of domestic production must be adjusted in order to provide an adequate amount of import substitutes. This adjustment presumably involves extra capital costs and certainly entails the usual input and import requirements. As a result, the resource gap changes. The balance-of-payments gap is adjusted mainly through the mechanism of import substitution until the required equality of the two gaps is attained.

One could add a long list of the limitations of the model. However, as long as the limited purposes for which the model was constructed are kept in mind, there is little need for such a list. The model exercises were also supported by a large number of detailed studies of feasible limits to variables, including exports of goods and services, the potential for raising taxes and savings, the growth potential of the agricultural sector, and the limits to import substitution. Studies of feasible magnitudes for all of these areas, with the exception of the limits on import substitution, were available at the time the model was being used for the preparation of the final Third Plan.

PLAN PREPARATION AND THE MODEL

A few words must be said about the capital coefficients. They were estimated from data for the First and Second Plan periods, assuming lags between investment expenditures and increased production. Because most coefficients were found to increase over time, further slight increases were assumed for the future. Later it was found that a considerable part of these increases resulted from underestimation of production growth. Thus, the model probably overestimated investment requirements for the Third Plan, but not by a very wide margin. Detailed studies of capital costs and physical targets of proposed projects were made later, which indicated relationships between growth and investment close to those assumed in the model. The only real test will be the results in 1970.

The Outline of the Third Five-Year Plan, completed by the Planning Commission in August 1964, included preliminary projections from 1965 to 1970. The central target was a 30 percent total increase of gross national product, or about 5.5 percent per annum. The Outline projected a slight increase in external resources (about 12 percent) and postulated a marginal rate of (gross) domestic savings of 23 percent. At that stage a simple macro-model was used in order to secure a reasonable degree of consistency between the balance-of-payments estimates and projected resources. At the time it was not possible to make an accurate analysis either of the relationship between overall and agricultural growth, or of the required level of imports, or of the implicitly assumed levels of import substitution.

The final version of the planning model used in the preparation of the Third Plan became available after the Outline was completed. Its first use was to check the estimates contained in the Outline and to widen the area of quantified variables examined. At the same time the preliminary evaluation of the Second Plan period was prepared.[3] In addition, some special studies on agricultural performance and prospects were well on their way. It then became possible to extend the number of variables for which alternatives could be studied and to gain insight into the consequences of alternative magnitudes for the shape and structure of the entire plan.

Initial test runs of the model on the Outline suggested that some of the problems would be of greater magnitude than presumed earlier. It was demonstrated that the projected rates of growth of production, savings, and exports, together with agricultural growth of 3.5 percent per annum, would lead to a serious imbalance between domestic supply and demand for agricultural products. The model showed a decline of about Rs.900 million in the agricultural export surplus, compared to an Outline estimate of increased agricultural exports of around Rs.350 million. If the plan in fact included effective measures for promoting exports of agricultural products at the levels envisaged, the country would be left with a deficit of agricultural products for domestic use of Rs.1,250 million, or nearly 5 percent of the total projected demand. The consequence would be a relative increase of agricultural prices. To permit that increase would be one of the necessary policies for attaining the planned export surplus.

Even if the planned level of agricultural exports were achieved, there would still be the need for a vigorous drive for import substitution. Under the assumption of growing agricultural exports, the model projected a required level of import substitution of around

3. Government of Pakistan Planning Commission, *Preliminary Evaluation of Progress during the Second Five-Year Plan* (Karachi, 1965).

Rs.2,550 million, or more than 20 percent of industrial production to be added during the plan period. Notwithstanding this considerable effort to substitute for imports, there would remain a slightly increased requirement for external resources.

The model indicated that higher rates of growth of the national product would result in even larger deficits in agricultural sector output — or, stated differently, in even heavier pressures on agricultural prices and greater difficulties in attaining the export target for agricultural products. This became a crucial issue in discussions on the revision of the Outline and the preparation of the final plan. Another important factor at this stage was the fact that preliminary estimates of economic growth during the Second Plan indicated that the increase in the gross national product (at factor cost) might approach 30 percent over the Second Plan period.

Thus, it became more and more obvious that an even higher rate of growth for the economy would be possible during the Third Plan, if only a solution could be found for the projected imbalance between agricultural demand and supply. At that point the first results became available of an analysis of agricultural performance and prospects in West Pakistan, later followed by a similar study for East Pakistan.[4] The studies made clear that the growth of agricultural production in the preceding years had already been at least as high, if not higher, than the rate projected for the future in the Outline. There also were strong reasons to believe that a further acceleration could be achieved, especially if forecasts of growth in the demand and supply of fertilizers and irrigation proved reliable. The Planning Commission accepted programs close to the proposed magnitudes and consequently an upward revision of the targets for agriculture.

Because the model includes agricultural exports as a balancing item between production on one side and domestic demands on the other — which would make it more appropriate to speak of agricultural surpluses than of exports — it was fairly easy to study the relationship between overall and agricultural growth. Given a specific projection of agricultural growth and alternative projections of overall growth, the model produced estimates of agricultural surpluses or deficits. These estimates are unattractive — requiring

4. A revised version of these papers is included as Chap. 9 of this volume: Walter P. Falcon and Carl H. Gotsch, "Lessons in Agricultural Development — Pakistan."

either an import of agricultural products or a relative increase in their domestic prices — with the result that a lower limit to the relationship between production and domestic demand was established. However, consideration had to be given to the growth of international demand and the price sensitivity of Pakistan's exportable agricultural products, constituting a feasible upper limit to the agricultural surplus.

The first exercise was addressed to finding the minimum rate of growth of agricultural production compatible with an overall growth target of 30 percent, a marginal rate of savings of 23 percent, and an exportable surplus of agricultural products of at least Rs.700 million. These magnitudes represented the Outline case with a modified target for exports. An agricultural growth rate of 4.3 percent per annum was found to be required, and slightly lower rates if higher domestic savings were assumed. It was, of course, possible to study the effects of higher rates of agricultural growth: the model implies that, with the above assumptions on exports and the rate of savings, for each .10 percent increase of the annual growth rate of agriculture, an increase of the overall growth rate of .14 percent is possible and necessary. A slight deterioration of the balance of payments on current account would occur simultaneously, it was found.

An agricultural growth rate of around 5 percent per annum would then permit and require a 6.4 percent annual rate of growth of the economy, or 36 percent for the period of the plan, on the assumption of a Rs.700 million exportable surplus of agricultural products. Since the possibility of attaining even higher agricultural growth rates could not be ruled out, the problem really became one of deciding on an upper limit to a feasible overall rate of growth. Serious thought also had to be given to the alternative of accepting larger surpluses of agricultural products. This would result in lower overall rates of growth despite a high exogenously determined rate of agricultural development. The question of agricultural exports above the tentative target of Rs.700 million became a critical issue.

Still another alternative would have been to retain a low export figure and to assume a relative decline of agricultural prices, that is, to accept worsening terms of trade for the agricultural sector in the domestic market. It was realized, however, that this would be a reversal of the agricultural policies followed during the Second

Plan. To a large extent agricultural growth in the preceding years was a direct consequence of creating a more favorable market for agricultural products by abolishing price ceilings and zoning regulations and drastically cutting export duties. The intention of the Pakistan government was not to let these beneficial policies be reversed.

Clearly, the one course that promised a reasonable degree of equilibrium between the agricultural and nonagricultural sectors, without endangering agricultural prices, was a target of higher overall growth. But its implications for investment, savings, and the balance of payments needed to be analyzed. At this stage the model was used to produce a set of alternative estimates, all based on the same agricultural assumption (an increase of value added by 30 percent) but with overall growth targets ranging from 30 to 40 percent and with slight variations in the marginal savings rate.

The model indicated that for every one percent increase of the annual growth of the gross national product, the agricultural surplus could be reduced by about Rs.250 million. A growth rate of 40 percent over the plan period and a feasible rate of savings would leave a surplus of around Rs.500 million. A 40 percent rate of national growth was considered the upper limit, because the growth required in East Pakistan had to be above the national average, and a much higher rate there just was not considered possible. At a growth rate of 40 percent for gross national product and a feasible rate of savings, the problem of agricultural deficits would not exist. An overall rate of growth of 42 percent, in fact, would make domestic demand for agricultural products practically equal to domestic agricultural output.

It was much more difficult to come to terms with the upper limit of agricultural surpluses. Because the model assumes that these surpluses will be exported, it is important to know which products are involved and their export possibilities. Here the model falls short. It does not even distinguish between food crops and non-food products — a distinction that would have been very helpful in that cotton and jute are at present the most important export products, while foodgrains must be imported.

The independent analysis and projections of agricultural growth were more specific. Since the growth target for agriculture, used as an exogenous input in the model, was based on those studies, more specific output data by crops could be used as a consistent set of specifications for the model. To these specifications were added preliminary estimates of industrial growth in sectors using agricultural products as inputs (especially the cotton and jute mills, but also vegetable oil manufacturing and the tobacco industry) and final demand for food and food products. On this basis, it was possible to obtain tentative projections of the composition of agricultural surpluses, given growth rates of 35 to 40 percent for the gross national product.

The analysis showed that additional exports of cotton, oilseeds, and other minor products, excluding rice and wheat, could already provide some Rs.700 million. These commodities could be marketed without risking significant adverse price effects. At the same time, it appeared that during the Third Plan Pakistan could change from a country with a foodgrain deficit to one with a surplus. Again, a foreign market could be found for foodgrains, because production in South and Southeast Asia lags significantly behind population growth, and prices show a tendency to increase. However, exports of rice or wheat would jeopardize Pakistan's position as a beneficiary under the American agricultural surplus disposal program (PL 480). Pakistan was receiving foodgrains, especially wheat, under this program, whose regulations prohibit the exports of "like commodities."

Foodgrain exports could therefore create serious problems, since part of the rupee-financing of the plan was supposed to be provided by PL 480 counterpart funds. In addition, the Indus Basin Replacement Works were to be partly financed from the same source, though they were not included in the Five Year Plans. It was clear that the Third Plan could not show exports of foodgrains on one page and PL 480 counterpart financing on another. The plan had to omit foodgrain exports, notwithstanding their probability. This omission resulted in a slight inconsistency but created a desirable cushion under the critical estimate of projected export growth. The urgency also became clear of starting negotiations with the U.S. government for a modification of the "like commodity" clause, to enable Pakistan to reap the full benefits of its agricultural development without risking a loss of external assistance.

Although the plan did not show an increase of agricultural exports beyond Rs.700 million, the model could show a higher figure, indicating the potential exports of foodgrains. It was considered unrealistic to assume foodgrain exports beyond Rs.800 million. This gave an outside total for agricultural exports of Rs.1,500 million. On the basis of these estimates — a low of Rs.700 million and a high of Rs.1,500 million — a closer look at the macro-economic frame of the Third Plan could be taken.

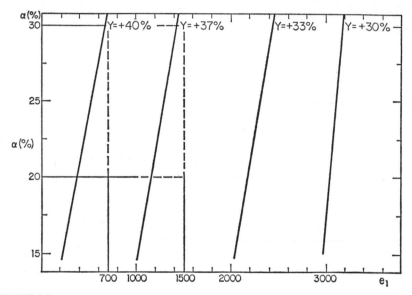

FIGURE 1.1

Growth of Pakistan's GNP as a function of savings and agricultural surpluses

As shown in the graph in Figure 1.1, the overall rate of growth must lie between 36 and 39 percent, to be consistent in terms of the model, assuming a marginal rate of savings between 20 and 30 percent.[5] The rectangular shape between the lines indicating the upper and lower boundaries of agricultural exports roughly demarcates the "feasible area." The range of choice of a macro-economic framework for the Third Plan is considerably reduced when the only constraints are the feasible savings rates and agricultural exports.

The next step was to consider the implications of the growth rates of gross national product for the balance of payments. Of course, it

5. Derivation of the graphs from the model relations is given in the Appendix to this chapter.

matters considerably at what level the marginal rate of savings is to be fixed. The target growth rate of the national product determines the investment requirements, and the rate of savings in fact distributes the financing over domestic and external resources. Once that distribution is made, the balance of payments must be adjusted to allow the flow of external resources to enter the economy. This adjustment was brought about in the model through the mechanism of import substitution, which reduced the import bill to the point where the gap in the balance of payments equaled the gap in the financing side of the plan.

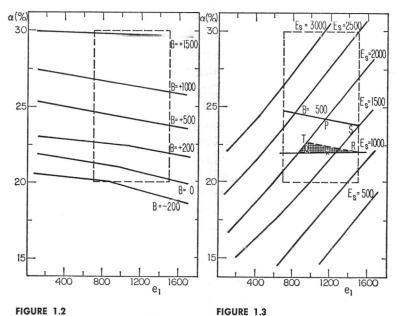

FIGURE 1.2

Projected effects of Pakistan's balance-of-payments improvements

FIGURE 1.3

Estimated feasible import substitution in Pakistan

The Pakistan government, having a long-term strategy of reducing dependence on external resources, imposed a constraint on the Third Plan by requiring the stabilization of foreign assistance around the level reached in the last year of the Second Plan. Small increases in the initial years were considered acceptable if compensated by decreases during later years, so that foreign assistance at the end of the Third Plan period would be slightly below that received at the end of the Second Plan. To what extent would such a target result in a further limitation of the "feasible area"? The answer is set out in Figure 1.2, where the changes in the balance-of-payments gap between 1965 and 1970 are shown as a function of a marginal rate of savings and the growth of agricultural exports.

Figure 1.2 demonstrates that limited reductions in the balance-of-payments gap are consistent with marginal rates of savings between 20 and 23 percent. Since the marginal rate of savings during the Second Plan was already estimated at 22 percent, it would be difficult to defend assumptions implying a lower rate for the next five years. As for higher rates, the range of choice becomes extremely narrow: higher rates of savings require larger improvements in the balance of payments, and such improvements can easily be proven improbable.

The proof is given in Figure 1.3, showing import-substitution requirements at different levels of saving and agricultural exports. It demonstrates clearly that higher savings require improvements of the external balance, which entail rapidly rising import substitution. The question then arises, what level of import substitution can be considered acceptable and realistic? The answer in Pakistan had to be vague in the absence of detailed studies concerning the composition of the import bill and the distribution of investment over industrial sectors. Although at a later stage such studies became available — indicating the possibilities of substituting for about Rs.1,200 million in the sector of intermediate products alone — in the earlier stage judgments had to be based on rules of thumb. It was therefore assumed that no more than 15 percent of additional production in the consumer and intermediate-goods sectors could substitute for imports. This percentage resulted in an upper limit of Rs.2,000 million, again reducing to a considerable extent the size of the feasible area.

If in addition it is assumed that the marginal rate of savings should not be lower than 22 percent, as in the Second Plan period, only the small area indicated by *QPSR* in Figure 1.3 remains. If the required improvement in the balance of payments is Rs.200 million rather than Rs.500 million, only a small triangle remains (*QTR*).

The ultimate choice of the macro-economic frame then becomes almost a question of taste and rounding. The Third Plan sets a target of a 37 percent growth of the national product and a 22 percent marginal rate of savings, which implies an increase of agricultural exports by Rs.1,200 million (or a "cushion" of Rs.500 million of rice exports). This increase in turn provides for an improvement of the balance of payments on current account by almost Rs.200 million. The corresponding import substitution is calculated at Rs.1,600 million, or slightly over 11 percent of additional production in the relevant sectors.

In evaluating the use of the model at the first two stages of plan formulation — providing macro-economic alternatives and analysis of critical issues — I can only conclude that it met most of the requirements reasonably well. Of course, one must always remember the limited reliability of basic statistics and of the coefficients derived from them. But these factors must be worked with in any case, and the model at least starts from data that are mutually consistent. Since the final product — each alternative set of projections — is also internally consistent and easily obtainable, the planner gains a tool that can give him quick answers to questions of alternative possibilities and of the magnitudes of responses to policy changes. The foregoing description of the way in which the model was used indicates also that Pakistan's planners did not accept the projections derived from it as the ultimate truth; they added common sense and specific detail wherever necessary.

Less use was made of the model with regard to the third stage, the sectoral detail. Sectoral plans and project lists are largely prepared outside the Planning Commission, and the decision on the inclusion of proposals depends sometimes as much on the organizational talent and persuasiveness of their sponsors as on economic justification. For both reasons the sectoral investment estimates of the model could be used only to a limited extent. In any case, the level of aggregation of the model made its sectoral estimates too cumbersome for framing the plan. The Planning Commission did refer sometimes to the sectoral investment estimates, but only as a guideline in the discussions on allocation for different executing agencies. Because the relationship between agricultural and non-agricultural growth played a crucial role in the formulation of the plan, it would be misleading to say that the sectoral specification was made entirely independently from the model. But it was generally agreed that separate analysis in considerably more detail would be needed as a basis for specific sector plans.

APPENDIX 1: THE BASIC EQUATION SYSTEM FOR PARAMETRIC VARIATIONS

The parametric variations with which Pakistan's planners worked are based on a set of five reduced-form equations, which contain the crucial endogenous variables for import substitution (E_s) and agricultural exports (e_1) and which relate the less interesting exogenous variables (the three exports e_2, e_3, and e_4) to endogenous ones. In this way a system was obtained of five equations with six unknowns. One coefficient was left undetermined.

In order to make savings (S) endogenous and to retain the marginal rate of savings (α) as an instrument variable, domestic savings were written as a function of the growth of the gross national product at market prices:

$$S = \alpha(Y + \Sigma t)$$

All indirect taxes and subsidies are endogenous in the model. Therefore Σt can be replaced by its reduced form equation, so that the expression for savings, above, can be transformed into a generalized savings function in which only exogenous variables remain and the marginal rate of savings is left undetermined. This is the first equation of the new system.

The second is the reduced form equation for agricultural exports.

The three export variables e_2, e_3, and e_4 are made endogenous by assuming fixed relations between these exports and additional gross outputs of the relevant sectors. The coefficients were derived from the first round of Third Plan projections, giving:

$$e_2 = .100\ X_2$$
$$e_3 = .070\ X_3$$
$$e_4 = .050\ X_4$$

Since the gross production variables are all endogenous, these can be replaced by their reduced form equations, resulting in three equations containing only exogenous variables.

The growth of agricultural production (X_1) and exports of services are assumed to be invariant: for the first one the 5.5 percent growth per annum of agricultural value added served as a basis, whereas exports of services are assumed to increase by Rs.100 million. As a result of this treatment the five equations mentioned above are all enlarged with a constant term.

The basic equation system can be written as shown in Table 1.1.

Table 1.1. Basic equations for parametric analysis in the Pakistan model.

Equation number	Y	S	e_2	e_3	e_4	e_1	Constant
1	1.117	.010–1/α	.026	.016	−.018	—	−704
2	−.634	.152	−.160	.073	.350	−1.000	10,772
3	.091	−.026	−.922	−.040	−.050	—	−474
4	.056	.030	−.033	−.982	−.063	—	−627
5	.005	—	—	−.001	−.946	—	−28

When e_1 is made the exogenous variable of this system of equations, solutions can be obtained for each specific value of α. The following values of α were chosen for this exercise:

$$\alpha_1 = .150$$

$$\alpha_2 = .175$$

$$\alpha_3 = .200$$

$$\alpha_4 = .240$$

$$\alpha_5 = .275$$

$$\alpha_6 = .300$$

$$\alpha_7 = .500$$

For each of these values for α, the endogenous matrix was inverted and the increase multiplied with the last two columns (e_1 and the constant term). The results — the reduced form equations for Y, S, e_2, e_3, and e_4 as functions of e_1 — are shown in Table 1.2 and Figure 1.4.

The "derived equations" for E_s and B are obtained by first substituting the reduced forms (in e_1) for Y, S, e_2, e_3, and e_4 and, second, substituting the assumed values for X_1 and e_7 in the original model-reduced form equations for E_s and B.

APPENDIX 2: THE BASIC EQUATION SYSTEM OF THE PAKISTAN GROWTH MODEL

The model consists of 98 equations and 105 variables. A solution to the equation system therefore requires that 7 variables be selected as exogenously determined. Although the model is of the static input-

Table 1.2. Reduced form equations for parametric analysis with alternative values of α.

Endogenous variable	α = .150		α = .175		α = .200		α = .240		α = .275		α = .300		α = .500	
	e_1	Constant	e_1	Constant	e_1	Constant	e_1	Constant	e_1	Constant	e_1	Constant	e_1	Constant
Y	−1.621	17,465	−1.633	17,588	−1.645	17,712	−1.663	17,905	−1.682	18,098	−1.694	18,230	−1.804	19,370
S	−.273	2,829	−.321	3,326	−.369	3,830	−.444	4,611	−.519	5,389	−.571	5,925	−1.015	10,535
e_2	−.147	1,103	−.147	1,100	−.146	1,097	−.146	1,092	−.146	1,088	−.145	1,084	−.143	1,056
e_3	−.096	410	−.098	432	−.100	455	−.104	490	−.107	525	−.109	549	−.129	755
e_4	−.009	63	−.009	64	−.009	64	−.009	65	−.009	66	−.009	67	−.009	72
Derived equations														
E_s	−1.155	1,839	−1.198	2,289	−1.242	2,744	−1.310	3,451	−1.378	4,155	−1.425	4,640	−1.826	8,810
B	.258	−1,231	.216	−791	.173	−347	.107	342	.040	1,028	−.005	1,501	−.397	3,890
$B - E_s$	1.413	3,070	1.414	3,080	1.415	3,091	1.417	3,793	1.428	5,183	1.420	6,141	1.429	12,700

output type, the structural equations are based on changes in the technical coefficients. That is, the technical coefficients are estimated as marginal coefficients implying further change in the average coefficients. The marginal coefficients were estimated on the basis of two 7-sector inter-

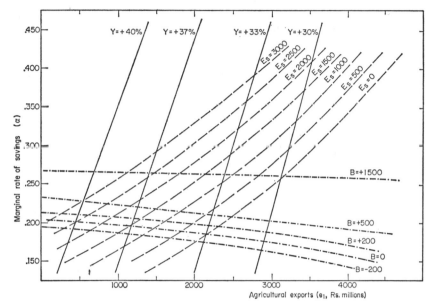

FIGURE 1.4

Summary results of parametric variations on marginal rate of savings, growth, and import substitution

industry tables for the years 1960/61 and 1964/65. The 1960/61 table is an aggregated version of the 30-sector table originally prepared by the Planning Commission, whereas the 1964/65 table was prepared from the "benchmark" projections which underly most of the work on the Third Five Year Plan. The 7 producing sectors identified in the model are shown in Table 1.3.

For each of the 7 sectors, subsequent tables show gross value added at factor cost, indirect taxes net of subsidies (including taxes on intermediate imported inputs), and imports at their c.i.f. prices by sector of destination. Valuation of output is therefore at market or user's prices, including margins on final products and inputs.

Final demand is defined as the sum of consumption expeditures, private and public, investment expenditure, changes in stocks and exports of goods and services. All values are at 1960/61 prices. Again, the equations for the components of final demand relate to changes. Table 1.4

Table 1.3. Sectoral definitions for the Pakistan model.

No.	Sector name	Major activities included
1.	Agriculture	All agriculture, forestry, fishing
2.	Consumer goods manufacturing	Food processing, beverages, tobacco, textiles, clothing, footwear, wood, furniture, paper and paper products, leather and leather products, rubber products, sewing machines, radios, bicycles, metal products[a]
3.	Intermediate goods production	Chemicals, nonmetallic mineral products, mining, coal and petroleum derivatives, public utilities, jute pressing, cotton ginning
4.	Investment goods industries	Metal products,[a] machinery, electrical goods, transport equipment
5.	Construction	All construction
6.	Transport and communications	All modes of transport, communication services
7.	All other services	Wholesale and retail trade, public administration, defense, banking and insurance, ownership of dwellings, other services

[a] Fifty percent of metal products sector allocated to consumer goods, remainder to investment goods.

presents the symbols used in the model in tableau form. The following four variables are not defined in the table:

B = balance of payments surplus on current account

S = gross domestic savings

E_s = import substitution

The equations of the model are given below.

A. Structural Equations

I. Inputs into agriculture

1. $x_{11} = 0.0516\ X_1 + 146.9$
2. $x_{21} = 0.0140\ X_1 - 148.4$
3. $x_{31} = 0.0479\ X_1 - 921.8$
4. $x_{41} = 0.0015\ X_1 - 30.0$
5. $x_{61} = 0.0272\ X_1 - 109.2$
6. $x_{71} = 0.0285\ X_1 - 194.5$

Table 1.4. Definition of symbols.

Sector	1. Agriculture	2. Consumer goods	3. Intermediate goods	4. Investment goods	5. Construction	6. Transport and communications	7. All other services	Final demand — Consumption	Final demand — Investment (fixed)	Final demand — Stocks	Final demand — Exports	Gross value of production
1. Agriculture	x_{11}	x_{12}	x_{13}	x_{14}	—	—	x_{17}	c_1	—	n_1	e_1	X_1
2. Consumer goods manufacturing	x_{21}	x_{22}	x_{23}	x_{24}	x_{25}	—	x_{27}	c_2	—	n_2	e_2	X_2
3. Intermediate goods production	x_{31}	x_{32}	x_{33}	x_{34}	x_{35}	x_{36}	x_{37}	c_3	—	n_3	e_3	X_3
4. Investment goods manufacturing	—	—	x_{43}	x_{44}	x_{45}	x_{46}	x_{47}	c_4	i_4	n_4	e_4	X_4
5. Construction	—	—	—	—	—	—	—	c_5	i_5	—	—	X_5
6. Transport and communications	x_{61}	x_{62}	x_{63}	x_{64}	x_{65}	x_{66}	x_{67}	c_6	i_6	—	—	X_6
7. All other services	x_{71}	x_{72}	x_{73}	x_{74}	x_{75}	x_{76}	x_{77}	c_i	i_7	—	e_7	X_7
8. Gross value added	V_1	V_2	V_3	V_4	V_5	V_6	V_7	—	—	—	—	Y
9. Indirect taxes (net of subsidies)	t_1	t_2	t_3	t_4	t_5	t_6	t_7	t_c	t_i	—	t_e	—
10. Imports	m_1	m_2	m_3	m_4	m_5	m_6	m_7	m_c	m_i	—	—	M
11. Gross value of production	X_1	X_2	X_3	X_4	X_5	X_6	X_7	C	I	—	E	—
12. Investment by destination	i'_1	$\longleftarrow\ i'_{2-5}\ \longrightarrow$				i'_6	i'_7					

II. Inputs into consumer goods manufacturing
1. $x_{12} = 0.3239\ X_2 + 3{,}702.3$
2. $x_{22} = 0.0660\ X_2 -\quad 45.7$
3. $x_{32} = 0.1292\ X_2 - 1{,}266.3$
4. $x_{42} = 0.0109\ X_2 -\quad 148.3$
5. $x_{62} = 0.0368\ X_2 +\qquad 0.6$
6. $x_{72} = 0.1556\ X_2 - 1{,}327.6$

III. Inputs into intermediate goods production
1. $x_{13} = 0.2005\ X_3 + 728.3$
2. $x_{23} = 0.0062\ X_3 +\quad 37.0$
3. $x_{33} = 0.1004\ X_3 - 241.8$
4. $x_{43} = 0.0051\ X_3 -\quad 15.1$
5. $x_{63} = 0.0575\ X_3 +\quad 18.2$
6. $x_{73} = 0.1579\ X_3 - 248.7$

IV. Inputs into investment good industries
1. $x_{14} = 0.0037\ X_4 -\quad 3.2$
2. $x_{24} = 0.0110\ X_4 -\quad 8.2$
3. $x_{34} = 0.1049\ X_4 - 81.4$
4. $x_{44} = 0.0878\ X_4 - 50.2$
5. $x_{64} = 0.1000\ X_4 + 18.2$
6. $x_{74} = 0.2987\ X_4 - 59.2$

V. Inputs into construction
1. $x_{25} = 0.0040\ X_5 +\quad 0.1$
2. $x_{35} = 0.1529\ X_5 -\quad 19.3$
3. $x_{45} = 0.0452\ X_5 +\quad 20.5$
4. $x_{65} = 0.0460\ X_5 + 127.6$
5. $x_{75} = 0.0576\ X_5 -\quad 56.0$

VI. Inputs into transport and communications
1. $x_{36} = 0.0061\ X_6 -\quad 8.8$
2. $x_{46} = 0.0061\ X_6 -\quad 0.8$
3. $x_{66} = 0.0109\ X_6 -\quad 6.9$
4. $x_{76} = 0.0242\ X_6 - 25.8$

VII. Inputs into services
1. $x_{17} = 0.0043\ X_7 -\quad 20.6$
2. $x_{27} = 0.0081\ X_7 -\quad 17.7$
3. $x_{37} = 0.0146\ X_7 - 110.7$
4. $x_{57} = 0.0086\ X_7 +\quad 11.8$
5. $x_{67} = 0.0120\ X_7 -\quad 85.1$
6. $x_{77} = 0.0334\ X_7 +\quad 68.2$

B. Final Demand

I. Consumption expenditures

1. $c_1 = 0.1438\ C + 2,954.1$
2. $c_2 = 0.5244\ C - 2,745.2$
3. $c_3 = 0.0885\ C - 1,558.1$
4. $c_4 = 0.0169\ C -\ \ \ 111.5$
5. $c_5 = 0.0081\ C +\ \ \ 139.7$
6. $c_6 = 0.0185\ C -\ \ \ 326.3$
7. $c_7 = 0.1219\ C + 2,700.3$

II. Investment by sector of origin

1. $i_4 = 0.0780\ i'_1 + 0.2380\ i'_{2-5} + 0.1460\ i'_6 - 193.1$
2. $i_5 = 0.7490\ i'_1 + 0.3140\ i'_{2-5} + 0.4180\ i'_6 + 0.9900\ i'_7$
3. $i_6 = 0.0100\ i'_1 + 0.0260\ i'_{2-5} + 0.0190\ i'_6$
4. $i_7 = 0.0180\ i'_1 + 0.0320\ i'_{2-5} + 0.0380\ i'_6$

III. Stock formation

1. $n_1 = 0.0015\ X_1$
2. $n_2 = 0.0019\ X_2$
3. $n_3 = 0.0032\ X_3$
4. $n_4 = 0.0103\ X_4$
5. $n_m = 0.0195\ M$

C. Imports

1. $m_1 = 0.0155\ X_1 -\ \ \ 216.4$
2. $m_2 = 0.1019\ X_2 - 1,260.8$
3. $m_3 = 0.1044\ X_3 -\ \ \ \ 60.1$
4. $m_4 = 0.1573\ X_4 +\ \ \ 114.0$
5. $m_5 = 0.1721\ X_5 -\ \ \ \ 84.6$
6. $m_6 = 0.1065\ X_6 -\ \ \ \ \ 1.9$
7. $m_7 = 0.0054\ X_7 -\ \ \ \ 27.8$
8. $m_c = 0.0697\ C - 1,051.5$
9. $m_i = 0.1230\ i'_1 + 0.3440\ i'_{2-5} + 0.3240\ i'_6 + 0.0100\ i'_7 + 193.1$

D. Indirect Taxes Net of Subsidies

1. $t_i = 0.0018\ X_1 -\ \ \ 16.0$
2. $t_2 = 0.0515\ X_2 - 285.7$
3. $t_3 = 0.0626\ X_3 +\ \ \ 88.1$
4. $t_4 = 0.0378\ X_4 +\ \ \ 37.7$
5. $t_5 = 0.0320\ X_5 -\ \ \ 13.9$
6. $t_6 = 0.0109\ X_6 -\ \ \ \ 1.9$
7. $t_7 = 0.0010\ X_7 -\ \ \ \ 0.9$
8. $t_c = 0.0082\ C -\ \ \ \ \ 1.5$
9. $t_i = 0.0220\ i'_1 + 0.0460\ i'_{2-5} + 0.0550\ i'_6$
10. $t_e = 0.0190\ (E - E_s) + 43.8$

E. Investment Output Relations

1. $i_1' = 0.1044\ V_1$
2. $i_{2-5}' = 0.3405 \sum\limits_{j=2}^{5} V_j + 0.0213\ E_s$
3. $i_6' = 0.4515\ V_6$
4. $i_7' = 0.1610\ V_7$

F. Definitional Equations

I. Production

1. $X_1 = x_{11} + x_{12} + x_{13} + x_{14} \qquad\qquad + x_{17} + c_1 + n_1 \qquad + e_1$
2. $X_2 = x_{21} + x_{22} + x_{23} + x_{24} + x_{25} \qquad + x_{27} + c_2 + n_2 \qquad + e_2 + .35E_s$
3. $X_3 = x_{31} + x_{32} + x_{33} + x_{34} + x_{35} + x_{36} + x_{37} + c_3 + n_3 \qquad + e_3 + .65E_s$
4. $X_4 = x_{41} + x_{42} + x_{43} + x_{44} + x_{45} + x_{46} \qquad\qquad + c_4 + n_4 + i_4 + e_4$
5. $X_5 = \qquad\qquad\qquad\qquad\qquad\qquad\qquad x_{57} + c_5 \qquad + i_5$
6. $X_6 = x_{61} + x_{62} + x_{63} + x_{64} + x_{65} + x_{66} + x_{67} + c_6 \qquad + i_6$
7. $X_7 = x_{71} + x_{72} + x_{73} + x_{74} + x_{75} + x_{76} + x_{77} + c_7 \qquad + i_7 + e_7$

II. Value added

1. $V_j = X_j - \sum\limits_{i=1}^{7} x_{ij} - m_i - t_i$

III. Foreign trade

1. Exports

$$E = \sum_{i=1}^{7} e_i + t_e + E_s$$

2. Imports

$$M = \sum_{j=1}^{7} m_j + m_c + m_i + n_m$$

3. Balance of payments

$$B = E - M$$

IV. Gross national product

$$Y = \sum_{j=1}^{7} V_j$$

V. Savings and investment

1. Investment

$$I = i_1' + i_{2-5}' + i_6' + i_7'$$

2. Savings

$$S = I + B + \sum_{i=1}^{7} n_i + n_m$$

By inverting the endogenous (98 × 98) matrix and multiplying the inverse by the exogenous (98 × 7) matrix, a set of reduced form equations is obtained, which still represents the full original equation system but presents the information in more useful form. These reduced form equations are given in Table 1.5.

Table 1.5. Partial matrix of reduced form equations.

Endogenous variables	Exogenous variables						
	Y	X_1	S	e_2	e_3	e_4	e_7
X_1	—	1.0000	—	—	—	—	—
X_2	0.9072	−0.6035	−0.2624	0.7828	−0.4017	−0.4973	−0.6938
X_3	0.8058	−1.1417	0.4260	0.4671	0.2606	−0.9017	−1.3254
X_4	0.1017	−0.0715	−0.0031	−0.0028	−0.0092	1.0777	−0.0843
X_5	0.1630	−0.0639	−0.0069	−0.0035	−0.0094	−0.0031	0.0094
X_6	0.1314	−0.0824	−0.0043	0.0017	−0.0016	0.0371	−0.1122
X_7	0.4726	−0.3002	−0.0985	0.0507	−0.0241	0.1025	0.6541
V_1	—	0.8120	—	—	—	—	—
V_2	0.1127	−0.0750	−0.0326	0.0972	−0.0499	−0.0618	−0.0862
V_3	0.2461	−0.3487	0.1301	−0.1427	0.0796	−0.2754	−0.4048
V_4	0.0202	−0.0142	−0.0006	−0.0005	−0.0018	0.2142	−0.0168
V_5	0.0799	−0.0313	−0.0034	−0.0017	−0.0046	−0.0015	0.0046
V_6	0.1098	−0.0688	−0.0036	0.0014	−0.0013	0.0310	−0.0937
V_7	0.4313	−0.2740	−0.0899	0.0463	−0.0220	0.0935	0.5969
m_1	—	0.0155	—	—	—	—	—
m_2	0.0924	−0.0615	−0.0267	0.0798	−0.0409	−0.0507	−0.0707
m_3	0.0841	−0.1192	0.0445	−0.0488	0.0272	−0.0941	−0.1384
m_4	0.0160	−0.0112	−0.0005	−0.0004	−0.0014	0.1695	−0.0133
m_5	0.0281	−0.0110	−0.0012	−0.0006	−0.0016	−0.0005	0.0016
m_6	0.0140	−0.0088	−0.0005	0.0002	−0.0002	0.0040	−0.0119
m_7	0.0026	−0.0016	−0.0005	0.0003	−0.0001	0.0006	−0.0035
m_c	0.0778	−0.0063	−0.0690	0.0018	0.0011	−0.0012	−0.0074
m_i	0.0831	−0.0740	0.0180	−0.0126	−0.0062	−0.0125	−0.0927
n_m	0.0079	−0.0055	−0.0007	0.0004	−0.0004	0.0003	−0.0065
M	0.4060	−0.2836	−0.0366	0.0201	−0.0225	0.0154	−0.3358
E	0.0812	−0.0690	0.9252	0.0490	−0.0006	0.0573	−0.1441
B	−0.3248	0.2146	0.9618	0.0289	0.0219	0.0419	0.1917
E_s	0.7277	−1.4836	0.7700	−0.8075	−1.0939	−1.3192	−1.6901
e_i	−0.6342	1.3877	0.1522	−0.1597	0.0725	0.3503	0.5166
I	0.3116	−0.2051	0.0380	−0.0293	−0.0214	−0.0499	−0.1788
Σn_i	0.0132	−0.0095	0.0002	0.0004	−0.0005	0.0076	−0.0129
Σt_i	0.1168	−0.0897	0.0099	0.0255	0.0156	−0.0177	−0.1058
C	1.1168	−0.0897	−0.9901	0.0255	0.0156	−0.0177	−0.1058
$i'_{1'}$	—	0.0848	—	—	—	—	—
$i'_{2'-5}$	0.1926	−0.2147	0.0541	−0.0374	−0.0173	−0.0790	−0.2326
$i'_{6'}$	0.0496	−0.0311	−0.0016	0.0006	−0.0006	0.0140	−0.0423
i'_7	0.0694	−0.0441	−0.0145	0.0075	−0.0035	0.0151	0.0961

Table 4.6. Partial matrix of reduced form equations

Alfred H. Conrad

2

~~~~~~~~~~~~~~~~

Econometric Models in Development Planning —
Pakistan, Argentina, Liberia

> *We make for ourselves internal pictures or symbols of external*
> *objects, and we make them of such a kind that the necessary conse-*
> *quences in thought of the pictures are always the necessary conse-*
> *quences in nature of the objects pictured . . . When on the basis*
> *of our accumulated previous experiences we have succeeded in con-*
> *structing pictures with the desired properties, we can quickly derive*
> *by means of them, as by means of models, the consequences which*
> *in the external world would only occur in the course of a long*
> *period of time or as a result of our own intervention.*
> *— H. R. Hertz.*[1]

My purpose here is to back away momentarily from the flow of empirical results and insights, to present some generalizations about the construction and use of econometric models for development planning. Elsewhere in this volume, theoretical models appear to grow explicitly from certain experiences or to show implicitly through the empirical generalizations. In particular, Development Advisory Service (DAS) experience is the source of theoretical inferences about economic development. I will reverse the order now — the reader must decide for himself where the cart and the horse are standing when I am finished — and describe some of the problems encountered in writing a model of the economy for policy purposes.

1. *Principles of Mechanics* (London, 1899), p. 1, as quoted in R. B. Braithewaite, *Scientific Exploration* (Cambridge: Cambridge University Press, 1955), p. 91.

I am conscious of two risks in this enterprise: first, that I will appear to be preaching or proselytizing; second, that I will be dismissed with some variant of Schumpeter's taunt that methodology is the last refuge of the scoundrel. For the first, I have no desire to preach, though it would probably be a healthy change for an econometrician to offer a sermon to some audience other than the usual assembly of the faithful. For the second, I would remind this group of specialists in the art of policy that Schumpeter adapted his advice to the scoundrel from an even more celebrated epigram about political skills.

One should refer to the *use* of growth models with a measure of reserve, if not of diffidence, for the fact is that models have been used relatively little in development policy. The amount of professional attention given to growth models has not been balanced by their use either by policy-makers or *for* policy-makers by their economic advisors. They may have been rejected because they ask the wrong questions. Many models are focused upon a few aggregates and define the relationships among such global variables as saving, investment, capital-output ratios, and the long-run rate of growth. But planning agencies are absorbed with specific policies for, say, trade or money supply or the allocation of resources among specific projects and industrial sectors. Global Harrod-Domar growth models don't help much with these planning tasks. Another complaint about the econometric models argues from the opposite pole: that optimizing models go too far. A development plan is the result of a great many political decisions based upon isolated, often intuitive judgments. No responsible planner is going to abdicate his responsibility to a linear programing model. No economist with a sense of proportion — not to mention the instinct for self-preservation — ought to recommend anything remotely resembling that abdication. I know of at least three models that have been developed in response to specific policy problems faced by DAS advisory groups. They are specific enough to avoid the first charge and modest enough to be innocent of the second. They will serve well to illustrate a discussion of the principles of economic policy.

Instead of beginning with the usual Theil-Tinbergen litany about objectives, instruments, and constraints, I will turn directly to the Devil's Advocate and try to counter some of the incisive skepticism expressed in Raymond Vernon's recent essay on these problems.[2] This combative posture will enable me to present the principles behind two of the models that are included in this book, as well as a third for which the DAS has paid hard cash. And in hopes that the reader will not think I am trying to feint him out of position by switching metaphors suddenly, I will meet the classic challenge to all kibitzers by picking up the cards held elsewhere in this book by Wouter Tims and Willy van Rijckeghem.

Professor Vernon started his criticism of model-building by outlining the multivalent nature of the economic objectives behind a national plan. In addition to such formal goals as consistency and optimality, he stated its other aims. Some are Machiavellian — like dressing up a bold and imaginative plan in the sober, dignified dress of an economic analysis. Other aims are distressingly complex, bringing together almost incompatible bedfellows, such as high savings rates and egalitarian income distribution. This multivalence is a trial for model-builders.

Second, he argued that the construction of a model for planning purposes presupposes the availability of enough information to implement the model. But venality, ignorance, and impatience all stand in the way of the free flow of information within the government bureaus of developing countries, just as in the mature economies. The ensuing game of blind man's buff is hardly what the econometric textbooks promise.

Third, complex models are expensive in trained manpower. To keep the apparatus within manageable dimensions, one must resort to a number of simplifying assumptions. A brief catalogue reads like a Cubist nightmare: linear equations, quadratic preference functions, triangular matrices, and rectangular isoquants. But beyond the economy of effort or admission of ignorance reflected in these simplifying assumptions, Professor Vernon noted that most of the parametric relationships used are stochastic or uncertain. The variance in our estimates ought to lead us to construction techniques that take chance and uncertainty frankly into consideration. Finally, Professor Vernon set in diametric opposition two urgent

---

2. Raymond Vernon, "Comprehensive Model-Building in the Planning Process: The Case of the Less-Developed Economies," *Economic Journal,* LXXVI (March 1966), 57–69.

and apparently incompatible demands upon the econometrician-cum-practitioner: to propose policies to meet immediate crises, like a fireman, and to develop comprehensive, consistent, and optimal long-run strategies, as he was presumably trained to do in graduate school.

Using the DAS experience for illustration, I can now make some general statements of these problems. Sometimes our practice will win high marks; sometimes we will get the hard lines we deserve. In order to save time and space, I will on occasion be terse and abstract. I hope I will not be incomprehensible. But I am really setting myself only one overriding constraint: I will not use the ad hominem argument that says the noneconometric planner or intuitive politician can not really do better.

The first problem arises from complex objective functions or preference functions. A distinction should be drawn between straight forecasting models — what Ragnar Frisch called the *"onlooker* approach" — and a broad class of decision models, including consistency, feasibility, and optimizing procedures. Preference functions are strictly relevant only in the latter class, but the line is necessarily indistinct. "Pure" forecasting models, when implemented by a simulation program or the introduction of alternative public spending patterns, begin to be operational policy models. I will concentrate here on models in which there are explicit objectives or goals to be reached, however informally they may enter the analysis.

Consider the nature of a preference function. It contains a set of variables or arguments, some of which are under the direct influence of the planners, some of which are uncontrolled. Further, some of the arguments will also appear among the structural limitations — I take this to be the essence of *multivalence*. The problem is to reach that vector of values of the noncontrolled arguments which is optimal, given the constraints in the structural system.[3]

Theil used the familiar theory of consumer demand to illustrate

3. H. Theil has shown that some instrument variables may also have direct effect on social welfare, just as the objectives do: tax burdens are the most obvious example. This section draws heavily upon Theil's *Optimal Decision Rules for Government and Industry* (Chicago and Amsterdam: Rand McNally, 1964), esp. chaps. 3, 6; and his *Economic Forecasts and Policy,* 2nd ed. (Amsterdam: North-Holland Publishing Co., 1961), chap. 7.

the nature of the preference function. Economists have all been taught to analyze the maximizing behavior of the consumer in terms of a utility function — in which all relevant commodities are listed — and a constraint, usually the consumer's disposable income. The solution to the optimizing problem is found at the point where the linear budget constraint lies tangent to one of the indifference curves or surfaces. We learn to introduce time, time preference, impatience, and myopia. Then we apply the theory in another setting, with regard to the production process, where time and, later, uncertainty are introduced in the form of inventory scheduling.

Now, suppose the simple linear constraint — the budget, in this instance — is replaced, to include more than one constraint. In the consumer case, a minimum consumption level might be introduced for a given commodity. In the more interesting planning case, one might wish to achieve a given change in the income distribution for its own sake and not simply as an instrument toward raising the savings ratio. Where the solution was previously given in terms of indifference, or transformation, curves in two-dimensional space, it now involves indifference surfaces in three-dimensional space. Where the previous solution was a point of tangency, now it is a set of points, a straight line along which the planner or policy-maker must choose.

In the approach outlined thus far — H. Theil's, essentially — the social welfare that can be achieved depends upon the combined values of instruments and objective variables. In Jan Tinbergen's treatment, the objective variables are given as targets, and the values of the instruments are to be chosen so as to reach them. As Professor Vernon argued, the objective function is multivalent — even worse, some of the objectives are nonquantifiable, and pairs or sets of them may be incommensurable. As I have suggested here, one way of formalizing multivalence would be to introduce several constraints. Without being able to specify a complete welfare function, the program could be constrained to fall within the bounds set by stated social or economic goals. If one of the bounds placed upon the instrument variables is violated, it may be substituted for one of the targets; the system might then be solved again, and possibly repeatedly, until a consistent solution is found. One is still faced, however, with the problem of establishing a basis for trading off one target against another. In practice, the procedure for solving this problem will probably be logrolling or some other exercise of political instinct around the pork barrel. The question here is whether the econometrician has a real alternative to offer. A simple analogue to this problem can be found among familiar capital budgeting procedures to maximize the discounted present value of net returns, taking the capital or construction cost as the fixed target constraint.[4]

It is now possible to consider the treatment of multivalence in two of the models presented in this volume. The growth model of Pakistan by Wouter Tims is a *consistency* model. It is, to begin with, a piece of general equilibrium analysis in the Walrasian tradition. The system extrapolates simultaneously several economic variables, which have been tied together by means of a fairly large input-output table and a set of income and expenditure relations and definitions.[5] Initially, there are 104 structural relations among the variables and 22 definitions. There are 135 variables, of which 9 are predetermined. The system is solved so as to obtain a reduced form, that is, a set of equations containing on the left of the equal sign the endogenous variables, one at a time, and on the right the predetermined variables. Then, since it is a policy model, the reduced form is compressed to a series of still further reduced forms, containing policy variables only.

Focusing for a moment on the two gaps, the domestic-resource gap $(S\text{-}I)$ and the foreign-exchange gap $(E\text{-}M)$, one can obviously write a reduced form to relate the gap variables to the exogenous variables: income, saving, agricultural output, and exports other than agriculture. Then, since consistency (determinateness, really) is achieved in the model by adding an *extra*-import-substitution variable to the endogenous set, the reduced form can be extended to include the balancing variable as a dependent variable. But this procedure still gives only consistency. At best, one can vary the

4. See Hollis B. Chenery, "A Model of Development Alternatives," in *Organization, Planning and Programming for Economic Development* (Washington, D.C.: Government Printing Office, n.d.), vol. VIII; Robert Dorfman, "Econometric Analysis for Assessing the Efficacy of Public Investment," in Pietro Salviucci and others, *The Econometric Approach to Development Planning* (Amsterdam and Chicago: Rand McNally, 1965).

5. I need not go into great detail here because the model is discussed by Wouter Tims in Chap. 1 of this volume. I want simply to give it sufficient setting to consider how policy and objectives are brought in.

predetermined variables in the *basis,* equal in number to the degrees of freedom, to evaluate the effect of the predetermined variables upon the objective variables under the equilibrium conditions of the consistency model. In the case under consideration, if *I, S, E,* and *M* are written as functions of Y, X_1, b (the marginal savings ratio), and the nonagricultural exports, it can be seen how the growth targets for GNP and agriculture are related to the crucial foreign exchange gap and savings ratio. This ad hoc procedure uses the complete model to focus upon a few relations of particular *policy* interest, because the government is in a position to influence, at least indirectly, the savings ratio or the resources applied to agricultural development.

A simple step carries one beyond this degree of "ad hockery": the feasible instrument technique that was introduced by Hollis Chenery and Michael Bruno and applied in the Pakistan Planning Commission case under discussion.[6] Consider the setting again. Tims was examining the question of the consistency of the Outline growth targets for national product and agriculture, given the constraints imposed by the marginal savings rate, which determines the domestic demand for agricultural produce, and by the foreign-exchange position, which would determine the amount of import substitution that must be achieved during the Third Plan. As if this were not multivalence enough, another constraint was imposed upon the planners in the requirement that consistency in the plan must not be allowed to violate the export regulations imposed upon "like commodities" under the U.S. PL 480 program.

Ideally, one would like to include in the basis as many controlled policy variables as there are degrees of freedom in the reduced form. It may, however, be necessary to include some of the predetermined variables in the basis set. By considering the limits — upper and lower, say, asymptotically, or perhaps as first and third quartiles of an intuitive probability distribution — the set of all feasible programs can be derived.[7] "Feasible" now means that the

6. Hollis B. Chenery and Michael Bruno, "Development Alternatives in an Open Economy: The Case of Israel," *Economic Journal,* LXXII (March 1962), esp. 93ff. See also Irma Adelman and Hollis B. Chenery, "Foreign Aid and Economic Development: The Case of Greece," *Review of Economics and Statistics,* XLVII (February 1966); Hollis B. Chenery and Alan M. Strout, "Foreign Assistance and Economic Development," *American Economic Review,* LVI, no. 4 (September 1966), pt. 1.

7. If there were nonlinearities in the model, it would be especially useful to

reduced form equations of the consistent growth model are satisfied *and* that the targets or the values of the controlled variables fall within predetermined limits. In Figure 1.1, Tims isolated the feasible range for income growth within the predetermined limits on savings rates and agricultural exports. The feasible area was further restricted by introducing the balance-of-payments limits, which was analogous, in this case, to adding another objective: reduced dependence upon foreign assistance. Finally, the macro-economic target was further constrained by bringing in the practical limits of import substitution. In this way the planner can trace the effect of changing the controlled variables between their minimum and maximum levels. The programing analogue to this cut-and-try procedure would be to write an explicit objective function and then describe the feasible area by varying the restraints on the system. The objectives can be read as restraints upon one another, and in this way their trade-offs or shadow prices can be obtained.

The Maynard-van Rijckeghem model, described in detail in Chapter 7, is drawn from a larger two-sector equation system for the Argentine economy. The sectoral model and the subsystem are stabilization devices. They are not exactly or even approximately consistent, in the sense that the two gaps, representing separate limits on the growth rate, introduce a built-in inconsistency. The stability properties of the submodel are implicit, without a set of constraints. It is not a growth model, properly speaking, and certainly not a *comprehensive* long-run growth model, but it is an imaginative policy tool that illustrates well some of the problems and possibilities under discussion.

The Argentine equation system replaces the technological basis of the Pakistan relationships by a set of decision functions in which

---

consider a Monte Carlo simulation procedure at this point. The procedure would require solving the equation system with values of the predetermined variables drawn either from a historical distribution or from a postulated, subjective probability distribution. This is not the place to essay a justification of Monte Carlo techniques or of subjective probabilities. Monte Carlo simulation is a way of making artificial trials with appropriate probabilities where the disproportionate costs of events generated by outlying values would make it misleading to use simple mean values. Subjective probability simply recognizes that, even in the absence of a record of relative frequencies, reasonable men are able to attach weights or probabilities to alternative events from their experience or judgments, or that they can do so by inference in situations where they have not had any direct, comparable experience.

credit availability and wage trends play a central role. In place of
the Chenery technique of locating the conflicting limits upon the
long-run (e.g., Harrod-Domar) growth process, the Buenos Aires
model substitutes short-run behavioral relationships to analyze price
and employment swings over the business cycle. In the debate
over inflation versus unemployment in the United States during the
late 1950's, several participants — following Tinbergen's discussion
— pointed out that there were two objectives, price stability and
employment stability, and that one instrument, monetary restraint,
could not possibly satisfy both, either in theory or in practice. The
Argentine model is addressed to the same *multivalent* problem.

The three equations presented by Maynard and van Rijckeghem
are not, properly speaking, a reduced form of the larger system,
but each structural equation contains one of the target variables
(production, prices, wages) and one or more of the controlled
variables. To achieve any one objective (such as price stability)
only at the cost of violating the others (output growth and real
wage improvement) would of course be undesirable. The problem
of finding strategies that avoid such one-sided achievements is
attacked by a simple simulation procedure. This is not simulation
in the Monte Carlo sense, where values of the uncontrolled variables are drawn from a probability distribution. Rather, by choosing plausible values for the controlled variables, one can trace the
paths in time of "actual" wages, prices, and output. The controlled
variables are the "agreed" wage increases, bank credit increases,
and money supply, each of which can be influenced experimentally
by changing policy parameters in the model. It would be instructive,
especially in the larger version of the model, to sample over the
probability distributions for gross agricultural output and a balance-
of-payments variable, which might replace the exogenous import
variable, and in that way to trace the path of the economy under
different stabilization strategies.

The exercise stops short of identifying an optimum. But suppose
that political acumen suggests that real wages can not be permitted
to decline if the risk of an opposition coup is to be avoided. Then the
range of wage policies alone is severely limited, and the feasible area
for a combined wage and monetary policy, or a combined wage,
credit, and monetary policy, can be traced, as was done by varying
the parameters in the Tims model. All of this tracing-out is to the

good; but with the information at hand, can we also help the planner set a price on each of the objectives? If the question implies a political price, in the sense of the changing probability of a regime's remaining in office next year, then the answer is no. (Every politician has to carry the opinion-poll findings in his own pajama pocket.) But the models can deliver shadow prices, trade-offs among the objective variables.

Suppose that for each objective a "production" function is written, containing as arguments the noncontrolled and policy variables that define it. The targets can then be set — a maximum rate of increase in the price case, perhaps, or a maximum variance in the employment variable — and the minimum "cost" of achieving the targets can be found. In the Pakistan setting as dealt with by Tims, for instance, one might minimize *extra*-import-substitution or investment expenditures; or if it was desirable to reduce dependence upon foreign assistance as quickly as possible, one might minimize the inflow of capital. Now the question arises, or returns, what could be gained or saved in terms of a "cost" variable by reducing or relaxing the targets that have been set? The solution to the optimizing problem contains the shadow prices or opportunity costs on each of the targets, around the presumably plausible values from which it started. Obviously, this full programing technique allows one, in theory, to incorporate multiple targets or objectives into the optimizing procedure. Furthermore, where the objectives are not directly commensurate — in terms of dollar cost, for instance — it allows one to find prices, in terms of the approach to one of the objectives, for each of the a priori targets. *In practice,* now, the question of those "production" relations is raised: where will one find such a set of functions among performance and policy variables?

Neither of the models examined thus far goes all the way to the shadow prices, but they both specify some of the functions looked for, in their reduced forms. In the Tims model one can specify the partial elasticities of each of the resource gaps, and therefore the *extra*-import-substitution objective, with respect to the income, saving, agricultural investment, and predetermined export variables. These would show, for example, by how much *extra*-import-substitution would change if agricultural investment were one percent higher. In the Maynard-van Rijckeghem model, Equation (5) writes the inflation objective to be minimized in terms of money supply, agreed wages, and bank credit. The full system brings in the relationship between bank credit, wage agreements, and output, via the production decision equation.

Finally, I want to suggest that the technique used for approaching the strategy solutions in each of the substantive models we have in hand may offer a practical shortcut toward the performance functions that are sought.[8] It will usually be possible to approximate the performance characteristics of each one of these functions, within plausible limits, by tracing the paths between solution-points of the reduced form when the controlled variables are set at assumed limiting (bracketing) values. In the Pakistan model a feasible area was defined by the intersecting limits of pairs of controlled variables, with none of the other predetermined variables being permitted to violate its boundary conditions.

I do not wish to suggest that this is easy. What I hope to have shown is how two of the econometric growth models drawn up in direct response to policy needs in DAS projects have dealt imaginatively and suggestively with the problems of multivalent, incommensurable, and possibly conflicting social objectives that Professor Vernon discussed. Further, I wanted to show that econometric models need not pretend to specify unambiguously the social welfare functions nor attempt to impose a welfare function upon the decision-makers. Rather, they offer the possibility of tracing one of the most important elements of the function, the trade-offs among the several objectives that must somehow be reconciled in the planning process. Incidentally, neither of the DAS econometric planners reacted to the multiplicity, even confusion, of targets with impatience, but they addressed themselves directly to the task of reconciling the multivalent objectives. Professor Vernon suggested that popular support may be more critical for the development process than a consistent plan. Turning to the sensitive Argentine political setting, the Maynard-van Rijckeghem exercise realistically *and* econometrically considers the crucial economic trade-offs that must be identified between the International Monetary Fund's demand for price stability and the popular demand for rising or at least stable real wages. Consistency may not be much of

8. The technique used by Tims in the Pakistan exercise is derived from the "feasible program" or parametric programing procedure introduced by Chenery and Bruno, "Development Alternatives in an Open Economy," sec. III.

an objective, but a serious economic *and political* price will possibly be incurred by ignoring it.

The third DAS model I want to mention in this regard was developed in the Liberian Advisory Group in response to some of the problems that began to appear in Liberia after the striking income growth of the 1950's. The balance of trade had shown a large annual surplus, a continuing inflow of foreign investment, and a large outflow of investment income. In the early sixties a deficit appeared on the trade account and was balanced almost entirely by net capital inflows. The picture for the next few years contained the additional sobering prospect of increasing fixed, contractual payments upon the debt service. The savings-investment gap brought the government crucially into the problem. While tax and other revenues have been generally sufficient to cover the current expenditures of the government, public investment projects have been financed primarily by credits, which are now falling due. In order to forecast the strains that would be imposed upon the growth process by the debt-service requirements, a very simple Harrod-Domar, two-gap model was written, relating the growth rate of national income to the external resource requirements and consequently to the debt-service constraints upon future income flows. (The model, prepared by me with the assistance of Poul Hansen and Peter Weisel, is shown in the Appendix to this chapter.) Multivalence appears in the conflict between an early, rapid rate of growth of income and the increasing strains imposed by the debt burden.

The second set of issues raised by Professor Vernon relates to the quality and, by implication, the cost of information required for these models. How sensible is it, he asks, to devote scarce manpower to a complicated procedure that requires more information than can reasonably be expected in an underdeveloped country? And there is a logical sequel to that question: are the models worth the cost of finding the information that they consume? He sets forth a sobering catalogue of all that can go wrong in the empirical specification of the model and adds to his list the fact — which does not partake of "rightness" or "wrongness" — that it is dealing with random processes. However well a model may have been specified and fitted, the constraints are random variables and not real constants. When a decision is taken or an action chosen, the outcome will depend upon the act only *in part;* the consequence will also depend upon the "state of the world," which can only be predicted to a particular level of probability. I will discuss these problems in two parts: first, the effect of error and misinformation; second, the possibility of acting optimally in the face of random constraints and uncertain consequences.

Under the first heading, one is dealing with the statistical quality of parameters. Measured input-output coefficients, for example, may vary in the short run because of a failure of supply or the illness of a specialist, neither of which are rare occurrences in a developing economy. Furthermore, the coefficients will change in the course of the process they are supposed to describe: investment in the latest-vintage, best-practice equipment will change the input ratios themselves. Similarly, a program of import substitution should, if successful, change the import and domestic input requirements and might even change the scale of operations in some industries by so much that the cost functions will themselves be altered. There may be a trend factor, which is likely to be correlated with the level of output and which will also subsume a great many elements of technological change not necessarily identified with the introduction of best-practice techniques. Prices may change. If so, factor proportions will alter, perhaps to such an extent that the assumption of fixed proportions is not appropriate.

The Tims model utilizes a number of devices for dealing with these threats. The most important of such adjustments is his use of constant-*marginal*, as opposed to constant-average, input ratios. That is, most of the input coefficients are fitted to points from two different years: the result is that there is an intercept, and the functions, though linear, are not proportional. This is an improvement, but it still involves the assumption that the relative changes (most of them declines) that occurred during the 1960/61– 1964/65 period will continue through the Third Plan to 1970. This is not a bad representation of the trend elements, probably, and it picks up some of the technological change features.

There are three ways to test the quality of the predictions from any set of "constant" input-output ratios: by using a given table to project the gross outputs of another, subsequent period and then comparing the projections to the actual outputs; by examining the variance of the ratios through direct observation; and by measuring those effects upon the key variables in the system that follow from given alterations in the parameters. The last of these tests has been performed on the Tims model by Richard Porter.[9] He found that 16 of the 39 nonzero input coefficients were "sensitive," in the sense that a 10 percent change in any one of them would produce a change of one percent or more in at least one of the 12 value-added and gap variables.

Projection studies have been made with the Netherlands Central Planning Bureau input-output table.[10] For all industries combined, the median root-mean-square error one year ahead (in terms of deviations between projected and actual deliveries in succeeding years) is between 7 and 8 percent. The mean error increases, but much less than proportionately, as the spread between table and forecast year increases. Forecasts of large sectors do better, on the whole. And finally, the input-output predictions are better than naïve methods (like final-demand-blowup extrapolations) as long as the table is not more than about two or three years older than the final demand ratios used for the extrapolations. I cannot believe that the Pakistan tables are comparable to the Central Planning Bureau tables, but I would expect the use of marginal coefficients derived from two separate years to improve the predictive ability of the system.

To complete the survey of Porter's sensitivity tests on the statistical relations outside of the input-output table, the effect of a 10 percent variation in the marginal propensities to consume is "rarely large," except for two induced changes of ±6 percent, respectively, in the import-substitution E_s variable, which would be effected through the export variable. About half the investment-by-origin coefficients were "significant," though not impressively so, and roughly the same was true of the accelerator-type investment coefficients. The effect of increases in import coefficients increases the "import substitution" required and reduces the relevant value added, as would be expected.

Certainly there are no alarmingly sensitive parameters; but the

9. Richard C. Porter, "Inter-Sectoral Analysis (the Tims Model)," in AID Office of Program Coordination, "Development Alternatives and Assistance Requirements in Pakistan" (United States Agency for International Development, October 9, 1965), pt. II, appendix 3.

10. The studies have appeared in a number of journals but are summarized in H. Theil *et al., Applied Economic Forecasting* (Chicago and Amsterdam: Rand McNally, 1966), chaps. 6–7.

results are not pure either. Thus, they raise a new class of doubt with regard to the operational qualities of the structure of the model, in the sense of being conceptually testable. There is some indication that *groups* of errors may be dangerous, as Professor Vernon warned. It would be better to test by simulation than by grouping, however, building up estimates of the mean and variance on each of the endogenous variables by drawing over probability distributions on the parameters. These distributions can be as rough-and-ready as necessary — perhaps nothing more than an explicit statement of the implicit hedges with which one works all the time. Ask the questions: what are the extreme values of this coefficient that are plausible? Then, how wide a bracket around the best estimate would enclose 50 percent of the occurrence — or, a little less formally, how wide a bracket about the best estimate would be a fair even-money bet? The answer to this question yields two more points — on the distribution quartile values, if the best estimate is taken to be the median. For the best estimate, take the value whose chance of turning out too high seems to be just equal to its chance of running too low — the median. There now are five points on the looked for probability distribution, counting the extremes.

Exhortation is cheap, of course, but if I am going to urge expenditure on data improvement, let me be more specific about its allocation. A major problem in all development models will be the effect of import substitution and technological change upon the domestic coefficients. The Tims model recognizes this, to a very limited extent, by the common-sense device of restricting *extra*-import-substitution to two sectors only and by using a somewhat higher capital coefficient for E_s, or import-substituting output, than for "ordinary" production. A more systematic treatment in general, not simply for one type of consistency model, would start from the separation of competing and noncompeting imports, already done in Pakistan. Then, the competing imports may be carried in the rows of the domestic sectors, with a balancing negative column in the final demand: intermediate flows equal domestic product plus competing imports. An alternative would be to enter the varying proportion for the supply of competing imports in the diagonal. If the competing import is specified as a proportion of domestic output — i.e., $m_i = k_i x_i$ — then $(I + k - A)x_i$ equals final demand. Adjustments owing to import substitution will henceforth need to be made only in the diagonal. The "total" effectiveness of import substitution is unambiguously determined by comparing the inverses of $(I + k_t - A)$ and $(I + k_{t-1} - A)$. A more difficult alternative would be to add a final demand category for import substitution and an entry in each column to pick up the differential inputs or limited effectiveness of production of "domestic imports." A similar range of possibilities is available for incorporating technological change into the table, and there have been interesting experiments in "predicting" technological improvements as a function of investment, which is almost necessarily channeled into new-vintage equipment.

With regard to the Argentine model, the obvious problem lies in the single-equation least-squares estimates of individual equations out of an essentially simultaneous structural set. It is hard to believe that the explanatory variables could be independent of the error terms. Without belaboring that point or speculating on the possibility that the model could be made fully recursive, I would commend the quality of the retrospective predictions and the fact that not a single turning-point has been missed in predictions with the individual equations of this or the complete model.

In the Liberian two-gap experiment there was no possibility of fitting parameters to time-series data. It was necessary to estimate the plausible values by inference from the tax schedules and anticipated ore shipments and by borrowing capital-output relationships from "comparable" economies. Without wishing to suggest that any relaxation of the raw-data-gathering effort is indicated, I would mention that useful untapped information is likely to turn up — in company records and even in forecasts — when a model is sufficiently bold to ask for the numbers.

Thus far, I have dealt only with the problem of uncertainty concerning the constraints and coefficients. But error aside, the problem remains of choosing among possible decisions now, as if their outcomes were known. In fact, a sequence of decisions is involved, each one of which may depend upon information that will not become available till later. How does one choose a path at the starting point as though one knew what would be the best decision later? There are a variety of techniques. The simplest in many ways is Theil's approach, which rests upon his use of a quadratic preference function. With a quadratic preference function, the decision-maker tries to minimize the weighted sum of squares of the deviations between his target values and the actual values. Then, by using the assumption of *certainty-equivalence,* acting as though the random coefficients are equal to their expectations, he can shift from maximizing the preference to maximizing its expectation. But, as Professor Vernon's argument suggested, it is not likely that the planner will anticipate positive and negative deviations as equally undesirable, which the quadratic function assumes. Indeed, it would be a rather special utility function that ascribed equally intense pleasure or pain in response to equally positive or negative deviations. The world, after all, is full of gamblers and risk-averters, even over-insured statisticians.

A second, less sophisticated possibility is simply to set a safety margin about the estimates. It may reflect the specific ex post standard error of measurement in estimated target variables or exogenous variables; it will more likely be a visceral or, one hopes, a common-sense estimate. The choice of bounds in the feasibility analysis on the Pakistan Plan is an excellent example of what this procedure can do.

A third possibility is to separate the elements that determine the desirability of each possible choice into three parts: the chance that different outcomes will occur, following a given decision; the consequences of those outcomes; and the desirability of the different consequences.[11] The decision process can then be subdivided to reflect each of these aspects. The decision rules that follow from this procedure are less simple and neat than Theil's quadratic preference function will support. In essence, they direct the decision-maker to choose in a sequence of gambles on the basis of his own cash certainty equivalent, which will depend upon his estimate of the chance of each payoff *and* his degree of liking for each payoff in comparison with every other.[12] Every uncertainty will be considered explicitly but need enter the decision only in proportion to its value. One

11. This procedure is exemplified in the work of Robert Schlaifer and Howard Raiffa at the Harvard Business School. The basic statement is in Schlaifer, *Probability and Statistics for Business Decisions* (New York: McGraw-Hill, 1959).

12. The cash-equivalent or certainty-equivalent in this sense is distinct from Theil's. I am concerned now with the cash in hand or "guaranteed" outcome that the decision-maker would be willing to accept in place of the gamble involved in the uncertain event in question. Obviously, it may be, but need not be, the mean or expected value.

advantage of this approach is that it provides a straightforward procedure for estimating the value of more information. Is more information, which is only available at a cost, worth that cost in terms of improving the expected value, or expected preference, of the best decision?

The Argentine stabilization model could more easily be adapted to fit this last sequential form of decision-making. The Pakistan growth model is more nearly self-contained as it stands. In the Argentine case, the economic team was faced with a choice among several monetary, bank credit, and wage policies, singly or in combination, including the choice of sitting tight and doing nothing. The Maynard-van Rijckeghem procedure predicts the consequences in terms of several objectives for a wide range of policies under consideration. As I have already suggested, the decision might be improved if the probability distribution of outcomes were approximated by a Monte Carlo procedure on the predetermined variables — that is, by choosing values from the probability distribution on the predetermined variables by some random process. Similarly in the Liberian case, while ore and rubber deliveries can be scheduled several months in advance, world market prices tend to fluctuate. The distribution of prices may affect the process described by the model both through export and revenue terms. It might obviously be an improvement also to apply Monte Carlo simulation over the distributions for the key parameters, rather than simply to use the least-squares estimates as fixed.

The Tims-Pakistan exercise predicts the consequences of a single complex set of decisions. By setting bounds on the predetermined variables, it can define an area of feasibility that includes political and administrative factors and economic considerations which are not accommodated elsewhere in the model. When the results of the reduced form and the feasibility analysis are in hand, a logical next step would be to define the transformation curve among the arguments that enter the implicit social welfare function. The sensitivity analysis tells which parameters would be most worth a further investment in research. As it stands, the model does not seem particularly amenable to simulation techniques, though its extreme sensitivity to the agricultural output assumption argues strongly for an investment in better crop forecasting methods and in a Monte Carlo procedure to reflect the chance element in the agricultural yields.

In place of a resounding coda, let me consider Professor Vernon's last point, which defines a dichotomy between short-run fire fighting and long-term global strategies. The models that have been considered here seem to bridge the long- and short-run gap most effectively. What is more important is the extent to which they facilitate the interplay of choice and constraints. Operationally, these models can not be judged without asking how much information must go into them and whether that input of data is not merely feasible, in terms of trained manpower and other resources, but even conceivable in the face of uncertainty. I submit that the two models that have been implemented come off remarkably well. I would emphasize that they permit the choice of policy and the definition of the objectives to proceed together, not as a bonus but as an essential part of their output. Professor Vernon is properly worried about optimizing models that produce policy directives mechanically, once they have been fed a real or imagined set of objectives. In the present examples, even with procedures as simple as the feasibility area in the Tims model and the cut-and-try simulation of the Maynard-van Rijckeghem experiment, the objectives and the policy are revised and refined in a real dialogue. That dialogue within the model seems to me to be essential to the dialogue among the practitioners.

*APPENDIX: A PRELIMINARY TWO-GAP MODEL
OF THE LIBERIAN ECONOMY*

The construction of the two-gap consistency model starts with familiar materials. National income is defined as follows:

(1) $$Y_n + T_f = Y - Y_f$$

where T_f is the tax paid by foreign income-receivers in Liberia, Y_f is expatriated income, and Y is net domestic product. Foreign wage earnings and consumption by wage earners are included, for convenience, with national households; the Y_f represents property income accruing to foreigners, and there is a basic assumption that reinvestment decisions are made "abroad" out of these expatriated earnings. In addition, the definition of Y does not include provision for capital consumption and indirect taxes; in this regard, the net may be read equally well as the gross.

The disposal of national income is exhausted by:

(2) $$C_h + S_h + T_h = Y_n$$

where the h subscript identifies the private sector, business and household, to include corporate savings and taxes. Investment is therefore exhausted by capital formation in the private and government sectors:

(3) $$I = I_g + I_h$$

The financing of private capital accumulation includes domestic, or national, savings and net borrowing from foreigners:

(4) $$I_h = S_h + B'_h$$

where the prime on B indicates net.

The treatment of the government account must be more complicated in order to bring the effect of the public debt service more clearly into the analysis. The outflow on foreign debt, interest and repayment of principal, are identified as r_o and D_o, respectively. Then:

(5) $$C_g + S_g + r_o = T_h + T_f$$

From Equations (3), (4), and $I_g = S_g + B_g - D_o$, one arrives at:

(6) $$I = S_h + S_g + B'_h + B_g - D_o$$

This last equation could be written in the more familiar form:

$$Y = C + I + E - M$$

where $Y - C$ is $S_h + S_g$ and $E - M$ is public plus private net borrowing from abroad: $B_h + B_g - D_o$. In the government investment-savings equation, B_g represents current and capital transfers from the rest of the world plus gross borrowing from abroad by the government. The I-S gap in this model focuses ultimately on inflow of capital to the government of Liberia.

Finally, the export-import gap is defined as:

$$E - Y_f - r_o = M + D_o - B_g - B'_h$$

in the usual receipts and disbursements form. The gap is more usefully indicated by rearranging:

(7) $$M + D_o + r_o + Y_f - E = B_g + B'_h$$

This completes the presentation of the definitions or balance equations. There are now nine structural or behavioral relationships to define.

The current expenditures of the government are taken as a function of domestic product, and the investment expenditures are counted as a share of total investment:

(8) $$C_g = gY$$

(9) $$I_g = pI$$

Both g and p, which are taken initially as structural parameters in estimating the gap, are obviously policy instruments as well and may be so used later in the adjustment process.

In the private sector taxes are defined as a function of domestic income, and savings are specified as a function of national income:

(10) $$T_h = t_h Y$$

(11) $$S_h = \alpha Y_n$$

Private-sector consumption is residually determined in (2).

In the foreign sector, imports, expatriate income, and expatriate taxes must be explained; exports are generally taken to be determined outside of the model. In some exercises it would be desirable to set other variables as given exogenously and to determine the required export volume; the possibility is noted only in passing it by. Imports are explained in part by the level of domestic income, in part by the level of investment:

(12) $$M = m_1 Y + m_2 I$$

Expatriate income (expatriate *property* income in the present setting) is taken to be a function of total domestic income and export volume, and expatriate income taxes are a fixed proportion of foreign earnings. Thus:

(13) $$Y_f = fY$$

(14) $$T_f = t_f Y_f$$

The final structural relation relates the target growth of income to the investment required. The link is the capital-output ratio (K):

(15) $$\Delta Y = 1/K \cdot I$$

In order to relate this incremental relationship to the rest of the system, it is necessary to add another definition:

(16) $$Y = \Delta Y + Y_o$$

If Y_o is base-year income, one of the set of given data, then:

(17) $$Y_o = Y_o$$

(18) $$r_o = r_o$$

(19) $$D_o = D_o$$

Interest payments and the repayment of principal are contractual and historically given. In the simplified exercise that follows, it is assumed that borrowing within the plan period will not affect r_o or D_o during that period. For long-term or perspective planning this will obviously not do. I shall later make some equally obvious remarks about the effect of different policy choices upon the future gap phenomena and growth prospects.

To recapitulate, there are nineteen equations in the model, of which eight — Equations (1)–(7), (16) — are definitions or accounting balances, eight are structural or behavioral relationships, and three simply state the values of the initial conditions. There are twenty variables, including the three givens. If two of the variables are now set — Y, as the target level of income, and E, which is essentially dependent upon external conditions — it really adds two more equations and the system cannot be solved. There are more than one, not necessarily equal, estimates for some variables. In this case the model has been set up to focus upon the so-called internal and external resource gaps.

Starting with an income goal and a given level of exports, the model determines the levels of national and expatriate property income, the disposal of those incomes among current and investment expenditures, and the size of the external or export-import gap and the internal or investment-savings gap. The gap is measured by $B'_h + B_g - D_o$. In this two-gap form there are two independent B_g estimates.

The main motive force in this model is the investment required to achieve the target change in gross domestic product. Once the income level is set, the necessary investment follows from the application of the incremental capital-output ratio. Given the investment estimate, one can divide it between the government and private shares in capital accumulation, which will subsequently be used to estimate the borrowing (or lending or debt repayment) that follows, once savings levels have been determined. Savings are calculated functionally for the private sector and residually, after taxes and budget expenditures are set, for the government. The tax functions depend primarily upon the rates set on incomes and import values, as well as upon the efficiency of enforcement. The rest of the forecast is arithmetic — up to the point at which the gaps are balanced and the feasibility of the targets is judged. In this two-gap model there is no automatic reconciliation or "slack" variable.

The first step in the consistency or feasibility analysis is to see whether the forecast values "make sense." Making sense is a criterion framed in terms of social and economic values: for instance, it would not make sense to provide growth by means of investment apparently paid for by reducing the consumption of urban laboring families by 50 percent. Similarly, if imports appear to be reduced by, say, 50 percent, then either import-substituting industries must have come into production during the base year or some producers are not going to have the imported materials they need. Minor shortfalls in terms of the targets proposed by Liberia's Planning Council would indicate that some policy variables might be changed to bring the economy closer to target. But the purpose of the model is to demonstrate what will happen to several, perhaps all, of the values of interest if any one of the structural relationships is changed.

Assuming that all other destinations seem to be within reach of the economy, consider the two gaps. It is always tempting to take the larger of the two as binding and to allow some slack in the other. If the *I-S* gap is the larger one, investment policies chosen so as to allocate a smaller investment total in directions that would increase the overall output per unit of capital might make possible a reduction in that gap without sacrificing the target rate of growth. Alternatively, the tax policy might be varied to increase government revenues and S_d out of the given income. If the *E-M* gap is the larger one, perhaps prohibitively large in terms of foreign assistance and borrowing prospects, the planned investment total might be directed toward the substitution of more domestic goods for some commodities that are being imported at the present time. Finally, it should be noted ruefully that it is possible to follow many less efficient routes. If the *I-S* gap is larger, and foreign capital is available to fill the gap, the *E-M* gap *may* be increased by imports of a relatively low order of usefulness. Or, if the *E-M* gap is larger and beyond the possibility of being covered with foreign savings, an inefficient reduction in raw-material imports might follow from an excessive attachment to the idea of capital expansion. The result would be a balance at a lower level of output and employment — with excess capacity to reward the zeal for capital accumulation. Most readers will be able to supply a list of even less edifying examples from their own experience; the object of this array is merely to emphasize that a *formal* adjustment mechanism is not the aim. It is to estimate the two gaps, identify the effective limit, and consider effective policy adjustments.

With these observations in mind, the model may now be set out in its entirety:

(1) $Y_n + T_f = Y - Y_f$

(2) $C_h + S_h + T_h = Y_n$

(3) $I = I_g + I_h$

(4) $I_h = S_h + B_h'$

(5) $C_g + S + r_o = T_h + T_f$

(6) $I_h + I_g = S_h + B_h' + S_g + B_g - D_o$

(7) $M + D_o + r_o + Y_f - E = B_g + B_h'$

(8) $C_g = gY$

(9) $I_g = pI$

(10) $T_h = t_h Y$

(11) $S_h = \alpha Y_n$

(12) $M = m_1 Y + m_2 I$

(13) $Y_f = fY$

(14) $T_f = t_f Y$

(15) $\Delta Y = \dfrac{1}{k} I$

(16) $Y = \Delta Y + Y_o$

(17) $Y_o = Y_o$

(18) $r_o = r_o$

(19) $D_o = D_o$

David Felix

3

~~~~~~~~~~~~~~~~~

The Dilemma of Import Substitution — Argentina

Economic growth in Latin American countries has traditionally occurred in fits and starts: a succession of booms interspersed with periods of relative stagnation. Until the 1930's the fluctuating fortunes of primary exports lay behind the cycles, but in the past three decades this export-economy pattern has been modified in varying degrees by industrial growth, impelled primarily by import substitution. The larger countries — Argentina, Brazil, Chile, Colombia, and Mexico — have since the 1940's most vigorously pursued import-substituting industrialization (hereafter called ISI) as their main growth strategy, although in the past decade a number of the smaller countries — Peru, Venezuela, Ecuador, and the Central American Common Market Countries — have also begun to adopt ISI with some vigor.

The spread of ISI has been paralleled, however, by growing concern in the larger countries and in such tutelary centers of Latin American economic thought as the Economic Commission for Latin America (ECLA) over its diminishing viability as a growth strategy. That is, ISI in these countries seems to have lost its capacity to lower the average import coefficient, so that the GNP growth rate

NOTE: I wish to thank the DAS for making possible two summers of research at the Instituto Torcuato Di Tella in Buenos Aires, the Instituto for generous access to its facilities and research staff, the Washington University Computer Center for the computations summarized here, and Daniel Schydlowsky of Harvard for a careful critique of an earlier draft that led me to rework the first part. Others to whom I am particularly indebted for helpful criticism and discussion are Raymond Vernon of Harvard, John Erickson of Williams College, and Richard Mallon of the DAS.

has again become closely tied to the growth of the capacity to import. To compound the dilemma, efforts to raise the capacity to import through industrial exporting have thus far been relatively ineffective. Those semi-industrialized Latin American countries with slow-growing foreign-exchange earnings in the postwar years have therefore suffered a decline in growth rate and a disturbingly large rise in foreign indebtedness.

My purpose here is to analyze the dynamics of ISI in order (1) to identify the relationships that make it lose its power to lower the average import coefficient and (2) to show how these tend to create an industrial cost-price structure that is a serious impediment to industrial exporting. Argentine data are used to support the major hypotheses advanced. Two caveats are in order. I smooth over the untidy reality of the Latin American industrialization effort in order to concentrate on a few key problems. Some of the relationships passed over may explain in part results attributed to those explicitly identified here.[1] The implication that generalizations supported by Argentine data are broadly relevant to, for instance, Brazil or Colombia is at this point merely an impressionistic judgment.

THE DIMINISHING DYNAMICS OF ISI

In economic growthmanship, import substitution may be viewed as either a tactic or a strategy. In two-gap planning models, for example, one possible tactic for eliminating the import gap is to produce import replacements in sufficient volume to allow a planned growth rate to be met without excess demand for foreign exchange. Since in such normative models the gap can also be closed by additional exports, the choice of import substitution over export promotion depends on whether the foreign exchange saved by the

1. For example, the comparative price data for Argentina presented in the second part of the chapter may well be influenced by a heedless fragmentation of firms within industries where demand would be inadequate — or at most barely adequate — to support one or two large firms at minimum efficient scale. The fragmentation stems partly from the fact that Argentine industrial promotion policy since Perón has been guided by a bowdlerized version of free enterprise in which, within a cocoon of almost prohibitive import protection plus subsidies, generous entry has been permitted to producers. Apparently this principle of nondiscriminatory access to discriminatory privileges is not unique to Argentina; witness, for example, the replication of fragmented and miniaturized automotive industries in one Latin American country after another. A fuller analysis of Latin American industrialization would need to incorporate the ideological and political crosscurrents that compound the ills besetting the process.

former can be obtained at a lower social cost than the additional exchange earned by the latter.[2] Implicit in such models is the assumption that the planners have effective policy instruments at hand to implement either alternative.

By means of additional premises that limit the range of feasible policy instruments, import substitution can be rationalized into a general strategy for accelerating industrial investment and the economic growth rate, as was done in the Latin American growthmanship literature of early postwar vintage.[3] A fundamental premise, also held by both sides in the polemics about balanced vs. unbalanced growth, is that pre-industrial economies are in a quasi-Keynesian state of underemployment — quasi-Keynesian in that despite a few supply constraints, notably a low capacity to import, surplus labor and other underutilized resources offer ample scope for augmenting capital formation and output through appropriate inducements that raise the prospective rate of return or reduce investment risks. Accordingly, investment can create its own savings, provided import constraint is overcome.

The policy instruments for promoting ISI are assumed to be able both to induce investments and to direct them toward foreign-exchange saving activities. Restrictions on consumer imports may raise the effective savings rate by, say, forcing local capitalists to make do with last year's Cadillac while concurrently providing profitable and protected investment outlets in import replacement for funds that might otherwise have gone into consumption or capital export. A high expected profitability could even induce them to

2. See Hollis B. Chenery and Michael Bruno, "Development Alternatives in an Open Economy," *Economic Journal* (March 1962), pp. 79–103.

3. Like M. Jourdain's philosophy teacher who made him conscious that he had been speaking prose, the Economic Commission for Latin America was principally responsible for conceptualizing an already ongoing process of import substitution in the early postwar years. ISI had gained momentum in the larger Latin American countries partly as a side effect of balance-of-payments difficulties in the 1930's and wartime barriers to imports. The commission elevated it into a more self-conscious growth strategy. Whether ECLA's efforts did much more than change the vocabulary of the industrial promotion effort is not so clear, particularly in Argentina. There the phrases "import substitution" and "saving foreign exchange" appear explicitly in the industrial promotion laws and decrees after 1950, whereas previously "anti-dumping," "diversification," and "economic independence" had predominated. But the industrial promotion policies pursued in the 1950's did not vary in essence from those of the previous decade. ECLA's efforts may, however, have given greater intellectual respectability to pressures from industrialist groups, military planners, and assorted nationalist intellectuals for accelerating industrialization.

repatriate funds from New York or Zurich. In addition, foreign manufacturers can be coerced into setting up local plants through fear of losing the local market through import restrictions. Even the inflation usually accompanying the ISI effort may function benignly by upping the profit share and hence the savings rate. The capacity to import constraint may thus be successively overcome, and more domestic labor and other resources may be drawn into productive activity. Finally, over the long run the skills and other favorable externalities created by industrialization should spread technical progress and investment to the agricultural and exporting sectors.

In contrast, export promotion as an immediate alternative to ISI is judged to be far less promising. The elasticity of foreign demand for traditional exports is assumed to be low, while the large competitive risks in open markets and the need for a high initial level of production and marketing competence make a rapid expansion of new export lines much more uncertain. The set of subsidies required to overcome these obstacles and ensure such expansion is far more economically sophisticated to devise and politically difficult to legislate than policies to promote ISI.

The factual validity of each of these premises has undoubtedly varied among countries and at different times in the past three decades; and perhaps even within the limited practical range of choice of policy instruments, industrialization may have been purchased in many cases at an excess cost in potential agricultural expansion or export growth.[4] I eschew such speculation, however,

4. The macro-evidence that ISI substantially depressed the growth of agricultural output or primary exports is inconclusive. Alfred Maizels, grouping newly industrializing countries of various geographic regions, found that between 1937–38 and 1955 the group kept its world market share of traditional exports and that there was no significant difference in the growth of similar exports between non-industrial and semi-industrial countries. He concluded that, "at least for the period from 1937 to 1955, the demand-deficiency argument has been nearer the truth than the supply-deficiency argument, if a broad generalization is sought . . . It cannot . . . be assumed that industrialization of a primary-producing country will, in itself, necessarily have adverse effects on the capacity to import and thus indirectly place limits on its domestic rate of economic growth." Maizels, *Industrial Growth and World Trade* (Cambridge: Cambridge University Press, 1963), Chap. V. Even where the supply-deficiency argument is clearly relevant, as in Argentina (whose market share of many of its leading exports fell between the 1930's and 1950's) or Chile (which shifted from being a net agricultural exporter to a net importer in the same interval), no prima facie case can be made against ISI as the cause. The slowdown in Argentine agricultural production dates back to the late 1920's, whereas the growth of agricultural output in Chile in the period 1949–57 was only slightly below the slow 1921–40 rate. Cf. O.E.C.E.I., *Economia Agropecuaria Argentina* (Buenos Aires, 1964), table 36; Tom E. Davis,

to concentrate rather on a narrower but more intriguing question. Why does ISI in time lose its power to sustain a GNP growth rate in excess of the growth in the capacity to import, irrespective of whether the import capacity is reduced by excessive reliance on ISI? That this seems to have happened to the Latin American countries that have most persistently pursued an ISI strategy is brought out in various recent ECLA studies.[5] Economists are, however, notoriously adept at discovering theoretical reasons that something need not have happened. It is not uncommon to charge that excessive dependence on ISI raises the economic costs of growth, but the consensus in the economic development literature — ECLA's current position being a major exception — is that no irremediable forces prevent a country that is willing to pay this cost from continuing indefinitely to grow faster than its capacity to import. My purpose here is to modify this consensus. I maintain that ECLA's empirical findings are not aberrations but a logical denouement of the interaction of consumer demand and industrial technology under an ISI strategy.

The following views seem to be the prevailing ones among non-ECLA economists. The most common view is that there are no reasons inherent in the ISI process why the import coefficient cannot continue to be lowered. Obstacles may arise from an unbalanced expansion of import substitution in consumer goods, but this expansion can be remedied by a compensating expansion of ISI in intermediate and capital goods so as to reduce the heavy reliance of the consumer-goods industries on imported inputs.[6] The remedy is

---

"The Growth of Output, Employment, Capital Stock, and Real Wages in Basic Sectors of the Chilean Economy," in Joint Economic Committee, *Hearings before the Sub-Committee on Inter-American Relationships* (87th Cong., 2nd sess. [Washington, D.C.: GPO, 1962]), p. 104.

5. See ECLA, "Preliminary Study of the Effects of Post-War Industrialization on the Import Structure and External Vulnerability in Latin America," in *Economic Survey of Latin America, 1956* (New York: UN, 1957); *The Economic Development of Latin America in the Post-War Period* (New York: UN, 1964); "The Growth and Decline of Import Substitution in Brazil" and "Protectionism and Industrialization in Latin America," *Economic Bulletin for Latin America,* IX (March 1964); "The Evolution of the External Sector in the Latin American Economy, 1960–63," in *Economic Survey of Latin America, 1963* (New York: UN, 1965).

6. Cf. *World Economic Survey* (New York: UN, 1961), pp. 42, 60. This view is still rather common in Latin American economic circles. In Argentina, for example, it is a basic tenet of the "Desarrollistas," the group of economists, politicians, military officers, and businessmen linked to former President Arturo Frondizi.

not painless, however. With tight foreign exchange, corrective measures put a short-term squeeze on import-intensive consumer-goods industries, which will consequently oppose shifting ISI to higher stage industries. For this reason, John Power suggested, many countries may have great difficulty getting past the consumer-goods stage of ISI.[7] Carlos Diaz-Alejandro added another qualification — the rate of decline of the import coefficient may be rather narrowly circumscribed because of the time lag between investment and output. Too rapid an acceleration of import-substituting investment raises income and hence the demand for imports in excess of the increase in output from maturing past investment.[8]

Apart from these qualifications, the consensus seems to be that as long as some additional domestic value is created within each successive import-substituting activity, there is no determinable lower floor to the economy's import coefficient. Continued ISI may cease to be efficient compared to a more flexible development strategy, but it remains feasible.[9]

Meanwhile, ECLA, whose early postwar views on ISI resembled those outlined here, has shifted to the position that ISI does become progressively harder to sustain.[10] This position is embedded in a series of empirical studies of ISI in the larger Latin American countries, from which the following general explanation for its declining efficacy may be extracted. As the consumer-goods phase of ISI is succeeded by a predominantly capital- and intermediate-goods phase, three sets of forces close in on the strategy. The import mix shifts predominantly to one of fuels, industrial materials, essential foodstuffs, and capital goods required by the industrial sector. The capital intensity of import-substituting projects rises,

7. John Power, "Import Substitution as a Development Strategy," paper presented to the World Conference of the Society for International Development, March 1966.

8. C. F. Diaz-Alejandro, "On the Import Intensity of Import Substitution," *Kyklos,* XVIII (1965), 495–511.

9. Much of the literature is concerned mainly with short-run problems of ISI rather than with its long-run feasibility. Since the long run is, however, a succession of short runs, it seems justifiable to deduce a long-run optimism about ISI's capacity to lower the import coefficient, in the absence of references in the writings to additional relationships that would gradually prevent the short-run solutions from being repeated indefinitely — particularly since the short-run analysis tends to be made in generic, theoretical terms. In the case of Diaz-Alejandro no imputation is needed; his article, in part a critique of ECLA's ISI pessimism, is explicitly directed to the long-run problem.

10. See note 6.

resulting in a rising import content of investment and causing the level of investment to be more severely constrained by the capacity to import. The projects tend to require increasingly large markets in order to reach minimum efficient scale, so that the ability of ISI to induce investment is progressively weakened by the thin domestic markets of even the larger Latin American countries.

The difference between ECLA's view and that of economists who believe in the long-run feasibility of ISI depends mainly on different appraisals of the same set of relationships, with one important exception. ECLA concerns itself explicitly with the inducement mechanism and finds, surprisingly, that Latin American industrial investors do worry about scale economies and relative costs, although ECLA does not make clear why this should be so in view of the normally high rates of protection provided Latin American industry and the established pattern of high-cost, underscale production. Apart from this concern with the diminishing effectiveness of ISI in encouraging industrial investment, ECLA's case is based on the premise that the rise in the imported capital intensity of investment more than offsets the savings in imports from completed projects. This premise, however, as Diaz-Alejandro has argued, requires extreme assumptions about the trend in the capital coefficient, which ECLA has not validated empirically.[11]

Nevertheless, I contend that ECLA's pessimism about ISI is justified. A major difficulty has been that both sides have worked within a framework that ignores the reciprocal effect of changes in the composition of final demand on the dynamics of ISI. If this effect is explicitly introduced, ECLA's pessimistic conclusion is greatly strengthened.

The more measurable determinants of an economy's import coefficient can be identified by means of the following equation:

$$(1) \quad M = \left(\sum_j r_{ij} m_j^{\mathrm{I}} + \sum_j \rho_{ij} k_j + m_i^C \right)_t Y_t$$

$$= \left(\sum_j r_{ij} m_j^{\mathrm{I}} + \sum_j \rho_{ij} k_j + m_i^C \right)_{t+1} Y_{t+1}$$

where Y is the vector of final demand, $\sum_j r_{ij} m_j^{\mathrm{I}}$ is a vector of direct and indirect current import requirements, $\sum_j \rho_{ij} k_j$ is a vector of direct and indirect imported capital requirements, and m_i^C is a vec-

11. Diaz-Alejandro, "Import Intensity of Import Substitution."

tor of ratios of individual consumer-goods imports to total supply of such goods. In each period the economy's imports, M, is the sum of the products of multiplying the vectors within brackets by the Y vector. For simplicity I assume the capacity to import to be fixed at a constant level through all periods — for example, by a zero rate of growth of exports — and that ISI pushes the level and composition of total activity in each period to the capacity-to-import ceiling, so that M has the same value each period. Following input-output convention, all values are assumed to be expressed in constant prices by appropriate deflation. The effects of changing relative prices, which in fact play a major role in investment inducement and in changing final demand under ISI, is introduced where necessary.

An increase in Y under these conditions obviously requires $M/Y_{t+1} < M/Y_t$. But it is also immediately apparent that the effect of lowering one or more of the components of the bracketed vectors can be negated by a shift in the final demand mix of Y toward more import-intensive products. Analysis of the dynamics of ISI requires, therefore, explicit hypotheses not only about the sequential pattern of domestication of industrial activities, their technological characteristics and import content, but also about the changing composition of final demand over time under ISI.

One possible demand hypothesis is that there is no persistent import bias to the changes in the final demand mix. Shifts toward goods with an import intensity above the previous period's average import coefficient are no more likely than shifts in the opposite direction. For analytic purposes, therefore, each period's Y vector can be assumed to be related to that of other periods by simple scalar multiplication.

Given this demand hypothesis, which is adhered to, implicitly at least, by Diaz-Alejandro and other ISI optimists,[12] can ECLA's pessimism be justified purely by plausible hypotheses about changes over time in the bracketed vectors? The answer is no if pessimism means that M/Y reaches a floor so that Y can no longer grow faster than M. It is yes if pessimism means that the rate of decline of M/Y decelerates. That is, there are convincing reasons to expect the capital-output ratios to rise and investment inducements to weaken

12. That is to say, income growth is treated by them as a process of scalar multiplication.

as the ISI strategy shifts more heavily to the substitution of capital and intermediate goods, but this trend alone is not sufficient to account for the leveling-off of M/Y.

ISI characteristically focuses first on consumer-goods substitution, on reducing m_i^C. To quote from an ECLA study, "Substitution usually begins in the easiest area, the production of finished consumer goods, partly because the technology is generally less complicated and less capital-intensive, but mainly because there is a larger untapped market for goods of this kind, either already existing, or brought into being as a result of the foreign trade policy adopted as a defensive measure." [13]

Each component of m_i^C has a theoretical lower limit of zero. But since protection raises the relative price of the import substitute, the practical limit is usually above zero, at what may be called the smuggler's floor, the amount of smuggling depending on the difference between the CIF price of the import and the price of its domestic substitute, on quality differences, and on the strength of enforcement of import controls. In Latin American countries the smuggler's floor for many imports is consequently well above zero, the floor manifesting itself either in increased smuggling or in the creation of legal import loopholes and quotas designed to restrain illegal importing. [14]

Lowering m_i^C by generating backward linkages also alters the other bracketed vectors. If ISI shifts to intermediate and capital goods, the zeros in the input-output and capital-output matrices decline in number and the values of the r_{ij} and ρ_{ij} coefficients in successive matrices tend to rise, while the import rows, the m_j's and the k_j's, correspondingly fall. Technological change may, of course, dampen the rise in the r_{ij}'s and ρ_{ij}'s. Its effect may even be greatest when the upward pressure on the coefficients from the creation of backward linkages is also greatest. That is, since technological change is usually correlated with output growth, productivity improvements in mimetic economies with chronic rationing of capital-goods imports tend in each period to be concentrated in the newer

13. "The Growth and Decline of Import Substitution in Brazil," p. 5.
14. For example, Argentine radio manufacturers complained in a recent petition to the government that over 25 percent of small transistor radios sold in Argentina were smuggled imports. In general, the official consumer-import figures in the semi-industrialized Latin American countries are considered to understate true imports by a substantial margin.

import-substituting activities, whose growth of demand is a function of ongoing import replacement as well as increasing income. The capital stock of the activity is then being augmented at a rapid rate by successive equipment imports, which incorporate the advancing technology of such industries in advanced countries, while the learning effect in new, fast-growing activities is likely to be relatively powerful.[15] Offsetting the effect of the new technology, however, is the likelihood that diseconomies of small scale will become increasingly prevalent as ISI pushes along the more specialized and technically complex backward linkages, which should raise capital-output ratios.

Even with no technological change, however, the rising capital intensity that occurs, as ECLA emphasizes, when ISI shifts more to capital- and intermediate-goods substitution is not likely to offset the fall in the m_j's and k_j's by raising r_{ij}'s and ρ_{ij}'s so much that the direct and indirect import coefficients cease to fall. Complete offsetting requires rises in the capital-output ratios far greater than those reported by ECLA for the semi-industrialized Latin American countries. Rising capital intensity may have slowed the decline of M/Y but could not have brought it to a halt.

The depressing effect on the economy's growth rate is compounded, however, according to ECLA, by weakening investment inducements as the capital intensity and minimum efficient scale of prospective ISI projects rise. Given the generous levels of protection under ISI, why should this be so? A plausible answer is that despite access to protection and subsidies the investor's risk appraisal is higher the greater the difference between the projected unit costs and the CIF price of the imported product. A large difference substantially reduces the credibility of protection, both because of an increased threat of smuggling and a greater danger of administrative policy reversals under pressure from user industries.[16] Thus, a

15. This is discussed in more detail in my "Structuralists, Monetarists, and Import Substituting Industrialization: A Critical Appraisal," in W. Baer and I. Kerstenetsky, eds., *Inflation and Growth in Latin America* (Homewood, Ill.: Irwin, 1964).

16. Argentine officials are continually adjudicating between firms pressing for special tariff concessions on equipment and current inputs and domestic producers of the items insisting on the exclusion of competitive imports. The resulting compromises have given Argentina a tariff structure whose nominal rates are the highest in the world, but through which about half of Argentine imports have entered in recent years free of duty, mainly because of ad hoc rather than generic tariff exemptions.

growing discrepancy between minimum efficient scale of operations and the size of the market may well weaken the potency of ISI as an inducement mechanism.

In a purely Keynesian world a decline in the willingness to invest increases liquidity and depresses output and employment; its effect on the price level depends on the stickiness of money wages and prices. In an ISI world with its strong inflationary expectations, reluctance to invest stimulates capital flight and hence lowers the capacity to import. If, however, one assumes no import bias to changes in the final demand mix, the M/Y ratio would still decline as long as some import-substituting continued to occur, though the decline would be small solace if M was also falling.

In point of fact, capital flight from the semi-industrialized Latin American countries has risen since the mid-1950's, while foreign direct investment has fallen in the past quinquennium.[17] But the depressing effect on the capacity to import was offset by a rise in foreign borrowing, and the fall in the rate of private investment was balanced by a rise in public investment financed by the increased foreign borrowing. The declining potency of ISI as an inducement mechanism can, therefore, explain the slowdown in industrial growth experienced by the semi-industrial countries in the past decade but can not explain the sustained increase in industrial excess capacity that has accompanied the reduced industrial growth, because neither the overall rate of investment nor the capacity to import has manifested a persistent downward trend. Apparently, only by postulating a persistent import bias to the changes in the final demand mix can the leveling-off of M/Y be adequately explained. What reasonable demand hypothesis will generate this bias?

One possibility for deriving this bias is to link Engel's Law to ISI and thus show that, as rising income shifts the demand mix toward products with high income elasticities, these tend to have higher import intensities than the products with slow-growing demand. ECLA's own planning advice for ISI emphasizes, in fact, a distinction between vegetative industries, the output of which have income elasticities of demand less than one, and dynamic industries, whose income elasticities are above one, with the dynamic industries increasing in relative importance as ISI proceeds. Both groups

17. See the detailed survey of capital flight estimates by country, 1946–62, in ECLA, *External Financing in Latin America* (New York: UN, 1965), pp. 77–87.

of industries include nonconsumer goods, so that the relationship to Engel's Law of the vegetative-dynamic industry classification is only approximate, although food and apparel, the income-inelastic items according to the "law," are in the vegetative group, whereas the income elastic durable consumer goods are in the dynamic group. Income elasticities and the vegetative-dynamic distinction are, in fact, treacherous guides to demand projections, since other factors affect the demand mix. But even if income elasticity were the overriding determinant of changes in the mix, would it impart an import bias to the changes, and would the bias be sufficient to set a lower floor to M/Y?

The answer to the first part of the question is yes. In accordance with the usual Engel's curves, the demand mix at low levels of Y should favor ISI in income-inelastic products; but if ISI succeeds in raising Y, demand will shift relatively to more income-elastic products, many of which will be pure imports. Excess demand for imports may again be overcome by distributing ISI investment between producing substitutes for these new imports and reducing the import content of the previously established industries by expanding backward linkages. There is, however, a lag between the domestication of a new product and its creation of a market for backward-linkage investment, which usually causes the new products favored by the income elasticity of demand structure to have initially a higher import content than longer established products.

The import bias is not likely to set a floor to M/Y if changes in the mix are purely a function of income, since a slowdown in income growth will lessen changes in the final demand mix. Slowing the growth rate thus becomes a self-correcting mechanism that should normally enable ISI to continue to lower M/Y at some reduced rate, even if the new activities are progressively more technologically sophisticated, requiring more varied and specialized inputs and greater capital investment. Such a trend might increase the import intensity of new activities in period $t + 1$ relative to t, and cause diseconomies of small scale increasingly to hamper the development of backward linkages, but the fall in the growth rate required to help close the import gap would also slow the shift in demand to more import-intensive products that had been widening the gap. A complete leveling-off of M/Y, based on special ad hoc propositions about trends in lags and other parameters, is possible, but it would be the extreme limit to the possible range of mutual adjustments rather than the general case.

The case would become more general, however, if import-biased demand shifts also occurred independently of income changes. This, I suggest, is what does occur via Ragnar Nurkse's "international demonstration effect," which formalizes the obvious fact that mimetic less developed economies borrow not only their new technology but also their new consumption tastes from advanced countries. Nurkse used the effect to explain low savings rates in underdeveloped economies, but it can be brought in more convincingly as a shift parameter causing the Engel's curves for new products in ISI economies to be persistently to the left of the curves for the same products in the advanced countries innovating the products.[18] At constant prices the demand for TV sets, wrist watches, or home permanents in Brazil or Argentina would be greater than Engel's curves would have predicted for these products in France or the United States. More formally, the import bias of consumer demand is positively related not merely to rising income but also to the rate of product innovation in advanced countries, to factors reducing informational lags concerning such products in borrowing countries, and to the trend toward greater technological complexity of these products and their components. Zero income growth is no longer the outer limit to the income adjustment required to overcome the import gap when the capacity to import is constant. Since the demonstration effect would make it possible for the gap to persist at zero income growth, the denouement of an ISI strategy could even be a rising M/Y — conjoined, if the capacity to import is constant, with a falling Y.

Presumably the demonstration effect operates in all underdeveloped societies open to foreign influence, but the intensity of the effect is probably strengthened by the stimulus that industrialization gives to urban growth, since urban centers are more accessible and

---

18. Nurkse disregarded the possibility that the demonstration effect may also increase investment opportunities for ISI. Provided the foreign-exchange constraint to realizing these investments can be overcome, the various mechanisms indicated earlier that raise the ex ante and ex post savings rates would be activated. This is the benign effect visualized by Albert Hirshman, *Strategy of Economic Development* (New Haven: Yale University Press, 1958). The overall impact of the demonstration effect on savings rates can thus be favorable or unfavorable. It is unfavorable when, by increasing the foreign-exchange obstacle, it prevents the investments from being realized.

responsive to new taste and product emanations than are rural cultures. The responsiveness is probably further increased as the industrializing economy imports, along with technology, the marketing skills and huckstering knowhow to titillate the sensitized urban centers with new products. ISI thus pushes against demand forces which increasingly counter its effort to lower M/Y. To conclude that pushing m_i^C to the "smuggler's floor" halts ISI in consumer products is to fall victim of a statistical illusion. It need only mean that the domestication of new products is taking place increasingly via licensing agreements, market surveys, promotional campaigns, and the like without the prior intercession of direct consumer imports. Like a sorcerer's apprentice, ISI stimulates changes in demand that are initially useful to growth but continue to press on even after the changes have become a deterrent to further growth.

ECLA's pessimistic finding that ISI has lost its effectiveness in the more industrialized Latin American countries, so that their growth rate has become closely tied to growth of the capacity to import, can thus be given stronger theoretical validation. This comforting support for reality turns out to depend not only on the progressively greater capital intensity and scale requirements of new import-substituting activities but also on an intensified import bias of demand shifts relative to the reduced M/Y. In time the interaction of these production and demand trends, aggravated by the propensity of ISI economies to borrow too freely the technology and consumption tastes of advanced countries, will bring a halt to the decline of M/Y.

One would expect the M/Y floor to be lower the larger the domestic market. This is roughly borne out in Latin America, where the ranking of the five most industrialized countries in order of absolute size of industrial output — Brazil, Argentina, Mexico, Colombia, and Chile — is approximately the reverse of their ranking by size of the M/Y ratio, which in each of these countries in the past five to ten years has oscillated around a horizontal or rising trend.

What happens if ISI is nevertheless continued, in an effort to sustain a positive growth rate? Since M/Y can no longer be reduced, growth requires running down foreign-exchange reserves or running up the external debt. Since these recourses are uncertain and exhaustible, it soon becomes necessary to curtail the level of

industrial activity by monetary-fiscal constraints or by tighter control of imports to the established industries. Chronic excess capacity
thus becomes a manifestation of this phase of ISI. Unable to sustain
full use of industrial capacity, the economy enters into stop-go contortions, the downturns being initiated by balance-of-payments
crises and the upturns by the reaccumulation of exchange reserves
during the industrial depression. When the given capacity to import
becomes an insuperable bottleneck, investment can no longer create its own savings, and both the quasi-Keynesian assumptions and
the expansionary monetary-fiscal policies that accompany ISI lose
their relevance.

Just how harmful the stop-go contortions will be depends on the
actual growth of the capacity to import. If, as in postwar Mexico,
it has risen rapidly, the economy can arrive at a constant or rising
M/Y with ample reserves, a strong line of international credit, and
a high income growth rate. It can continue to pursue ISI with only
mild cyclical distortions and decelerating growth. If, however, the
capacity to import has been growing slowly — the more typical
case for the semi-industrialized Latin American countries — the
contortions will be frequent and severe.

Greater stress on capital- and intermediate-goods ISI does little
to alleviate the problems as long as the final demand mix is allowed
to shift freely to more import-intensive goods. Under these circumstances the effort to increase backward-linkage investment, if realized, need not reduce M/Y but may in thin domestic markets
merely increase the incidence of underscale high-cost activities in
the producer-goods sector. Parallel measures to shift consumer demand toward less import-intensive goods would be needed to enable
the backward-linkage investments to lower the M/Y ratio, the
measures having the additional virtue of deepening markets for a
narrower array of backward-linkage activities. That is to say, selective purchase taxes or a reduction of income inequality, by shifting
demand from more import-intensive products, could increase the
volume and efficiency of investment and the growth rate. The validity of the standard argument that an increase in income inequality
increases capital accumulation disappears when the composition of
final demand is a major obstacle to overcoming the import bottleneck.

A STATISTICAL TEST OF THE DEMAND-SHIFT HYPOTHESIS

Support for the hypothesis that the import bias of final demand shifts is a critical factor in diminishing the effectiveness of ISI is provided by the following test on Argentine data. The test findings show that the intermediate import requirements per composite unit of Argentine output were higher in 1960 than in 1953 despite considerable ISI in the intervening years, the shift in demand to the dynamic industries being responsible for the increase.

The test compares $M' = (\sum_j r_{ij} m_j^I) Y$ for the 1953 and 1960 composition of Y in Argentina, using, alternatively $\sum_j r_{ij} m_j^I$ vectors for 1953 and 1960, where M' are intermediate import requirements. Although the availability of inverted 24×24 Argentine input-output tables determined the choice of years for comparison, the period is not inappropriate, being one of particularly active ISI, with a considerable emphasis on import substitution of technically complex products. Tractors, farm machinery, motor vehicles, and various consumer durables were first "domesticated" in this period, while the production of fuels, finished steel products, and various chemicals and synthetics expanded markedly at the expense of competing imports. Especially notable was the rapid rise of domestic production and fall of imports of crude petroleum in 1960 compared to 1953.

For the comparison, the 1960 final demand of each of the 24 sectors was deflated by its sectoral price index to 1953 prices and total final demand normalized at a constant m$n 1,000,000, so that Y_{1960} differed from Y_{1953} in composition but not in level. The import requirements obtained by vector multiplication were also deflated by $\dfrac{11.9}{6.4} \times \dfrac{1}{1.32} = 1.41$ to correct for the greater rise of the exchange rate than domestic prices between 1953 and 1960 (the first fraction) and the drop in the dollar price of current Argentine imports (the second fraction).[19] Imports were thus deflated to 1953 c.i.f. peso prices at the 1953 average exchange rate.

The results, summarized in Table 3.1, show that despite the ISI

19. The basic data and a detailed description of the methodology used are given in David Felix, "Did Import Substituting Industrialization in Argentina Save Foreign Exchange in 1953–1960? A Report on Some Findings" (mimeo, Instituto Torcuato Di Tella, 1965).

Table 3.1. Intermediate imports required in Argentina to produce one million pesos of final demand, with 1953 and 1960 compositions (in 1953 c.i.f. peso prices).

Sectors	1953 final demand mix	1960 final demand mix at 1953 prices	Percentage change
	$(\sum_j r_{ij}m_j^I)_{1953}$		
Manufacturing[a]	23,769.6	26,792.2	+13.3
Dynamic industries	10,123.4	15,452.9	+52.6
Vegetative industries	13,095.8	10,578.8	−19.3
Remaining sectors	12,435.2	12,483.1	+0.4
All sectors	36,204.8	39,275.3	+8.5
	$(\sum_j r_{ij}m_j^{I'})_{1960}$		
Manufacturing[a]	26,754.7	33,110.7	+23.8
Dynamic industries	13,829.8	22,766.7	+64.6
Vegetative industries	11,548.3	9,423.3	−18.3
Remaining sectors	12,247.0	12,494.7	+2.0
All sectors	39,001.7	45,605.4	+16.9

Source: Consejo Nacional de Desarrollo, *Actualización de la Matriz de Insumo-Producto del año 1953 al año 1960* (Publicación No. 18, Buenos Aires, 1965).

[a] Includes minor sector, "miscellaneous manufactures," not classified under either dynamic or vegetative.

of the intervening period a given quantity of final demand with the 1960 composition required 8.5 percent more intermediate imports using the 1953 *I-O* coefficients and 16.9 percent using the 1960 *I-O* coefficients than it did with the 1953 final demand mix. With either set of coefficients, the relative increase in the output of the manufacturing sector accounted for virtually all of the increase in import requirements. More specifically, the responsibility is attributable entirely to the substantially greater growth of the dynamic industries with their above-average import coefficients.[20]

By reading down each column of Table 3.1, one can see that between 1953 and 1960 there was also a rise in the $r_{ij}m_j^I$'s for the dynamic industries and a decline for the vegetative industries. Some

20. The share of manufacturing in GDP rose from 30.3 percent in 1953 to 34.8 percent in 1960, with the physical output index of dynamic industries rising by 90.8 percent and of vegetative industries by only 18.2 percent. Consejo Nacional de Desarrollo, *Cuentas Nacionales de la República Argentina* (Buenos Aires, 1964), tables 18, 82. For the list of dynamic and vegetative industries at the 2-digit level, see Table 3.3 below.

of the rise for the dynamic industries may reflect changes in relative prices of inputs between the two years, or shifts to more import intensive technologies in some activities. Probably most of the rise, however, reflects changes in output weights within the rather aggregated sectors between the two years, while similar shifts in weights may have dampened the fall of $r_{ij}m_j^I$ for the vegetative industries. That is to say, in a more finely disaggregated set of tables, much more of the difference between $(\sum_j r_{ij}m_j^I)_{1953} Y_{1953}$ and $(\sum_j r_{ij}m_j^I)_{1960} Y_{1960}$ — obtained by comparing the upper half of column 1 with the lower half of column 2 — would probably turn out to be a result of demand shifts rather than of higher $r_{ij}m_j^I$'s.

Although the demand-shift hypothesis is supported by the findings of Table 3.1, one important qualification tempers the euphoria. The shifts that frustrated ISI in this period can not be attributed entirely to income elasticities and the international demonstration effect. They also reflect the drop in the wage share between the two years, which undoubtedly helped turn demand toward more import-intensive goods.[21] Unfortunately, the data to weigh the relative importance of the various demand influences are lacking.

Finally, capital-goods imports rose even more sharply than current imports, thanks to external borrowing and a flurry of foreign investment in 1959–60; foreign investment in particular was directed almost entirely to the dynamic industries. However, the resultant rise of the overall M/Y in constant prices from 0.083 in 1953 to 0.116 in 1960 exaggerates the upward trend of M/Y in the 1950's, because capital-goods imports were unusually restricted in 1953.[22]

RELATIVE PRICE AND OUTPUT PATTERNS UNDER ISI

Industrial exporting suggests itself as an obvious way of cutting through the balance-of-payments bind. A basic obstacle to such

21. The income distribution and import effect of the 1959 devaluation, which helped substantially to lower the wage share, is analyzed in detail in C. F. Diaz-Alejandro, *Exchange Rate Devaluation in a Semi-Industrialized Country* (Cambridge, Mass.: MIT Press, 1965).

22. Tight import restrictions also affected current imports in 1953, but to a much lesser degree. In any event, the *I-O* coefficients exclude the effect of changes in inventories of imports. A crude test described in Felix, "Did ISI Save Foreign Exchange?" suggests that there were no cumulative biases in the corrections for inventory changes.

efforts is, however, the growing incompatibility between ISI as an investment-inducing mechanism and the investment allocation required for effective industrial exporting. ISI increasingly favors the so-called dynamic industries, whereas it is among the slower-growing vegetative industries that activities with the least unfavorable comparative costs for exporting are principally to be found. Were individual dynamic industries truly dynamic with sustained growth rates, this peculiar cost-price structure, in which the more technologically progressive industries have the higher relative costs, would not persist. But in fact the vegetative-dynamic dichotomy is misleading. Dynamic industries, despite a higher income elasticity of demand than vegetative industries, tend individually under ISI to have a shorter duration as growth industries, because the growth of demand does not depend primarily on income elasticity but on a more complex set of factors, including the growth of income. Since their "domestication" coincides with the diminishing effectiveness of ISI, individual dynamic industries have been unable to sustain high rates of growth long enough to benefit substantially from the various cost-reducing forces associated with rapid growth. The divergence between the comparative costs of the vegetative and dynamic industries tends, therefore, to remain large and relatively invariant. Policies that persist in favoring dynamic industries because of their high income elasticity of demand or because of the more rapid growth of world trade in dynamic than in vegetative products tend only to accentuate the stop-go pattern and to increase the obstacles to industrial exporting.

To explain industry growth and relative price trends, I must first drop the assumption of constant relative prices. An essential part

Table 3.2. Rank correlations between output growth rates and changes in relative prices for Argentine industries, 1946–61.

Industries	1946–53	1953–61
41 vegetative	−0.3354	−0.3352
49 dynamic	−0.2038[a]	−0.3257

Source: Consejo Nacional de Desarrollo (CONADE) revised industry price and output series (unpublished).

[a] 48 industries for 1946–53, since complete data for Radiofonia were not available for this period.

of the ISI inducement mechanism is an initial rise in price of the product being domesticated, because of restrictions on competitive imports. This rise enables the new industry to overcome the high production costs that result from production inexperience, lack of externalities, or diseconomies of small scale. However, while the industry's output is growing faster than overall industrial output, its relative price usually declines from an initial peak. Evidence for an inverse relation between relative price and output growth in Argentina is given in Table 3.2. The industries referred to in the table represent Argentina's industrial gamut, although many of the industries are rather aggregative, not enough data being available for a finer breakdown.

Some general propositions on industry growth and retardation can be formed by comparing the secular growth of the array of dynamic and vegetative industries. Secular industry-output curves, as Arthur Burns showed, can be usefully described by a second-degree logarithmic parabola of the form: $\log Q = c + t \log a + \frac{t^2}{2} \log b$.[23] Applying this function to an array of U.S. output series covering a forty- to sixty-year period, Burns found that $\log b$ is almost always negative, so that b, the "retardation coefficient" or second derivative of the antilog function, is less than one. That is, the growth rate, $\frac{d \log Q}{dt} = \log a + t \log b$, declines secularly, eventually turning negative.

A basic reason for retardation is that demand in an economy with changing technology and wants shifts to new products as they enter the market, depressing the income elasticity of demand for older products and usually raising their price elasticity. The structure of price and income elasticities thus undergoes continual change, with the underlying changes in technology and factor supplies that raise income in a progressive economy ensuring that high income elasticities for individual products do not remain high indefinitely. The changing demand structure requires, in turn, parallel changes in the capital structure and investment mix.[24]

23. A. F. Burns, *Production Trends in the United States since 1870* (National Bureau of Economic Research, 1934), chap. IV.
24. This does not mean that changing consumer wants necessarily initiate the changes in the investment mix and capital structure, but only that regardless of

The same set of retardation factors beset individual output curves when technological change and industrial growth are induced by ISI, but they are supplemented by additional factors that make the retardation more pronounced. These factors are illustrated by the following model:

(2) $$Q_j = f\left(Y_c, \frac{P_j}{P}, M_j\right)$$

where Q_j is the output of the jth industrial good, Y_c is per capita income, P_j is the price of the jth good, P is the industrial price index, and M_j is imports of the jth good. Differentiation with respect to time produces:

(3) $$\dot{Q}_j = \frac{\partial Q_j}{\partial Y_c}\dot{Y}_c + \frac{\partial Q_j}{\partial\left(\frac{P_j}{P}\right)}\frac{\dot{P}_j}{P} + \frac{\partial Q_j}{\partial M_j}\dot{M}_j$$

In addition,

(3.1) $$\frac{\partial Q_j}{\partial Y_c} = E_{Yj}\frac{Q_j}{Y_c} \quad\text{and}\quad \frac{\partial Q}{\partial\left(\frac{P_j}{P}\right)} = -E_{Pj}\frac{Q_j}{P_j}$$

where E_{Yj} is the income elasticity of demand and $-E_{Pj}$ is the price elasticity of demand for the jth good; and, since a unit fall (rise) of M means a unit rise (fall) of demand for j,

$$\frac{\partial Q_j}{\partial M_j} = -1$$

Substituting these terms in Equation (3) and dividing by Q_j gives the growth rate of j as

(4) $$\frac{\dot{Q}_j}{Q_j} = E_{Yj}\frac{\dot{Y}_c}{Y_c} - E_{Pj}\frac{\left(\frac{\dot{P}_j}{P}\right)}{\frac{P_j}{P}} - \frac{\dot{M}_j}{Q_j}$$

Moreover,

(5) $$\left(\frac{\dot{P}_j}{P}\right) = -g\left(\frac{\frac{\dot{Q}_j}{Q_j}}{\frac{\dot{Q}}{Q}}\right)$$

where the change begins, the capital and demand structure will undergo further alteration as socio-economic forces push them toward some mutual adjustment.

That is, the relative price of j falls when the growth rate of j is above the growth rate of the industrial sector, $\frac{\dot{Q}_j}{Q_j}$. Further,

$$(6) \qquad \frac{\dot{I}_j}{I_j} = h\left(\frac{\dot{Q}_j}{Q_j}\right)$$

The percentage change in investment in j capacity is a positive function of the growth rate of j, where h is an investment accelerator. And,

$$(7) \qquad \frac{\dot{Q}}{Q} > \frac{\dot{Y}}{Y}$$

Industrial output grows faster than GNP, as expected under ISI.

Since $\dot{M}_j$ is negative and Q_j initially small when j is first domesticated, $-\frac{\dot{M}_j}{Q_j}$ gives an added initial impetus to the growth rate beyond the income elasticity of demand, so that $\frac{\dot{Q}_j}{Q_j}$ is considerably higher than the growth rate for the industrial sector. The higher growth rate of j normally causes its relative price to fall again, so that the price-elasticity effect also helps sustain a high $\frac{\dot{Q}_j}{Q_j}$. Industry j is thus for a time a leading industry, contributing a rising proportion to total investment and income growth.[25]

How long does industry j continue as a leading industry? $-\frac{\dot{M}_j}{Q_j}$

25. Note that if imports of the jth good were restricted by a nonprohibitive tariff, its domestic price would be its CIF price plus tariff, and Equation 5 would be inconsistent with Equation 4. The two are consistent when the techniques used to restrict competitive imports largely divorce domestic prices from movements of CIF prices, as was the case in postwar Argentina. The techniques used in Argentina over and above formal import tariffs were quantitative controls, multiple exchange rates, and variable tariff surcharges that were raised and lowered frequently by administrative fiat, mainly to minimize competitive imports and to encourage investment in domestic substitutes. Prices of these goods therefore tended to reflect production costs and the degree of local competition rather than CIF prices.

Table 3.2 lends empirical support to the explanation. So does a comparison of the Argentine/U.S. industry price ratios, listed in Table 3.6, with the average tariff for these industries in 1958, as estimated by Bela Balassa, "Integration and Resource Allocation in Latin America" (paper presented at the Conference on the Next Decade of Latin American Development, Cornell University, April 1966). For each of the eleven industries in Table 3.6, the Argentine/U.S. price ratio is well below the CIF price plus average industry tariff. In addition, the rank correlation between the relative height of the industry tariffs and the relative size of the Argentine/U.S. price ratios is −0.20.

approaches zero as Q_j rises, but the larger the initial volume of imports, M_j, the longer does $-\dfrac{\dot{M}_j}{Q_j}$ remain positive and $\left(\dfrac{\dot{P}_j}{P}\right)$ negative; hence, the longer is the period of high growth. During this phase the income elasticity of demand makes a rather subordinate contribution to the growth of j, unless per capita income is rising at a very high rate.

As $-\dfrac{\dot{M}_j}{Q_j} \to O$, E_{yj} becomes the main support for $\dfrac{\dot{Q}_j}{Q_j}$. But since $\dfrac{\dot{Y}}{Y} < \dfrac{\dot{Q}}{Q}$, unless income per head is growing and E_{yj} is substantially above unity, $\left(\dfrac{\dot{P}_j}{P}\right)$ will turn positive and further depress $\dfrac{\dot{Q}_j}{Q_j}$, the adverse substitution effect partly offsetting the positive income effect. Industry j thus ceases to be a growth industry, its contribution to total investment falls off, and new products must be domesticated in order to sustain the rate of investment. But this process of rapid substitution is an additional depressant to $\dfrac{\dot{Q}_j}{Q_j}$, since the new products tend to push the demand curves for older products leftward, which gradually dampens E_{yj} and raises E_{pj}.

The fitted industry-output curves in an ISI economy like Argentina should therefore have lower values for b, the retardation coefficient, than was shown by Burns's U.S. industry series. The basic reasons are (a) the importance of M_j in first raising and then depressing the growth of demand and (b) the depressing effect on income elasticity and rise in price elasticity of existing products because of the rapid rate of introduction of substitutes relative to the growth of income in the ISI economy. Moreover, since ISI in dynamic industries tends to be concentrated in the period when the income growth rate is slackening, the retardation of growth in dynamic industries is likely to be even greater, and their span as leading industries less, than for vegetative industries.

To test these conclusions, the logarithmic parabolic function was applied to the output of the ninety-two industries making up the Argentine manufacturing sector. The series were constructed by CONADE (Consejo Nacional de Desarrollo, the national planning agency), mainly by revising the official Dirección Nacional de Estadísticas y Censos industrial-output series to cover new products and activities that the DNEC series ignore or underweight.[26] The CONADE series cover only the period 1946–64, but since thirty of them were unrevised DNEC series, they could be extended back to 1939. Thus, the log function was fitted to nineteen annual observations in the case of sixty-two industries and to twenty-six observations in the case of thirty industries.

Table 3.3 summarizes the information only for the sixty-one

Table 3.3. Average retardation coefficients for 61 Argentine industries.[a]

Industry class	Number of component industries	Average R^2 of fitted function	Average retardation coefficient	Average years from index $Q_i = 25$ to $\dot{Q}_i/Q_i = 3\%$
1. Processed food, beverages	11	.777	.996	20
2. Tobacco	1	.960	.997	21
3. Textiles	4	.607	.992	16
4. Clothing, cloth products	3	.514	.996	20
5. Wood products	6	.448	.993	17
6. Printing, publishing	1	.626	.999	37
7. Leather goods	2	.235	.996	19
Vegetative (weighted average)	28	.616	.995	19.4
8. Paper, paper products	1	.817	.994	16
9. Chemical products	8	.804	.993	17
10. Petroleum refining	1	.987	.998	33
11. Glass, tile, ceramics	5	.760	.992	16
12. Metals, metal products	10	.796	.992	17
13. Vehicles, machinery	5	.784	.988	14
14. Electrical equipment	3	.941	.983	14
Dynamic (weighted average)	33	.810	.991	16.6

Source: Calculated by fitting $\log Q = c + t \log a + \dfrac{t^2}{2} \log b$ to annual output series for 1939–64 or 1946–64, as provided by CONADE. 1960 = 100 for all series.

[a] Includes only industries with statistically significant retardation coefficients less than 1.0. All averages are unweighted means of the individual component industries.

industries with statistically significant retardation coefficients, *b*, less than 1.0.[27] However, as shown by Table 3.4, twenty of the

26. There are actually 94 CONADE series, but they include two sets of identical pairs. Evidently each pair was constructed from a common input measure.

27. Five percent significance by *t*-test was the cut-off, but most *b*'s <1.0 were significant up to 1 or 2 percent.

Table 3.4. Growth and retardation coefficients for all Argentine industries.

Industry class	Number	Growth rate at $t = 0^d$	Average R^2	Average retardation coefficient	Years from index $Q_i = 25$ to $\dot{Q}_i/Q_i = 3\%$
Growth rates of 4 percent or less at $t = 0^a$					
Vegetative					
$b < 1.0$	9	2.7	.543	.998	24
$b > 1.0$	6	−3.6	.551	1.006	—
$b = 1.0$	3	1.8	.598	1.000	—
Traditional export industries[b]	2	−6.7	.231	1.006	—
Dynamic					
$b < 1.0$	1	4.0	.569	.996	20
$b > 1.0$	6	−4.0	.646	1.008	—
$b = 1.0$	1	3.2	.758	1.000	—
Traditional export industries[e]	2	−0.5	.430	1.001	—
Growth rates greater than 4 percent at $t = 0$					
Vegetative					
$b < 1.0$	19	9.8	.651	.993	19
$b > 1.0$	1	4.6	.960	1.003	—
$b = 1.0$	1	5.2	.975	1.000	—
Dynamic					
$b < 1.0$	31	16.4	.829	.991	16
$b > 1.0$	2	7.3	.949	1.001	—
$b = 1.0$	8	9.5	.843	1.000	—

Source: Calculated by fitting $\log Q = c + t \log a + \frac{t^2}{2} \log b$ to annual output series for 1939 64 or 1946 64, as provided by CONADE. 1960 = 100 for all series.

[a] $t = 0$ at 1939 for 9 series, at 1946 for 21 series.
[b] Meatpacking and washed wool.
[e] Linseed oil and quebracho extract.
[d] $t = 0$ at 1939 for 21 series, at 1946 for 41 series.

thirty-one excluded industries were declining, slow-growing, or stagnating during the postwar period. Their calculated growth rate, $\frac{d \log Q}{dt} = \log a + t \log b$, was below 4 percent at $t = 0$, being negative for fourteen of the twenty slow-growing industries.[28] In other words, they represent industries that were domesticated before World War II and had run through their rapid growth phase by the end of the war.

28. For six of the thirty-one industries, $t = 0$ in 1939; for the rest, the initial year is 1946.

How does the Argentine pattern compare with that depicted for the U.S. in the Burns study? In the U.S. pattern the average annual retardation coefficient was approximately 0.998, as compared to 0.995 for the vegetative and 0.991 for the dynamic industries in Table 3.4.[29] Thus, an industry with a 10 percent growth rate at $t = 0$, would take thirty-three years to fall to a 3 percent growth rate with the average b for the U.S., thirteen years with the average b for Argentine vegetative industries, and only 7.5 years with the average b for Argentine dynamic industries.

This result is not surprising, given the smaller size of the Argentine market and the fact that only a handful of Argentine industries are exporters. Yet the comparison can be taken as only roughly illustrative. Burns's series range from forty to sixty years, long enough to permit him to expunge cyclical fluctuations and use overlapping decades for further smoothing, whereas, even if cyclical deflators were available for Argentina, such smoothing would sacrifice too many degrees of freedom in a nineteen- to twenty-six-year period. The Argentine series are, however, not obviously biased by the choice of terminal years; both 1946 and 1964 were mid-years in a cyclical upswing, and 1939 was not apparently a depressed year.

Differences in the choice of output series also mar the comparison. Burns selected mainly standardized, semiprocessed goods, whose wide array of uses can sustain their growth rate for long periods. Since the Argentine series cover the gamut of industries, they include a large proportion of finished products. As Burns suggested, the growth span for "luxuries, superfluities and style goods" is likely to be much shorter than for basic goods.[30] However, the Argentine data aggregate finished products into rather broad industry classes, whose output indices are therefore more stable than those of the component products.[31]

29. Burns, *Production Trends in the U.S.*, obtained his b estimates by taking the average differences in the growth rate of each industry for overlapping decades. The average drop for all his series and for the manufacturing series was about 1.2 percent between overlapping decades, which works out to slightly more than a 0.2 percent drop per annum.

30. Burns, *Production Trends in the U.S.*, pp. 169–73.

31. In addition, CONADE in a number of cases estimated output of finished goods by indices of one or more key raw-material inputs — e.g., cotton, wool, and synthetic fiber inputs in the case of textile products.

A more fundamental difference arises in the interpretation of the two patterns. The U.S. pattern reflected more accurately the way in which a continually progressing economy changes its output mix as technological and want changes alter comparative industrial efficiency. The slow-growing industries were more truly mature, and the declining industries were truly passing out of the picture. Few of them were likely to revive merely because of a sustained revival of the income growth rate. The rapid fall in the Argentine industry growth rates, however, has represented a decline into precocious maturity, reflecting the scrambling of a rapidly widening array of industries for shares of a domestic market whose modest growth resulted in good part from industrial widening. A more rapid rise of income would spark many of those industries into renewed growth, but the widening process as such was incapable of effecting this rise.

The righthand columns of Tables 3.3 and 3.4 are equally illuminating. Since the output series had a common base year, 1960 = 100, but were in different stages of maturation during the postwar period, all were extrapolated by means of the fitted function to get the estimated value of t when $Q_j = 25$ and the value of t when $\frac{\dot{Q}_j}{Q_j} = 3$ percent. The span of years between the two t's is taken as the time when each industry ceased being a leading industry, 3 percent being below the annual growth rate of the Argentine industrial sector as a whole in the postwar period. The righthand column averages the time span for the components of each two-digit industry. The method breaks down for $b \geq 1.0$, but as indicated earlier, twenty of the thirty-one industries with such b values were clearly no longer growth industries in the observed period. Typically, the vegetative industries lasted longer as growth industries than did the dynamic.

Not all vegetative industries were slow-growing in the postwar period, nor were all dynamic industries fast-growing, as shown in Table 3.4, where component industries were reclassified into those with a growth rate under 4 percent and those with a growth rate above 4 percent at $t = 0$. As can be seen, twenty-one industries called vegetative, including two with no evidenced retardation, were growth industries for at least part of the postwar period. Conversely, ten dynamic industries were stagnating or declining in the same period. Again, the vegetative industries on the average lasted longer as growth industries than did the "dynamic" ones.

Table 3.4 also indicates the growth characteristics of the industries with $b > 1.0$. The average growth of sixteen of the nineteen industries showing acceleration was strongly negative at $t = 0$. Four of the sixteen were traditional exporters, their growth being restrained by agricultural supply limitations or by technological substitution abroad rather than by lagging domestic demand. On the other side of the ledger, ten dynamic industries showed both high growth rates and no significant retardation. However, no less than five of the ten — iron and steel, automobiles, tires and tubes, batteries, radios and phonographs — were new ISI industries, still in the process of replacing imports during the past decade.[32]

An additional piece of evidence helps explain why dynamic industries quickly lose their dynamism. Table 3.5 gives cross-sectional income elasticities for various categories of durable consumer goods calculated from a detailed survey of 1962 expenditures of urban families.[33] With the exception of furniture, jewels, and fur coats, the items in Table 3.5 are classified as dynamic goods, yet two-thirds of them show income elasticities below unity.

The survey data combined with production figures suggest an explanation. In 1962 the lower half of family income units bought over 50 percent of refrigerators and washing machines, almost 40 percent of all TV sets, and about one-third of all stoves, heaters, radios, and vacuum cleaners, while the upper 25 percent of all income recipients purchased from two-thirds to three-fourths of the automobiles and remaining goods in the table. However, 44 percent of all durable-goods expenditures were on automobiles alone, and another 18.6 percent was spent on TV sets, leaving little more than one-third of all expenditures to be shared by the remaining items. In addition, peak production for the utilitarian household durables — refrigerators, washing machines, stoves, and heaters — was reached in the later 1950's, after which output tended to level off

32. The output growth of TV receivers offset the decline of two other subcomponents, radios and radio-phonograph combinations, making up the radiophonic industry.

33. The survey, sponsored by Organization of American States–Inter-American Development Bank, covered 4,564 family units randomly selected from all Argentine cities of over 10,000 population.

or decline. Thus, trickling-down to the lower income units was associated with a cessation of output growth.

Evidently the pattern is for cross-sectional income elasticity to be high when durables are being newly domesticated and the upper-income families are stocking up. As this phase terminates, replacement demand plus trickling-down are not sufficient to sustain a strong positive growth rate.[34] That is, the cross-sectional income elasticity of demand for refrigerators and washing machines would have been much higher in 1957 and, conversely, the elasticity for automobiles will probably be much lower in 1967 than the estimates in Table 3.5. Multivariate analysis with a stock-adjustment param-

Table 3.5. Cross-sectional income elasticities of demand among urban families in 1962 for selected durable consumer goods.

Class of item	Regression equation	R^2	Standard error of estimate of income elasticity
Automobiles	$\log Y_1 = -9.785 + 2.459 \log X_1$	.776	.100
Furniture	$\log Y_2 = -9.519 + 2.288 \log X_2$	.702	.413
Jewels, fur coats	$\log Y_3 = -7.251 + 1.816 \log X_3$	.867	.198
Radio-phonograph combinations, air conditioners	$\log Y_4 = -6.309 + 1.598 \log X_4$	.850	.172
Vacuum cleaners, radios	$\log Y_5 = -2.575 + 0.961 \log X_5$	.905	.074
Stoves, water heaters	$\log Y_6 = -0.831 + 0.695 \log X_6$	.761	.103
Television sets	$\log Y_7 = -0.619 + 0.513 \log X_7$	.561	.020
Refrigerators, washing machines	$\log Y_8 = 1.122 + 0.378 \log X_8$	.447	.017

Source: OAS-IADB survey of family expenditure in 1962 in Argentine cities of 10,000 and over.

eter would probably produce more stable income elasticity estimates, but it would also place income elasticity in a properly subordinate place as a determinant of demand.

What are the consequences for the industrial price structure? If dynamic industries tend to be more capital intensive and more subject to diseconomies of small scale than vegetative industries, one would expect them to have a higher initial rise in relative prices

34. For example, the ratio of household refrigerators per family unit rose to one-third by 1959, and has remained at this level through 1966, the most recent year for which information was available.

at the beginning of their domestication. If they also tend to have a shorter growth span, their prices should continue to show a higher ratio to international prices than would vegetative products.

To test this conclusion, ratios of Argentine to U.S. prices were computed for a wide array of industrial products produced in both countries for the period 1960–65. That is, U.S. industrial prices were assumed to be representative of international prices for the respective products; the assumption would, of course, be a treacherous one if used for more than broad comparisons. Two separate data sources were used for the comparisons. The first were worksheets from an ECLA study of comparative purchasing power of Latin American currencies in 1960 and 1962.[35] From these sheets 217 domestically manufactured items were selected. The Buenos Aires peso prices of each item for June 1960 and June 1962 were converted to dollar prices at the average exchange rate for the respective months and divided by the June 1962 average of Los Angeles and Houston prices for the items. The resulting price ratios were then assigned to appropriate two-digit industries, and the mean and standard deviation was computed for each industry. The prices were those charged to final purchasers; that is, they were retail prices for all except capital and intermediate goods. The results are summarized in columns (1)–(3) of Table 3.6.

The second set are wholesale prices, obtained for May 1963, 1964, and 1965, primarily from worksheets for the DNEC wholesale price index and the Central Bank's wholesale price index. These prices, converted to dollars, were compared with prices for items of the same or similar specification in the U.S. wholesale price index for the corresponding months. Since the Argentine indices are very light on capital goods and durable consumer goods, automobile, truck, and agricultural machinery prices were obtained through direct inquiry from U.S. manufacturing subsidiaries in Argentina and added to the list. The elimination of underspecified items left only 101 price ratios for each of the three years. In order to broaden the list for metal products, building materials, and machinery, 44 such items from the ECLA list were added to the 101 items. The resulting ratios and standard deviations for each industry group are given in columns (4)–(6) of Table 3.6.

35. These were made available to me through the generosity of Stanley Braithwaite of ECLA, who directed the study, "A Measurement of Price Levels and the Purchasing Power of Currencies in Latin America, 1960–62" (mimeo, E/CN. 12/653, March 1963).

Table 3.6. Ratios of Argentine to U.S. prices in 2-digit industries, 1960–65.

Industry class	Mean ratio 1960, 1962 (1)	σ (2)	Number of ratios (3)	Mean ratio 1960, 1962, 1963–65[a] (4)	σ (5)	Number of ratios (6)
Vegetative	0.87	—	184	1.02	—	73
Processed food, beverages	0.69	.33	80	0.97	.29	27
Textiles, clothing	1.16	.33	82	1.37	.80	33
Wood products	0.94	.55	16	1.10	—	4
Leather goods	0.68	.41	6	0.65	.15	9
Dynamic	1.22	—	250	1.58	—	362
Paper, paper products	1.17	—	4	1.64	.34	12
Chemical products	0.79	.40	50	1.92	1.25	114
Rubber products	1.20	.68	10	1.55	1.02	11
Stone, glass, ceramics	0.63	.28	22	0.78	.40	35
Metals, metal products	1.14	.66	58	1.45	.63	47
Vehicles, machinery	2.00	.78	70	2.17	.70	125
Electrical equipment	1.64	.68	36	1.57	1.05	18
Total	—	—	434	—	—	435

[a] Wholesale price ratios for 101 products for May 1963, 1964, 1965, plus 44 capital-goods, building materials, and metal-product prices for June 1960–June 1962.

The mean ratios by industry bear out the hypothesis that prices of dynamic industries averaged considerably higher in recent years than those of vegetative industries in relation to international prices.

Table 3.7. Argentine relative industrial prices, 1960–65.

Industry class	1960, 1962 average	1960, 1962, 1963–65 average
Processed food, beverages	68	74
Textiles, clothing	111	105
Wood products	90	85
Leather goods	65	50
Vegetative average	83	78
Paper, paper products	112	126
Chemical products	76	148
Rubber products	115	119
Stone, glass, ceramics	60	60
Metals, metal products	109	112
Vehicles, machinery	192	167
Electrical equipment	157	121
Dynamic average	117	122
Average all industries	100	100

Source: columns (1) and (4) of Table 3.6.

This pattern is seen more clearly in Table 3.7, where industry mean ratios of each period's prices are expressed as percentages of the average for all prices of the period. With the large exception of chemical products, there is not much change in the relative price structure between the two periods. In the earlier period price ratios of dynamic products averaged 41 percent higher than those of vegetative products; in the later period they were 56 percent higher.

The price structure also seems to be fairly stable. This stability is indicated by the high coefficients of the correlation matrix in Table 3.8. It is further evidenced by the fact that despite frequent devalua-

Table 3.8. Rank-correlation matrix for price-ratio rankings, 1960–65.

Year	1960	1962	1963	1964	1965
1960	1.000	0.818	—	—	—
1962	0.818	1.000	—	—	—
1963	—	—	1.000	0.961	0.919
1964	—	—	0.961	1.000	0.960
1965	—	—	0.919	0.960	1.000

Source: columns (1) and (4) of Table 3.6.

tion and considerable inflation in 1960–65, the industries with mean ratios below 1.0 in 1960–62 remained below 1.0, with two exceptions, while all those with mean ratios above 1.0 remained above unity. Dynamic industries were evidently unable to whittle down their high price ratios; nor did leads and lags between devaluation and domestic inflation greatly affect the ordering of the price ratios.

These conclusions are tempered, to be sure, by the crudeness of the comparisons. Since the items were chosen from basic collections that were structured samples of sorts, they are broadly representative of the range of Argentine industrial output.[36] But in order to select manufacturing items from the ECLA collection

36. The ECLA study is based on weighted samples designed to express the distribution of expenditure among all categories of goods and services, including imports. The study concluded that the Argentine peso's purchasing power parity was substantially greater in 1960 and 1962 than was its dollar exchange rate. It also found, however, that Argentine capital-goods prices at the official exchange rate were the highest of all Latin American countries included in the study. The DNEC and Central Bank wholesale price indices formed the core of the second price collection, although as indicated, they are light on capital goods and metal products, which were therefore added on an ad hoc basis.

and choose from the wholesale price indices on the basis of the availability of U.S. price equivalents, any notion of weighting had to be abandoned. Simple averages were used instead. The simple averaging partly explains the large standard deviations around many of the industry means; proper weighting would probably reduce the sigmas but would also alter the means in one direction or another. As it stands, therefore, the mean ratios do not represent strong central tendencies in many cases, and one's confidence in their representativeness must rest heavily on their relative invariance over the observation period.[37]

To summarize, the Argentine ISI pattern has been one of comparatively short periods of rapid growth for each domesticated industry, with the rapid-growth phase of dynamic industries usually of shorter duration, despite their allegedly higher income elasticity of demand, than the corresponding phase of vegetative industries. In both classes of industries rapid growth has been associated with falling relative prices, but since dynamic industries typically begin with a greater rise over CIF import prices than vegetative industries and experience shorter periods of rapid growth, vegetative industries have tended to reach a more favorable cost-price position for entering industrial exporting. This comparative cost advantage of vegetative industries has been relatively invariant to the successive devaluations of the Argentine peso in recent years. Since Argentina's industrial market is second in size among Latin American countries, it is reasonable to assume that its industrial growth pattern and comparative cost structure is at least roughly representative of other Latin American ISI countries.

IMPLICATIONS FOR INDUSTRIAL POLICY

The broad policy implications of both sections of this chapter thus coincide. In order to prolong the ability of ISI to lower M/Y, it is necessary to reduce the import bias of changes in the demand mix, which broadly means shifting demand toward the less import-

---

37. Some of the large discrepancy between the two ratios for chemical products is probably due to the fact that the ECLA collection is mostly composed of simple household items such as soap, perfume, toilet articles, and pharmaceuticals, for which U.S. prices are notoriously high, whereas industrial chemicals predominate in the 1963–65 collection. It is also possible that the subtleties of industrial chemical specifications may have led me into error in my matching efforts.

intensive vegetative products and those dynamic products sharing this characteristic.[38] Comparative cost considerations also favor concentrating export promotion efforts on the vegetative industries. Both objectives are complementary in that expanding domestic demand for vegetative products should also, by reviving their growth momentum, help lower their relative prices and bring some of them down to profitable exporting level. Since egalitarian income redistribution is one obvious means of shifting demand toward vegetative products, the dismal science would seem for once to be on the side of virtue.

Unfortunately, when exports consist of agricultural wage goods, as in Argentina, the feasibility of this virtuous solution is considerably weakened.[39] Rather, there is a conflict between the income redistribution required to achieve a short-term improvement in the trade balance via devaluation and that required to encourage the long-run reallocation of resources necessary for sustaining the improvement in the trade balance through industrial exporting. The conflict strengthens the case for using variable purchase taxes, selective export subsidies, and other discriminatory devices rather than global measures such as general wage increases or devaluation in order to break through the balance-of-payments bind. Since proponents of general wage increases to solve balance-of-payments problems are scarce, we shall concentrate only on showing why, given the preceding analysis, general devaluation tends also to be an ineffectual solution.

The short-term improvement in the Argentine trade balance after each postwar devaluation should, as Diaz-Alejandro showed in some detail, be attributed chiefly to the income rather than the substitution effect of the rise in the domestic price of imports and exportable goods. Short-term price inelasticity of demand for imports and short-term inelasticity of agricultural exportables has put the burden of adjustment on a fall in real income and level of activity to reduce the demand for imports and release additional agricultural goods for export. The basic income mechanism has been the decline

38. The import-intensity characteristics reflect only central tendencies of the aggregates. The variance of the two aggregates undoubtedly overlaps.

39. The succeeding argument also applies when imports are an important source of agricultural wage goods, as in Chile and Brazil, because the essence of the case is the short-run supply inelasticity of domestic agriculture and the higher marginal propensity to consume of wage earners.

in real wages resulting from lags between the immediate rise in the price of agricultural exportables and money wage adjustments, which transfers income from workers to farm owners and operators producing exportables. Because the latter groups have a higher marginal propensity to save than workers but are less disposed to invest than the industrial sector, aggregate effective demand declines, the incidence falling on industrial demand, because unconsumed exportables can be freely exported. The trade balance therefore improves because of a decline of imports by the depressed industrial sector and an increase in agricultural exporting, with an anti-egalitarian redistribution of income playing the key role in effecting the improvements.[40]

The tenability of a balance-of-payments improvement that depends on wage lags is likely to be short-lived unless devaluation also sets in motion longer-term resource reallocation to sustain the improvement. Devaluation has had contradictory effects, however, on relative costs within the industrial sector. Apparently it should favor the less import- and capital-intensive vegetative industries, but many of these, such as food processing, leather goods, and textiles, also have a heavy input content of exportable raw materials whose relative prices rise with devaluation. Similarly, since the fall in real wages results from the rise in the price of exportable foodstuffs, labor costs fall relatively for more labor-intensive manufacturers only if their prices rise *pari passu* with food prices.[41] Such price rises are restrained, however, by the anti-egalitarian income redistribution, which shifts the demand mix toward dynamic products, reinforcing the long-run demand forces guiding industrial development toward the more import-intensive dynamic industries. The favorable long-run effect of devaluation has therefore had to depend primarily on the long-run responsiveness of agricultural output to improved relative prices. Since this response has been sluggish, Argentine devaluations have been condemned to repeat themselves

40. See Diaz-Alejandro, *Exchange Rate Devaluation*, chaps. II–VI. The general model has been common tender in Argentine economic circles in recent years, but the Diaz-Alejandro study is by far the most rigorous theoretical and empirical exposition and testing of the model.

41. Most labor-intensive products are probably in the vegetative category, although there are undoubtedly many exceptions because the categories are rather heterogeneous aggregates. The impending publication of the 1963 Argentine industrial census may make possible an up-to-date ranking of industrial activities by labor intensity.

at frequent intervals, despite a downward trend in the wage share from the early postwar peak.

The modest expansion of industrial exporting since 1962 does not seriously impair this conclusion. The list of products exported indicates that new exporting activities fall broadly into two categories: domestically owned steel and metal-products firms, whose capital intensity makes their unit costs particularly sensitive to cutbacks in output, and subsidiaries of multinational corporations who can reduce short-term unit costs up to a point for the corporation as a whole by diverting orders to high-cost subsidiaries with considerable excess capacity.[42] Exports of these dynamic products have been facilitated by the favoritism of Latin American Free Trade Association (LAFTA) tariff concessions toward dynamic products and a similar bias in the Argentine drawback and tax rebate system instituted in 1962 for nontraditional exports, which offers higher subsidies to dynamic products. However, the fact that industrial exports reached a peak in the 1963 depression and fell off in the 1964–65 revival of domestic activity reinforces scattered direct evidence that much of the exporting, despite the tax and tariff concessions, was at less than full cost. In other words, this pattern of industrial exporting has been triggered by severe excess capacity and further stimulated by discriminatory tariff and tax subsidies rather than by improved relative costs and prices brought about by devaluation.

Devaluation remains an unavoidable short-term mechanism for reducing excess demand for foreign exchange; but the experience of Argentina with successive devaluations refutes the notion that, with the industrial cost-price structure created by ISI, devaluation by stealing a short-term advantage for external over domestic prices can unleash a sustained expansion of industrial exporting to help maintain the advantage. If that expansion is to be achieved, policymakers must choose between alternative sets of discriminatory measures. The wisdom of concentrating tariff and tax subsidies on the high-cost dynamic products depends on whether LAFTA succeeds in resolving the policy conflicts and institutional obstacles

42. There was also a sharp but brief increase of refined sugar in 1963 — a "non-traditional export" to the United States as a result of the U.S. boycott of Cuban sugar. By 1964, however, Argentine sugar exports had dropped to pre-1963 levels and, given high sugar-cane production costs, are unlikely to rise again in the foreseeable future.

hampering its development, since high costs and high risks make the prospects for a significant growth of dynamic exports outside of a protected regional market unlikely. If LAFTA continues to be a disappointment, then policy measures will have to focus on the other end of the industrial cost gamut — on products whose costs with moderate subsidy can be brought to profitable exporting levels in international markets. These are likely to fall primarily though not exclusively in the vegetative category.

The measures may have to range broadly. It is doubtful that these vegetative industries, which lack the foreign market connections of multinational corporate subsidiaries and which reputedly are often run by rather vegetative management, would respond vigorously to cost subsidies alone. As essential parts of the policy package, measures would be needed to enforce consolidations, plant modernization, quality control, and market research, as well as other measures similar to those successfully employed by French and Italian industry rationalization policy. Selective purchase taxes to reduce demand for import-intensive consumer products would help release foreign exchange to finance the external cost of the rationalization effort. The political difficulties of pushing through a policy package of this sort are no doubt formidable, but so also are the balance-of-payments problems confronting Argentina and most other ISI countries in Latin America.

John Sheahan

4

~~~~~~~~~~~~~~~~~

Imports, Investment, and Growth — Colombia

Colombia has the skills and resources necessary to achieve a significantly higher rate of economic growth than it has accomplished in
the last decade. It is well on the way toward a modern economy;
it already has a wide range of industries and a start toward efficient
commercial agriculture. Initiative and organizational capacity have
proven adequate for high rates of growth in the periods in which
foreign exchange has been available for imports of necessary
materials and equipment. But the country's potential has been badly
underutilized. The growth rate has been mediocre: probably more
people are stuck in miserable conditions in agriculture and on the
urban fringe now than ten years ago, and opportunities for more
productive employment have been rising at an infinitesimal pace.[1]
The present chapter examines ways in which changes in the pattern
of investment decisions and in trade policy might work together to
help Colombia realize its own potential more fully.

THE PATTERN OF GROWTH

The rates of growth registered in the years of high earnings from
coffee exports, 1950–56, provide an indication of what the economy

NOTE: Of the many people who registered helpful objections to earlier drafts
of this paper, particular thanks are due to Richard Bird, Lauchlin Currie, and the
whole economics department of Williams College. Release from teaching assign-
ments for work on this study was made possible by an AID research grant to
Williams College. AID is in no way responsible for the results.
1. Lauchlin Currie, *Accelerating Development* (New York: McGraw-Hill,
1966), pt. II.

can accomplish. In this period, gross domestic product increased at
a rate of 5.1 percent per year, and value added in manufacturing
rose at a rate of 7.0 percent. Gross fixed investment averaged approximately one-fourth of total product. Prices increased persistently
but at relatively manageable rates: 7 percent per year for the wholesale index, or 5 percent for the national product deflator. The external current account was kept in almost perfect balance for the
first five years, though deficits did begin to be serious in 1955–56.[2]

This effective performance was aided greatly by the ability to
finance rapidly rising imports, which permitted both high investment
and quick reactions to specific bottlenecks. Imports rose 80 percent
between 1950 and 1956, financed chiefly from the greater earnings
made possible by higher prices for coffee. Between 1950–53 and
1954–56 the increase in receipts from coffee accounted for 91
percent of the total rise. The unusual luck with prices for this commodity gave the industrialization process a chance to develop
without requiring the diversion to exports of any significant share
of gains in production.

Investment in this period of unusual opportunity took a direction
similar to that in many other newly industrializing countries: concentration on replacing imports of consumer goods with domestic
production oriented toward the internal market. Natural tendencies
in this direction may have been accentuated by a policy of providing almost automatic protection to any firm wishing to undertake
production of goods previously imported, provided that the restrictions on imports did not involve shutting off supplies for sensitive
users, such as agricultural producers or established industrial firms.
Potential investors could count both on protected markets for their
own products and on access to imports of the capital equipment and
materials needed for production. This combination of protection
plus assured supplies made investment highly profitable and biased it
toward the consumer end-products for which import restrictions
were least likely to be contested by existing firms.

According to the rough classifications given in Table 4.1, imports of finished consumer goods in 1956 were only 6 percent higher

2. Banco de la República, "Cuentas Nacionales," 1950–61, 1962–65 (mimeo,
Bogotá); Banco de la República, *Informe Anual de Gerente a la Junta Directiva*
(Bogotá, annual issues); Departamento Administrativo de Planeación, *Plan Ge-
neral de Desarrollo Económico y Social* (Cali, 1962), pt. I, p. 16.

Table 4.1. Composition of Colombian imports, 1950–64 [a]
(in millions of $, c.i.f.).

Year	Consumer goods	Fuels	Construction materials	Raw and intermediate materials	Capital goods	Unclassified	Total
1950	76.1	10.2	25.0	130.5	121.0	1.8	364.7
1951	74.1	16.6	26.9	160.1	136.5	2.2	416.4
1952	74.3	19.3	27.8	141.3	150.4	2.2	415.4
1953	104.9	25.6	43.9	158.8	210.3	3.2	546.7
1954	144.1	29.8	52.5	193.9	246.9	4.5	671.8
1955	114.8	24.7	51.9	210.2	263.4	4.3	669.3
1956	80.6	23.2	56.6	229.6	263.3	3.9	657.2
1957	53.3	19.1	40.0	213.5	152.0	4.7	482.6
1958	32.8	9.8	32.9	191.4	128.8	4.2	399.9
1959	30.3	8.6	20.4	204.2	149.3	2.8	415.6
1960	34.6	10.3	23.6	229.7	216.4	4.0	518.6
1961	48.1	12.5	24.7	238.2	228.3	5.3	557.1
1962	36.0	13.5	25.7	243.9	208.1	12.8	540.3
1963	31.4	9.3	24.2	234.0	195.7	11.4	506.0
1964	37.1	6.4	27.3	268.0	236.5	11.0	586.3

Source: For 1950–57, Departamento Administrativo de Planeación y Servicios Tecnicos, *Informe al Congreso Nacional, 1961–1963* (Bogotá, 1963), p. 134; for 1958–64, typewritten study by Departamento de Planeación, "Importaciones Nacionales segun su uso y destino" (1965).

[a] Many arbitrary decisions enter into any broad import classification, and it is not possible to check the consistency of all those that underlie this table. In particular, the figures for 1950–57 are quite doubtful, in view of the results of a recheck of previously published data made by the Department of Planning for the years 1958 through 1964. The data from 1958 have a more solid basis, although even for this period contraband imports are registered nowhere.

than in 1950, although total consumption increased 32 percent. The total of all other imports exactly doubled: production materials went up in line with the growth of domestic industries, and nearly all capital goods had to be imported.

Continuation of this process would have required rising export earnings, which might have come either from further improvement of markets for coffee or by a redirection of other outputs away from domestic use to exports. Neither happened. Coffee prices plunged in 1957, and nothing significant was done to replace the loss in earnings. As indicated in Table 4.2, coffee exports for 1957–59 averaged one-fourth or $134 million less than in the preceding three years. All other exports combined increased just $3 million.

Table 4.2. Exports of commodities, 1950–66 (in millions of $, f.o.b.).

Period	Coffee	Petroleum	All other[a]	Total[a]
1950–53 (average)	385.1	71.5	25.5	482.1
1954–56 (average)	503.0	69.1	39.8	611.9
1957–59 (average)	369.4	70.4	42.2	482.0
1960	333.5	80.4	51.8	465.7
1961	307.9	68.2	58.7	434.8
1962	331.8	60.5	70.9	463.2
1963	303.0	76.6	66.5	446.1
1964	394.1	75.0	76.6	545.7
1965	343.9	88.1	105.0	537.0
1966	328.3	70.6	107.6	506.5

Source: IMF, *International Financial Statistics* (August 1967), and *Supplement* (to 1965–66).

[a] Export data do not include domestically produced gold, which has varied between $11 million and $15 million per year, without trend.

With earnings down sharply, imports had to be cut back. Since current production materials were needed to supply the newly established consumer goods industries, the reductions were concentrated on capital goods. Investment in machinery and equipment, given in Table 4.3, was brought down in 1957–59 to one-

Table 4.3. Colombian investment-GDP ratios and GDP growth rates, 1950–65 (in millions of pesos at 1958 prices).

Years included in columns (1)–(3)	Average gross fixed investment (1)	Average investment in machinery and equipment (2)	Fixed investment as percent of GDP[a] (3)	Rate of growth of GDP (4)
1950–53	3,126	1,695	19.9	(1950–53) 5.2
1954–56	4,763	2,667	25.1	(1953–56) 5.0
1957–59	3,480	1,353	16.6	(1956–59) 3.9
1959–62	4,484	2,072	18.4	(1959–62) 4.7
1963–65	4,495	2,089	16.3	(1962–65) 4.3

Source: Banco de la República, "Cuentas Nacionales" for 1950–61 and 1962–65 (mimeo, Bogotá).

[a] Ratios calculated from data in constant 1958 prices for each year separately, then averaged for the period.

half the average of the three preceding years. It has never since regained the levels of 1954–56.

External equilibrium was restored in the years 1957–59, while the growth of domestic production was greatly slowed. By 1959, on the basis of the improved balance-of-payments position and new possibilities of official foreign lending, the decision was taken to allow greater freedom for imports and investment. The economy responded promptly by resuming rapid growth, assisted this time by the existence of considerable underutilized capacity.

In the new period of expansion, from 1959 to 1962, imports of consumer goods were allowed to rise along with consumption. Imports of materials for production increased at a closely similar rate. But the rate of growth of consumption was half again as fast as that of real national income, which reduced the savings ratio substantially. Total exports did not grow at all. The brakes had to be put on expansion once again, leading to a new slowdown that lasted through 1965.

Comparing the structure of Colombia's national accounts in 1965 to that of 1956 gives a fairly dismal picture. In terms of constant prices, fixed investment fell from 25 to 15 percent of gross domestic product. Real national income, corrected for changes in the terms of trade, increased during these nine years at a rate of 3.5 percent, barely faster than the growth of population. Consumption grew 4.3 percent per year. Total exports in dollar terms decreased.

The problem of developing exports is especially difficult for Colombia because its main traditional source of earnings has such doubtful long-term prospects. Coffee is too tempting a commodity at present prices for too many producers. Significant improvement in Colombia's prospect for growth is unlikely to come about as a result of better luck with coffee. This means that progress has to be made in two directions at once: increasing the proportion of output of other goods that is directed to export markets, and achieving a greater degree of vertical integration in the structure of production.

SAVING, INVESTMENT, AND FOREIGN EXCHANGE

Colombia's slower rate of growth since 1956 is primarily attributable to the decrease in its rate of investment. One possible interpretation of the situation is that the propensity to save has been too low; that investment and the growth rate could be raised by greater restraint on consumption. An alternative interpretation is that investment has been limited rather by the lack of foreign exchange. Demand for licenses to import types of capital equipment not produced in Colombia has persistently exceeded the rate of licensing actually permitted, indicating that investment would have been higher if more exchange had been available. This second explanation seems to lead to a different policy conclusion than the first: restraint on consumption appears to be an unnecessary sacrifice that contributes nothing to a solution of the real problem. The appeal of the second interpretation is that it is closer to the immediate facts. Its danger is that it may obscure the necessary path of corrective policy.

A major study of the Colombian economy by Jaroslav Vanek attempted to disentangle the roles of domestic saving and of foreign exchange by calculating separately the savings-investment and the export-import gaps that might be expected to occur at specified future dates for various possible rates of growth.[3] For the most plausible sets of forecasts the effective constraint turned out to be foreign exchange. Vanek concluded that the growth rate could be raised by increased aid, but not by greater savings. In conditions in which effective saving is limited by lack of access to imports, an attempt to increase savings "might leave the savings rate unchanged and at the same time have disastrous effects on the economy, such as deflation, excess capacity, unemployment, and other effects." [4]

This problem of an apparent supply limit on investment has often been noted in developing countries, but the more usual conclusion is that it should be subject to reasonably rapid correction. Henry Bruton agreed that a "high marginal saving rate may be wasted if the capital goods sector is small and incapable of expansion in the short run and if export markets are weak. In such conditions, the high-saving rate simply means lower income or less rapidly growing income than a lower saving rate would mean." But the problem should not be lasting: "The capital goods sector is generally expansible. Especially if effective wage rates to firms reflect true relative scarcities, then it will be unusual for the

3. Jaroslav Vanek, *Estimating Foreign Resource Needs for Economic Development* (New York: McGraw-Hill, 1967).
4. Vanek, *Estimating Foreign Resource Needs,* p. 144.

marginal-saving rate to outstrip the capacity of the economy to use the released resources effectively." [5]

The capital-goods sector in Colombia is expansible, but after more than ten years of responding in the right direction, the net gain is still insufficient. Production of machinery and equipment increased at the rate of 16 percent per year between 1950 and 1963.[6] But it started from such an infinitesimal fraction of total supply that it fell far short of compensating for the decrease in imports. Combined domestic and imported supply in 1963–64 was 21 percent lower than in 1954–56. It is easier to see that greater domestic production of capital goods must be a part of the eventual solution than it is to be confident that it can relieve the supply restraint on investment in the near future. Does this mean that Vanek was right, that restriction of domestic consumption is irrelevant or harmful? On the contrary. Greater saving is a necessary condition for the structural changes that would permit faster growth.

The savings-investment and the export-import gaps are not independent of each other. They may be treated as if they were for purposes of statistical projection on the assumption of a given policy framework, but not for purposes of analyzing the consequences of changes in policy. The rate of growth of consumption is intimately related to the supply of foreign exchange available to purchase capital goods for investment.

Every increment of domestic consumption has some foreign-exchange cost. For manufactured goods, the import costs involved in production are low for textiles and range up to quite high ratios for consumer durables. They are not zero for any branch of industry. For primary products other than coffee, potential exports are directly reduced by domestic consumption. This reduction is particularly true for such important products as oil, cotton, sugar, and meat. During the acute world shortage of sugar in 1963 and early 1964, with export prices rising steeply, an embargo was placed on exports to make sure that domestic consumption would not be adversely affected. Efforts to develop exports of meat have been

5. Henry J. Bruton, *Principles of Development Economics* (Englewood Cliffs, N.J.: Prentice-Hall, 1965), pp. 159–60.
6. John Sheahan, "El Desarrollo de la Producción de Bienes de Capital en Colombia," *Revista del Banco de la República* (June 1965), p. 4 (table 1). According to figures supplied by the Banco from unpublished data, domestic production of capital goods in 1963 is estimated at 332.9 million pesos in 1958 prices.

troubled by the sensitivity of the government to complaints that sales abroad will raise prices at home. Except for coffee, increases in consumption and increases in exports compete with each other.

It is difficult to conceive of any general reduction in the rate of growth of consumption that would not make more foreign exchange available for possible investment. But reducing consumption would not by itself raise the rate of growth. If additional exchange were made available and then used to establish new consumer-goods industries on the pattern previously followed, nothing would be accomplished. As soon as the capacity was activated, investment would have to be cut back again. This process created the present situation. Against a ceiling of foreign exchange that did not rise, increasing requirements for production materials cut down progressively on the scope for purchasing machinery and equipment. The change needed is to divert as much of such investment as possible into the expansion of facilities for providing the inputs that will be required as growth continues. Import substitution in the past was misdirected in the sense of yielding a structure of production not well suited to the limitations imposed by foreign-exchange availabilities.

The preceding analysis has neglected questions of comparative advantage. The reason is ignorance. No one has yet been able to disentangle the opportunity costs and external repercussions of Colombian investment decisions in such a way as to make a convincing case for any specific structure of production. The study of Argentina by David Felix in this volume gives good grounds for a presumption in favor of relatively simple consumer goods as against complex products and capital goods in particular. This presumption runs counter to the idea of fostering the production of intermediate materials and capital goods rather than consumer products, but the point is too general. Some capital goods can be produced efficiently now. Others, particularly the most capital intensive, should not be attempted until the economy is much richer.

The dividing line between the products that should be developed at home and those that should be imported depends on the availability of foreign exchange.[7] If the Colombians could raise exports

7. Cf. the empirical calculations for alternative import-substitution and export-supplying industries in Israel, given in Michael Bruno, "Optimal Patterns of Trade

20 percent per year by selling consumer goods, they would be well advised to concentrate on them. If they can not raise total exports at all, which they have not been able to do over the last ten years, they will have to begin to produce practically everything for themselves. As it is, they could do a great deal more to raise exports and also to raise the rate of growth by clearing away more of their own specific bottlenecks for materials and machinery. They should try to go in both directions at once, to close the gap from both sides, paying due deference to any solid information on relative efficiency that may be established but recognizing that the presumption in favor of producing more materials and capital goods is at least as strong as any general argument against it.

INVESTMENT AND THE RATE OF GROWTH

Some of the best Colombian economists are inclined to doubt that higher investment is necessary, because of evidence that the country has a great deal of idle capacity. The difficulty is that this capacity is not well suited for producing the inputs that are wanted to expand further production. Some of it might well be put to use if greater competition forced lower prices or if favorable exchange rates encouraged production for exports. Some of it is probably bound to remain idle because of organizational inefficiency or poor location. Much of it could be activated if the underlying foreign exchange restraint could be eased to allow a greater rate of expansion of aggregate demand. Investment in the right directions, raising either exports or the supplies of inputs to other industries, could both relieve specific supply restraints for some industries and raise demand for all of them.

On the hypothesis that access to capital goods is a key limitation, the possible rate of growth may be defined in terms of the factors that determine their supply. Assume that a relatively fixed level of foreign exchange is expected from coffee, oil, and foreign lending and that imports of consumer goods are held to a low, fairly constant rate. The net inflow from these factors could be considered a parameter, designated A. Imports of production materials are related to current production Y by a coefficient m. Capital goods are

and Development," Harvard University Project for Quantitative Research in Economic Development, Memorandum No. 14 (August 1966), table 1.

supplied both by imports, designated as K_1, and by domestic supply, K_2. Exports other than coffee and oil are designated as X.

The possible growth in output in any period is given by the following two relationships:

(1) $$\Delta Y = \frac{K_1 + K_2}{c}$$

where c is the marginal capital-output ratio, and

(2) $$K_1 = A + X - m(Y + \Delta Y)$$

Substituting (2) into (1) indicates that the expected growth of output is:

(3) $$\Delta Y = \frac{A + X + K_2 - mY}{c + m}$$

If A, c, and m are regarded as fixed, the rate of growth of domestic product is then limited by the rate at which exports other than coffee and oil, plus domestic production of capital goods, grow relative to total output:

(4) $$\frac{\Delta Y}{Y} = \frac{1}{c + m} \left(\frac{A + X + K_2 - mY}{Y} \right)$$

The coefficients should not be regarded as fixed in fact: they can be changed by better economic policy. Equation (4) simply permits separate consideration of the effects on the growth rate of each factor individually. Filling in the relationship with export and production data for 1963, and with long-run average coefficients, gives the following illustrative results.[8] Structural coefficients are:

$$c = 2.16$$

$$m = 0.077$$

Parameters as percentages of gross domestic product are:

$$A/Y = 12.33$$

8. The estimated capital-output ratio refers to that for machinery and equipment for 1950–62 as calculated in Sheahan, "El Desarrollo de la Producción," and in a typewritten study by Colombia's Department of Planning, Division of Global Studies, revised May 1965. The import coefficient refers to the last period of sustained expansion, 1959–62. Minor exports in dollars were converted to a basis comparable to national accounts in constant 1958 prices by using the average 1958 exchange rate of 6.41 pesos per dollar. Imports and exports as defined here mean commodities only: the invisibles on both sides are left out.

$$X/Y = 1.61$$
$$K_2/Y = 1.36$$

From which, $\Delta Y/Y = 3.4$ percent.

The scope for legitimate doubt about the accuracy of all these figures can scarcely be overestimated. They may nonetheless be considered to cast some light on Colombia's difficulties in trying to come anywhere near the target growth rate of 5.5 percent set in the development plan. If minor exports and the production of domestic machinery and equipment are considered the two more dynamic variables under direct policy influence, it is pitiful how small they are. By 1965, after a year of better exchange-rate policy, minor exports increased 60 percent over the 1963 rate, which brought them to about 2 percent of gross domestic product. This change by itself, if sustained, could be expected to raise the growth rate by about 0.3 percent yer year. The road is long.

The illustrative values also point to the deadly handicap of inefficient allocation of capital, a point rightly stressed by John Delaplaine.[9] The coefficient as calculated refers to machinery and equipment only and is unusually high on a comparative basis. This low productivity of capital is probably a result both of misallocation among fields and of the sheer waste of underutilized capacity.

Significant improvement of the growth rate could be achieved by reducing the capital-output ratio without requiring any decrease in the share of consumption in national product. Any chance of raising efficiency by reducing capital requirements should be seized, but it would be a mistake to rely on this possibility as an excuse for avoiding restraint on consumption. Efficiency must be considered a tough factor, unlikely to change so rapidly as to make unnecessary a shift toward increased exports and toward the production of investment goods and materials. Such redirections of resource use imply that consumption ought to be reduced relative to total output if it is to be raised more rapidly in the long run.

DEVALUATION AND PRICES

All the structural changes needed — more exports other than coffee, greater use of domestic inputs, and greater economy in the

9. John W. Delaplaine, "The Structure of Growth in Colombia and Argentina" (mimeo, presented at the Bellagio Conference of the Harvard Development Advisory Service, June 1966), p. 34.

use of capital — would be encouraged by an increase in the relative price of foreign exchange. The case for devaluation, or for
continuous adjustment by using a free exchange rate, appears
overwhelming. The trouble is that misuse of exchange-rate variation
in recent years has reduced its effectiveness by weakening the
society's previous resistances to inflation. The last several changes
in the exchange rate have not helped increase the relative price of
foreign exchange, and the defense mechanisms of all groups in the
economy are now more oriented toward preventing successful use
of this previously powerful technique.

The principal exchange rate was left practically unchanged for
the twenty years up to 1932, then again from 1935 to 1949. From
1951 to 1966 there were five devaluations, which are listed in
Table 4.4. They refer only to changes in the principal rate applied

**Table 4.4. Changes and principal exchange rates applied
to commodity imports and domestic prices, 1950–66.**

Devaluation sequence	Change in price of dollars	Percent increase in price of dollars	Change of cost-of-living index	
			Period	Percent increase
March 1951	1.96–2.51	28.1	December 1950–December 1951	−3.5
June 1957	2.51–4.86 in June 1957, to 6.40 by October 1958	93.6 initially, to a total of 155.0	June-December 1957; June 1957–June 1959	8.3 / 24.1
March 1960	6.40–6.70	4.7	December 1959–December 1960	6.7
November 1962	6.70–9.00	34.3	October 1962–October 1963	38.6
September 1965–August 1966	"Basic" imports initially unchanged, but majority: 9.00–13.50	50.0 for about 60 percent of total imports initially, for 75 percent by January 1966, and for all by August 1966	September 1965–September 1966	20.6

Source: Banco de la República, *XL y XLI Informe anual del Gerente a la Junta
Directiva* (Bogotá, 1965), Pt. II, Tables 75 and 134; IMF, *International Financial
Statistics* (1951–1966).

to commodity imports, not to the special rates often used for coffee,
oil, minor exports, or capital transactions. The consequences of

devaluations for domestic prices varied a great deal, but only in one direction: they got progressively worse.

Among the multitude of factors operating on domestic prices in the periods following these devaluations, observation suggests that great importance should be given to changes in the supply of food. Agricultural production happened to increase more rapidly in 1951 than in any other year of the period considered. It also rose in 1957 and 1958 but fell in both 1960 and 1963.[10] Food prices alone accounted for the fall in the overall index in 1951 and greatly aggravated the inflationary situation in 1963.

Another critical variable on the supply side is the quantity of imports available. Increases in imports can either make up for shortfalls in agricultural production or, more generally, relieve supply bottlenecks and facilitate a more rapid response of production to increases in monetary demand resulting from devaluation. The favorable result of devaluation in 1951 was aided not only by higher agricultural production but also by increasing total imports. Conversely, the grim results in 1962–63 were aggravated by the necessity of reducing imports.

The experience of 1957–58 would seem to represent a contradiction in that, although imports were drastically reduced, the increase in prices was held to a small proportion of the degree of devaluation. In this case it should be noted that the simultaneous fall in export earnings (because of lower coffee prices) was a strong deflationary factor, or would have been in the absence of devaluation. The increase in the peso price of dollars shielded money incomes from the deflationary impact of the decrease in exports. Another way of saying the same thing is that the decrease in foreign-exchange earnings softened the expansionary effect of devaluation.

Another important aspect of the 1957–58 experience was the ability of the government to count on general acceptance of the need for restraint and cooperative effort. The new government, which succeeded a military dictatorship in May 1957, had to cope with falling exports and a considerable overhang of short-term foreign debt at the same time that it attempted to end a long period of

10. The measure used here is the volume index of agricultural production, table 14, in "Cuentas Nacionales, 1950–61." No one really knows the level of production even for the major crops, let alone for those consumed chiefly in the rural areas. This particular index is simply a careful guess, based on estimates of twenty of the most important crops.

violence approaching civil war. The problems were understood, the government enjoyed unusually wide popular support, and it exercised a high quality of leadership. It did not have to cope with the riots, protest strikes, and aggressive behavior of price-setting groups that contributed so much to the inflationary climate after the 1962 devaluation.

The 1951 devaluation also benefited greatly from special surrounding circumstances. At that time there was no crisis at all. Prices were stable, the balance of payments was not under pressure, and devaluation was undertaken calmly as a discretionary device to stimulate growth. In the slightly paraphrased words of one of the architects of that operation: "I was sitting on the beach one day thinking how calm the economy was, and it occurred to me that if we ever wanted to devalue, now would be the time to do it."

The three preceding considerations — agricultural production, import supply, and *ambiente* — go far to account for the sharp contrast in results between the first two devaluations and the 1962–63 experience. A more conventional interpretation is that the money supply was more effectively restrained in the first two cases. An exponent of this view can point out that the supply was held constant from June 1950 to June 1951. A skeptic might add that it increased 20 percent in the following six months with no noticeable effect on prices. Again in 1957 the money supply was held constant in the second half of the year, but it was allowed to expand quite rapidly in 1958 and 1959 without causing explosive effects. For the period 1950–62 in general, Jorge Ramírez Ocampo concluded that the connection between money supply and prices was so indefinite that money supply could not be considered an important determinant of price changes.[11] Still, monetary management was so bad in 1962 that it surely made the situation worse than it would otherwise have been. The government financed its substantial budget deficit by direct recourse to the central bank and thereby helped increase the money supply by 27 percent in the last three months of 1962. Another aggravating factor in early 1963 was the government's decision to decree a nationwide increase in wages to lessen the impact of the devaluation on workers. This measure added to

11. Ramírez, "Inflation in Colombia, 1950–62" (mimeo, Williams College Center for Development Economics, May 1965).

the money incomes of workers an amount equal to roughly 27 percent of national product.[12]

The more complex operation of September 1965 avoided an immediate explosion. No devaluation was announced; in fact, all goods considered likely to have a direct bearing on the cost of living were left initially at the original exchange rate. Approximately 60 percent of imports were moved to the new rate of 13.5 in the first instance. In a deft series of subsequent decisions the government moved a few more items over to the new rate from time to time, usually with a special explanation for each one. By January 1966 about 75 percent of all imports were at the new rate, and by August the transfer was completed.

Devaluations can work. When they do, they help a great deal. But it would be a serious mistake to think of them as simply working or failing to do so. They are not merely neutral when they go wrong; they are seriously harmful. The key changes needed in the Colombian structure of production were all made more difficult as a consequence of the 1962 devaluation. The most evident result was that prices of domestic goods rose relative to prices of imports before the end of 1963, discouraging exports and stimulating efforts to use imported rather than domestic inputs. Wage rates for hourly workers rose 38 percent in the course of 1963 alone, making it more advantageous than ever to substitute imported machinery for domestic labor wherever possible.

The frequent recourse to devaluation in recent years seems to have moved Colombia closer to the threshold beyond which high degrees of inflation become a way of life. In the 1962–63 devaluation, in contrast to the preceding ones, major economic groups struck out promptly for self-protection by demanding or establishing higher wages and prices. Cotton farmers refused to plant in 1963 until guaranteed what they thought to be an adequate increase in the negotiated price for cotton; house-owners pushed up the rent component in the cost-of-living index for employees by 20 percent in the year ending October 1963; political pressure raising national minimum wages was quickly followed by bargaining pressure on above-minimum salaries in industry; and those companies not in-

12. Miguel Fadul, in Fadul, Peñalosa y Asociados, untitled study of the impact of devaluation on wages and other costs for Bavaria, S.A., September 1964.

cluded among the unlucky few subject to effective price control
quickly moved up their charges. Naturally, the government responded by attempting more intensive controls, without any pronounced success.

The 1962–63 experience stimulated everyone's awareness of
inflation, encouraged greater group organization for self-defense
through cooperative pricing, enlarged the area of administrative
decision on prices, and weakened confidence in the ability of the
government to control the process or distribute the burdens of
adjustment fairly.

Monetary restraint is essential to limit the additional inflationary
pressure created by exchange-rate depreciation, but it may not be
enough. Except in some parts of agriculture, the economy is not
competitively organized. The typical industry has very few firms;
many have only one. The two cotton-growing federations, the
single buyer for the textile industry, the handful of meat dealers able
to shut off supplies to Bogotá whenever they decide that prices are
not going up fast enough, and other well-organized groups in many
fields are all capable of raising prices no matter what is happening
to aggregate demand. The government generally supports wage
claims when it seems that workers may be falling behind, "and the
larger and wealthier the companies, the more they are expected to
do for their workers. It is accepted as a matter of course that the
companies will pass along any increase in labor costs to the consumer." [13]

One possible response is to conclude that control of inflation is
hopeless and the best way to live with the situation is to cut the
exchange rate loose to allow continuous depreciation. This reaction
is understandable but may involve an underestimate of the possibilities for limiting inflation in the absence of devaluation. More active
government leadership, working out group agreement to minimize
money claims that react back and forth on each other, might
possibly restore a little of the maneuverability that the government
possessed in 1957–59. Both the introduction of a sales tax in 1965
and the important reforms of monetary institutions accomplished
since establishment of the Junta Monetaria in late 1963 have
increased possibilities of effective action on the side of demand.
The chances of gaining anything by devaluing frequently are now

13. Currie, *Accelerating Development,* p. 193.

quite low, but the chances of holding down the rate of price increase in the absence of devaluation are by no means zero.

Repeated devaluations or a floating rate in the present state of
Colombian market organization and expectations should not be
considered as simple offsets to a given rate of inflation. They would
instead be likely to add pressures raising the rate of inflation. A
floating exchange rate is an appealing recommendation for any
country that can keep prices well under control, but it is rather like
pouring gasoline on the flames in Colombia's situation. Ragnar
Nurkse's study of the consequences of frequent devaluations by
continental European countries in the 1920's, in the absence of
effective control of domestic inflationary pressures, brought out
clearly the process of mutual aggravation between exchange rates
and worsening inflation. Although these countries possibly had a
higher degree of internal competition and social discipline than is
yet the case in Colombia, successive devaluations got nowhere:
"The fall in the exchange rate became literally the leading factor
in the mechanism of inflation, driving up the cost of living and
creating an irresistible pressure for wage adjustments, which in
turn called forth demands for additional currency on the part of the
government as well as businessmen." [14]

A freely fluctuating exchange rate would have the special defect
of going down fast whenever financing for imports proved particularly difficult, which is just when the economy would be facing
supply difficulties and least able to respond effectively without increased inflation. If increased aid could be fed in over an extended
period, in which the rate was allowed to drop gradually, the chances
of success would be distinctly better. If the economy had to do its
best without such outside support, a free rate or frequent devaluation would amount to a race between depreciation and the added
intensity of inflation that it would surely create.

The Colombian economy would develop more effectively if the
relative price of foreign exchange could be raised; the question is
how to accomplish this at minimum cost. If more serious inflation
seems an unimportant cost, frequent change of the exchange rate
probably would not have any worse results there than in Argentina
or Chile. To do better, Colombia would need the patience and

14. League of Nations, *International Currency Experience* (Geneva, 1944), p.
115.

political stamina to create appropriate prior conditions before adopting a policy of frequent rate changes for imports. Such conditions probably include a period of relative stability to calm down inflationary expectations, explicit arrangements for limiting the arbitrary reactions of price-makers, and a prior approach by alternative methods toward a structure of production that can yield a more flexible supply response to the impact of devaluation on demand.

MEANS TO IMPROVE THE STRUCTURE OF PRODUCTION

If it were considered preferable to avoid recourse to devaluations until more favorable conditions had been created, it would be important to make all possible improvements in the other conditions operating to orient incentives in ways adverse to development. Three areas of corrective policy that seem particularly promising are the tariff system, other domestic taxes bearing on the competition between imports and domestic inputs, and the separate exchange rate applied to minor exports.

The tariff system has operated to bias incentives against needed structural changes. A sample study of the degree of protection afforded by tariffs and equivalent charges indicated approximate levels of protection in 1962 of 211 percent for manufactured consumer goods, 57 percent for industrial raw materials, and 18 percent for capital goods. Of the eight Latin American countries included in the study, Colombia had the highest ratio between protection for manufactured consumer goods and protection for capital goods.[15]

Taxes other than tariffs bear on the structure of imports in many ways, but that particular jungle is too nearly impenetrable to enter here, except for one important possibility: the use of sales taxes to reduce the distortion of investment incentives that arises from efforts to limit imports of nonessential consumer goods. Prohibiting these imports or subjecting them to high tariffs has the familiar effect of encouraging investment in their production at home. If tariffs were accompanied by high sales taxes to discourage possible domestic production, this effect could be controlled. Protection intended to stimulate domestic production, as in materials and

15. Santiago Macario, "Protectionism and Industrialization in Latin America," *Economic Bulletin for Latin America* (March 1964), p. 75 (table 5).

equipment or essential consumer goods, could continue to operate without offsetting taxes, while protection intended to reduce the use of resources for purposes of nonessential consumption could accomplish its objective instead of distorting investment.

Apart from policies affecting choices between domestic production and imports, there is important scope for corrective action with respect to incentives for minor exports. Unlike coffee, for which external market limits are the dominant constraint, the issue with most other exports is ability to produce and effort to sell.

Domestic protection in general raises relative returns for investment in industries selling to the home market and decreases relative returns in export industries. This effect may be countered by special subsidies to exporters, which in Colombia are substantial. They include tax privileges and the right, under certain restrictions, to import freely without tariffs the materials that go into producing exports. These privileges work out unevenly among firms, and they also have the disadvantage of encouraging the use of imported materials. A more favorable exchange rate for minor exports, raising incentives equally among firms and eliminating the present complicated and counterproductive system of special privileges, should be more efficient.

Colombia experimented with a free rate for minor exports from 1958 to November 1962 and again from November 1964 to June 1965. Minor exports responded well in the first period, increasing 13 percent per year from the 1957–59 average to 1962. When the export rate was reduced and fixed at ten pesos per dollar in November of that year, the growth of minor exports promptly stopped. The costs of supporting the rate of ten proved too great by November 1964, so it was released again in that month. Minor exports reacted almost immediately. In the first half of 1965 they ran approximately 100 percent higher than in the first half of 1964.[16] The policy response was to bring the export rate down again in June 1965 and peg it at 13.50.

The reasons given for bringing the rate back down in 1965 were that the use of a higher value for dollars in converting export earnings than in purchasing imports encouraged inefficient industries and involved a loss to the government (or the central bank) in

16. Departamento Administrativo de Estadistica, *Boletín Mensual de Estadistica* (October 1965).

paying out more for dollars than the rate charged in selling them. Accepting the judgment that the gap between the import and export rates might have been too high, it seems unfortunate that the concern for possible encouragement of inefficient industries did not lead to reduction of protection for those unable to export, before reducing incentives for those that could. The monetary imbalance between the buying and selling costs of dollars has to be countered somewhere in the system; but when the results are so strongly positive in such a crucial matter as export stimulation, it would seem better to make the offset somewhere else rather than to take away the export incentive.

Stimulation of exports and greater protection for domestic production of materials and equipment would gradually alter the structure of production in directions favorable for more rapid growth. All these changes are similar to those sought by devaluation, and all would work in the direction of higher prices, but they are somewhat less likely to provoke interacting wage-price defensive spirals. Changes in tariffs occur all the time. They affect the prices of the goods involved, but they do not serve as signals for generalized inflation. Further, the corrections needed in the tariff structure go in both directions. The increases on materials and equipment should be accompanied by decreases on the more highly protected consumer goods.

Stimulating minor exports by a higher exchange rate need not raise costs at all. Unit costs might often decrease as existing industries use their capacity more fully. Demand would be increased, but that effect should not be overestimated: minor exports accounted for about 2 percent of national product even at the sharply higher level reached in 1965. When minor exports jumped upward in the first half of 1965, they did not provoke any noticeable change in prices. Still, higher peso earnings from exports could be a source of trouble in conditions of strong aggregate demand, and it would be desirable to offset the stimulus by adequate domestic taxes.

More generally, the changes needed in the economy imply that the rate of increase of consumption should be held below the rate of growth of national product. The policies suggested differ from devaluation in their probable impact on group-determined price spirals but they could, like devaluation, be made useless by failure to control excess monetary demand. They differ in avoiding the signals of inflation to which the community has become progressively more acclimated and in aiming directly at the correction of important forms of unhelpful bias that would remain even after a successful devaluation.

CONCLUSIONS

Given Colombia's entrepreneurial capacities and organizational flexibility, its rate of growth of production in the last ten years could have been substantially higher than actually achieved. It could have been higher if investment in the periods of ready access to capital equipment had been directed more toward increasing the production of materials and equipment and if minor exports had been stimulated as a means of getting needed equipment in exchange for consumer goods. The trouble did not come from pushing import substitution too fast but from shaping substitution in such a way as to increase dependence on imported supplies and equipment, which then used up so much foreign exchange for current production that adequate imports of capital goods became impossible.

The existing system of tariffs and exchange rates is not well designed to promote necessary changes in the structure of production. Tariffs and other taxes are too low on imports of supplies and equipment and too high on consumer goods, discouraging investment in the directions in which it is most needed. Temporary use of an exchange rate distinctly more advantageous for minor exports than for imports resulted in a strikingly positive response, but the exchange rate operation of 1965 again took away this advantage, apparently under the misapprehension that the technique constituted a distortion of incentives. It was actually an offset to the otherwise strong bias toward investment in protected domestic industries and a promising way to turn excess capacity for producing consumer goods into needed production materials and capital equipment through trade.

Devaluation has been misused so badly that it is unlikely to be of much help until better conditions are created in which to use it. In 1962–63 the consequences of devaluation were such as to set back growth, move incentives adversely, bring the economy closer to the danger zone of runaway inflation, and weaken public support for the government.

Apart from special circumstances making the odds in favor of successful devaluation higher or lower in a given case, a key point is the availability of imported materials and equipment with which to carry out supply adjustments. If imports can not be increased, the attempt is almost certain to be self-defeating. This consideration suggests that a freely fluctuating rate would not be a promising technique in the present stage of Colombian development. The rate would presumably fall most rapidly precisely when the country encountered unusual difficulties in financing imports.

The question is not one of accepting or rejecting devaluation as a basic policy technique. Rather, the step should be taken only under conditions in which it has a good chance to work. It can easily fail to work, failure can be extremely costly, and alternative devices can do a considerable share of the job that needs to be done with much less risk.

The Colombian position resembles those that have proven so difficult to handle in Argentina and Chile. The similarity is probably not because of any peculiar Latin American characteristics but because these countries managed to advance a considerable distance toward industrialization without developing their exports at the rate necessary to balance rising import requirements of new industries focused on domestic markets. Although it looks today like a specifically "Latin problem," it could easily be "the African problem" a decade or two from now.

Part II

STABILIZATION AND SHORT-TERM POLICIES

Harold B. Dunkerley

5

~~~~~~~~~~~~~~~

Exchange-Rate Systems in Conditions of Continuing Inflation — Lessons from Colombian Experience

The rate of inflation in the less developed countries in recent years has generally been more rapid than in the developed countries. Weaknesses of monetary and fiscal policy, in part reflecting deep-seated socio-political conditions, have undoubtedly been a major cause. The "structuralists" deduce additional reasons from the basic conditions of underdevelopment and the need for price and wage increases in eliminating obstacles to ·adequate growth rates. Among the less developed countries, inflationary pressures may be relatively mild in the ones where income, population growth, and public social spending are low and where labor movements are weak. As such countries move higher up the development scale, and as others with stagnant economies strive to accelerate growth, the underlying inflationary pressures may become even more prevalent. It is not my purpose, however, to review yet again the arguments for greater susceptibility to inflation in developing countries. It is simply assumed that many of these countries will be unable in the near future to find an acceptable and sufficiently potent method to curb inflation to developed country levels. On all evidence such an assumption appears reasonable.

It follows that many developing countries will be prone to severe balance-of-payments difficulties. There are additional well-known reasons for such difficulties. For some developing countries, expansion of markets for traditional exports has proved particularly hard as a result of technological development, income inelasticities, or protective policies in the developed countries: terms of trade have worsened. Growth accentuates a developing country's demand for imported capital goods, and this pressure is often compounded by the expanding import requirements of consumer-goods substitution industries. Foreign borrowing for infrastructure leaves a legacy of high debt-servicing charges. Again, it is not my purpose to review the arguments for and against the inevitability of such pressures as a concomitant of development. It is sufficient to note that the pressures demonstrably exist in many developing countries and are unlikely to be rapidly eradicated.

If so much is accepted, presumably the developing countries experiencing such problems will from time to time be forced to devalue. The pressure of increasing overvaluation of a currency can not be contained indefinitely under the conditions prevailing in such countries, even with exchange controls, import taxes and quotas, and export subsidies — all of which are notoriously difficult to administer effectively. The contention here is that the choice of exchange-rate systems can in such circumstances have a very wide and significant influence on growth, and that existing policies in this field are often seriously inadequate. The choice can exacerbate or diminish existing tendencies to inflation and to monetary, structural, and balance-of-payments disequilibria.

The choice is essentially one of alternative methods of adjustment of exchange rates that must inevitably be depreciated. Accordingly, a major part of the current debate on the relative merits of flexible exchange rates versus permanently fixed rates is irrelevant. By contrast, the impact on resource allocation of the choice of method of making exchange adjustments can assume great importance for developing countries, even though it is of limited interest to developed countries and has been largely neglected in the debate. A reappraisal of alternative exchange-rate systems in the specific context of developing countries therefore seems warranted.

In the following account I have tried to draw some lessons from Colombia's experience from 1960 to 1966, a period covering its first attempts to achieve accelerated growth in the framework of an overall development plan supported by exceptional levels of foreign aid. In the first part, a case summary is presented, describing the

devaluations of 1962 and 1965. Case studies are notoriously difficult to construct; perhaps they are even harder to digest. Nevertheless, it has seemed useful to try to convey to readers unfamiliar
with such experience the type of difficulties, the confusion, and the
disruptive policy switches and political reactions that may in practice be encountered with the traditional devaluation-stabilization
approach. Following the case study is a largely self-contained analysis of the choice of exchange-rate systems in conditions of continuing inflation. Some underlying reasons for the failure of the traditional approach are diagnosed and the alternative is examined of
a flexible exchange-rate system with simple proportional differential
rates for certain types of transaction. It is clearly not possible here
to cover all relevant considerations, but it is hoped that the examination of several aspects that have perhaps been unduly neglected
may contribute to a more rigorous and comprehensive analysis.

THE COLOMBIAN DEVALUATIONS OF 1962 AND 1965:
A CASE SUMMARY

The late 1950's were years of relative stability in Colombia.
Annual national product growth averaged probably about 1 percent
per capita. Austerity in monetary and import policies had eliminated the large foreign short-term debt incurred during the preceding dictatorial regime and reduced the price rise to less than
10 percent a year — a rate above the average of the early fifties in
Colombia but notably below other South American countries.
Heavy dependence on coffee for nearly three-quarters of export
earnings of $400–$500 million a year gave cause for concern in
view of the inelastic international market and growing competition.
Calculations for the National Plan 1960–70 underlined the prospect of a large balance-of-payments gap; subsequent revisions put
annual gross borrowing requirements at over $200 million a year
on the basis of maintenance of coffee prices and a 1½–2 percent
growth rate in GNP per head. Fortunately, the support given by
international agencies to the National Plan indicated that Colombia, as the proposed "showcase for the Alliance for Progress," might
receive help of this order.

A few other aspects of the setting should be noted. A population
growth of over 3 percent per year and heavy migration to the

towns, in part stimulated by insecurity in the countryside, had produced large and growing urban unemployment. Although industry
had expanded relatively rapidly to pass 20 percent of gross domestic product, industrial employment was failing to keep pace with
the labor influx. Moreover, for a country with a per capita income
around $250, which places it among the wealthier members of the
developing community, the low 11 percent ratio of public revenues
(including departments and municipalities) to national income constituted an obvious obstacle to public investment to promote growth
and employment.

The new Constitution of 1958 had brought political stability,
ending the spasmodic civil war between the traditional Liberal and
Conservative parties, but it also created a political system biased
toward inaction. The two-thirds majority required in Congress to
pass all important legislation provided insurance against domina-
tion of the legislature by either of the two parties — each of which
is allotted 50 percent of the seats. It correspondingly increased the
power of minority opposition groupings. The President, chosen
alternately from the two parties for a four-year term, has concentrated executive power but only limited means to overcome legislative prerogatives. Even under state-of-siege powers, the decree
laws require the signature of all ministers, drawn equally from the
two parties and often strongly influenced by leaders of particular
groupings. The biparty system stretches down to appointment of
senior civil servants and often below. In practice, "officialist"
groups have formed in both of the parties to support the "Frente
Nacional" government and the existing political system. Reflecting
the strong influence of a comparatively small oligarchic class, they
have displayed little basic policy divergence. The opposition has
consisted primarily of right-wing Conservative followers of the ex-
dictator Rojas, on the one hand, and of the left wing of the Liberal
Party, on the other. Splinter groupings of "officialists" have often
voted with them against economic and fiscal measures.

The exchange-rate system comprised three tiers, with in 1960 a
relatively small spread between them. The Central Bank (Banco
de la República) applied a fixed rate of 6.70 pesos to the dollar for
imports, government transactions, and most freights. On the legal
"free market" for most private capital, tourism, and some miscellaneous items, the rate stood around 7. Coffee and net petroleum

exports were penalized by the Central Bank's "coffee rate" of around 6.40.[1] Other "minor" export proceeds were at any given time converted by the Central Bank at the free market rate of the previous week.

The 1962 Devaluation. National budget deficits stand out as a major proximate cause of the December 1962 devaluation. From a small overall budget surplus in 1960, the situation deteriorated progressively to a deficit equivalent to about 30 percent of total expenditures in 1962. In the absence of long-term borrowing facilities, government recourse to the Central Bank in 1961 and 1962 provided an expansionary force equivalent to roughly half the money supply existing at the end of 1960.

The steps by which such a drastic deterioration occurred are more difficult to trace. The enthusiasm engendered by the Ten Year Plan probably accounts for much of the abrupt increase of more than 50 percent in budget allocations for investment between 1960 and 1961 and the accompanying gross overestimating of revenues. Insufficient account of exemptions added by Congress to the 1960 income-tax reform appears also to have been important. It is particularly significant that no advance consideration seems to have been given to the cut in export taxes that proved unavoidable with rising local costs, though declining world coffee prices were also a factor. A further worsening occurred when, in reaction to growing pressure on local government budgets, Congress in 1961 legislated a progressive transfer of police and education expenditures to the national budget with no corresponding increase in national taxation. Nineteen hundred sixty-two was an election year! Serious attempts to halt the slide into deficits are seen in the 20 percent cutback in the investment budget in early 1962 and in the increasing delays in various payments; but these were more than offset later in the year when, to "clear the decks" before the devaluation, the government paid off its large accumulation of short-term debts.

Attempts were also made, again rather tardily, to counteract the inflationary pressure by credit restrictions. The commercial banks retaliated by increasing their capital and by not complying fully with banking regulations. Nevertheless, their loan expansion was

1. To simplify the exposition, the special problems of the exchange system for petroleum are not treated in this study.

cut from 21 percent in 1961 to 11 percent in 1962. Monetary measures alone could not, however, cope with government borrowing
on the scale at which it continued. Although stabilization of the
money supply was achieved during the first half of 1962 after the
rise of 20 percent in the second half of 1961, a similar expansion
again occurred in the second half of 1962, despite the contractive
effect of diminishing reserves. (See Figure 5.1.)

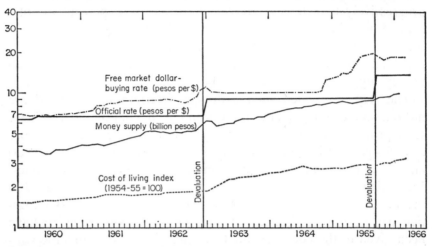

FIGURE 5.1

Colombia's free market and official exchange rates, money supply, and cost
of living, 1960–66 (log scale). *Source:* Exchange rates, Central Bank (Banco
de la República); cost-of-living index, National Bureau of Statistics (Departamento Administrativo de Estadistica).

The monetary expansion of 1961–62, twice as great as in the
preceding two years, did not find immediate reflection in an accelerated price rise. The yearly average cost-of-living index increased
by 8.5 percent in 1961 but by only 4.3 percent in 1962, the small-
est increase since 1955.[2] The cost of living was kept in bounds at
this time primarily by the stabilizing influence of a rapid expansion
of imports. Licenses for reimbursable imports increased about 25
percent between 1959 and 1961, seemingly as a result of a delib-
erate policy to bring raw materials and capital-goods imports up
to a level consistent with the ten-year plan growth targets. Not
until the early summer of 1962, when importers escalated license

2. The cost-of-living index for workers is used throughout this chapter. Other
indices, including the implicit GDP deflator, show a closely similar pattern.

applications under the threat of an imminent balance-of-payments crisis, did the government clearly reverse its policy by progressively transferring items from the automatic-license list to the prior-approval system. In November all licensing was suspended during the six weeks of congressional debate on the proposed devaluation measures.

The liberal import policy transferred much of the pressure of the monetary expansion from prices to the balance of payments. As the crisis developed, the balance-of-payments deterioration intensified, due in large part to the rush by importers to secure payment for already licensed imports, which more than counterbalanced the tardy restriction of new licenses. Payments for reimbursable imports in 1962 reached $423 million, as against $284 million in 1959. There is also some evidence of increasing delays in repatriation of export earnings. A 10 percent fall in the international coffee quotation exerted a further pressure on the current balance, which swung from a surplus of over $40 million in 1959 to a deficit of about $120 million in both 1961 and 1962. Not surprisingly, repayment of private credits contracted abroad — mostly to finance import deposits and supplier credits — also accelerated, leading to a sharp deterioration in the recorded short-term private capital account. Undoubtedly, unrecorded capital flight in order to place savings abroad before the devaluation, or to speculate on the exchange depreciation, increased substantially. These pressures on official reserves produced both a widening imbalance in authorized transactions and increased Central Bank intervention to restrain the upward trend in the free market rate.

Despite the intervention, the free market rate rose fairly rapidly to reach 9 by April 1962 and then, after a pause influenced by new aid receipts and monetary measures, to reach 11 at the time of the devaluation. As Figure 5.1 shows, the rise in the free rate was considerably more rapid than the climb in prices, though roughly proportional to the increase in money supply. The widening of the spread between the free and fixed rates also affected reserves through a diminution of net receipts from normal trade. That is, the spread led to under- and over-invoicing and to the smuggling of coffee exports, which increased rapidly during this period.

Clearly evident in Figure 5.2 is the cumulative impact on gross reserves, even with increased official short-term borrowing and

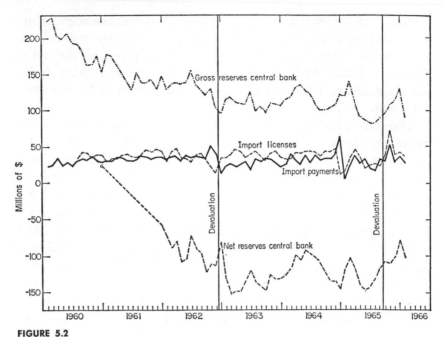

FIGURE 5.2

Colombian reserves and imports, 1960–66. *Source:* Central Bank; IMF, *International Financial Statistics* (monthly issues).

"swap" operations, which were reflected in an even more rapid deterioration of net reserves. In the first half of 1962 a temporary improvement followed negotiation of an aid package totaling $151 million, of which a considerable part took the form of direct balance-of-payments assistance; but from mid-1962 reserves again plunged downward. By early November they had declined to $100 million, less than half the early 1960 level, and a substantial part of this total represented bilateral balances and other assets not readily mobilizable. Payments due on official debts for the remainder of the year and amounts shortly due on imports already received totaled over $500 million. Only immediate further aid could save the situation; but the international agencies had already made clear several months earlier that no further aid would be provided without devaluation. They had underlined this decision by repeated deferment of the Consultative Group of donor countries and international agencies to consider long-term international finance for a $370 million project list, the establishment of which had been agreed to in 1961.

The Terms. After protracted discussion and great political op-position, the devaluation took place in December 1962. The terms were largely determined by the International Monetary Fund (IMF) — future aid from the international agencies being, in effect, tied to acceptance of the IMF proposals. At first, the IMF tentatively suggested a unified flexible rate for all transactions, to be allowed to find its own level prior to stabilization. The idea of flexibility was quickly abandoned, however, and although the objective of unification was maintained, it became accepted that this could not be achieved in a single step. As a transitional measure, agreement was reached that the free rate would be pegged by Central Bank intervention at slightly above the fixed import rate, with the expressed hope that the premium could later be eliminated. For coffee export proceeds, a rate below the import rate was agreed upon, accompanied by a somewhat equivocal promise to the coffee growers that the differential would be progressively reduced. The devaluation that emerged amounted to 34 percent for the import rate, fixed at 9 pesos to the dollar as against 6.70 previously. The free market rate, pegged at 10, represented a similar devaluation as compared with 1960 but amounted to an appreciation of 10 percent on the level effective immediately prior to the pegging. The coffee rate, which had been adjusted from 6.10 to 6.50 during 1960, was devalued a further 9 percent to 7.10.

The causes of the modifications to the original IMF suggestions are important. No close examination seems to have been made of the initial Colombian reaction that flexibility of the exchange rate might cause difficulties to importers and lead to speculation. The continuing differential rate for coffee, however, was accepted only after strong Colombian insistence on the need to restrain coffee production and, perhaps even more, after consideration of the large contribution that receipts from the differential could make in alleviating the fiscal position.[3] No alternatives were immediately available for these purposes. The IMF strongly pressed for unification of the minor export rate with the import rate, apparently both to prevent "subsidization" and to avoid possible peso losses if export proceeds bought at a premium were sold for imports at the 9 rate. Only under strong pressure from the Colombian Congress did the

3. Carlos Sanz de Santamaria (Minister of Finance, 1962–64), *Una Epoca Difícil* (Bogotá: Tercer Mundo, 1965), pp. 111–12.

IMF accept the compromise formula of allowing minor exports to receive the free rate but pegging the free rate at a maximum of 10 to the dollar.

Early projections by the IMF pointed to a much improved fiscal situation after the devaluation. These projections were based on a proposed increase in income and certain minor taxes, as well as on the automatic increase in customs receipts and a share in the enlarged coffee exchange differential — the rest of which was to go to the Coffee Federation to pay off its debt to the Central Bank. Adding in also the projected budget-support foreign aid, an increase of roughly 50 percent in budget investment allocations without net Central Bank borrowing seemed possible, even after allowing for salary increases.[4] This increase in allocations would permit the National Plan levels of budget investment to be reached. Doubts seem nevertheless to have arisen on the validity of the revenue estimates, leading to a condition that the government abstain from net Central Bank borrowing. The desire to ensure a greater margin of credit for the private sector probably influenced this decision as well.

In the monetary field, the agreements stipulated a maximum expansion of net Central Bank domestic credit, defined as Central Bank assets less international reserves, public deposits, and "sterilized" private deposits. Foreign credits to the Private Investment Fund, a new institution to provide long-term finance for private "development" projects, were specifically excluded, and changes in counterpart funds appear surprisingly to have been overlooked. The basis for the allowable credit expansion seems to have been a projected 5 percent direct effect of the devaluation on prices, with a maximum 15 percent increase in the cost of living and in wages after allowing for secondary effects.[5] The IMF insisted that the government immediately, prior to the devaluation, pay off short-term internal debts equivalent to as much as a sixth of 1962 budget expenditures, while proposing many measures for tightening overall control of banking credit.

The policy of "starting with a clean sheet" while relying primarily on monetary controls and the free play of market forces to

4. Sanz de Santamaria, *Epoca Difícil,* p. 88.
5. *Devaluacion 1962: Historia Documental* (Bogotá: Tercer Mundo, 1964), p. 117.

bring about stabilization may also be seen both in the IMF's stip-
ulation that price controls be abolished and in the strong pressure
exerted by the IMF for liberalization of import restrictions. As to
the liberalization, it seems to have been estimated that the devaluation would reduce potential import demand by about 20 percent,
in which case exchange receipts, including the projected increase
in aid and private capital, would be adequate to meet the strain of
import liberalization.[6]

The impressive external aid offered in reward was to be channeled mainly through the Consultative Group, which was to be
convened immediately to consider financing of $450 million worth
of projects during the period up to the end of 1964. Total net long-
term aid effectively utilizable was expected to reach $150 million
in 1963 and more in subsequent years.[7] This level implied more
than doubling the 1961–62 average; in 1960 net long-term aid had
been zero. Additionally, the IMF provided a new "stand-by" of
$52.5 million, and commercial banks in the United States made
available $40.5 million of acceptance credits.

The Aftermath. In almost all respects the aftermath of the devaluation diverged dramatically from the projections. The price
rise accelerated sharply. By April the cost-of-living index had
jumped 23 percent above the predevaluation level. Although inflation then moderated, it did not stop until mid-1964, with the index
55 percent above the predevaluation level, or more than one and
a half times the depreciation of the main exchange rate. Wages,
which had risen about 10 percent in 1962, moved sharply upward
following the enactment early in February of statutory increases
estimated in retrospect to have raised total wage costs to the private
sector by about 25 percent and to the public sector by 30 percent.

Nor did the devaluation halt the pressure of capital flight on the
free market. Intervention by the Central Bank to maintain the rate
of 10 proved far more costly than anticipated. In the first four
months following the devaluation, almost all the IMF's stand-by
had to be drawn, though the pressure then slackened. Demand for
imports continued at high levels. Under these conditions the Colom-

---

6. Sanz de Santamaria, *Epoca Difícil,* pp. 82–83.
7. Including drawings on the $200 million remaining from the $350 million of
aid committed between 1959 and early 1962, as well as new AID program and
PL 480 loans. Disbursements from previous commitments had become more
difficult as devaluation approached.

bian authorities found it impossible to liberalize imports. The new system of automatic and prior-approval lists constituted a more restrictive policy than that prevailing before the devaluation crisis developed.

The credit restraint policy did not work as planned. Although basic legal reserve requirements were raised progressively, the effect was weakened by granting an option of increased investment in specified types of development when financial stringency in those sectors became acute. A parallel attempt to tighten credit by a 100 percent reserve requirement on deposits in excess of those existing on the date of devaluation proved ineffective for a time, mainly because of the high level of deposits at the base date — a level consequent on the government's repayment of internal short-term debts. Similarly, a reduction of rediscount quotas proved initially ineffective because of unused quotas at the time of devaluation and the failure of the banks to meet legal limits. Complete failure of the credit restraint was averted only by continuation of import deposits at existing rates on the new higher peso import values, in contradiction to an agreement to reduce these rates. Largely as a consequence, the money supply actually declined by 5 percent during the first four months of 1963. But by its nature this decline was a "once and for all" effect.

Although still more restrictions on the banks' reserve ratios and rediscount facilities were introduced in May, by the end of 1963 the IMF's ceiling of 3,625 million pesos for domestic operations of the Central Bank had been exceeded by 657 million. It is important for the subsequent analysis to note that this excess was not attributable to the government's operations: indeed, the public sector's use of Central Bank credit in 1963, including counterpart funds and repayments by the Coffee Federation, proved roughly neutral.[8] The commercial banks, nevertheless, under increasingly severe pressure for credit, contrived to expand their position with the Central Bank by more than 850 million pesos, continuing to make full use of the development loan option and failing to meet reserve and credit ratio regulations. Despite the reduction in the early months of the year, the money supply increased by 12 percent from December to December — which was notably less, however, than the 35 percent rise in the cost-of-living index.

8. Sanz de Santamaria, *Epoca Difícil,* p. 230.

The success in balancing the fiscal position in 1963 unfortunately owed as much to restriction of investment expenditures as to higher revenues. After much delay Congress gave the government extraordinary powers to impose new revenues, including a 20 percent surcharge on income tax for two years and a forced subscription to government bonds by the commercial banks. As a result of these and a few minor new taxes, together with increased receipts from the coffee differential, central government current revenues rose by 850 million pesos, or 45 percent. Budget-support foreign aid provided an additional 325 million pesos. Even so, to avoid Central Bank borrowing in the face of the greatly increased salary bill, investment expenditures had to be held at the 1,100 million pesos level of the previous year, which represented a further reduction of 20–25 percent in real terms and as much as 45 percent below National Plan targets.

The balance of payments did not respond as expected, despite the failure to liberalize imports. The fall in coffee earnings by $30 million, both volume and prices falling, can be attributed to bad luck. But the so-called minor exports, which had doubled from 1959 to 1962, now fell back slightly. Net aid reached only $101 million rather than the $150 million projected. Private long-term capital receipts dropped further, and recorded private short-term capital remained slightly negative. Although payments for imports declined sharply after the predevaluation rush (import arrivals maintained their 1962 level), net international reserves deteriorated from $92 million in excess liabilities at the end of 1962 to $127 million at the close of 1963 (as shown in Figure 5.2). Only by heavy use of the IMF credit was it possible to achieve a marginal improvement of gross reserves.

The 1963 record of production proved little short of catastrophic. Industrial expansion slowed down, which the business community attributed mainly to the credit restrictions. A poor harvest compounded the difficulties. GDP growth dropped to little more than 3 percent, barely equal to the population growth. The national income showed no rise at all; per head it fell by about 3 percent.

Some Technical Aspects. The reasons for this melancholy debacle have their roots in the basic policies underlying the exchange reform-stabilization plans, which are examined later in this study. From a more limited technical point of view the devaluation program also appears to have had serious faults. Action in the fiscal, import, and monetary fields should clearly have been pushed more strongly at an earlier date: for example, at the time of the aid discussions late in 1961. In the previous major devaluation of 1957, the main exchange rate had been depreciated almost 100 percent, from 2.51 to 5 pesos per dollar; further adjustments to 6.70 at the beginning of 1960 represented an additional 34 percent depreciation. In contrast, the rise in the cost-of-living index from the 1957 devaluation through 1961 had been no more than 30 percent. Moreover, prices had been relatively stable well into 1962, and aid was offsetting the decline in terms of trade. At the least, a much smaller devaluation with far less disruptive effects would have been possible had action been taken earlier. As it was, the aid granted in 1961, and the prospect of more to come from the promised Consultative Group, enabled the Colombian authorities to delay changes in basic policies till growing lack of confidence, suspension of aid, and exhaustion of reserves forced them to accept the devaluation-stabilization proposals. Largely as a consequence, the devaluation occurred in advance of measures to increase government revenues.

It has proved tempting to put the blame for the subsequent inflation primarily on the "demagogic" wage legislation that increased wages by roughly double the estimates of the IMF. But this is surely only a part, if a very important part, of the story. Even on the wage front the announcements of government policy in Congress before the devaluation made a wage increase of this order entirely foreseeable in the absence of much stronger undertakings in the devaluation agreements.[9] Nor can the extent of the price rise be attributed solely to the wage increase. Although some price controls were maintained and even reinforced on certain essentials in the first months after the devaluation, large price rises elsewhere spread quickly in many parts of the economy in advance of higher wage costs. Often these increases covered goods and services whose price had been held down under anti-inflationary policies for a considerable time. A suppressed price-lift force was freed at the same time that higher import prices took effect and in conditions of excessive liquidity much increased by the IMF's insistence on the prior repayment of the country's floating debt.

9. A prior statement by the Minister of Labor, Belisario Betancur, for example, is given in *Devaluacion 1962*, pp. 116–27.

The decision to hold the free rate at a maximum of 11 percent above the import rate as a preliminary to unification also seems to have been conceived with little respect for warnings of the capital flight that might ensue. Given the traditional propensity to hold balances abroad and the evident extent of smuggling, pressure to establish a wider premium was foreseeable in the liquidity position prevailing. The run on Central Bank reserves for intervention came as a natural consequence.

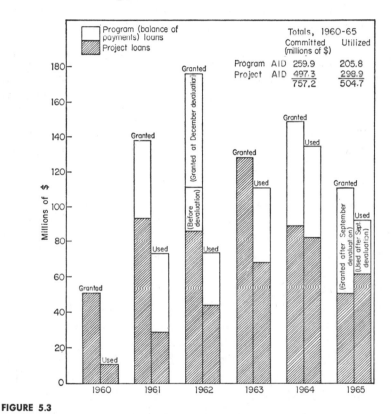

FIGURE 5.3

Long-term aid, commitments, and utilization, 1960–65. Includes loans from IBRD, Inter-American Bank, AID, Ex-Im Bank, and Federal Reserve Bank short-term finance in anticipation of AID loans. Excludes PL 480. *Source:* Data provided by the agencies and the Central Bank.

Projected receipts from foreign aid were clearly overoptimistic. Previous experience had demonstrated the difficulties of disbursement on project aid (see Figure 5.3). Delays could also have been anticipated from the requirement for increases in utility rates as a prior condition for disbursement on several important projects. Moreover, as could have been expected, the enforced budget stringency led to shortages of local funds to match the foreign contribution.

Little consideration appears to have been given to the crucial importance of developing minor exports. Even if the IMF's rosy estimates of the domestic price and wage repercussions of the devaluation had been accurate, the rise in the price level since the end of 1961 would not have been offset by the rate of 10 chosen for minor exports — still less by the proposed rate of 9.

The 1965 Devaluation. Already by the beginning of 1964 the internal-external price relationship had deteriorated to a position worse than in the latter months of 1962 at the time of the devaluation. In the first half of 1964 the cost-of-living index rose a further 12 percent under the double influence of shortages of foodstuffs, following poor 1963 harvests, and higher incomes in the coffee sector, stemming from a 25 percent jump in world prices. Discussion of the possibility of a new devaluation inevitably became more open. Substantial new aid negotiated at the end of 1963 — $135 million of program aid and IMF facilities — and the higher receipts from coffee exports enabled Colombia to hold its reserve position for some months. But it could do little to restore confidence in face of the price rise and the increasing probability of political and fiscal crises.

The renewed fiscal disequilibrium reflected a much more rapid increase of costs than of revenues, which was primarily the outcome of the time lag in the income-tax base. A contributory factor was a sharply higher debt amortization charge. Thus, although the ending of direct budget-support foreign aid was balanced by higher receipts from the temporary taxes and bond sales, and the coffee differential yielded more with higher world prices, rising expenditures outstripped the higher receipts. Despite a further cut in budget investment in real terms, borrowing from the Central Bank had to be resumed. The net total for the year reached 400 million pesos, roughly the same as in 1961. Inflationary pressures of a similar magnitude were added by Coffee Federation borrowing, both from the Central Bank and from foreign buyers through advance payments, for purchase of the new crop. This borrowing reflected higher local support prices, which more than offset the rise in world coffee prices and which the government agreed to on consideration of increasing local costs and as an alternative to raising the coffee exchange rate.

The prospect became even more gloomy with the mid-term elections of March 1964. The main opposition groups campaigned on the issue of the rise in prices, stressing profiteering and other inequities of the devaluation. Their combined representation in Congress rose to almost exactly one-third, and the government effectively lost control of the crucial two-thirds majority required for all major legislation.[10] When Congress reconvened in July, it immediately became apparent that no hope existed of securing approval of new taxes to replace the important revenues provided for the two years following the 1962 devaluation. Even the limited sales tax, approved in 1963 but postponed to 1965, came under danger of further postponement.

In the early months of 1964 monetary policy was transferred from the board of the Central Bank — consisting primarily of commercial bank nominees — to a Junta Monetaria of four government ministers and the president of the Central Bank. The new Junta progressively gained control of Central Bank credit creation through a further series of severe restrictions and increased penalties for noncompliance. Nevertheless, although net Central Bank credit to the banking system actually fell marginally over the year, the much more rapid expansion of private deposits, fed by public-sector borrowing, permitted an expansion of total bank credit of 18 percent for the year, the same as in 1963. In consequence, the year's expansion in money supply totaled 21 percent, approximately the same as in 1961 and 1962 and substantially above the 12 percent for 1963.

In these circumstances some general improvements in the economy experienced in the latter part of 1964 could do little to restore confidence. Arrival of supplies from the new harvest led to a fall in the cost-of-living index of 5 percent from June to October, limiting the December to December rise to 8.5 percent, as against 35 percent in 1963. The swing from a poor to a relatively good

10. Only 37 percent of the registered electorate voted, as compared with nearly 60 percent in the 1962 and 1960 elections and 70 percent in the 1958 elections. The low turnout reflected growing frustration with the political system.

harvest and the pickup in industrial production after the stagnation of 1963 produced an estimated growth of over 5 percent in GDP. Helped by the rise in coffee prices, the national income per capita increased by about 3 percent — the largest increase since 1959 — whereas 1963 had been the worst year of this period. Nevertheless, as rumors of a serious fall in reserves became more insistent, a new run began on the free market.

The first casualty was the pegging of the free rate. In September and October 1964 the cost of Central Bank intervention to maintain the rate at 10 rose precipitously, with another acceleration in payment of private foreign debts before an expected change in the rate. Despite some $42 million borrowed abroad by the Coffee Federation, gross reserves fell to minimal levels (as shown in Figure 5.3). Late in October the Central Bank had to suspend its intervention. Credit restrictions were tightened yet again, and a series of ill-conceived measures were introduced to supply the free market automatically with additional resources — for example, by routing 40 percent of minor-export proceeds into this market via the commercial banks. These hurried measures singularly failed to restore confidence. The free rate moved up from 10 to around 13 by the end of the year, and the pressures quickly spread to the official market. By November, monthly allocations for payment for imports had reached $40 million, as against an average of about $30 million in the first six months of the year, and in the early part of December as much as $65 million had to be provided.

Throughout these months political leaders had declared their strongest opposition to a new devaluation, which they considered would have "suicidal" price and political repercussions. The President had gone on record as saying that while he remained in office, there would be no further devaluation. Nevertheless, by the beginning of December the reserve position had become so critical that no escape seemed possible from the alternatives of a new devaluation or a moratorium. The international agencies and the United States had during the summer already made it clear that they regarded a new devaluation as inevitable and were firmly opposed to further aid while capital flight continued. Technical difficulties, particularly the transfer of program aid to a "forward procurement" basis, had virtually stopped the release of aid already contracted. Finally, when it became evident that another week of exchange allocations for imports at prevailing high levels would completely exhaust available reserves, the Finance Minister obtained authorization to negotiate a devaluation of the official rate from 9 to 12.50.

While the hurried discussions with Washington proceeded, pressure from importers on the official market suddenly eased, apparently as a result of the tightening credit position of the commercial banks. Probably influenced also by intense pressure from political leaders against a new devaluation, the President suddenly reaffirmed his previous strong antidevaluation stand. At this point the United States agreed to immediate release of the remaining $40 million of program aid already contracted. Presumably the United States government wished to avoid being held responsible for a devaluation or, alternatively, for the chaos of a moratorium. A new regulation requiring importers to deposit 95 percent of the peso equivalent twenty days before allocation of exchange achieved an effective breathing space of about one month's imports payments. The Central Bank managed to arrange some additional short-term credits.

That the respite given by the December 1964 measures proved temporary is scarcely to be wondered at; none of the underlying causes of the balance-of-payments pressure had been removed. Of more interest is the tenacity with which the almost inevitable new devaluation continued to be postponed, to the detriment of the economy as a whole. As the problems became more intense, so did opposition to effective action on foreign-exchange rates.

Heralding the drama of the ensuing months came the threat of a general strike at the end of January 1965, in protest at the rise in prices and general weakness of government policy. The inflationary dangers of meeting the union demands, including repeal of the new sales tax, were obvious; the threat of serious disorders and a possible military coup were perhaps even more evident. As a compromise, the government agreed to a special session of Congress, first to approve further strengthening of labor and social security legislation, second to reconsider the sales tax and introduce new taxes on the wealthy. For the drafting of detailed proposals the President convened an Alta Comision, which consisted of representatives of the unions, employers, and officialist political groups. Meanwhile, the fiscal situation deteriorated further. Strong pressure from the coffee growers, whose costs continued to rise, forced the government to accept an increase from 7.10 to 7.67 in the coffee exchange rate. The increase cut government revenue from the "differential" by about one-third. Although budget operating expenditures had been pruned and real investment levels cut still further, deficit borrowing from the Central Bank accelerated. Even more important, as the free market exchange rate rose, so did the Central Bank's credit creation as a result of the purchasing of dollars from minor exporters at the free rate while selling them to importers at the fixed rate of 9.

For a few months the "sterilization" of the growing peso deposits required on application for foreign exchange more than counterbalanced the fiscal and foreign-exchange account losses. Postponement in use of counterpart funds also helped. In consequence, the money supply expanded only marginally during the first three to four months of 1965. Prices nevertheless resumed their upward trend, rising a further 6½ percent in the first half of the year. Actual shortages of imports, and even more the prospect of intense shortages as the reality of the closing off of aid became appreciated, were already affecting both prices and production. After some erratic movements at the beginning of the year the issue of reimbursable import licenses became stabilized — at little more than half the 1964 average!

Against this background the President reconvened Congress at the end of April. The Alta Comision's proposals included continuation of a slightly modified sales tax and various new taxes, along with the strengthened labor laws. But the extent of the fiscal deficit remained clearly underestimated, and that of the new revenues overestimated. Congress showed no disposition to take any positive measures, and the violence of the reaction to a suggested use of "state of siege" powers led to the public abandonment of that avenue. At this point student rioting occurred, touched off by events in Santo Domingo. Tensions mounted rapidly. With one student killed, and expectations of much greater casualties added to fears of a coup by the Rojas faction, the government rushed 10,000 troops into Bogotá and proclaimed a state of siege after all.

The temporary nature of the late 1964 measures became increasingly obvious. The movement to obtain rapid payments for imports rebounded after the respite given by the advance-application system. Although in comparison with the previous year minor exports doubled under the stimulus of the higher free rate, the increase represented only a small additional foreign-exchange inflow in absolute terms. A wave of kidnapping of rich people added to the upward pressure on the free rate. The routing of part of the minor-exports proceeds to the free market had to be abandoned to meet import payment obligations. The free rate responded with a bound reaching 19 at the end of May. Meanwhile, reserves had again fallen below the level they had occupied at the time of the 1962 crisis (Figure 5.2).

Once again devaluation appeared inevitable. During May the Finance Minister obtained authority to hold talks with the Washington agencies on the action necessary to obtain a resumption of balance-of-payments support aid. These talks led to agreement on the introduction of a tax of 3.50 pesos per dollar on foreign-exchange sales at the 9 rate as an alternative to a formal devaluation; the 7.67 coffee rate was to be maintained, so as to provide much larger revenue from the "differential" to ease the fiscal situation.

The two weeks following the reporting of this agreement to the full cabinet provided a classic example of the strength of opposition to large devaluations. Several ministers opposed the proposals on the familiar grounds of their disastrous political consequences. Leaks to the press immediately occurred. The Finance Minister referred to "saboteurs in the Cabinet." Congress suspended consideration of the proposed tax measures until the government clarified its position. Within a week the President let it be known that he "remained" completely opposed to any devaluation. The Minister of Health suggested a crusade of Latin American countries against the IMF and raised the possibility of loans from "socialist" countries. The political parties and almost everyone else found it expedient to proclaim redoubled opposition to devaluation. The cabinet, after meeting almost every day until the small hours of the morning for over two weeks without reaching any decision, announced that reports of divergencies among its members were erroneous. The press tried to find out who was really to blame for the preceding three or four devaluations. Immediately available reserves fell almost to vanishing point.

During the next three months the chaos became widespread. Gross reserves fell to $84 million in June. In a desperate effort to protect what remained, administrative delays in allocating exchange became pronounced. The delays could not, however, stop the run on the free market, particularly as the monetary situation rapidly worsened. The temporary sterilizing effect of the introduction of deposits for import-exchange allocation had ended, but the fiscal deficits continued. Action taken under state-of-siege powers at the end of June, substituting a fixed rate of 13.50 pesos for minor exports in place of the free rate, reduced but did not eliminate Central Bank losses in selling the exchange to importers at the 9 rate, and it immediately reduced minor exports. Money supply rose 10 percent from April to September. The free market rate touched 20 in August.

Just how far production was depressed is still unclear, though curtailment was undoubtedly drastic. Repercussions from the cuts in import-licensing, inevitably including some hoarding of supplies, were increasingly reflected in short-time work in industry and threats of complete stoppage. Substantial firing of workers could be prevented only by administrative regulation. The postponement of foreign private investment in centers such as Cali became almost complete. Budget investment expenditures were reduced 15 percent for the year in current prices and more in real terms.

One Finance Minister had resigned in February 1965, following the December 1964 debacle. His successor resigned in mid-June in protest at the repudiation of the May agreements. A new minister proved hard to find. In mid-July, reportedly under the strongest pressure from the investment-banking community, the President appointed a leader of the industrial sector. Using state-of-siege powers, the minister quickly introduced a series of tax measures and then at the beginning of September — almost a year after abandonment of the free-rate pegging — instituted the long-awaited devaluation.

The Terms. To save face and reduce the psychological impact, the official rate of 9 pesos was maintained as a "preferential rate" for some 25 percent of imports of a "basic necessity" type.[11] For other imports, invisibles, and certain types of private capital previously transacted at 9, the rate was devalued 50 percent to an "intermediate rate" of 13.50 — the rate previously applying and

11. The devaluation was presented as a "revaluation" to bring down the free rate while the official rate was maintained at 9!

still maintained for minor exports. An agreement between Colombia and the IMF stipulated that import items once placed in the "intermediate" market would not subsequently be restored to the preferential rate. An understanding was also reached that imports on the preferential list would gradually be moved to the intermediate market. Thus, the rate for all imports and minor exports would be progressively unified. Some theoretical flexibility was provided in the published "letter of intent" by undertaking to maintain the intermediate rate at a level "adequate to the situation of the balance of payments." The free market rate, then standing around 19.50, would be left to "fluctuate freely in accordance with demand and supply" with no net Central Bank intervention. The coffee rate was devalued from 7.67 to 8.50 pesos, with an additional 0.50 pesos for financing of coffee-sector institutions.

The Colombian authorities committed themselves to progressive liberalization of imports with the avowed purpose of reducing protection and distortions in industry. Specifically, they agreed to reduce the prohibited list and to place not less than half of total reimbursable imports on the automatic license list at the intermediate market rate within 6 months; control of capital-goods imports to permit direction of investment was to be continued. The backlog of exchange allocations for imports was to be paid off at once, and administrative delays were to be avoided in the future. A pledge was given to build up international reserves, after deduction of these delayed payments, by not less than $45 million by the end of 1966.

The fiscal and monetary limitations laid down at this juncture were more complex than those devised in the 1962 devaluation agreements, although the underlying philosophy showed little change. The government undertook not only to avoid net Central Bank borrowing but also to increase revenues sufficiently to ensure a current-account budgetary surplus of 1,600 million pesos for 1966. This surplus, it was estimated, would permit an investment budget of roughly the same real magnitude as in 1965, though still far below the 1961 level and even farther below the ten-year plan targets. Central Bank domestic credit ceilings at each quarter-end were meticulously worked out on the basis of the agreed international reserve buildup, and an increase of money circulation of 12–13 percent in 1966 was envisaged, to equate the anticipated rise in prices and growth of national production. Severe restrictions were placed on use of counterpart deposits and Coffee Federation borrowing from the Central Bank. The government undertook to reduce import deposits as a first step toward their complete elimination.

The new revenue measures introduced in September were again of a temporary nature and remarkably similar to those of 1963. An extension of the income-tax surcharge for two years at rates of 15 percent for 1965 (plus a 5 percent forced bond subscription) and 10 percent for 1966 accompanied provisions for compulsory government bond purchases by nonbank financial institutions. These measures, together with the additional receipts from customs and coffee differential as a result of the devaluation, were originally projected as being sufficient to produce the agreed current budget surplus in 1966. However, following strikes in public agencies and pressure for large pay increases in the armed forces, the government had to concede salary increases which, on the assumption that they became generalized, indicated a 25–30 percent increase in the government's wage bill. Obtaining assurances of additional revenues in 1966 was apparently an important cause of the delay in signing the aid package until December.

The aid package again proved to be of an exceptional size. Commitments of over $300 million for the year to October 1966 were envisaged, with over $150 million in program-type aid for support of the balance of payments, including $80 million of IMF facilities. Since the new project aid could hardly affect the 1966 balance of payments, a speedup of disbursements on unutilized balances of previous loans was agreed to, the Colombian government promising in this context to introduce a more automatic system for adjusting tariffs in the utilities sector. Release of much of this aid package was made conditional on quarterly reviews of the execution of the government's program. The program also undertook to reinforce agricultural policy and the planning mechanism, make improvements in the educational system, and review industrial policy.

The Aftermath. First reactions to the new devaluation have been more favorable than those that came soon after the previous one. Helped by an immediate doubling in reimbursable import licenses, short-time work in industry rapidly declined, and the investment climate noticeably improved. The hiatus in foreign private investment, however, had by March 1966 not yet been overcome.

The improvement in the reserve position has been striking. Continuing buoyancy of coffee prices has helped, as well as exhaustion of the long import-payment run and the delayed effects on payments of the import-license cuts of the first nine months of 1965. Following advances against the first *tranche* of aid, Central Bank reserves ended the year about $45 million above the pre-devaluation level. By early February 1966 net reserves showed an improvement of $12 million, even though $50 million of delayed import transfers had been paid off. The free market rate declined a little from 20 before the devaluation to stabilize in the range of 18–18.50 around the turn of the year.

Other aspects have been less favorable. Although tight credit restrictions were maintained, money supply rose 10 percent from August through January. The cost-of-living index rose substantially more than allowed for in the IMF's calculation — 13 percent from August to March — and further inflation appears inevitable. Rate increases in various utilities and steel are long overdue; the impact of higher duties on many imports and the transfer of additional items to the 13.50 rate have still to be fully absorbed. Producers of several important products are holding back supplies or reducing production to force acceptance of price increases. A further spread of the wage rise is to be expected.

The Coffee Federation's finances had been brought into balance at the time of devaluation. They became unbalanced again in January 1966 when the government yielded to pressure for a higher domestic coffee-support price at the same time that it further devalued the coffee exchange rate from 8.50 to 8.94. To offset the monetary repercussions of the reduced differential on the budget, additional import items were transferred from the preferential rate of 9 to the intermediate rate of 13.50.

Although the fiscal situation has benefited from increases in tariffs accompanying the import liberalization and a large quota for automobile imports, recourse to Central Bank borrowing is being avoided only by the continued holding down of government investment expenditures well below the projected level. Congress still shows no inclination to pass the additional tax proposals submitted by the government, and even though state-of-siege powers can still be used, disruptive delays in public investment are now inevitable. The very limited investment budget targets seem most unlikely to be achieved. The restrictions placed on use of counterpart funds, presumably to achieve a deflationary sterilization of counterpart funds from the new program loans while building up reserves, will further reduce public investment possibilities. Local-currency finance will not be available to match the anticipated receipts of project aid.

More generally, the exceptional level of aid and particularly the lines of short-term credit provided the wherewithal for the government to continue policies of increased imports and to allow easier credit beyond the elections in March–May. The promotion of a better economic climate during this period was doubtless an important consideration in the whole devaluation-stabilization package.

Some Technical Aspects. The more favorable first reactions to the 1965 devaluation can be attributed largely to the severer difficulties that preceded it. Compared with the 1962 devaluation, the preceding price rise had been far greater; to a much larger extent, the devaluation represented an adjustment to an already prevailing price situation. Physical shortages were much more severe in advance of the 1965 devaluation, particularly of imported supplies; consequently, the sudden increase in imports following devaluation had a marked impact in holding down prices and in stimulating domestic production. The free market rate had already risen prior to the devaluation to more than double the main import rate. When the worst fears about the effects of further delays in devaluation, of fiscal disequilibrium, and of the impact of the devaluation itself were not realized, pressures on the free market fell. Similarly, the better response in reserves appears largely attributable to the draconian cut in import licenses prior to the devaluation, as well as to better luck with coffee prices.

The fiscal and monetary measures accompanying the devaluation were better timed. The simultaneous announcement of new fiscal measures to balance the budget stood in marked contrast to the 1962 devaluation. No repetition occurred of the sudden prior repayment of floating debt. On the contrary, a fairly tight grip was maintained on the credit situation both immediately prior to and after the devaluation, permitting some relaxation after the first shock of the devaluation had been absorbed.

The new devaluation has not, however, fully offset the preceding rise in prices. Against the 60 percent increase in the cost-of-living index between the devaluations, the main import rate has been depreciated by 50 percent and the average import rate by roughly 37.5 percent. If the 1962 devaluation was too large, the latest devaluation appears on the low side. This is particularly evident in the devaluation of the minor-export rate by 35 percent from its 1963 level.

The import-liberalization policy, the two rates for imports and the commitments for nonintervention in the free market are also open to question. The general policy issues involved are discussed later. From a narrower viewpoint, the experience of the first few months indicates that licenses for nonliberalized imports may be unduly squeezed by the high level of applications for liberalized goods. Although the two-rate system for imports is presumably temporary, it has obvious disadvantages. Many products at the 9 rate compete directly or indirectly with domestic production; the implied subsidy to these imports appears to have been adopted primarily for psychological reasons. The spread of over 100 percent in exchange rates is making effective control of export smuggling and false invoicing extremely difficult.

How substantial is the flexibility theoretically introduced into the exchange system is difficult to judge. In the early months of 1966 the Colombian authorities reiterated that the 9 rate would be maintained for roughly the present volume of imports at least through 1966. Similarly, though the 13.50 rate is theoretically flexible, the policy is apparently to defend this rate by raising tariffs and using balance-of-payments lines of credit to the full if necessary.

The relative "success" of the 1965 devaluation in terms of smaller immediate price rise, improvement of reserves, and the pickup in production may possibly be used as justification for this type of devaluation-stabilization policy. After the setback in 1965, when the GDP per head may not have risen at all despite normal harvest conditions, an above-average GDP rise for 1966 could of course be anticipated; industrial production previously held back by import shortages could be expected to rebound. It is a far step, however, to deduce that growth has been re-established as a result of the devaluation. The timing and technical details of large-devaluation stabilization policies can alter the extent to which unfavorable repercussions fall before or after devaluation. What is more important is that the cycle leading to future disruptive difficulties does not seem to have been broken. Inflation continues, the long-term fiscal problem is unresolved, and the seeds of a new harvest of distortion and another devaluation are already sown.

THE CHOICE OF EXCHANGE-RATE SYSTEM

The record of development in Colombia since 1960 is disappointing. As shown in Figure 5.4, the conventional measure of growth,

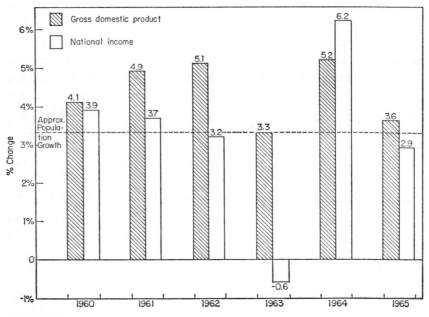

FIGURE 5.4

Growth of Colombia's domestic product and national income, 1960–66. *Source:* Central Bank national accounts (Cuentas Nacionales), 1960–63; Planning Department (Departamento Administrativo de Planeación) estimates, 1964–65.

the annual GDP increase, has, despite exceptionally high levels of foreign aid, averaged only about 1.5 percent per capita, and national income has advanced at a rate of less than 1 percent per capita — more slowly, on available evidence, than in the 1950's. Private consumption has been allowed to rise at twice this rate, but nonunionized labor has shared little, if at all, in the consumption growth. With growing unemployment, now probably exceeding 10 percent in the towns, income distribution has apparently worsened. After a temporary increase in 1961, fixed capital formation has fallen to the lowest level for more than a decade, with both public and private investment sharing the decline. National budget investment for 1964 and 1965 averaged roughly 40 percent below the 1961 level. Even if local governments and autonomous agencies are included, some decline in real levels appears to have occurred, which becomes more pronounced when taken as a proportion of national product. Other public development expenditures have been inadequate for the needs of the growing population; for instance, probably a smaller proportion of children is now at school than five years ago. Making due reservations for the fallibility of the national accounts, the contrast is striking between these trends and the 1960–70 Plan projected growth of roughly 2½ percent per head in national product and 1.3 percent in consumption, accompanied by a sharp rise in savings and investment. Furthermore, there has been a growing rate of inflation and a fundamental worsening of the balance of payments, with debt servicing and import needs rising more rapidly than exports.

How far have the exchange-rate-system stabilization programs contributed to the failure to achieve a better development? To provide an answer, it is necessary to look more closely at some consequences of the approach adopted and to consider whether an alternative approach could be expected to fare better. First, it will be useful to examine briefly a common apologia.

Other underlying influences, which would in any case have been operative, evidently hold an important share of the responsibility for Colombia's dismal record from 1960 to 1966. The opposition of the governing class to new fiscal and exchange measures, expressed through strong pressure on political groups and the press, undoubtedly played a crucial role. A weak coalition government, with little interest in planning in its wider as well as its narrower sense, became further incapacitated by the deteriorating political situation. A poor civil service with minimal coordination — nowhere more evident than in the relations of the monetary authorities with other agencies — complicated the formulation and implementation of development policies. Even these handicaps, however, were magnified by the devaluation-stabilization programs. The 1962 devaluation fiasco greatly strengthened the opposition to further exchange reform and directly contributed to the political deterioration and loss of the two-thirds congressional majority. Foreign financial support for stabilization may also at times have been conceived more to shore up the unsatisfactory political system for fear of alternatives than as an integral part of a development process. Even the condition of the civil service, which has been worsened by salaries increasingly lower than those in the private sector, can be partly attributed to the impact of the exchange-stabilization policies on the fiscal situation.

Such handicaps or equivalent ones are, however, common to the "developing country" status. Whether or not it is fair to say that with better government the devaluation-stabilization approach adopted would have enjoyed greater success, it seems more rewarding to investigate how far this approach increased the difficulties the government had to face as compared with practical alternatives.

For this purpose, it is necessary to examine some consequences inherent in the once-and-for-all devaluation approach — the "traditional approach" — when applied in conditions of continuing inflation, as well as the possible advantages of a flexible exchange-rate structure. It is convenient to break into the circle of closely interrelated consequences by a general examination of the direct price impact of the traditional approach.

Direct Price Repercussions. The underlying purpose of big devaluation-stabilization exercises is to enforce a fairly drastic reduction in domestic demand to bring it back into line with current resources. The need to rebuild reserves, exhausted while devaluation was delayed, usually necessitates an even greater devaluation and reduction in domestic demand.[12] Insofar as a country seeks to reduce imports sharply and expand exports within a short period following the devaluation, an abrupt cut in real consumption is necessary, and the restraints required on monetary demand are raised to draconian levels. Such abrupt cuts are bound to be fiercely resisted via wage demands, price increases, opposition to taxes, and evasion of monetary controls. The policy measures actually feasible in a developing country are most unlikely to be adequate to offset these pressures.

12. "Stand-by" loans may afford temporary alleviation of pressures to rebuild reserves, but they increase future balance-of-payments problems. It also becomes difficult for a country to escape from the policies of the agencies concerned when refinancing of the large amounts falling due is offered as part of the aid packet to overcome the next crisis.

A flexible exchange rate, whether adjusted continuously or in small steps, has evident advantages in this general analysis. The problem of cutting excessive consumption financed by a deficit in the balance of payments is greatly reduced by progressive devaluation: action is taken before the situation has gotten out of hand. The cuts required at any time will therefore be much smaller and can perhaps be absorbed in the normal growth of GNP.

Inflationary "ratchet" effects of the traditional approach, deriving largely from spasmodic shortages and the stickiness of prices and wages to downward adjustments when the temporary pressures ease, produce an additional, overlapping family of reasons for anticipating that progressive devaluation would be preferable. The sudden swing in demand from imports to domestic production involved in a large-devaluation stabilization exercise inevitably creates a strong temporary pressure on prices of the domestic products; a rapid expansion of exports following the devaluation will magnify that effect. With a smoother growth of demand for domestic products under progressive devaluation, supply can be more readily adapted and pressure on prices reduced. Other examples of ratchet effects on prices from the traditional approach can be found in the exaggerated impact of sudden import-license cuts to defend the exchange rate and in the price increases by manufacturers and traders during the period of a large devaluation exercise as a defense against expected further large general price increases and imposition of price controls. A rush by consumers to buy "sensitive" goods before the expected large price rise, building up personal stocks and reducing liquidity, can be a contributory factor. Progressive devaluation by dampening such abrupt movements should lessen the ratchet effect.

The pattern of wage movements under the traditional approach tends to be similar, reflecting shortage-produced price rises before a large devaluation and anticipation of a drastic upward price movement afterward. Temporary improvement in the fiscal situation may encourage the government to yield to postdevaluation pressures. The large wage increases granted — in the event necessary to offset the price rise — set a pattern of high-percentage wage settlements that is difficult to reduce substantially at subsequent wage negotiations, particularly since "leap-frogging" tends to occur.

Additional pressures may arise from black market or free market exchange rates. In countries such as Colombia, if the free rate is not pegged, it tends increasingly to be considered the "true" value of the currency whenever the main rate becomes progressively overvalued. Many domestic prices may then be adjusted in accordance with the free rate which, as the Colombian experience shows, can be forced to very high levels as the disequilibrium within the exchange system grows. If the free rate is absorbed in a flexible exchange rate or, to anticipate the subsequent analysis, is linked through a fixed differential to a flexible main rate, this pressure on the price level should be much alleviated.

The exaggerated price effects produced by large devaluations have a self-reinforcing nature. Expectations of rapid inflation are increased by the abruptness of the price rise at the time of a large devaluation. Experience in many countries has shown that increased anticipation of inflation makes much more difficult the task of monetary and fiscal policy in controlling inflation. With cost-push pressures, or more exactly "seller's inflation," intensified by the occasional large devaluation, the stabilization monetary measures are more likely to result in reduced output than reduced inflation to the extent they are in fact successful in restricting the money supply. The reduction in output may even lead to higher prices in some sectors, where unit costs are thereby increased.[13]

Fiscal Repercussions. In conditions of continuing inflation the progressive overvaluation of the exchange rate between the occasional large devaluations inevitably tends to create serious fiscal difficulties. Most developing countries depend heavily on taxes on foreign trade. While prices and the national income (in current prices) rise between devaluations, customs duties based on the local-currency value of imports converted at the fixed rate remain stable — that is, decline in real terms. If aid is reduced to exert

13. The argument of E. V. Morgan and others that improvement of the foreign balance from the devaluation under conditions of domestic inflation will be only temporary because the implied reduction of resources for domestic absorption will intensify the inflation, and therefore that flexible rates are useless in such circumstances, appears to miss the real issues. Morgan, "The Theory of Flexible Exchange Rates," *American Economic Review,* XLV (June 1955). First, the direct effects on domestic prices should be *less* than the extent of the devaluation, with *some* improvement of the trade balance. (Michael Michaely, "Relative Prices and Income Absorption Approaches to Devaluation: A Partial Reconciliation," *American Economic Review,* L [March 1960].) Second, the initial foreign imbalance can not continue indefinitely. A choice of depreciation methods *must* be made. One has then to consider which system will lead to fuller and more efficient use of domestic resources and minimize the inflationary impact. See also Arnold C. Harberger, "Some Notes on Inflation," in *Inflation and Growth in Latin America* (Homewood, Ill.: Irwin, 1964).

pressure for a new devaluation and if imports are cut, the customs duties will even fall. Similarly, if a differential rate on exports (or export tax) exists, such as the coffee rate in Colombia, receipts from this source fall in money terms between devaluations and even more in real terms. Governments are forced to yield to pressures to reduce such levies in the face of rising local costs and in response to increasing spread to the free market rate. Average fiscal revenues from foreign transactions are reduced, and a cycle is formed. Table 5.1 demonstrates the importance of the swings in

Table 5.1. Colombia's foreign-trade tax receipts, 1960–66 (in millions of pesos).

Year	Customs[a]	Exchange differential	Total[b]	Index at constant prices[c]
To devaluation of December 1962				
1960	617	1	619	100
1961	617	6	626	83
1962	548	—	550	78
To devaluation of September 1965				
1963	599	469	1,070	120
1964	693	626	1,320	126
1965, January–August (annual rate)	680	337	1,025	94
After devaluation of September 1965				
1965, September–December (annual rate)	766	345	1,113	95
1966 (estimate)	1,000	585	1,587	129

Source: Informes Financieros, Contraloria General de la Republica de Colombia.

[a] Includes some small additional import taxes.
[b] Includes some small direct export taxes.
[c] Using as deflator the average cost-of-living index for period.

Colombia in recent years, with peak points up to 50 percent above lows. Insofar as the large devaluation leads to *acceleration* of the price rise, income-tax revenues, based on previous years' incomes, rise proportionately less than national income and government expenditures.

On the expenditure side, subsidies to minor exports have to be raised between devaluations to offset rising internal costs, or the increase may come automatically through a rise in the free rate; the cost of such subsidies accordingly grows. At the same time, subsidies for public utilities tend to rise as the government tries desperately to avoid rate increases that might precipitate a devaluation. The longer the delays, the greater the opposition to such adjustments, since the potential adjustment and the devaluation threat become larger. The devaluation sequence thus leads to an increase in budget costs and introduction of a cycle on the expenditure side. Real fiscal revenues are seriously reduced, while expenditures increase from the time of one devaluation to the next. The natural consequence is a tendency to increased fiscal deficits and cuts in budget investment between devaluations.

This cycle is probably a major cause of the inadequacy of the measures taken in Colombia to correct a fiscal disequilibrium so serious that it has represented the main proximate cause of the inflation, the insufficiency of development expenditures, and the ineffectiveness of planning. Not only has no basic change in the tax structure been undertaken, but even the sizable gains obtainable from improved tax administration have until recently been neglected. The additional revenues that became available from the international sector at the time of the devaluations largely obscured the underlying need for more far-reaching reforms: the "once-and-for-all" philosophy effectively precludes consideration of the deterioration in the fiscal situation to be expected as the cycle proceeds. Moreover, the last-minute nature of devaluation-stabilization exercises militates against the inclusion of basic tax reforms as part of the agreements. Instead, the easiest course tends to be taken, which is higher rates of taxes on sectors already contributing relatively heavily. The difficulties are compounded if, as in Colombia, the additional taxes are imposed for limited periods to reduce opposition to the devaluation-stabilization exercise and on the grounds that the stabilization will provide a more productive tax base for the future. It is then argued that the "sacrifices" demanded at the time of devaluation were presented as sufficient; new taxes would give a further lift to prices and reduce funds available for private investment.

The violent cycle in budget revenues and expenditures produced by periodic large devaluations, as well as the worsening of the average fiscal situation, should be mostly eliminated by a more gradual exchange-rate adjustment. The more constructive approach to long-term fiscal problems thereby made possible can be of pivotal importance to the whole development effort in countries such as Colombia. Moreover, insofar as inflation decelerates as a result of a smaller direct price impact, so that prices of the base period for taxes such as income tax approach the price level of current expenditures, revenues in real terms will improve. The fiscal problem is clearly much more easy to handle to the extent that additional revenues accrue from existing taxes. A smaller reaction on savings in the private sector can also be anticipated than under the traditional alternative of sudden large increases in tax rates falling almost inevitably on sectors already heavily taxed, such as company profits. New tax measures required to offset internal demand effects can be introduced in small doses in contrast to the massive, and so often unattainable, tax measures required to contain the price impact of a large devaluation.

Foreign Exchange Repercussions. Foreign-exchange earning potential is evidently reduced by the impact on exports of the progressive overvaluation inherent in the traditional approach. In Colombia the rapid growth of minor exports in 1961–62 and again during the latter months of 1965 and the first half of 1966 contrasts sharply with their stability or decline during the rest of the period, when their exchange rate was pegged despite rising local costs. There is

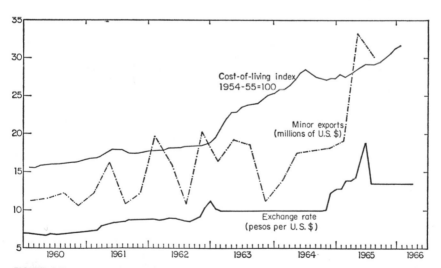

FIGURE 5.5

Minor exports: value and exchange rate, 1960–65. *Source:* Minor exports and cost-of-living index, National Office of Statistics; minor-export exchange rate, Central Bank; value, customs control data.

evidence of considerable price elasticity (Figure 5.5). A policy of unification or near-unification of the minor-export exchange rate with a fixed and increasingly overvalued import rate is clearly not conducive to development of such exports. Moreover, abrupt changes in exchange rates and hence profitability are inherently prejudicial to the long-term growth of exports; constancy of supply to foreign markets is jeopardized. Investment in this crucial field — as, for example, in meat for export from Colombia — is inevitably depressed.

The inflow of private long-term capital is also reduced. Reference has been made to the long periods of expectation of a new devaluation in Colombia during which the inflow almost ceased. Risks, including fears of exchange control and violent swings in import or fiscal policy, are enlarged. The ground lost is unlikely to be recovered. The foreign capital will probably have been used elsewhere. Fear of recurrent instability is increased. As Jan Tinbergen stressed, avoidance of violent swings in exchange rates that affect the transfer of dividends can be one of the most important aspects of improving the climate for foreign investments.[14]

The net effect of the traditional approach on private short-term capital and on long-term investment abroad by nationals is difficult to assess in the absence of reliable statistics, but again it appears to be strongly unfavorable. During periods of pronounced over-valuation — the period of pegging the Colombian free rate at 10 is a good example — the capital outflow may become considerable. The virtual certainty of a large devaluation provides a one-way option to a considerable appreciation in terms of local currency. Even if the free rate is allowed to rise, the increased spread from the overvalued main rate enhances possibilities of false invoicing, which also stimulate an outflow. Should the funds return after the devaluation, reserves are nevertheless lost on average, and the complication of a cycle accentuates the exchange crisis. In fact, there is evidence that the funds return only partially.[15] Although after devaluation some compensating movement may occur as local companies borrow abroad short-term to alleviate tightening credit restrictions, such

14. Jan Tinbergen, *The Design of Development* (Baltimore: Johns Hopkins Press, 1958), p. 60.

15. Colombian liquid dollar assets, excluding bank and official holdings, reported by the U.S., for example, rose from $62 million at the beginning of 1960 to $87 million at the end of 1962 and $115 million at the end of August 1965.

balances are extremely volatile. The immediate contribution to reserves is at the expense of accentuation of the next exchange crisis.

It is not possible here to examine other adverse influences on the balance of payments from the overvaluation of the exchange rate, such as the increased smuggling, the stimulation of tourism abroad, and the servicing of wasteful foreign borrowing. Unfortunately a statistical basis does not usually exist for a good assessment of the total cost of the adverse repercussions. From the fragmentary evidence available for Colombia, it seems probable that for the period 1960–65 the cost exceeded net aid receipts.

A flexible rate system on this analysis should have marked advantages. It should reduce dependence on imports and increase foreign-exchange receipts from minor exports and from long-term foreign private capital by eliminating the cyclical swings and average overvaluation of the exchange rate inherent in the traditional approach. The risks of sudden policy changes will be reduced. The special case of "major" exports, such as coffee, where limitations on export have to be applied, is considered below; here it is sufficient to note that exchange receipts for such categories will not be diminished by adoption of a flexible system.[16] Short-term speculative capital movements present particular problems considered in more detail among the possible "objections." For the present, it may be noted that the stimulation of domestic capital outflow for permanent investment abroad inherent in the average overvaluation of exchange rates under the traditional approach will be removed. The flow of aid should be less subject to interruption, and less of it should be required for general "balance of payments" — overconsumption — support. A flexible exchange rate system should also help wider trade agreements. Overvaluation and cyclical swings constitute a major obstacle to regional integration schemes with other countries. A better, more stable relationship of relative domestic-foreign prices and of import policies should assist the development of intraregional markets.

Other Repercussions on Resource Allocation. The effects of the

16. Such cases need to be distinguished from others where a depression of foreign sales of "wage goods" by an overvalued rate has led to increased domestic consumption — e.g., meat at certain times in Argentina. Primarily to avoid too drastic repercussions on the standard of living, quotas or export taxes may then be introduced following a large devaluation. Such distortions and loss of export earnings are evidently reduced by a flexible rate moving approximately parallel with local production costs.

traditional approach in leading to a misallocation of resources include but spread beyond the repercussions so far examined. With imports relatively and increasingly cheap between large devaluations, local demand is switched progressively from domestic supplies to imports. For international finance projects, the requirement for purchase of foreign supplies of domestic quotations are higher by more than a small percentage reinforces the natural tendency of the entity concerned, short of local financing, to include as many items as possible under the foreign financing. Demand for local products competing with imports becomes depressed on the average and also becomes cyclical. Periods of overimporting moreover lead to the building of industrial capacity dependent on imported supplies at higher levels than can be maintained. When imports are cut back, output is restricted. Investment is dissipated in the process, leaving a legacy of surplus capacity. Colombia provides extreme examples. The inevitable, abrupt switches in import policy and the erratic incidence of licensing in the face of multiplying applications create further distortions.

An additional effect of overvaluation on investment is likely to be cumulatively significant. With capital goods mainly imported, a strong impetus is given to use capital-intensive processes; they are cheap in relation to domestic labor. This tendency is strikingly evident in Colombia, even in "traditional" industries such as breweries and tobacco. It may well be a major cause of the very low relation observed between growth of industrial output and employment. Industrial-output growth averaged 5–6 percent in 1960–65, whereas industrial employment probably expanded not more than 1 percent. In cases where international finance is provided — in Colombia to the private as well as to the public sector — at below market interest rates, with the government bearing the exchange risk, the tendency is magnified.[17]

The fiscal cycle has a profoundly adverse effect on the efficiency

17. When large tax exemptions for investment and monopolistic trade union wages are also operative, it is small wonder that the perpetual "shortage" of foreign exchange for capital-goods imports appears so great. A naïve use of tautological Harrod-Domar type models then exaggerates the role of imports as the determinant of growth and overplays the need for additional aid, with scant concern for the misallocation and underutilization of labor and capital resources. Nor does the use of "shadow prices" obviate the difficulty unless they are translated into actual prices, since demand, profits, and further investment pressure will evolve mainly on the basis of actual prices.

of public investment. This is accentuated by the stop-go tempo in foreign aid: availabilities are increased markedly after a devaluation and suspended some time before the next. Investment projects are started — and a foreign financing contribution obtained — at the peak of the cycle, only to become difficult to maintain at an adequate rate of completion during the downturn. Colombia shows many examples of half-finished projects held up for lack of local finance, representing a serious waste of investment. Nor can the process of cutting back the public investment level be carried out easily in a logical way. Political intervention necessarily involves a far from rational distribution of the reduced financing available. Pressures from international agencies requiring priorities in the meeting of past commitments for local funds as a condition for further support may add substantially to the difficulties.

Space limitations do not permit extended treatment of domestic sectoral price distortions. The agricultural sector, as Arthur Smithies pointed out, will tend to keep up with industrial wages and profits if the exchange rate is adjusted *pari passu* with the domestic price level; whereas "if the exchange rate is adjusted periodically, the fortunes of agriculture will fluctuate correspondingly." [18] To take another sector, resistance to adjusting utility rates in line with inflation may be reduced if the danger that these will precipitate a major devaluation, with all its consequences, is removed by a flexible rate system.

If the analysis so far is generally correct, the benefits for investment from adopting a flexible exchange-rate policy should be considerable. The benefits flow both from the higher level of investment made possible and from the removal of the distortions introduced by the traditional approach. The elimination of pauses in the flow of aid and foreign investment, as well as the reduction of permanent private capital outflow, represent an addition to resources for investment. The better fiscal position is unlikely to reduce private savings commensurately and should therefore lead to an improved overall situation. Furthermore, it will lead to more foreign project aid where the aid has been held up for lack of local finances. The reduction of the risks — as well as of losses of output and profits — associated with the swings in fiscal, monetary, and

18. Arthur Smithies, "Lectures on Latin American Inflation" (mimeo, 1963). He concludes, "Reducing inflation may itself be a main factor in increasing agricultural supply."

import policies should encourage investment more generally in the private sector and a smaller distribution of profits. Personal domestic savings should also be promoted by the better general investment climate and the reduction of the downward pressures on stock-exchange values of the type noted in the Colombian experience.

Repercussions of the Monetary Ceilings. The overall monetary ceilings stipulated in typical stabilization programs have been based on superficially sophisticated but anachronistic money-supply models in which causation is implicitly assumed from definitional relationships. To prevent price and international-reserve deterioration, money-supply limits have been rigorously related to the assumed production and net import availabilities at an assumed price level consistent with maintaining the exchange rate.

It can readily be agreed that a country can not consume more than the resources available, including foreign earnings and loans, and that an excess of money will tend to produce either inflation or a balance-of-payments deficit, or both. It may be useful for the IMF to emphasize this fact, even though no precise causal relationship can be established in the equation Foreign Trade Balance equals National Income less Consumption (public and private) and Investment.[19] Probably most development plans are too ambitious in their projections of public and private savings, and both national and foreign agencies are generally unwilling to face squarely the degree of austerity required for the development targets proposed.

Nevertheless, limitations of the overall monetary-management approach should by now be clear in the light of the bitter experience in many developing countries. The commitments that Colombia made in the 1962–65 period point up some of the weaknesses. The overall net domestic credit ceilings place any one form of credit expansion on an equal footing with others. Credit for consumer purchases is implicitly assumed to have the same repercussions as credit for public investment or working capital or credit to sectors where the influence on production and savings may be particularly favorable.[20] A government deficit financed by the Central Bank

19. Fritz Machlup, "The Analysis of Devaluation," *American Economic Review,* XLV (June 1965), provides a useful discussion.

20. It is difficult to prevent selective credit from being used for purposes other than those intended, but partial success is possible in conditions such as prevail in Colombia. The converse is also clear, that general credit restriction may particularly affect crucial sectors, such as working capital, with a more than commensurate effect on output. There also is pressure on businesses and other organi-

has to be offset by a decline in credit to the private sector. The Colombian commitments not to use Central Bank borrowing for budget deficits are designed presumably to liberate more credit directly for the private sector. To this limited extent, therefore, a general value judgment has been introduced that credit for the private sector is "better" than for public purposes — without weighing whether private or public borrowing at the margin might have the greater benefit under the conditions prevailing. To the IMF, all government deficits apparently have much the same significance. The composition of the government expenditure is generally irrelevant; although the last Colombian agreements contained a commitment on the current budget surplus to be achieved, it is secondary to avoidance of Central Bank borrowing.

Under the IMF formulas, monetary management tends to become divorced from the measures rationally required to meet the changing economic situation. Severe problems are created if prices *do* rise above the IMF projections — as they usually do. A strong deflationary policy is then required to bring down the value of production at the higher price level into line with the monetary ceiling. Similar problems arise if the money supply is influenced by the deflationary or expansionary effects of an unprojected fall or rise in reserves. If reserves fall as a result of lower coffee prices, the ceiling provides no margin for the Central Bank to offset deflationary repercussions on domestic production. If reserves rise — as a result of reduced capital flight, for example, or "swap" operations, or a rise in world coffee prices and hence domestic coffee-sector incomes — a margin is provided for an expansion of Central Bank credit that may be singularly inappropriate at the time. No account is taken of changes in credit requirements following from changes in relative outputs between sectors or from stock movements — for example, because of a swing from an abundant to a poor harvest. Nor does account appear to have been taken of changes in liquidity preference or, to judge by the 1962 Colombian experience, in the degree of liquidity at the time of devaluation.[21]

---

zations short of domestic credit to borrow abroad — sometimes officially, as in the case of agricultural credit in Colombia.

21. Velocity of turnover of checking deposits in Colombia showed fairly substantial variation during 1960–65, rising during the periods of rapid price increase after the two devaluations. Changes in the form of liquidity are also relevant: demand deposits of the public in the banks rose by 113 percent from 1959 to 1964; money outside the banks rose by only 92 percent.

In these circumstances, why should one be surprised that the money supply often cannot in practice be contained within the IMF rules? In retrospect it seems inevitable and probably fortunate that in Colombia the strait jacket of the basic philosophy had to yield in some places to the pressures of private industry and public sentiment. Despite ever more complicated banking regulations governing overall monetary supply, evasion of regulations has continued to occur, and extrabank credit has grown sharply.[22] Unfortunately, such surreptitious alleviations bring further distortions. In Colombia, favored-customer treatment at banks lending at 12–16 percent has contrasted with rates often well over 24 percent per annum for nonbank financing. Such rates, together with emergency fiscal measures such as forced government bond sales, have reacted unfavorably on stock-exchange prices and on savings through this channel.

The difficulties of accomplishing the monetary undertakings and the constant preoccupation with plugging holes inevitably require so much attention that basic reforms in the general credit structure are neglected. Worse, serious distortions of the banking structure tend to be introduced, such as by ceilings established with reference to a certain date. It is symptomatic that the policies for restraining credit creation have been aimed almost entirely in the direction of reducing credit availability; possibilities of reducing demand through a higher bank interest rate structure have been ignored. The assumption of being able to achieve stability may also be a factor in the lack of concern at low interest rates paid for savings accounts: in Colombia the rate is around 4 percent, in no way sufficient to compensate for the inflationary trend or to discourage capital flight. The secrecy surrounding the IMF negotiations and the lack of discussion with other agencies about the implications of the far-reaching commitments proposed, often known in full only by the monetary authorities, also militate strongly against a monetary policy adequate for the wider requirements of development.

The swings in credit policy as successive new measures are introduced to try to conform with the IMF approach become particularly pronounced around the time of a new devaluation (see Figure 5.6). Credit restrictions have to be very severe indeed to curtail the

22. Acceptances and other paper guaranteed by commercial banks had reached a level in September 1965 equivalent to over 20 percent of commercial bank credit.

speculative capital outflow. The squeeze on investment finance comprises both the outflow of capital that does occur and the reduction in normal credit availabilities. Private foreign long-term capital inflow is subject to a similar swing as optimistic forecasts of the country's prospects after a devaluation give way to pessimism, which fades in turn when a new devaluation, a new aid package, and a green light from the IMF restore optimism for the moment. The problem for private investment programing is obvious.[23]

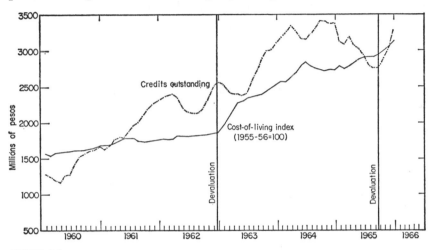

FIGURE 5.6

Commercial bank credits, 1960–66. *Source:* Central Bank; National Office of Statistics.

Repercussions of Import Liberalization Policy. Elimination of import quotas and cuts in prohibited lists to improve efficiency through increased competition and to reduce the anomalies of import licensing have clearly much to commend them. When protection is justified, the case for tariffs rather than quotas is well known. Nevertheless, sudden drastic undertakings, such as Colombia has now assumed, present serious dangers *in the context of the basic exchange policies pursued.* The door is opened to speculative stocking when the exchange rate again lags behind inflation.[24] In these

23. High private investment in luxury housing and office buildings, as in Colombia, may represent not only an inflation hedge but also the need for premium collateral to obtain favored treatment in credit squeezes.

24. Tariffs to stem excessive demand can not suffice for long under conditions of continuing inflation, nor can they in practice be raised again and again after each new devaluation. Moreover, in the absence of equalizing excise taxes on domestic production, higher tariffs will again increase protection unduly in some sectors and lead to misuse of the limited import resources.

circumstances, too, low-priority goods that have been liberalized will tend to be imported at the expense of items more essential to development, particularly if, as in Colombia's case, many of the latter remain in the nonliberalized sector. While small industry receives insufficient time to adapt to the abrupt increase in competition, better organized groups secure piecemeal increases in import duties. The result will frequently be a distortion of the tariff structure between raw materials and processed products, or among competing goods such as different textiles, or between necessities and luxury goods. Inefficient quotas and tariff arrangements are primarily a reflection of the underlying disequilibria, particularly the overvaluation of the exchange rate. An attack on one symptom, quotas, is unlikely to provide a remedy.

Repercussions of an Uncontrolled "Free Market" Exchange Rate. The policy of nonintervention on the "free market" as contained in the 1965 Colombian agreements apparently reflects a philosophy of letting market forces play freely to establish a "true rate." Another reason for the policy may have been fear of criticism that intervention had provided a channel for diverting foreign aid into capital flight. Presumably also the negotiators reacted strongly to the failure of the free rate pegging adopted in the 1962 devaluation. Whatever the background, it is difficult to find any underlying logic. The extent of transactions on exchange markets such as the Colombian "free market" are largely unknown. It is entirely possible that the Colombian free market is fundamentally out of equilibrium in the sense that a free rate level close to the main import rate would result in a sizable surplus of demand, even in the absence of capital flight. Without intervention, the free-rate premium must then rise appreciably to choke off the excess demand; in the process, quite legitimate requirements for foreign exchange will be penalized, and incoming transfers unduly subsidized. The higher level of the free rate will also undermine, psychologically in part, the main import rate. The continued existence of the wide spread between the 13.50 main import rate and the level of 17–18 for the free rate since the 1965 devaluation provides some indication that this is in fact the position in Colombia, even though a temporary influx of capital may further reduce the gap. In any case, there is no evident rationale for a policy of maintaining an exact balance between the many miscellaneous items in such a free market — including long-term private capital transfers, tourism, short-term capital of many kinds, or a proportion of freights. As an example of the idiosyncracies involved, a reduction in tourist expenditure abroad as a result of a foreign-travel tax would lower the free rate and encourage capital flight, reduce the premium on foreign capital inflow and foreign tourism, and make import smuggling more profitable. The giving up of the Central Bank's powers to intervene in the market represents less the adoption of a policy than an abdication of management.

A Flexible Exchange-Rate System. The highly unfavorable repercussions of the "traditional" devaluation-stabilization approach on the economy, not only for short-run growth but also in the long term, make much harder the achievement of rapid development. That its distortions are difficult to measure and perhaps impossible to sum up does not make them the less significant. The advantages to be expected from a flexible exchange-rate system lie primarily and simply in removing some of the most distortive consequences inherent in the traditional approach and in the abrupt corrective measures to counter them. It appears that a progressive exchange-rate adjustment in conditions of continuing inflation should have a far less unfavorable direct impact on prices, on the fiscal situation, and on the level of investment, and a more favorable impact on the balance of payments. Distortions in the use of resources should be substantially reduced.

These benefits should be strongly self-reinforcing. Smaller price reaction to devaluation improves the fiscal situation; a smaller fiscal deficit improves the monetary situation, which in turn lessens the stimulus to inflation and devaluation. Higher levels of foreign financing and more efficient investment increase domestic supplies, which tends to reduce inflationary pressures. The better use of resources reduces import needs for any given output. In these conditions, credit and import policies better suited to development needs can more readily be adopted. It follows that the total extent of devaluation necessary over a given period of years is also likely to be substantially less, for there will be less inflation, more production from better use of resources, and a stronger underlying balance-of-payments position.

Nor should the importance of reducing the demoralizing effect of the traditional approach on policy-makers concerned with long-term development be overlooked. The Colombian experience from 1960 to 1966 is instructive. The sequence of foreign-exchange and fiscal crisis, violent swings in aid, declining investment, and increasing distortions in the use of resources left little foundation on which to evolve practical programs and policies for development. Inevitably, a considerable part of the planning staff, seriously weakened by disillusionment, had to concentrate on emergency measures such as cuts in already programed investment. In the private sector, too, the sudden changes in fiscal position, credit conditions, and balance of payments necessarily concentrated attention on critical short-term problems. The overall restraint on the growth of national income and savings and the difficulties placed on investment form a vicious cycle, which conventional exchange-stabilization policies make exceedingly difficult for the policy-makers to break.

The Case for Limited Differentials. Limited differentials surrounding a flexible main rate may be justified on different grounds. The Colombian experience shows that a unified rate may be unsuitable where strong arguments exist for taxes or subsidies on various international transactions handled most conveniently through the exchange structure. Colombia's performance also demonstrates that both an inflexible and a completely uncontrolled free rate for capital transactions have serious inconveniences. Much confusion on exchange-rate differentials derives from poor experience in countries where multiple rates have been developed as a *substitute* for devaluation of the main rate. In these cases proliferation of rates and increasing "spread" have rapidly outdistanced the possibilities of effective control of the system.[25]

Given a flexible main rate, however, several types of transactions may justify a favorable differential fixed in relation to the main rate. In Colombia, minor exports are an evident candidate. The balance-of-payments projections indicate a continuing large structural gap seriously constraining development. World overproduction and international agreements restrict the value of coffee shipments, which now account for two-thirds of exports. The foreign-exchange content, both direct and indirect, of the minor exports,

25. For some cases of successful use of multiple exchange rates in Thailand, Costa Rica, and Nicaragua, see Margaret G. de Vries, "Multiple Exchange Rates," I.M.F. Staff Papers. XII, no. 2 (July 1965) 292ff. Abandonment of multiple exchange-rate systems may not always signify inherent weaknesses in the systems; pressure by international agencies to conform to IMF standards and the absence of general flexibility have been contributing factors.

both actual and potential, is generally small. Most can be considered "infant" exports. A large proportion are from agriculture, where expansion can make an important contribution to employment with relatively small investment. Unit foreign-exchange values are primarily determined by international markets and are unlikely to be appreciably affected by an expansion of Colombia's exports. For these and other reasons, a policy of minor-export incentives is indicated. As part of such a policy, a premium on the central exchange rate has much to commend it. Administratively simple and uncomplicated in its operation, and direct in its effects, in contrast to many tax incentives, such a subsidy readily lends itself to cost calculation. If the free rate is also maintained above the main rate, as will be suggested, the premium given to minor exports will reduce problems of false invoicing and failure to repatriate earnings.

There are practical limits to the desirable size of the premium. The danger of re-export of imported goods rapidly grows as the premium widens. Moreover, a fluctuating premium — for instance, one linked to an uncontrolled free rate — is too unstable to serve as a basis for long-term export promotion. A small fixed percentage premium to a flexible main rate avoids these difficulties. A single limited premium rate for exports can indeed be considered as use of a "shadow price" related to the crucial balance-of-payments bottleneck. For Colombia, a premium of 15–20 percent might provide a reasonable balance in conjunction with limited tax incentives.

There is a further argument for such a premium where import-substitution industries are protected by tariffs on the familiar infant-industry or external-economy justifications, as is customary. The domestic costs and price of the protected products are then high relative to the general domestic price level. Markets are thus limited internally, while exports are generally rendered impossible. An efficient production level may never be achieved. As Jacob Viner, Nicholas Kaldor, and others have observed, this limitation would be reduced if protection were given in the form of a subsidy permitting prices to be aligned with international prices rather than with domestic costs.[26] Unfortunately the fiscal problems in-

26. Jacob Viner, *International Trade and Economic Development* (Glencoe, Ill.: Free Press, 1952), p. 60; Nicholas Kaldor, "Dual Exchange Rates and Economic Development," in *Essays on Economic Policy* (London: Duckworth, 1964), II, 184.

volved generally make the subsidy approach impractical. A differential exchange rate for minor exports can provide compensation for the higher initial costs of the substitution industries — or the excess of marginal private costs over social costs — at least so far as international trade is concerned. It is not a complete remedy, but at least some exports will become possible. Total markets will thereby be expanded, lowering unit manufacturing costs and at the same time aiding the balance of payments.

A similar case can be made for pegging the free rate at a premium on the flexible official exchange rate to serve, on the one hand, as a subsidy to encourage the inflow of foreign capital and tourism and, on the other, as a tax on holidays abroad and the placing of savings abroad. For many of these transactions the tax or subsidy *can not* be effectively administered except via the exchange-rate mechanism, because of the nature of the transactions and the administrative limitations on exchange control. A free rate — or black-market rate — substantially above the main rate will exert strong upward pressures on the official rate by undermining confidence, encouraging false invoicing, or stimulating price rises. If too close to the main rate, it will not be effective in discouraging outward private capital movement and promoting foreign capital or tourist inflows. These considerations point to pegging the free rate above the flexible main rate by Central Bank intervention at a fixed percentage level that balances the advantages and disadvantages of moving to a higher or lower premium. To peg the free rate at a fixed level, even more to unify it with a fixed main rate, is bound to fail in conditions of continuing inflation; to allow the premium to fluctuate freely makes impossible a rational determination of the implied subsidies and taxes and is likely to disrupt the whole exchange system.

Import smuggling provides a further reason for holding the free market rate above the main rate. In Colombia, smuggling may well exceed $50 million annually. If smuggled goods can be financed at roughly the same exchange rate as legal imports that have to pay tariffs, control over long frontiers becomes inefficient. A free-rate premium acts as a uniform tariff on smuggled goods.

The optimal premium on the flexible main rate, and whether more than one premium rate should be established, must obviously depend on conditions in the country. For Colombia, a single premium of 15–20 percent covering both minor exports and free market transactions might be appropriate as a balance between economic advantages and disadvantages and administrative convenience.

For certain export proceeds a strong case may exist for an exchange rate less favorable than the main rate. Coffee is an obvious candidate in Colombia, given the world tendency toward overproduction. Coffee export receipts converted at the exchange rate needed to restrain import demand without inefficient controls would, on all evidence, stimulate Colombian coffee production available for export to well above present international quotas or probable future market possibilities. Financing of the surplus stocks created would have direct inflationary consequences. Taxation of coffee production is thus an obvious policy, preferably with a sliding-scale arrangement to offset external price movements. A small fixed percentage discount on the main exchange rate appears to have many advantages as part of such a policy. To the simplicity of collection and directness of the exchange differential is added the convenience of lessening the rates of the other forms of coffee taxation and hence increasing their administrative effectiveness.[27] The problem of coffee smuggling makes it desirable for the exchange rate spread to be relatively small.

To summarize, the case for limited exchange differentials is primarily one of administrative convenience as compared with formal taxes and subsidies, with the exception of differentials for those free market transactions that can not be effectively reached by other means. For this reason a system of differentials can be sensibly assessed only in the context of the total tax system, not in terms of restricted monetary exchange-rate concepts. Where tax possibilities are weak, as they are in the majority of developing countries, the efficiency of administration of differentials through the banking system and the partial removal of the implied taxes or subsidies from the political arena make a strong

27. Psychological and political pressures create difficulties for a formal export tax. Pressures for progressively reducing a differential also exist but should be more manageable with a fixed percentage differential, provided that there is a flexible main rate to compensate roughly for changes in local costs. However, it is quite possible to argue that flexibility to compensate for world price fluctuations should be provided through a limited range by a variable coffee rate discount, say, between 5 and 25 percent, with a more passive role for other parts of the coffee taxation system.

case for integrating differentials into the general tax policy. The practical limitations need to be kept in mind, nevertheless, particularly the avoidance of an excessive spread of rates and the desirability of simplicity and permanence, without which the advantages are much reduced. Differentials are best regarded as specific taxes and subsidies and never as a replacement for rational policies in other fields, not least the field of general exchange-rate adjustment.

Objections to a Flexible System with Fixed Differentials. Will the authorities in the developing countries be under less pressure to contain inflation under a flexible rate system than under a fixed rate system with occasional abrupt changes, as is often contended? Will inflation without the hazards of shock corrections become too comfortable? These are questions of judgment, to which no absolute answers can be given. However, strong reasons exist for a contrary view. First, the traditional approach tends to hide the consequences of inflation or excessive stimulation of demand until the pressures have built up to a new crisis. For instance, actions such as large statutory wage increases, improved social security benefits, or extravagant public investment are not immediately reflected in the need for exchange-rate adaptation, particularly in the early stages of the cycle. To establish clearly and quickly the causal connection between inflationary action and the exchange rate is one of the merits of a flexible system. The ostrich attitude induced by attempted once-and-for-all stabilization exercises surely holds much of the responsibility for failure to adopt policies realistically adapted to the underlying pressures. Second, a flexible system should be inherently less inflationary than the traditional approach and create fewer distortions. The extent of the problems with which the authorities have to contend will be smaller in aggregate and less cyclical. Monetary and fiscal measures are most unlikely to be sufficiently powerful to contain the massive repercussions of a large devaluation; under the flexible system there is much more chance of a consistent policy and of avoiding the usual chaotic "hole-plugging" and eventual breakdown of disinflationary policy. Third, the international agencies could better promote disinflationary measures, both fiscal and monetary, if the struggle for immediate and complete price stabilization and fixed exchange rates were abandoned in favor of a more gradual reduction of inflation in the basically less inflationary conditions of a flexible rate system. Finally, even if a flexible rate system led to some relaxation of disinflationary discipline, this disadvantage would still need to be weighed against the distortions inherent in the traditional approach.

A similar objection based on some unfortunate experiences in the past is that a flexible rate structure with differentials will yield to pressure to multiply rates for dubious economic purposes — for example, to hold down the price of imported food. But this pressure is at least as strong during attempts to hold down a progressively overvalued exchange rate. It is possible that other pressures to obtain favored rates for politically strong private interests may be somewhat larger with a differential system. However, provided the system is introduced with the simple structure suggested here, avoiding a multiplicity of import and export rates and supported by international agencies, such additional pressures would not appear dangerous.

A second set of objections, closely connected with problems of speculation to be discussed subsequently, concerns the difficulties of administering a flexible rate system where Central Bank intervention is required to maintain differentials or to smooth temporary pressures. More administrative skill is certainly required in the continuous operations of such a system than under a fixed rate, but such competence certainly does not seem outside the capacity of a monetary system such as Colombia's. Space does not permit discussion of the technical detail of operations — or problems of transition — but some brief observations may be appropriate even at the risk of being too dogmatic. The guide for adjustment of the rate should be the movement of reserves; price indices, whether of domestic goods, all goods, internationally traded goods, or goods excluding exports, do not provide an adequate barometer of underlying pressures where structural changes, varying foreign trade coefficients, and changes in world market conditions are involved. A policy of reserve changes — and of debt payments and aid — in relation to changes in world prices of principal exports should be worked out in advance, if possible in conjunction with the international agencies. If these reserve limits are exceeded, the rate should be adjusted progressively until the limits are again entered. Seasonal and other temporary pressures should be countered in part by use of a stabilization fund — in part only, since the degree of transitoriness can never be accurately gauged, and it is desirable to make a partial adjustment to induce stabilizing private speculation. Price indices may help in judging the temporary or permanent nature of pressures, but the subsequent movement of reserves will indicate whether the judgment was right or further corrections are needed.

In considering the difficulties of such a system, one should contrast with them the difficulties of determining an adequate rate after a long period of overvaluation under the traditional approach. Similarly, the political opposition to small devaluation steps, often cited as a barrier, needs to be contrasted to the extreme political opposition to large devaluations. Opposition should be inherently less for a progressive devaluation with its smaller repercussions, and the influence of international aid-giving agencies should correspondingly have a greater chance of timely success.

The dangers of speculation provide the basis for a further set of objections that seem to hold a particular fascination for the more theoretical economists. These objections fall into two groups: apprehension that speculation under flexible rates may become "explosive"; and the less dramatic worry that speculation may involve "overtracking" of the equilibrium rate at any time, forcing up import prices and in consequence the general price level, thereby inducing a monetary expansion, and thus bringing about a higher equilibrium position. That speculators may "overtrack" is postulated mainly on insufficient information and expectation of continuing exchange depreciation based on the experience of the recent past. The historical evidence that with flexible rates speculation may be destabilizing beyond the equilibrium point is not convincing. Irving Friedman, in his trenchant critique of this thesis as put forth by Ragnar Nurkse, concluded that even in the exceptional post-World War I European conditions studied by Nurkse the evidence pointed to speculation as being on balance equilibrium-promoting.[28] Robert Z. Aliber, examining examples of flexible rates of developed countries, generally of international currency status, reached inconclusive findings.[29] Nor are the theoretical mod-

28. Irving Friedman, "The Case for Flexible Exchange Rates," in *Essays in Positive Economics* (Chicago: University of Chicago Press, 1953); Ragnar Nurkse, *Internal Currency Experience* (Geneva: League of Nations, 1944).

29. Robert Z. Aliber, "Speculation in the Foreign Exchanges: The European Experience, 1919–1926," *Yale Economic Essays* (1962), pp. 171–245.

els satisfactory, particularly in relation to conditions of continuing inflation in developing countries. The drawbacks of the models arise partly from a static equilibrium approach, partly from lack of comparisons of alternative policies, and partly from oversimplifications, such as neglect of the relation of the risk for the speculator to size of exchange adjustment required and to level of reserves.

Some general conclusions may be drawn from the debate, however. It is clear that speculation depends on expected gain discounted for risk as compared with the costs involved in holding assets abroad pending the devaluation. The costs are relatively high in developing countries, since the spread between short-term interest rates in the international money centers and domestic interest rates (perhaps more precisely the profit on use of the funds locally) is much larger than it is between international centers. Thus, the prospect of a large gain is needed to make speculation worthwhile. Such a prospect is provided by the traditional large-devaluation stabilization approach, whereby to an increasing magnitude of required devaluation is added a declining risk as reserves are allowed to fall to minimal levels — even more so if aid is suspended. If the authorities do not react quickly to such a situation, the conditions are favorable for self-reinforcing speculation.

With a flexible system, the lessening of underlying inflationary and other pressures should *per se* reduce the extent of devaluation needed over a given period. Even more important in the present context, the magnitude of devaluation to be anticipated in relation to the costs and risks involved should never be large. The risks can also be raised considerably if reserves are maintained at adequate levels and the backing of international agencies is known to be available to counter speculative runs; the possibility of occasional downward movements appreciating the exchange rate can be added to the more general depreciating trend. In such conditions the balance of considerations seems to lie strongly toward private speculation becoming a stabilizing factor, which can be reinforced if the authorities yield a little to what they may believe are merely temporary pressures on the reserves.[30] These considerations apply

30. See Robert A. Mundell, "The Monetary Dynamics of International Adjustment under Fixed and Flexible Exchange Rates," *Quarterly Journal of Economics*, LXXIV (May 1960), for a demonstration that the speed of reaction of a Central Bank to a fall in reserves is a major factor in determining whether speculation is stabilizing or destabilizing. Egon Sohmen, *Flexible Exchange Rates* (Chicago: University of Chicago Press, 1961), argues that speculation with a well-managed

even more strongly to speculation in stocks of imported goods, because "carrying costs" are higher. Similar considerations apply to smuggling.

If the argument so far is accepted, the fear that a fluctuating rate will cause serious difficulties to importers and exporters in making or accepting quotations has very limited validity. Prices of almost all imports and most exports for importers and producers in Colombia, for instance, are within narrow limits fixed in terms of foreign currency; the problem is whether a profit can be made at the relatively fixed international price converted by the exchange rate.[31] Under a flexible exchange-rate structure of the type suggested, the fluctuation of the applicable rate over a period of two or three months should be small and should tend to move roughly parallel with domestic prices, or production costs. There seems no reason to assume a significantly greater margin of error in calculation of profitability than under the fixed rate with rising domestic costs. It should also be feasible for a central bank under such a system to guarantee a rate at a small premium or organize a forward market. In any case, it is once more necessary to consider the objection not *in vacuo* but in comparison with the existing system with its inherent pressures toward speculative movements, long periods of uncertainty in advance of a devaluation, abrupt price-level changes, and the tendency toward overimporting and reduction of exports resulting from overvaluation.

Another set of objections, connected with the use of differentials, has to do with the problem of credit or debit balances arising in local currency on exchange-equalization accounts. These balances

---

system of flexible rates will promote stabilizing speculation. Gottfried Haberler, *Money in the International Economy* (Hobart Paper No. 31 [London: Institute of Economic Affairs, 1965]), p. 29, concludes that "the system of occasional but fairly frequent changes in the exchange rates [as promoted by the IMF approach] is calculated to maximize disequilibrating speculative capital movements." See also James Meade, "Exchange Rate Flexibility," *Three Banks Review* (June 1966): "The use (of the I.M.F. approach) builds a paradise for anti-social speculation." Opposing views often seem to assume a lesser degree of monetary and fiscal discipline and a long-term fixity of exchange rates as a practical alternative. See, for example, Robert Triffin, *Gold and the Dollar Crisis,* rev. ed. (New Haven: Yale University Press, 1961), pp. 82–85; Jacob Viner, "Some International Aspects of Economic Stabilization," in L. E. White, ed., *The State of the Social Sciences* (Chicago: University of Chicago Press, 1956).

31. Insofar as export prices in terms of foreign currency are in fact adjusted to win markets, foreign demand is likely to be more elastic under a gradual adjustment than under occasional large adjustments following big devaluations.

should not present great difficulties so long as they are considered as part of the total fiscal and monetary position. In conditions resembling those in Colombia, a policy of differentials for minor exports, free market transactions, and coffee can result in a small net sterilization of money supply by partitioning net differential receipts between the monetary authorities and the budget. This sterilization can ease central bank control of money and credit. What is clearly *not* justified is moving items to differential rates not because of general tax-subsidy policies but simply, as in the past, to achieve a "better" balance of transactions at these rates — in the free market, for example.

Many of the objections to the use of flexible rates and differentials center on the prospect of retaliation by other countries whose exchange rates have been thereby appreciated. This consideration may in certain circumstances be a valid one for developed countries. It is difficult to believe, however, that international trade partners will retaliate against a developing country for its adoption of flexible rates with limited fixed differentials of the type suggested. Differential rates for imports are specifically not proposed, and a flexible import rate moving generally in line with inflation may well be preferred to periodic exchange crises and violent swings in import policy.[32] Export taxes, in the form of differentials on such items as coffee, are likely to be welcomed rather than criticized. Nor is there reason to expect opposition to a premium rate favoring foreign capital and tourism and penalizing domestic transfers abroad. To judge by past experience, neither should a limited premium for minor exports from developing countries present serious difficulties. In all these respects the danger of retaliation is likely to be much greater with occasional large devaluation changes than with a more gradual depreciation. In the intervals between large devaluations other countries build up trade at the expense of the country with the overvalued currency; they are then more likely to react to a sudden loss of these markets than if the advantage had not been given them.

These seem to be the main objections to a flexible rate in con-

32. Eugene Schlesinger, *Multiple Exchange Rates and Economic Development* (Princeton Studies in International Finance, No. 2 [Princeton: Princeton University Press, 1952]), argues the case for multiple rates for imports in certain circumstances. But with a *flexible* main rate for imports, the problems appear better handled by tariffs.

ditions of continuing inflation. Certain risks or inconveniences can not be entirely excluded. But the risks appear small. If set against the risks and inconveniences of the large-devaluation stabilization approach, the balance seems strongly in favor of the flexible-rate approach.

CONCLUSIONS

The preceding analysis of exchange policies for developing countries such as Colombia in conditions of continuing inflation leads to conclusions diametrically opposed to the "traditional" devaluation-stabilization approach. Rather than fixed rates moved occasionally and abruptly, the country would be better off with a flexible rate. Rather than a unified rate, differentials around the main rate offer strong advantages. Rather than attempting to peg the free rate at a fixed level or alternatively leaving it to the free play of market forces, Central Bank intervention to maintain the free rate in a constant relation to the flexible main rate seems advisable.

The adoption of the traditional approach has been greatly influenced by the attitude of the international agencies, particularly the tying of aid to acceptance of IMF proposals. The developing countries may, and often do, have genuine doubts about the validity of the proposals. Yet under the pressure of vanished reserves, the proposals are accepted because of the sugar coating of aid. It should be emphasized that the criticisms of the IMF's approach are not directed against members of the IMF's staff, who often go to the limits of their terms of reference to introduce flexibility into the agreements. But they are inevitably circumscribed by the views enshrined in the IMF's articles and the myth that they are dealing with a temporary balance-of-payments problem.

The use of highly aggregative and often tautological models by both monetarists and macro-economists has been partly responsible for the lack of attention given to the distortions and other adverse "side effects," often of a qualitative nature, introduced by the traditional approach. So has the use of constant price models in national plans. Yet based on the experience of Colombia and other countries, these distortions appear to be highly important. The traditional approach seems provocatively destined to magnify the inflation it is designed to end and to increase aid requirements, even though in the process it results in periods of economic stagnation. Although the adverse consequences are likely to be particularly severe in developing countries with relatively rapid inflation, such as those of Latin America, the analysis of inherent tendencies to distortion indicates that greater attention to the "side effects" may be appropriate even where inflation is considerably less pronounced.

An examination of the consequences would probably reveal that existing exchange-rate policies are one of the major deterrents to growth in a considerable number of developing countries and that for many of them a flexible main rate with a simple system of limited differentials would have considerable advantages. Obviously the exchange-rate system needs to be considered as a whole and adapted to the institutions and conditions of the country. Differentials without flexibility of the main rate, however, seem doomed to failure in conditions of continuing inflation, while a unified flexible rate without differentials is unlikely to meet the needs of many developing countries for an administratively simple and effective method of taxing or subsidizing certain types of foreign transactions.

The relative merits of different administrative patterns for a flexible rate system offer a justifiably large area for debate. The important practical problems involved should not, however, be allowed to obscure the need for a change from the present approach of disruptive jerks in exchange rates interspaced with increasing and cumulative distortions. In working out the precise framework for a flexible system, a pragmatic approach is needed to take account of the state of development in the country, the degree of underlying inflation, the extent and nature of its balance-of-payments problem, the importance of the foreign sector in the economy, the tax system, and the complementary policies practicable. The framework will accordingly need to be revised as development proceeds and the underlying problems change. There is no simple panacea suitable for all developing countries, least of all the present standard devaluation-stabilization formulas.

If the pressure of the international agencies and the work of foreign advisory missions were directed toward promoting exchange policies suited to the dynamic conditions of a degree of continuing inflation, monetary-fiscal discipline needed to curtail excessive inflation could in all probability be achieved with a higher degree of success than in the past. The difficulties encountered by many ill-conceived, multiple-rate and flexible-rate systems in the past, which have not been backed by such discipline or foreign aid, do not give valid grounds for opposing selective application of more carefully designed systems. Rather, the failure of existing policies even with the pressures and aid of the international agencies should be considered.

As Javier Marquez noted some years ago, no anti-inflation cum balance-of-payments policies are basically simpler to put into operation than the type of devaluations practiced in the past in combination with credit restriction on banks and government.[33] A minimum of analytical penetration, administrative skills, and detailed preparation has been demanded. Today a better approach to problems of exchange-rate adjustment is demonstrably required — one that is both more sophisticated and more realistic, that relates to the conditions of the particular country, and that is backed by more thorough analytical work on the root causes of the inflationary trends and balance-of-payments disequilibrium.

33. Javier Marquez, "Financial Policy as an Anti-Inflationary Instrument," in *Inflation and Growth in Latin America* (Homewood, Ill.: Irwin, 1964), p. 417.

6

~~~~~~~~~~~~~~~~~

Exchange Policy — Argentina

Instead of trying to speculate on the consequences of the revolution of June 28, 1966, in Argentina, I shall focus on Argentina's economy as it stood before the revolution. At that time an important sector of opinion, particularly among exporters and the international financial community, alleged that the current exchange rate was grossly overvalued and should be depreciated further to improve the country's long-term balance-of-payments position. Other groups asserted that the current rate was close to its long-run equilibrium level and that current pressure on the balance of payments was exclusively a problem of excessively high service payments on the foreign debt inherited from previous governments. This was not, of course, a new issue or one that was relevant only for Argentina. It is, in fact, one of the most persistent and burning policy questions in a large number of developing countries.

The stop-and-go performance of the Argentine economy during the fifteen years prior to 1966 was closely related to balance-of-payments difficulties. Each period of expansion was cut short by an external-payments crisis, the temporary correction of which involved a consolidation of arrears into a rapidly rising foreign debt, which by the end of 1963 exceeded $3 billion. What started as primarily a current-account problem caused by the stagnation of exports was therefore turned into a capital-account squeeze caused by heavy annual service payments on external obligations.

Every conceivable policy was applied at one time or another to tackle the balance-of-payments problem, from strict quantitative regulations to prior import deposits and exchange surcharges, from multiple exchanges to freely fluctuating rates. The frequent changes in policy reflected not only the rapid turnover of government officials with different policy prescriptions but also the successive failure of the measures previously adopted — sometimes because they were ill-conceived, frequently because they were not executed in conjunction with a consistent set of policies, and occasionally because of external factors beyond the control of policy. Such is the backdrop to past efforts to determine an appropriate exchange policy in Argentina.

One of the main reasons that exchange-policy management has proved so difficult in practice is that, unlike the majority of other developing countries, Argentina exports mostly basic domestic wage goods: principally meat, grains, fresh fruit, textile fibers, and leather. Its imports, however, are chiefly raw materials, intermediate products, and capital goods, few of which are directly competitive with domestic output because of the exceedingly high tariffs on competitive imports, and most of which are essential for maintaining or expanding the level of economic activity. Exchange-rate adjustments, therefore, have an immediate impact on the general cost of living. Such adjustments generate pressure from the country's strongly organized labor unions for wage increases, and these increases, together with the rise in other costs, quickly tend to be passed on in the form of higher prices by the strongly cartelized producers.

Under these circumstances it is exceedingly difficult for devaluation to bring about a significant change in relative prices lasting long enough to help induce the shifts in demand and in allocation of resources between domestic and internationally traded goods necessary to solve the balance-of-payments problem. With persistent and relatively high rates of internal inflation, the exchange rate tends to become progressively overvalued between devaluations. As long as inflation continues, policy must be concerned not only with the *level* of the exchange rate at any particular moment but also with its *flexibility* over time.

RECENT POLICY: AIMS AND BACKGROUND

The National Development Plan promulgated prior to the revolution stated the aims of exchange policy as: "(1) Maintenance of a flexible exchange rate adjusted in accord with changes in the domestic price level; fluctuations in foreign prices of individual (export) commodities to be compensated by a flexible policy of taxes and exemptions. (2) Continuation of exchange regulations until heavy service payments on the accumulated foreign debt are normalized." [1] The specific measures used to implement this policy can be summarized as follows.

(1) The Central Bank stood ready to buy or sell foreign exchange at predetermined rates, adjusted in small increments when necessary. Between the beginning of 1964, when the new policy came into force, and the end of 1965, the exchange rate was adjusted six times, the largest adjustment amounting to about 13 percent in April 1965.

(2) A well-organized futures market was permitted to enable dealers to hedge against rate adjustments.

(3) Visible trade transactions were mostly free, with the exception of a small list of prohibited imports and occasional export quotas for goods that were considered in short supply on the domestic market.

(4) Most invisible transactions were regulated by a system of permits and quotas, and conditions were specified for new credits to finance imports of capital goods.

(5) A flexible system of prior import deposits and export "retentions" (taxes) was applied in conjunction with adjustments of the exchange rate. The introduction of a 100 percent prior import deposit in 1965 and the progressive reduction in the percentage thereafter were designed to discourage inventory accumulation.

Exchange policy was coordinated with other policies through an annual financial plan, subsequently reviewed by the World Bank, which included projections of the fiscal deficit and its financing, money supply and bank credit, and the balance of payments. The plan and the supporting report of the Bank were used to estimate annual debt refinancing requirements to be negotiated with creditor countries.

Before analyzing the rationale of recent policy, it will be useful to review briefly the balance-of-payments experience of Argentina during the fifteen years prior to 1966. In Table 6.1 the figures are arranged according to the three-year cycle of expansion and con-

1. National Development Plan, p. 405, freely translated from the Spanish.

Table 6.1. Argentine balance of payments, 1951–65 (annual averages in millions of $).

Items	1951–52	1953 (Recession)	1954–55	1956 (Pause)	1957–58	1959 (Recession)	1960–61	1962–63 (Recession)	1964–65
Exports	927	1,125	978	944	985	1,009	1,022	1,291	1,449
Imports	1,330	795	1,076	1,128	1,272	993	1,355	1,168	1,137
Trade balance	−402	330	−98	−184	−287	16	−333	123	313
Services[a]	1	−6	7	53	6	−5	−62	−142	−212
Current-account balance	−401	324	−92	−131	−281	11	−395	−20	101
Capital	175	30	−19	398	83	240	452	−77	−147
Foreign exchange and gold reserves (increase—)	227	−354	111	−268	198	−251	−57	96	45

Source: Central Bank of Argentina.

[a] Series not comparable, particularly before and after 1960.

traction, each year of recession being associated with a shift in exchange and/or other policies to correct the balance-of-payments disequilibrium of the previous period of expansion. During the period 1951–61 the cause of the periodic external-payments crises shows up very clearly: export earnings, which remained stagnant at about a billion dollars per annum, were not sufficient to pay for the increase in imports generated during periods of economic recovery. The main changes in policy carried out in each of these years can be summarized as follows.

1953: The state export board (IAPI) shifted from a policy of buying cheap and selling dear to the opposite policy; the subsequent losses suffered by IAPI were in effect subsidies to farmers. Imports were restricted by a system of multiple exchange rates and strict quantitative regulations. Price controls and subsidies were employed to offset the effect on the cost of living of the increase in prices of internationally traded goods.

1956: IAPI was liquidated, the exchange rate was devalued, and export "retentions" were applied to absorb windfalls. The multiple rate system was gradually unified, quantitative import restrictions were progressively replaced by import surcharges, and price controls were gradually lifted, except for those on beef.

1959: All import restrictions and price controls were terminated, and the exchange rate was left free to find its own level, after which it was stabilized at about 83 pesos per dollar. The system of export "retentions" and import surcharges was continued, although many exemptions were permitted for the import of capital goods.

1962: A freely fluctuating rate was introduced, and export retentions were eliminated.

The picture that emerges from this sequence of policies is the transformation of a thoroughly controlled economy into a virtually free one, which should have been accompanied by substantial shifts in relative prices and a corresponding reallocation of resources and demand. But the changes that did occur did not bring about a greater shift toward balance-of-payments equilibrium. This apparent paradox is used by the so-called "structuralist" school as evidence for their contention that agriculture is not responsive to price incentives and that the price elasticity of demand for imports is very low. Thus, in their view a long-term solution to balance-of-payments difficulties requires not only institutional changes, such as land reform, to make output more elastic, but also greater efforts to force down the import coefficient through import substitution. The fact is, however, that little systematic research has been carried out to test the "structuralist" hypothesis or to analyze policy options.

Moreover, the paradox, which is very pertinent to the selection of an optimum exchange strategy, does not seem quite so paradoxical on closer examination of even the fragmentary information available. It is true that up to 1959 relative prices of agricultural goods appear to have increased significantly, but until 1955 this was achieved on the basis of administrative decisions by officials in whom farmers had little confidence. Between 1955 and 1959 the improvement in overall agricultural prices was accompanied by a much more significant change in relative prices within the sector in favor of crops and against beef. Thus, the response of producers was mainly in the direction of substituting cropland for pastures.[2] Between 1959 and 1961, however, overall relative prices of agricultural goods suffered a sharp decline, mainly as a result of fixing the exchange rate at 83 pesos per dollar while internal in-

2. The relation between the price of steers and the weighted average price of wheat, corn, and linseed declined from about 4.0 in 1955 to 2.9 in 1956 and 2.7 in 1957; it did not recover its previous level until 1959. Cattle stocks are estimated to have declined from almost 47 million to 41 million head between mid-1956 and 1959, whereas during the same period total cultivated area in Argentina rose by about 2.5 million hectares, or by almost 10 percent.

flation continued. It appears that considerable investment was nevertheless being carried out by farmers during this period, mainly in mechanization to replace labor that had emigrated to the cities and to expand cultivated acreage after 1955.[3]

Up to 1959 measures to divert demand from internationally traded products to other domestic goods were restrained, understandably so in view of the fact that most of Argentina's exports are basic wage goods with a heavy incidence in the cost-of-living index. Pent-up demand for imports after many years of quantitative restrictions also made it difficult to reconcile the policy of liberalization of import controls with the need to contain import demand. Finally, after five years of almost continuous economic expansion with the exception of the 1956 pause, the economy in 1958 showed signs of heating up, particularly as a result of the massive increase in wages granted that year.

In 1959 strong measures were first taken to reduce both demand for internationally traded goods and global demand by lifting all price controls and imposing severe restraints on monetary expansion. Because the general price level almost doubled that year, the changes in relative prices were not very significant or long-lived, except for beef, but the drop in the level of economic activity and real wages was pronounced. Exports expanded, and current imports (excluding capital goods) were cut back to their lowest level since 1953.

Because the stabilization measures adopted at the time fell mainly on wages rather than profits and were accompanied by broad import-surcharge exemptions for imports of investment goods and efforts to attract foreign capital, the rapid recovery that followed was spurred mostly by an unprecedented investment boom. Imports rose by 37 percent between 1959 and 1960–61, almost half of the rise corresponding to increased purchases of capital goods. The resulting trade deficit did not create immediate balance-of-payments

3. Between 1950 and 1960 the agricultural labor force is estimated to have declined from 2.2 million to 1.5 million (National Development Plan, p. 133, Table 69). With respect to agricultural investment, see "La Producción, Ingresos y Capitalización del Sector Agropecuario en el Período 1950–60," a study prepared in 1961 for CAFADE (Comisión de Administración del Fondo de Apoyo al Desarrollo Económico, an ad hoc agency set up to disburse U.S. PL 480 counterpart funds) but unfortunately not published. See also unpublished estimates available in CONADE (Consejo Nacional de Desarrollo, the official planning council).

problems because it was offset by the inflow of foreign capital, a large share of which was short-term. This feature led to the collapse of the boom, beginning in the second half of 1961, when depressed export receipts resulting from a poor harvest obliged the Central Bank to sell large amounts of foreign exchange from its reserves to support the pegged rate. This development, combined with growing uncertainty over the future political stability of the country, undermined the confidence of foreign creditors. They began to recall their loans — a process that was accelerated after the government fell in March 1962.

The heavy use of foreign credit in 1960–61, added to large external financing received in connection with the balance-of-payments adjustments of 1956 and 1959, was responsible for the foreign debt burden inherited by the government. In 1956, 1959, and 1960–61 the *net* inflow of largely short- and medium-term capital amounted to over $1.5 billion. This sum was approximately equal to the debt-service payments that the country was obligated to pay during the following *three* years, because of the short-term maturi-

Table 6.2. Argentina's estimated annual foreign debt-service obligations as of December 31, 1963 (in millions of $).

Items	1964	1965	1966	1967	1968	1969	1970/90	Total
			Public sector					
Central Bank	258	226	129	30	22	12	27	703
National Government, decentralized organizations, and state enterprises	208	182	171	167	156	138	555	1,577
Provincial governments	20	19	16	14	10	4	7	89
Other	33	63	54	46	36	28	88	348
Subtotal	519	489	369	257	223	183	677	2,717
			Private sector					
Amortization	418[a]	195	117	71	44	34	184	1,064
Interest	32	23	14	9	5	2	6	92
Subtotal	450	218	131	80	49	37	190	1,156
Grand total	969	707	500	337	272	220	867	3,873

Source: Unpublished Central Bank survey.

[a] Includes obligations on revolving commercial credits, which normally turn over as payments on old import credits are offset by credits on new imports. It is also likely that private debt obligations were exaggerated by respondents in the bank survey.

ties of much of the debt (see Table 6.2). Annual contractual debt-service payments thus equaled 50 percent of the export level that had prevailed in the 1950's, although export earnings fortunately increased, so that debt service was a smaller proportion of increased earnings.

THE RATIONALE OF RECENT POLICY

The question arises as to whether recent exchange policy is the most appropriate policy in the light of past experience and current conditions in Argentina as compared with other feasible alternatives. In the following analysis a rather artificial division is made between the choice of an optimum exchange-rate strategy, on the one hand, and the problems of implementing policy, on the other. The implementing problems are dealt with first.

When the new administration came to power toward the end of 1963, it inherited a freely fluctuating exchange rate, a large trade surplus ($385 million for the whole year), a heavy foreign debt, and a depressed economy that only recently had begun to show signs of recovery. The net outflow of financial services and capital, which amounted to about $450 million in 1962–63, had apparently been held down by the depressed level of economic activity and monetary liquidity.[4] Moreover, any substantial recovery in GNP and liquidity would evidently be accompanied by larger payments of external obligations on private account, which, added to the service of the public foreign debt, would exert heavy pressure on the balance of payments. The choice of policy was clearly between allowing the exchange rate to rise sufficiently to equilibrate supply and demand or adopting controls to regulate the flow of financial transfers.

The first alternative would have required both continuation of a relatively tight money policy to limit the demand for exchange and reliance on a substantial reflow of speculative private capital to prevent the rate from running away. But a tight money policy would have been inconsistent with the government's desire to re-

4. Total money supply in 1962 increased by only about 60 percent as much as GNP in current prices. Even more significant, net bank credit to the private sector, excluding agriculture and adjusted for the net increase in government debt to private suppliers, rose by only 1 percent in comparison with a 22 percent increase in the current value of output (see Table 7.7).

activate the economy, and a substantial reflow of speculative capital was considered neither probable in the short run nor desirable over the long term. The appropriateness of a tight money policy at this juncture depended upon the diagnosis of the causes of balance-of-payments disequilibrium and domestic inflation. If both were chiefly the result of an excess of total demand over supply, the classic medicines of monetary restraint and other measures to hold down the level of demand was obviously called for. But the trade balance was highly favorable; the difficulty was with financial services and capital account. Moreover, real GNP in 1963 was below the level of 1958, in contrast with the large expansion that had taken place since 1958 in productive capacity as a result of the investment boom, and unemployment was estimated at about 9 percent of the labor force in Greater Buenos Aires and even higher in the interior of the country.[5]

The question of whether the Argentine inflation is the result of excess demand, as has frequently been stated or implied in policies prescribed for the economy, or of other largely autonomous factors is so basic to the choice of an exchange policy that further clarification seems called for. Research carried out in CONADE for the period 1950–63 indicates clearly that inflation has been related mainly to the wage-price spiral and the built-in momentum of inflation itself, including expectations of future price increases. The effect of general monetary and balance-of-payments restrictions was to depress the level of economic activity, not to reduce the rate of inflation.[6] Monetary liquidity, in fact, steadily declined from .370 in 1955 to .198 in 1963 (relation of total money supply to GNP in current prices), and at least since 1958 productive capacity has been only partially utilized. Recent investigations indicate that even by 1965 the percent of installed industrial capacity utilized had not yet reached the modest 1961 level of about 67 percent, even though real output had risen by more than 12 percent. Detailed results of these investigations and recent estimates of the relation of capital stock to current output are given in Table 6.3.

5. When in October 1964 the CONADE employment survey was broadened to include four other major urban centers, it was found that unemployment still exceeded 9 percent in three of them and in all cases was higher than the 5.7 percent recorded at the time in Buenos Aires.

6. National Development Plan, chap. 4, 2nd part.

Table 6.3. Value of machinery and equipment and gross product of manufacturing sector (in billions of 1960 pesos).

Year	Fixed capital in machinery and equipment, net of depreciation[a]		Gross product of manufacturing (3)	(3)/(1)	(3)/(2)
	(1)	(2)	(3)		
1935	288.0	161.3	94.0	.33	.58
1936	293.1	159.3	99.9	.34	.63
1937	308.1	164.1	106.1	.34	.65
1938	324.4	169.5	111.7	.34	.66
1939	330.1	165.2	116.2	.35	.70
1940	327.4	157.1	115.0	.35	.73
1941	320.3	147.1	120.9	.38	.82
1942	315.0	135.9	125.4	.40	.92
1943	301.9	123.5	131.0	.43	1.06
1944	283.0	112.5	145.6	.51	1.29
1945	265.2	103.1	143.1	.54	1.39
1946	251.5	101.3	157.7	.63	1.56
1947	260.8	120.6	178.4	.68	1.48
1948	281.8	155.3	187.1	.66	1.20
1949	279.6	170.6	188.5	.67	1.10
1950	282.6	183.2	193.9	.69	1.06
1951	297.4	194.4	195.6	.66	1.01
1952	317.9	205.1	190.5	.60	.93
1953	337.0	214.0	190.5	.57	.89
1954	359.1	226.2	207.9	.58	.92
1955	378.7	238.6	233.1	.62	.98
1956	397.2	250.4	246.3	.62	.98
1957	407.7	260.5	265.4	.65	1.02
1958	424.6	277.8	285.1	.67	1.03
1959	445.3	289.2	263.7	.59	.91
1960	483.2	313.2	280.6	.58	.90
1961	533.3	345.7	304.4	.57	.88
1962	585.5	376.4	283.9	.48	.75
1963	625.7	390.7	268.2	.43	.69
1964	668.3	405.2	306.7	.46	.76
1965	712.1	420.2	342.0	.48	.81

Source: CONADE.

[a] Column (1) is based on the assumption that value of equipment remains intact during its average useful life, after which it is retired from the capital stock 100 percent. For column (2), depreciation figures are based on estimated annual consumption of each type of equipment by the straight-line method.

The conviction that a substantial reflow of speculative capital to prevent the exchange rate from running away was neither probable nor desirable stemmed from several considerations. First, it would not be reasonable to expect capital to return to Argentina as long as there existed a large backlog of payments pending on previous credits. Since annual debt-service obligations amounted to about 7 percent of total GNP at 1963 prices, it was not likely that this backlog could be eliminated over the short run. On the contrary, the diversion of such a large share of national income abroad, even after assuming a certain amount of refinancing, would retard economic recovery and prolong the period of adjustment. Because of large existing excess productive capacity it was also not reasonable to expect any substantial inflow of new equity investment or increase in supplier credits for capital-goods imports. Second, reliance on private speculation for the success of a country's exchange policy would be risky. "Hot money" is extremely volatile and can quickly flee a country at the first signs of economic difficulty or political instability, as it did in 1961–62. Finally, government was concerned about the inflationary effect of sharp upward adjustments of the exchange rate, because exports consist mainly of basic domestic wage goods or important ingredients in their manufacture, and labor is strongly organized. The impact of devaluation on the domestic price level is therefore likely to be larger than might be assumed on the basis of the relation of total trade to GNP of approximately 20 percent.

In the cost-of-living index for Buenos Aires, based on a 1960 survey of working-class budgets, bread, cereals, meat, and fresh fruit — whose prices are extremely responsive to changes in world market prices or the exchange rate — have a combined weight of over 30 percent. If to these are added goods that have a high component of exported or imported materials — wool and cotton clothing, leather goods, paper, and tobacco products — the combined weight rises to well over 50 percent. Similarly, in the wholesale price index agricultural and imported goods have a weight of over 30 percent; goods manufactured from agricultural materials, 25 percent; wood, paper, and textile products, 15 percent; and so forth. To identify any major category in these indices that does not have an important export or import component is in fact difficult.

It is not surprising, therefore, that during the twelve months following each of the last three major devaluations the most notable result was not so much a change in *relative* prices as an increase in the *general* price level, even though on the last two occasions devaluation was accompanied by severe monetary restrictions and a drop in total internal demand. For example, observe in Table 6.4

Table 6.4. Wholesale price increases (in percents).

Period	Agricultural	Nonagricultural
September 1955–September 1956	51	43
December 1958–December 1959	89	100
April 1962–April 1963	51	34

the relationships between the wholesale price indices of agricultural and nonagricultural goods. Or compare the indices of the peso price of the dollar, general wholesale prices, and the cost of living as set out in Table 6.5.[7]

Table 6.5. Rise of exchange rates, prices, and cost of living (in percents).

Period	Peso-dollar exchange rate	Wholesale prices	Cost of living
December 1958–December 1959	113	97	102
April 1962–April 1963	44	39	33

These figures should not be interpreted as signifying that relative prices of internationally traded goods did not improve significantly during the period under study. On the contrary, between 1950 and 1963 relative prices of the agricultural sector rose by no less than 37 percent, and relative prices of individual export commodities did even better (wheat — 50 percent, steers — 70 percent, linseed — 80 percent, sunflower seed — 120 percent, corn — 130 percent).[8] By 1963 it could be said that relative agricul-

7. Because of the complicated multiple exchange-rate system and price controls existing in 1955–56, it is not possible to give comparable figures for that period. To avoid this problem in 1958–59, when the change from a multiple-exchange to a single-rate system was completed, the exchange rate was estimated by dividing monthly export values in pesos by export values in dollars.

8. The figures represent changes in the ratio of two factors — implicit GNP prices of the agricultural sector as a whole and of the individual wholesale commodity prices listed — to a third, the general implicit GNP price index. See CONADE, *Cuentas Nacionales de la República Argentina* (Buenos Aires, April 1964); R. D. de Ravizzini, *Investigación sobre precios agropecuarios* (Buenos Aires: National Secretariat of Agriculture, n.d.).

tural prices had returned roughly to their pre-World War II level, and relative prices of imported goods also appear to have increased substantially.[9]

The conclusion to be drawn is that the effort to correct the distortion in relative prices which occurred during the decade prior to 1952 was very costly in terms of the general inflationary pressures generated by the corrective measures during the following decade. These measures also led to underemployment in the economy during a considerable part of the decade and brought about a redistribution of income against wage earners.[10] A policy of allowing the exchange rate to fluctuate freely to equilibrate supply and demand for foreign exchange under conditions existing at the end of 1963 implied a continuation of the same measures and almost surely would have produced the same results.

The second policy alternative — regulation of financial transfers abroad and a managed exchange rate — first required a decision on the appropriate initial level of the rate. It would be false to give the impression that the rate actually chosen was based on careful research; this kind of decision seldom is, because official intentions must be held secret until the decision is put into effect. Furthermore, expert judgments differ widely on such crucial factors as to whether existing prices are sufficiently remunerative to farmers or what is likely to happen to world market prices of export goods; there is always a good deal of arbitrariness in determining ex ante an equilibrium rate of exchange.

But at the time it could reasonably be maintained that relative prices of Argentina's main export goods provided sufficient incentives to expand output, in view of the improvement in prices. Furthermore, since the volume of exports had risen by 60 percent be-

9. Capital-goods prices rose 80 percent between 1950 and 1961; raw materials and intermediate products rose 40 percent from 1953 to 1963. But trends were very irregular.

10. Between 1950 and 1963 wages and salaries are estimated to have declined from 42.7 percent of gross national income to 35.6 percent. This decline is probably partly explained by the increase in the share of the labor force self-employed, particularly in agriculture, but statistics on real wages in manufacturing also confirm that remuneration per worker increased much less than GNP per capita. Professor Julio Olivera of Buenos Aires University prepared an interesting inflation model in which the downward rigidity of prices combined with sharp changes in relative prices stimulates increases in the general price level. Olivera, "La Inflación Estructural y el Estructuralismo Latinoamericano," presented at the Conference of Economic Research Institutes in Mendoza, Argentina, December 1965.

tween 1956 and 1963, representing a much larger margin than the increase in agricultural output, it could not reasonably be argued that an even larger proportion of supply should be diverted to exports.[11] Real per capita personal consumption in 1963 was 6 percent *below* the level of 1950 and 16 percent below the peak reached in 1958. A more logical and certainly more palatable strategy would be to try to maintain existing incentives and concentrate on improving agricultural productivity and output through an appropriate agricultural extension and development program.

This discussion has been framed with reference to Argentina's traditional agricultural export products. It could be argued that diversification of exports to include an increasing share of manufactured goods would require a higher exchange rate, or even an undervalued one, particularly in view of the relatively high domestic prices of most manufactures. For instance, after the exchange rate was freed in 1962, miscellaneous exports rose from $29 million to $129 million in 1963, whereas after exchange regulations were introduced in 1964, these exports fell back to an estimated $75 million in 1965. The statistics are misleading, however, because 60 percent of the increase in 1963 was attributable to sugar as a result of the failure of the Cuban harvest. Exports of manufactures, excluding sugar, tea, and tobacco, have fluctuated between $55 and $75 million during 1963–65.

Still, the sharp expansion between 1962 and 1963 was noteworthy, and in 1965 a decline in exports of certain manufactures was clearly evident. A relatively higher exchange rate would certainly help promote nontraditional exports if the general inflationary impact of devaluation could be kept to a minimum. One way of accomplishing this would be to ensure that increases in the "real" exchange rate — that is, relative to the general internal price level — would be accompanied by appropriate increases in retentions on traditional exports and by compensating reductions of import duties and surcharges. Such a compensated devaluation would help place Argentine industry on a more competitive footing vis-à-vis other developing countries, many of which have for some time given exchange premiums of one kind or another to

11. This 60 percent figure, taken from official export statistics published in the *Boletín* of the National Statistical Office, is so high as to inspire doubt, but no other source is available.

their nontraditional exporters, with notable results in some cases.[12]

On the import side, the presumption has always existed in Argentina that the price elasticity of import demand is very low. Final consumer goods represent a small share of total imports, purchases of fuel are made only to cover the gap between total demand and domestic supply, and imports of capital goods are regulated by a system of high tariffs and import surcharges to which exemptions are granted for equipment that can not be supplied by domestic producers. Similarly, the high level of protection of local industry would tend to reduce the price elasticity of substitution between domestic and foreign supplies of raw materials and intermediate goods. Under these conditions total imports would be mainly a function of the level and composition of real domestic demand. Although no research has been carried out to test this hypothesis, the figures given in Table 6.6 suggest that the price elasticity of

Table 6.6. Relation of imports to GNP (in percents).

Change	1955	1956	1957	1958	1959	1960	1961	1962	1963	1964
Import volume ÷ industrial GNP	5.0	−25.8	19.6	5.1	22.9	0.4	10.3	−10.8	−17.1	18.9
Import prices ÷ implicit GNP deflator for industry	−19.5	143.0	−0.7	−20.1	32.7	−14.4	−10.2	3.8	−6.3	−14.1

import demand for raw materials and intermediate goods, which constitute more than half of total imports, may be higher than has usually been assumed.

At any rate, the long-term strategy of the National Development Plan was to reduce gradually what is generally considered to be an uneconomically high level of protection.[13] The aim was to induce industry to become more efficient and competitive in export markets, which would diversify exports and increase foreign-exchange earnings. Development of domestic production of steel, chemicals, paper, wood, and automobile components —

12. Daniel M. Schydlowsky of the Harvard Advisory Group has been giving a good deal of attention to compensated devaluation and export incentives for manufactures in Argentina.

13. Ad valorem surcharges on imports of goods that compete with domestic production generally range from 80–150 percent of "essential" consumer goods, raw materials, and intermediate products; 100–150 percent on capital goods; and 300 percent or more on "luxury" goods. In addition, import duties and several other lesser taxes are levied.

which together account for over 60 percent of total imports of raw materials and intermediate products — would meanwhile help to hold down the rise in import demand. If short-term balance-of-payments difficulties cropped up, they could best be corrected by short-term measures, such as temporary prior import deposits, which were not built into the more permanent relative cost-price structure.

On the basis of these considerations, the initial rate chosen was the one prevailing toward the end of 1963 in the free market.[14] The other decision that had to be made was on the criteria for determining when and by what amount the new "sliding parity" rate should be adjusted to keep domestic and world market prices in line.

THE "SLIDING PARITY" RATE POLICY

For a number of years the Central Bank has compiled two indicators of the parity between domestic and foreign prices. One is simply the ratio between the exchange rate (unadjusted for changes in import surcharges, export retentions, and the world market price level) and the internal cost of living and wholesale price indices. The other is an estimate of the implicit exchange rates of individual export commodities, calculated by dividing the FOB peso price of each commodity by its foreign market price, adjusted for maritime and insurance costs to put it on an equivalent basis. Each of these measures of parity are deficient for measuring short-term changes in the relation between domestic and world market prices, even aside from the well-known long-term shortcomings of the purchasing-power parity doctrine.[15]

The simple ratio between the exchange rate and internal price indices, even if the exchange rate is adjusted for the incidence of taxes on foreign trade and changes in the world price level (by whatever method such a level might be estimated), does not adequately reflect shifts that may occur in relative costs and prices

14. The Central Bank had actually begun to support the rate in November 1963, bringing it back down to the vicinity of 135 after uncertainty over the future policy of the new government had pushed it up from 134.65 pesos per dollar in August to 148 pesos in October. Prior to August the rate had fluctuated within the narrow range of 134 to 138 since the beginning of 1963.

15. See, for example, Frank W. Taussig, *International Trade* (New York: Macmillan, 1927), chap. 26; G. Haberler, "The Choice of Exchange Rates after the War," *American Economic Review*, XXXV (June 1945).

of internationally traded goods as against domestic ones. A drop in world primary-goods prices or a serious drought affecting domestic costs and prices, for example, might well require adjustment of the exchange rate by an amount that would not be adequately indicated by the above-mentioned ratio. The implicit exchange rates of individual export commodities are tautological, however, since as long as a commodity continues to be exported, all they indicate is that the price at which it is sold equals the price at which it is bought. These implicit rates ignore completely the supply side of the equation.

An attempt was therefore made to develop another indicator of exchange parity, which would provide information as to whether peso export prices of principal export products were sufficiently remunerative to induce an expansion of output. Behind this attempt lay the premise that prices in the recent past were indeed satisfactory and that measures other than exchange policy would be used if necessary to influence short-term fluctuations in imports. Since this question can not be determined in absolute terms — that is, a "remunerative" price for farmers depends on relative costs and prices, which can change rapidly under inflationary conditions — the indicators were based on a comparison over the last few years of the estimated cost-price relation of wheat, corn, linseed, beef, and wool, which together account for about 90 percent of Argentina's export earnings.

To illustrate the method employed and the kind of problems encountered, wheat and beef are used as examples. In the first place, annual estimates of the cost of production per *quintal* (100 kgs.) of four major agricultural commodities are available from the Secretariat of Agriculture. These estimates are based on old production functions, which have changed in recent years, but the annual variations probably reflect rather accurately the effect of inflation on costs, and the difference between market prices during the harvesting season and these cost estimates probably reflects the order of magnitude of recent *changes* in net receipts of producers (see rows 1–4 of Table 6.7). The unit value of exports and the implicit exchange rate (rows 5–7) are taken from official trade statistics, and the value of taxes and retentions (row 8) are estimated from the relevant rates ruling during each year. Finally, the difference between the f.o.b. export price (less taxes and reten-

Table 6.7. Estimated margin received by Argentine wheat producer.[a]

Items	1958/59	1959/60	1960/61	1961/62	1962/63	1963/64	1964/65
1. "Real" cost of production (pesos/ton)[b]	1,445	2,542	3,452	3,823	4,376	5,550	6,656
2. Internal price harvesting season (pesos/ton)[c]	1,540	2,628	3,689	4,007	6,531	8,047	7,560
3. Producer's margin (2) − (1)	95	86	237	184	2,155	2,497	904
4. Ratio (3)/(1) × 100	6.6	3.4	6.9	4.8	49.2	44.8	14.1
5. Average f.o.b. price ($/ton)[d]	57.80	59.05	60.31	59.36	58.74	61.55	53.29
6. Implicit exchange rate (pesos/$)[d]	78.6	83.0	82.8	98.1	138.5	138.1	166.5
7. F.o.b. price (pesos/ton)[d]	4,541	4,901	4,994	5,822	8,134	8,500	8,875
8. Export taxes and "retentions" (pesos/ton)[d]	938	1,259	811	686	638	444	484
9. Price received by exporter (pesos/ton)	3,603	3,642	4,183	5,136	7,496	8,056	8,391
10. Exporter's margin (9) − (2)[e]	2,063	1,014	494	1,129	965	6	831
11. Ratio (10)/(2) × 100	134.0	40.2	13.4	28.2	14.8	0.0	10.9

Source: Official published statistics, with the exception of export taxes and "retentions," which were estimated by the Central Bank.

[a] Producer and exporter margins are gross of internal taxes.
[b] Estimated by National Secretariat of Agriculture. "Real" costs include the effect of variation in yields per hectare on unit costs. Although production functions on which these estimates are based are antiquated, year-to-year changes in "normal" costs (excluding the effect of variations in yield) are roughly parallel to changes in the wholesale price index of nonagricultural goods.
[c] The harvesting season is November–January; prices are for grain delivered at Buenos Aires port.
[d] Averages for calendar years 1959–65. The implicit exchange rate is computed by dividing the average f.o.b. peso price by the f.o.b. dollar price.
[e] Normally wheat is bought up by traders during the harvesting season, and exports are made from their stocks. In 1958/59 devaluation occurred too late to help most farmers, which thus gave windfall profits to traders.

tions) and the internal market price indicate the exporter's margin (rows 9–11).

The sharp increase in the rate of return in 1962/63 (row 4) was sufficient to boost the area sown to wheat from less than 5 million hectares to 6.28 million in 1963/64. On the basis of these results and of estimated unit costs for this harvest, a domestic price of about 7,800 pesos per ton would have provided an adequate incentive to producers. But by the beginning of the harvest season the f.o.b. price of wheat had approached 67 dollars per ton, which even at the existing rate of exchange would have given windfall profits to exporters. So it was decided to pass part of the windfall on to farmers by raising the domestic support price. Quite unexpectedly during the following months the f.o.b. price of wheat dropped by no less than 15 percent, thus placing the government in the dilemma of either reneging on the support price guaranteed farmers, permitting the exchange rate to rise by an equivalent amount, or obliging the National Grain Board to buy up the large harvest and sell it abroad at a loss. This experience demonstrated the inconveniences that volatile world prices and rigid domestic price support and exchange policies can create. If monetary and fiscal objectives are not consistent with the credit financing of large official grain purchases and the absorption of possible losses on Grain Board sales, price support and/or exchange policy must be made more flexible.

The market for beef posed entirely different problems, as reflected in Table 6.8. In the first place, it is not possible to estimate

Table 6.8. Estimated margin received by beef exporter.

Items	1960	1961	1962	1963	1964	1965
1. Unit value f.o.b. ($/ton)[a]	455	412	413	391	568	667.5
2. Exchange rate (pesos/$)[b]	83	83	115	138	140	168
3. Unit value f.o.b. (thousands of pesos/ton)	37.7	34.1	47.4	53.9	79.5	112.1
4. Export retentions (thousands of pesos/ton)	5.2	4.0	5.8	0.7	0.7	10.8
5. Price received by exporter (3–4)	32.5	30.1	41.6	53.2	78.8	101.3
6. Equivalent price of steer on hoof (pesos/kg.)[c]	18.8	17.4	24.1	31.0	46.0	58.7
7. Average price Liniers market (pesos/kg.)	15.6	14.8	18.6	25.6	42.6	52.1
8. Difference (6)–(7)[d]	3.2	2.6	5.5	5.4	3.4	6.6
9. Quotient (8) ÷ (5)	9.8	8.6	13.2	10.1	4.3	6.5
10. Steer/grain price ratio[e]	4.27	3.19	2.76	3.01	5.06	n.a.

Source: Official published statistics, with the exception of export retentions, which were estimated by the Central Bank.

[a] Unit value of chilled and frozen beef.
[b] Value of exports in pesos divided by their value in dollars.
[c] A yield of 58 percent in meat is assumed.
[d] This difference is only a very approximate measure of the gross profits of packing houses. Normally the sale of by-products (hides, glands, tankage, etc.) more than covers the cost of converting steers into beef, but obviously the margin depends on the prices of by-products and the degree of utilization of packing-house capacity.
[e] The price for grains is the weighted average price of wheat, corn, and linseed.

the cost of producing a steer, because the main inputs are fodder (mostly from natural grasslands) and other animals (cows and bulls for breeders, calves for fatteners). A remunerative price for steers was therefore estimated in relation to the weighted average price of a representative basket of grains (wheat, corn, and linseed), which in the economic sense compete with cattle for use of the scarce factor land. It has been observed that when this relationship exceeds about 4.0, pasture area is expanded, and more animals are retained for breeding and fattening; when the ratio falls below 4.0, herds are reduced, and a greater area is sown to crops.[16]

With the end of the severe 1962–63 drought, rapid improvement in the carrying capacity of pastures enabled ranchers to rebuild their herds. Deliveries of animals to market declined, and prices soared, approximately doubling in the space of twelve months. The steer/grain price ratio, which in 1962–63 averaged less than 3.0, rose to more than 5.0 in 1964 and kept rising in 1965. Instead of unremunerative prices for ranchers, therefore, a shortage of beef for consumption and export arose — exactly the reverse of the wheat situation.

The exchange rate became a problem for the packing houses, whose margins were squeezed between rising domestic prices and not so rapidly rising foreign prices. But more rapid devaluation of the exchange rate at this time would probably have been of very little benefit to the packing houses. Exports were already absorbing over 28 percent of total slaughter — the highest percentage in at least two decades — with total supplies 20 percent below those of 1963; per capita domestic consumption was at the lowest level since before World War II, and the relative price of beef (retail price deflated by the cost-of-living index) was 50 percent higher than prewar and double the 1950 level.[17] Rather than devalue further or levy taxes on internal consumption, the government decided to prohibit domestic beef consumption two days a week and try to hold up foreign prices by means of commercial policy until the cattle cycle ran its course. Beef supplies began to recover toward the end of 1965 as expected.

In conclusion, attempts to implement a sliding parity exchange-rate policy have demonstrated the difficulty of taking into account the different and rapidly changing market conditions of various export products and of reconciling exchange with price support and other domestic policies. These difficulties could be reduced by making the effective exchange rate for each export commodity more flexible. This flexibility could be achieved under the present system by carrying out a compensated devaluation and by adjusting

16. "Agricultural Development and Economic Growth," a study prepared for CAFADE in 1962 by a group of Argentine and AID experts.

17. The figures upon which these percentages are based were taken from "Evolución y Perspectivas de la Producción de Carne Vacuna," a report prepared by CONADE in December 1965.

higher export retentions in accordance with fluctuations in world market prices so as to maintain domestic support price and exporter margins at stable "real" remunerative levels, or the problem could be met through the use of export-retention receipts to subsidize packing houses when a price-cost squeeze occurs.

EVALUATION OF THE 1964–65 RESULTS

During 1964–65 the value of exports continued to rise, almost reaching $1.5 billion in 1965. Although imports rose even more rapidly with the expansion of GNP by more than 16 percent between 1963 and 1965, the trade balance remained highly favorable, falling only from $385 million in 1963 to $293 million in 1965. The cumulative trade surplus was sufficient to cover most of the $700 million net outflow of financial services and capital in 1964–65, gold and foreign-exchange reserves declining by only about $95 million.[18] Thus, at the macro-level balance-of-payments developments were not unsatisfactory, although further comment will be made on the long-term viability of the strategy so far pursued with respect to solving the external debt service problem.

Evaluation of results at the micro-level requires analysis of trends in relative prices. The general measurements of exchange-rate parity can be divided into two kinds: those that attempt to compare the real internal purchasing power of a currency with that of another country, usually the United States, which is taken as a standard for international comparison, and those that simply compare changes in the exchange rate of a country with variations in domestic price indices.[19] Of the first kind, two long-term series have been estimated for Argentina, one by Colin Clark and the other by ECLA.[20] Although long-term purchasing-power parity series are not necessarily good indicators of the equilibrium exchange rate at

18. The decline actually took place in 1964, with 1965 registering a small improvement of $22 million.

19. On the first type of measurement, see, for example, Bela Balassa, "The Purchasing Power Parity Doctrine: A Reappraisal," *Journal of Political Economy* (December 1964).

20. Colin Clark, *The Conditions of Economic Progress* (London: 1957); United Nations Economic Commission for Latin America, *Medición del Nivel de Precios y el Poder Adquisitivo de la Moneda en América Latina,* Doc. No. 1/CN. 12/653, April 1963. Both series have been brought more or less up to date in Techint, *Boletín Informativo* (Buenos Aires), no. 146 (March–April 1965).

any particular moment in time, they are useful for putting recent rate fluctuations in perspective and for judging the appropriateness of different base years for the second kind of parity measure.

The purchasing-parity rate series of Clark and ECLA run parallel for most of the period 1935–64, with Clark's somewhat below ECLA's (see Figure 6.1); and the actual exchange rate remains

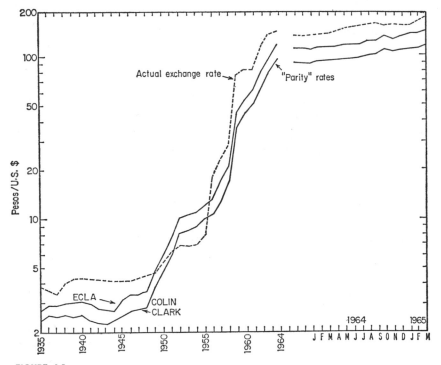

FIGURE 6.1

Argentine exchange-rate parities

above the parity series for most of the period, except from the beginning of rapid domestic inflation in 1949 to the devaluation of 1956.[21] This latter period was one of tight foreign-exchange restrictions, which clearly were used to keep the peso overvalued. If one were to attempt to draw conclusions with respect to the selec-

21. Probably the main reason that the one series ran below the other is that the relative price of a representative basket of goods increased between 1951, when Clark made his estimates, and 1960–62, the base period for the ECLA calculations. During the period of multiple exchange rates (1950–58) the actual rate appearing in Figure 6.1 was estimated by dividing the value of foreign trade in pesos by its value in dollars. No dollar trade figures are available before 1950.

tion of an appropriate base period for the second kind of parity measure, it would clearly be advisable to exclude the period 1946–55 and probably also the abnormal war years. The year 1959 was also exceptional, since the initial increase in the rate reflected the final and sudden elimination of all quantitative controls and the unification of the multiple rate system.

For the other years the percentage differential between the ECLA parity series and the actual exchange rate, averaged for groups of years and with parity divided by actual rate, is as follows:

1935–39	1956 58	1960 63	1964
77%	73%	70%	83%

These figures indicate that the differential between purchasing power parity and the actual rate tended to widen over time but that this tendency was reversed in 1964. If the same relationship had existed in 1964 as in the three previous periods, then instead of the actual level of 140 pesos per dollar the figure would have been between 151 (the 1935–39 differential) and 166 (the 1960–63 differential). The average uncontrolled parallel rate for the year was 155.7.[22]

These differences are not very significant, however, in relation to the effect that underlying structural changes in the economy could have had on the long-term equilibrium rate. The substantial increase in export receipts above the previous billion-dollar ceiling (if based on fundamental and continuing improvement in agricultural output and productivity), the reduction of the import coefficient (if related not only to temporarily depressed demand but also to long-term progress in import substitution at economic prices), and other similar structural changes might have been sufficient to more than justify the smaller differential observed in 1964 between the actual exchange rate and "purchasing-power parity." [23] But it is unfortunately impossible to establish with any certainty whether and to what extent recent changes in export and import coefficients

22. Not much confidence can be placed on the parallel rate as an indicator of what the general rate would be without controls, because the parallel market appears quite thin and highly susceptible to relatively small shifts between supply and demand.

23. The Argentine differential between purchasing-power parity vis-à-vis the United States and the actual exchange rate may be compared with those estimated by Bela Balassa for a number of other countries in 1960: Canada — 92.8, United Kingdom — 82.4, Germany — 77.9, France — 77.4, Italy — 70.1, Japan — 62.6. Balassa, "The Purchasing Power Parity Doctrine," p. 588, table 1.

reflect fundamental and enduring structural changes. The impression exists that a technological breakthrough is beginning in agriculture and that the gestation period of the automobile, steel, and other industries with high initial import content is coming to an end. But other factors could be listed that operate in the opposite direction.

It is necessary to fall back on the kind of relative price analysis described in the previous section, which would still be highly relevant for policy guidance even if fuller information were available on basic structural changes of the economy. In Figure 6.2 relative

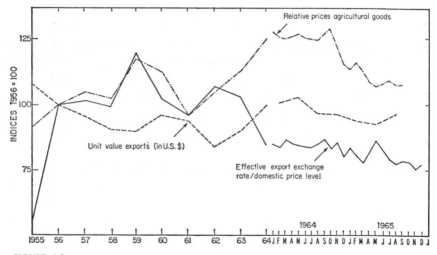

FIGURE 6.2

Relation of agricultural prices to export exchange rate

price series are given for agricultural goods and the effective export exchange rate, annually for the period 1955–64 and monthly for 1964–65.[24] Although the export rate was lower in 1964 than in any year since 1956, relative agricultural prices were at their peak. Part of the explanation lies in the improvement in the unit value

24. Relative agricultural prices are implicit GNP prices for the agricultural sector divided by the implicit GNP deflator; monthly figures have been extrapolated by using the ratio of the wholesale agricultural price index to the general wholesale price index. The effective export exchange rate was estimated by dividing the peso value of exports, less export retentions, by the dollar value of exports; this rate was in turn divided by the implicit GNP deflator. The monthly series were extrapolated by using the ratio of the official exchange rate to the cost-of-living index.

of exports, whose deterioration, beginning in the second half of the year, was accompanied by a sharp decline in relative agricultural prices, although by mid-1965 they still remained above the level of all previous years except for 1959, 1960, and 1963. Another possible explanation is the shrinkage of exporter margins, particularly in the cases of wheat and beef, thus passing on to the producer a larger proportion of the export price than in previous years. Finally, general agricultural price indices may not be representative of the

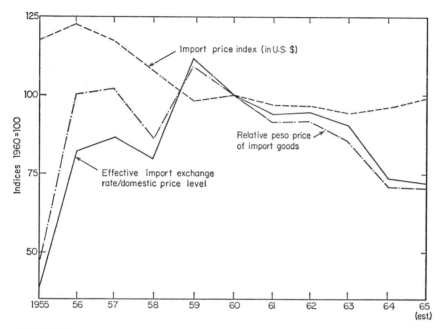

FIGURE 6.3
Relation of import prices to exchange rate

movement of individual commodity prices because of the heavy weight given to beef, whose relative price rose swiftly in 1964. But in any event, the area sown to wheat, corn, linseed, and sorghum — the four most important agricultural exports — expanded from about 38 percent of the total area devoted to grains and oilseeds at the beginning of the period to 48 percent in 1964–65.

In Figure 6.3 similar relative price series are given for imports.[25]

25. The dollar import price index was compiled by CONADE from a sample of standardized import goods composed mainly of raw materials and intermediate products and representing between 70 percent and 86 percent of total imports. The

A somewhat different picture emerges in comparison with the export series: although the 1964–65 level of the relative import exchange rate is below that of any year since 1955, it is considerably closer to the 1956–58 level than the export rate, because of the sharp increase in import surcharges that occurred in 1959. But the relative peso price of imported goods has in more recent years run much lower than the 1956–63 level, unlike agricultural goods, particularly because of the considerable decline in dollar import prices between 1956 and 1959.[26] Although the relative exchange rate continued to decline somewhat in 1965, its effect on the peso price of imports was probably offset by the introduction of prior import deposits.

CONCLUSIONS

A managed sliding-parity exchange policy was adopted by Argentina at the beginning of 1964 because the alternative of permitting the rate to remain free would probably have led to violent fluctuations, unless complemented by measures that were inconsistent with other policy objectives. The continuation of a tight money policy to restrain demand for foreign exchange, which had been bloated by large payments obligations on the foreign debt accumulated in previous years, would not have been compatible with a policy of economic recovery from the recession of 1962–63, which had initially been provoked by a sharp decline in monetary liquidity. The existence of large unemployed resources, rising exports, and a highly favorable trade balance indicated that excess demand was not the cause of either inflation or balance-of-payments difficulties. The latter were entirely the result of scheduled debt payments, which during the next three years would have absorbed approximately 7 percent of GNP.

A substantial reflow of private speculative capital to damp down exchange-rate fluctuations appeared neither probable in the short

peso price of imports was calculated by multiplying this index by the effective import exchange rate, computed by dividing the peso value of imports (adjusted to include duties and surcharges) by the dollar value of imports. Both the peso price of imports and the effective exchange rate were expressed in Figure 6.4 in relation to the implicit GNP deflator.

26. The decline in the dollar import price is specious to the extent that it reflects a change in the composition of imports or overinvoicing at the beginning of the period when quantitative import controls were in force.

run, because of the magnitude of the projected payments gap and the large accumulation of payments pending on previous foreign credits, nor desirable over the long term. It is very risky to depend on volatile "hot money" to equilibrate the exchange market, particularly under conditions of uncertain economic and political stability, as was demonstrated by the experience of 1961–62 and again in 1966.

Even though the initial exchange rate established at the beginning of 1964 appears somewhat low in comparison with the relationship between the rate and measures of exchange parity in previous years, relative prices and exports of agricultural goods do not appear to have been adversely affected. The effects of the relatively lower exchange rate were offset by an improvement in world market prices, internal price supports, and a reduction in exporter margins. In fact, the area sown to major export crops, the size of cattle stocks, and foreign-exchange earnings expanded significantly. So-called nontraditional exports declined, but principally because of the fall in shipments of refined sugar and the rise of domestic demand, which made it more unattractive to export manufactures at less than full cost, as had been done in 1962–63.

The relative price of imported goods, however, appears to have fallen substantially below the level of 1956–63, not only because of the decline in the relative exchange rate, which was partially offset by the increase in import surcharges after 1958, but also because of the sizable reduction in the dollar import price index. But assuming that because of the way in which import protection operates, import demand is mainly determined by the level of economic activity and not by relative prices, the fall in relative prices of imported goods should pose no threat to the balance of payments. In fact, such a fall is consistent with the long-run policy of gradually reducing excessive protection to make industry more efficient and competitive in export markets, assisted at the same time by special tax and financial incentives. It is preferable to solve short-term balance-of-payments problems by short-term measures, such as temporary prior import deposits, which do not become built into the more permanent price-cost structure of the economy.

Subsequent adjustments of the sliding parity rate (six during 1964–65) kept the exchange rate well in line with the rise in domestic prices until the first part of 1965, after which the rate

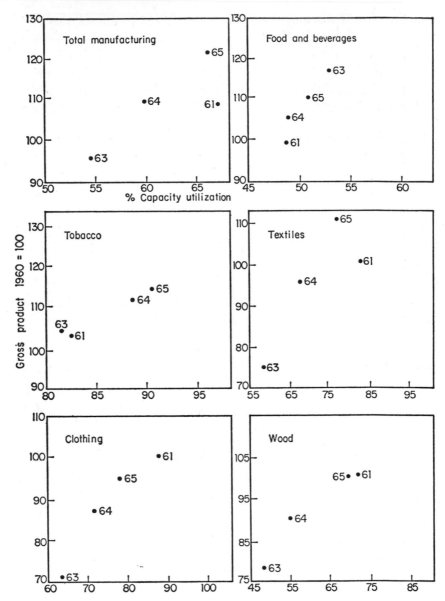

FIGURE 6.4

Utilization of manufacturing capacity, 1961 and 1963–65

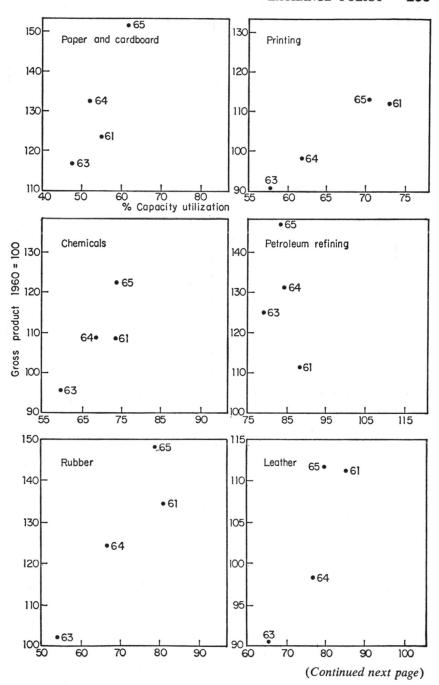

(*Continued next page*)

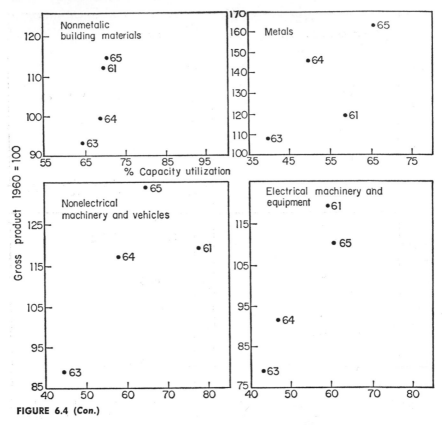

FIGURE 6.4 (Con.)

tended to lag somewhat behind. This lag coincided with a tightening of domestic anti-inflationary policy in response to an acceleration in the rise of internal prices. It is understandable that officials should be reluctant to accelerate exchange-rate adjustments at such a time, particularly in view of the impact that devaluation appears to have on the general internal price level. Furthermore, although the share of most Argentine export commodities in world markets is not sufficient to exert much influence on foreign prices, shipments of beef and perhaps one or two other major products (such as linseed oil) do exert such an effect, so that more rapid devaluation could be accompanied by a worsening of the terms of trade (see, for example, the fluctuations in the unit value of exports and the effective exchange rate in Figure 6.2).

Any effort to keep the peso "overvalued" in the long run, whether for anti-inflationary or terms-of-trade reasons, would tend to discourage production of export goods and encourage substitution of Argentine exports in foreign markets. If, however, internal stabilization policy were successful in reducing inflation and future adjustments permitted the exchange rate to recover its previous relative level, no serious difficulties would arise, assuming that foreign prices did not suffer an important decline.

Contracyclical measures to cushion the effect of fluctuations in foreign prices and domestic supplies on the internal prices of export goods have proved difficult to reconcile with general fiscal, monetary, and exchange-policy objectives. A partial solution would be to fix agricultural support prices closer to the break-even point for producers and permit the Grain Board to enter the market during the harvesting season at a higher price level if conditions warranted.[27] But a more fundamental solution could be achieved through greater exchange-rate flexibility by moving the rate above "parity" and compensating fluctuations in the foreign-internal price ratios of individual commodities through appropriate changes in differential export retentions and subsidies. This has already been contemplated in the official policy position and was in fact attempted in connection with the larger-than-average devaluation of April 1965. Some economists suggested that if this policy were carried further, so that increases in the "real" exchange rate were compensated for not only by retentions on traditional exports but by reductions of import tariffs and surcharges as well, more powerful incentives could be provided for exports of manufactures (utilization of manufacturing capacity is shown in Figure 6.4).

Finally, very little has been said up to now about the broader, long-term issues of Argentina's foreign economic policy. Adequate treatment of this subject would exceed the limits of this chapter, but a few closing remarks are in order concerning the long-term viability of present official balance-of-payments policy. The fundamental question is whether the effort to maintain a considerable trade surplus over an extended period will not inevitably retard economic growth, at least below the rate that could otherwise be achieved if a smaller trade surplus would permit fuller utilization of Argentina's abundant resources.

27. This policy implies that in effect the Grain Board would be arbiter of the distribution of margins between private traders and producers. But the formulation of fairly objective criteria should not constitute an insuperable problem.

There is little doubt that present policy, both Argentine and foreign, will sooner or later affect the rate of growth. Foreign-exchange reserves adequate to offset the effect of serious drought or other catastrophes on export earnings can not be built up while foreign debt refinancing continues on a hand-to-mouth basis, supplemented by the issue of short-term dollar bonds that only postpone the problem. Meanwhile, the inflow of new long-term foreign capital has been limited by regulations, imposed by the Paris Club agreement on the financing of capital-goods imports, uncertainty with respect to the future possibility of remitting profits and interest on private investment in Argentina, and the slow process of developing aid-worthy projects to be financed by international credit institutions. Added to these are the inevitable uncertainties about the future economic and political stability of a country walking on the razor's edge between recession and continued inflation.

Eventually an agreement will have to be reached between Argentina and the international financial community. It would greatly facilitate such an agreement if conditions were limited to policies bearing directly on the country's balance of payments. Along those lines, the following commitments would be reasonable: to devote some reasonable share of export earnings to foreign debt retirement, in exchange for long-term refinancing of the balance; to follow policies that encourage export expansion and foreign investment, in return for a guarantee that annual debt-service obligations will be appropriately reduced any year that export receipts decline for reasons beyond the control of policy;[28] and to take drastic corrective measures if the economy shows signs of heating up, in exchange for agreement on a program similar to Chile's for progressive reduction of the fiscal deficit and the rate of monetary expansion.

28. A flexible debt-service schedule is Argentina's only line of defense against export fluctuations, unless creditors are willing to finance a rebuilding of the country's gold and foreign-exchange reserves.

Geoffrey Maynard and Willy van Rijckeghem

7

Stabilization Policy in an Inflationary Economy — Argentina

It is well known that the growth performance of the Argentine economy since 1950 has been very modest and that it has been accompanied by continuous inflation. The average annual growth rate of GNP between 1950 and 1963 barely exceeded 2 percent, while the rate of inflation was seldom below 10 percent, averaged over 25 percent, and in one year approached 100 percent. Recent data have shown that the poor growth performance resulted less from the inability of the economy to expand rapidly over a number of years than from the extreme instability of the development process: severe recessions tended to follow periods of fast expansion.[1] The recessions themselves seem to have been the direct result of attempts to stabilize prices and improve the balance of payments, but the rate of inflation was not checked by these attempts; on the contrary, it tended to accelerate as output fell.

The outstanding instance of accelerated inflation accompanying sharp recession occurred in 1959. It followed six years of rapidly rising output, when real GNP probably increased at the rate of nearly 6 percent per annum. Prices were also rising rapidly, at something like 18 percent per annum over all six years and by about 39 percent in 1958 alone. In 1959, however, nonagricultural output fell by 6 percent, while the rate of inflation jumped to over

1. The instability of the growth process is illustrated by the fact that the standard deviation of the annual growth rates of GNP in the period 1960–63 is 4.65 — more than twice the average annual growth rate.

90 percent. Output picked up again in 1960 and 1961, rising by between 7 and 8 percent in each of the two years, while the rate of inflation fell back to 23 percent and then to 15 percent. The years 1962 and 1963 saw a further sharp fall in output, again as a result of stabilization policies, and the rate of inflation once more accelerated to over 25 percent.

This combination of recession and accelerated inflation in recent Argentine economic history has been attributed to the nature of the policies recommended by the International Monetary Fund.[2] While we believe that these policies were in a number of respects inappropriate, it is not our purpose to join in an attack on the IMF. Nor are we concerned with the monetarist versus structuralist debate that has dominated the economic literature on Latin America in recent years. The aim here is to throw light on the *modus operandi* through which the stabilization policies produced the result they did, mainly with a view to discovering whether policies might be framed that would successfully slow down inflation without at the same time causing output to fall. More precisely, we wish to establish the quantitative basis of short-run money, credit, and wage policy, which in our view must play an essential role in any stabilization strategy for Argentina. Thus, we do not aim at providing a complete and exhaustive explanation of postwar inflation in Argentina; rather, we seek to trace the impact on prices, wages, and output of changes in the variables that the government can control, or at any rate influence, in the short run.

Various theories have been advanced for explaining why stabilization policies tend to produce a decline in output, at least in the early stages of application. They usually emphasize the impact that these policies have on effective demand. Investment expenditure may show a temporary fall, not only because of the money and credit restrictions that are invariably included among the policy measures, but also because of a change in expectations, which alters the relative attractiveness of different forms of investment.[3] Consumption demand may be affected directly, apart from multiplier effects, if, for instance, a successful attempt to restrain wage increases reduces the wage share in national income. A fall in the

2. Ephraim Eshag and Rosemary Thorpe, "Economic and Social Consequences of Orthodox Economic Policies in Argentina in the Post-war Years," *Bulletin of Oxford Institute of Statistics* (February 1965).

3. See G. Dorrance, "The Effect of Inflation on Economic Development," *IMF Staff Papers*, X (1963).

wage share is held to have been an important element in Finland's experience with a stabilization program.[4]

But a fall in effective demand, whether produced by a fall in investment, consumption, or both, does not necessarily produce a fall in output. For that to happen, either the policy for reducing demand must have been carried to excess — that is, beyond the point where aggregate demand and aggregate supply are in equilibrium at a stable price level — or there must exist some cost- and price-raising force independent of aggregate demand, at least in the short run, which keeps prices rising even when aggregate demand is falling. Moreover, explanations stressing the prime role of effective demand can not easily explain why inflation should accelerate when output is falling, which seemed to happen in Argentina.

Quite apart from these considerations, a preliminary econometric analysis of the investment and consumption functions for Argentina led to the conclusion that an attempt to study the effect of stabilization policies through their influence on demand would not be very fruitful. The investment function did not show a significant relationship between monetary variables, such as total money supply, bank credit, and interest rates, and the rate of fixed capital formation; the absence of a reliable series for inventories made it impossible even to look for a relationship here. Splitting consumption expenditure between spending on agricultural and nonagricultural goods showed the former, but not the latter, to be influenced by changes in the distribution of income between wage and non-wage income.[5] Agricultural output was influenced mainly by weather conditions, especially rainfall, rather than by demand and was largely absorbed by home consumption or exports.

The best investment function we were able to obtain explains the annnual percentage changes in gross fixed capital formation (i) by the percentage changes in gross output of the nonagricultural sector (z_r) and imports of capital goods (m_i):

$$i = 0.87 \, z_r + 0.38 \, m_i + 0.41 \qquad R^2 = 0.89$$
$$\quad (0.27) \qquad (0.06) \qquad (1.43)$$

4. See A. S. Gerakis, "Recession in the Initial Phase of a Stabilization Programme: The Experience of Finland," *IMF Staff Papers,* XI (1964).

5. See, however, Carlos F. Diaz-Alejandro, *Exchange Rate Devaluation in a Semi-Industrialized Country* (Cambridge, Mass.: M.I.T. Press, 1965). Alejandro gives more weight to the income distribution effect of exchange-rate depreciation than is suggested here.

The annual percentage changes in the consumption of agricultural commodities (c_a) seem best explained by percentage changes in national income (y), changes in income distribution as measured by the difference between the percentage changes of total income and wage income $(y - w)$, and relative prices $(P_a - P_r)$:

$$c_a = 0.75\,y - 0.19\,(y - w) - 0.23\,(P_a - P_r) + 0.47 \quad R^2 = 0.90$$
$$\ (0.21)\quad (0.09)\qquad\qquad (0.06)\qquad\qquad\ (0.94)$$

The annual percentage changes in the consumption of "rest" or non-agricultural goods was best explained by the annual percentage change in national income (y) and the relative availability of the outputs of the agricultural and rest sectors $(z_a - z_r)$:

$$c_r = 0.92\,y - 0.22\,(z_a - z_r) - 0.39 \quad R^2 = 0.93$$
$$\ (0.08)\quad (0.04)\qquad\qquad (0.41)$$

These results led to the exploration of a rather different line of reasoning concerning the relationship between stabilization policy and output. It stressed the impact that monetary restriction would have on output decisions, independent of the influence it might have on effective demand. There was, in fact, considerable direct evidence in Argentina that at times when commercial bank credit to the private sector was being severely restricted (and monetary restriction usually tended to fall much more heavily on the private sector than on the public sector), firms often had to dismiss labor and cut back output because they literally could not get the working capital to finance current production at continuously rising costs. Many tried to meet the problem by resorting to the extra-bank credit market, which because of the severe restrictions imposed on the ordinary commercial banks in recent years had grown extensively; but either they were unsuccessful in getting any credit at all or were forced to pay such high interest rates that they could not afford them for long. There was also a tendency for firms not to pay their own suppliers, which simply pushed the problem farther down the production line, and a liquidity crisis quickly spread throughout the economy. Money wages, however, had eventually to be paid in cash, although it was not unusual for employees to go without their wages for many weeks at a time, and the difficulty of obtaining this cash led to cuts in employment and production. Argentina, in fact, provides an interesting and perhaps extreme

example of a country in which rapid inflation, sustained principally by cost pressures, has produced a severe and chronic shortage
of money and credit in relation to circulation needs. The whole
financial system has become less efficient and more costly, so that
any further measures to restrict money and credit quickly produce
a liquidity crisis.

To check this line of reasoning, a model was set up for the Argentine economy which attempted to "explain" the annual growth
rate of prices, wages, and output in the rest sector of the economy
over the period 1951–64, in terms of changes in total money supply,
bank credit to the private sector, and money wages.[6] The model is
a rather restricted one in that it abstracts from important secular
changes, such as those affecting production functions, which may
influence price behavior in the long run. Moreover, many important
short-run factors, such as changes in the weather, in foreign capital
inflows, or in international terms of trade, are introduced implicitly
rather than explicitly by assumptions about wages and imports,
which are exogenously determined as far as the model is concerned.
In particular, the model assumes as given what happens in the
agricultural sector, so that agricultural gross output and relative
prices between the agricultural and rest sector are exogenous to the
system. It is not denied, of course, that sharp changes in agricultural output do have a significant direct impact on the general price
level, but their effect on the price level of the rest sector is mainly
indirect and occurs as a result of the response, usually quick and
full, of money wages to a rise in food prices. It is therefore sufficient to include only money wages as a direct determinant of prices
in the rest sector. Similar reasoning leads to the exclusion of
exchange-rate changes as a direct determinant of the nonagricultural sector price level, since a major consequence of exchange-rate
depreciation is a rise in food prices, again with rather full, quick
repercussions on money wages. Changes in money wages are therefore a fairly adequate proxy of the rise in costs to the rest sector as
a result of devaluation. Imports in the sector are treated as being
determined outside the model rather than being a function of sector output, primarily because in the short run, particularly at times
of balance-of-payments crises, quantitative and exchange controls,

6. This model is part of a larger and more general model of the Argentine
economy.

as well as credit restrictions, have a major direct effect on them. Finally, the government sector does not enter the model as a producing sector but influences the course of events by the policies it pursues.

A SHORT-RUN PRICE AND OUTPUT MODEL FOR THE ARGENTINE ECONOMY

Output Function for the Rest Sector. The function obtained for the 1950–64 period was as follows:

$$(1) \quad z_r = 2.30 + 0.13\,(B_r - \eta) + 0.22\,m_{o-\frac{1}{3}} + 0.13\,z_a \qquad R^2 = 0.81$$
$$ (0.04) (0.05) \phantom{\,m_{o-} + } (0.09) d = 1.74$$

where

z_r = the annual percentage change in gross output of the rest sector;

B_r = the annual percentage change in bank credits to the rest sector;

η = the annual percentage change in "agreed" wages paid by the rest sector ("agreed" wages mean the wage rates agreed upon during the annual wage negotiations; their increase is measured as the geometrical average of the monthly increases obtained by twelve representative occupations, all in the rest sector);

m_o = the annual percentage increase in "other" imports, that is, imports that are not capital goods. An implicit lag of a third of a year is obtained by taking two-thirds of the percentage change of the current year and one-third of the change during the previous year;

z_a = the annual percentage change in agricultural gross output.

(The statistical series relevant to our model is presented in Table 7.1.)

Imports of noncapital goods (mostly intermediate goods and raw materials) were the most important factor determining year-to-year fluctuations in the growth rate of output, but bank credit deflated by agreed wages also had a very significant effect. In most years "actual" wage increases (the implicit wage earnings derived by dividing the total wage bill by employment) differed from agreed wage increases, sometimes falling short of, but usually exceeding, them. However, inclusion of actual wages in the output function in place of agreed wages produced a less satisfactory result. Although

Table 7.1. Statistical series.

Year	$M_{-\frac{1}{2}}$	B_r	B_r^o	η	S_r	z_a	z_r	P_r	$m_{o-\frac{1}{3}}$	c_r	c_a	y	$y-w$	P_a-P_r	e_r
									Variables						
1950	—	—	—	19	—	—	—	—	—	—	—	—	—	—	—
1951	18	36	36	19	26	6	4	34	8	3	0	4	7	4	2
1952	15	10	10	28	26	−15	−5	22	−14	−4	−8	−6	−8	18	0
1953	18	11	11	4	7	29	1	7	−27	−1	7	6	3	1	−2
1954	20	21	21	17	13	0	7	8	27	6	5	5	−2	−2	2
1955	17	24	24	3	11	4	10	13	30	10	5	7	6	−7	4
1956	18	28	26	37	22	−4	4	19	−2	3	5	2	1	−6	2
1957	17	18	17	3	23	0	8	21	6	6	−1	5	3	12	5
1958	29	31	16	47	44	5	6	39	11	6	1	5	−4	−6	3
1959	39	18	14	70	62	−1	−6	91	−3	−5	−20	−5	12	66	2
1960	31	36	54	18	31	0	7	23	1	5	8	6	−3	−5	0
1961	23	30	36	24	26	−2	8	15	16	4	14	6	−4	−15	0
1962	13	12	1	25	23	1	−4	24	−3	−6	−3	−3	2	12	−4
1963	21	13	21	25	30	−2	−6	28	−23	−5	−4	−5	2	—	−7
1964	37	23	30	32	36	10	8	24	7	—	—	—	—	—	—
1965[a]	32	25	—	30	33	10	8	27	13	—	—	—	—	—	—

Source: Data on money supply and bank credits are taken from the *Boletin Estadistico* of the Banco Central de la Republica Argentina. Data on gross output, consumption, income, income distribution, imports, rate of inflation, and relative prices are taken from CONADE, *Cuentas Nacionales de la República Argentina* (Buenos Aires, 1964). The series on wage agreements is taken from the *Boletin de Estadistica* of the Direccion Nacional de Estadistica y Censos.

[a] Provisional.

its coefficient was not significant, agricultural output was left in the equation because it was an important factor in the 1952 recession, when agricultural output fell by 15 percent as a result of a severe drought.

The explicit introduction of variables such as population changes and increases in the nation's capital stock did not yield significant results. Their effect is probably included in the constant term, the other variables explaining the short-term fluctuations around this trend. The implication is that our output equation can satisfactorily describe short-term behavior only in a situation where ample labor and productive capacity are available. There are sufficient indications that such conditions existed in Argentina during the period studied and afterward.

A conclusion seems to emerge quite clearly from our output equation: a stabilization policy that makes use of quantitative restrictions or substantial exchange-rate devaluation to reduce imports, and which effectively restricts bank credit available to the private sector while not producing a correspondingly restrictive effect on wage agreements, is likely to have a severe depressive effect on nonagricultural output. The sensitivity of output to the availability of imports results, on the one hand, from the fact that a long process of import substitution has produced a situation where current imports consist almost entirely of raw and intermediate materials for industry and, on the other, from the rigidity of production functions. Industrial output is therefore crucially geared to the availability of foreign exchange. There is, however, a significant trend term in the equation. If agricultural output were to expand at about 2 percent per annum, which has been about its rate of increase in Argentina over the last fifteen years, and if imports were to grow at the same rate as rest sector output, our output equation could be written as follows:

$$z_r = 3.0 + 0.17 \, (B_r - \eta)$$

Thus, it appears that if bank credit to the private sector could be adjusted to offset the increase in costs as reflected in wage agreements, output would expand at about 3 percent per annum.

Price Function for the Rest Sector. The most satisfactory price function proved to be:

(2) $P_r = 7.16 + 0.70 \, M_{-\frac{1}{2}} - 0.89 \, z_r - 1.82 \, \pi_c + 0.30 \, \eta \quad R^2 = 0.86$
        $(5.85) \quad (0.47) \qquad (0.57) \quad (0.72) \qquad (0.26) \qquad d = 1.85$

where

$P_r =$ the annual percentage change in the price level of the rest sector;

$M_{-\frac{1}{2}} =$ the average of the percentage changes in the money supply (which includes term deposits as well as currency and demand deposits) in the current and previous year, measured at the end of the year;

$z_r =$ the annual percentage change in gross output of the rest sector;

$\eta =$ the annual percentage change in agreed wages;

$\pi_c =$ price controls, a dummy variable that is given a value of 10 in 1953 and 1954, when price controls were in operation, and minus 10 in 1959, when all were abandoned.

Both money supply and money wages appear to be important

determinants of the price level, although all standard errors are very high because of the presence of multicollinearity. The money-supply variable had a higher coefficient when introduced in the form of the average of the percentage increases of both current and previous years than when introduced simply as the increase for the current year. If money had been defined as currency and demand deposits only, excluding term deposits, its coefficient would have been nearer one, while that of the wage variable would have been reduced; but there are advantages in working with the more inclusive concept. The advantage of using agreed wages, as distinct from actual wages, is that they are a more autonomous variable — that is, they are less likely to be affected by the behavior of the *current* price level.[7] When actual wages are substituted for agreed wages in the equation, the relative importance of money supply and wages is reversed: money wages have a higher coefficient than money supply.

Wage Function for the Rest Sector. The model is completed by the inclusion of a function relating changes in actual wages (S_r) to changes in agreed wages. We make use of this function when discussing possible stabilization policies, since what happens to real wages (that is, the change in actual wages deflated by the change in prices) may have an important influence on the choice of policy. The wage function takes as given the outcome of the wage negotiations and translates them into actual wages. The function is:

$$(3) \qquad S_r = 3.95 + 0.68 \ \eta + 0.25 \ \eta_{-1} \qquad R^2 = 0.87$$
$$\qquad\qquad (6.75) \quad (0.08) \qquad (0.08) \qquad\qquad d = 1.99$$

It can be seen that actual wages of the current period are affected not only by wage negotiations of the same period but also by negotiations of the period before. The sum of the elasticities for both current and previous years is 0.93, suggesting that wage agreements are not entirely translated into actual wages. Nevertheless, there is a positive trend term which ensures that actual wages normally tend to increase at a faster rate than agreed wages.

7. A similar line of argument was followed by A. C. Harberger in an inflation study of Chile. He introduced wages in the way of legal minimum wages for white-collar workers (which did not operate in Argentina during the period covered by the series). He found an elasticity with respect to money supply of about one, and with respect to minimum wages of 0.13 with a standard error of 0.22. Harberger, "The Dynamics of Inflation in Chile," in C. F. Christ, ed., *Measurement in Economics* (Stanford: Stanford University Press, 1963).

THE 1959 AND 1962–63 RECESSIONS

We can apply these functions to the 1959 and 1962–63 recession periods to find out how well they "explain" what happened. The background to those recessions has been fully described by Ephraim Eshag and Rosemary Thorpe, and only one or two main features need be mentioned here.[8] The background to the 1959 recession was a severe foreign-exchange crisis during 1958, which in turn was the culmination of a number of years when the growth of imports greatly exceeded that of exports. By the end of 1958 Argentina's foreign-exchange reserve position was in a precarious state. IMF assistance was obtained at the expense of a number of restrictive measures in the field of budgetary, monetary, and wage policies. These could hardly have been avoided, given the state of Argentina's balance of payments, but other measures in the foreign-exchange field, such as a large devaluation of the exchange rate, were perhaps more controversial. The net result was a sharp fall in industrial production, which improved the current balance of payments somewhat by reducing home consumption of beef and therefore expanding exports.

The most important result of IMF assistance was the restoration of confidence felt by the foreign investor and foreign creditor. In 1960 and 1961 a large inflow of capital took place, in the form of both direct investment in industry and official short- and medium-

8. Although Eshag and Thorpe provided a reasonably accurate account of developments in the 1958–63 period, we do not fully support their attack on "IMF type" policies. They gave the impression that the IMF was wrong to put pressure on the Argentine government to reduce or eliminate its budget deficit or to try to restrain wage increases. In our view both of these aims are absolutely essential if price stability is to be obtained without a serious restriction of output. Moreover, one can not ignore the fact that Argentina had massive current-account balance-of-payments deficits in those years; and although it may be better to try to correct these without reducing output and employment, the fact remains that the balance-of-payments situation had to be corrected quickly. Eshag and Thorpe did not suggest what should have been done about these short-term balance-of-payments crises. One can not overlook the main difficulty facing Argentina in the 1950's. The negligible growth of agricultural output in the second half of the decade simply did not permit the industrial sector to maintain a growth rate in excess of 6 percent per annum without quickly producing a balance-of-payments crisis. Imports rapidly outstripped exports. It could thus be argued that unless foreign creditors were willing to cover the current balance-of-payments deficit over the long run, a sharp fall in industrial production was inevitable in order to restore a long-term balance between the growth of industry and of agriculture.

term loans. Supplier credits provided another important element. Industrial activity quickly picked up from the 1959 recession, as the result to some extent of the foreign direct investment in Argentine industry, which had as its complement a large inflow of capital goods imports, but more as the consequence of monetary expansion and credit relaxation associated with the inflow of foreign capital. Exports remained stagnant, however, so that once again the balance

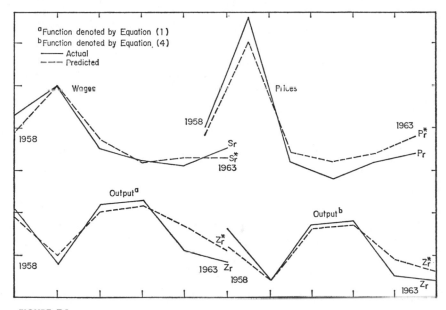

FIGURE 7.1

Actual and predicted percentage changes in output, prices, and wages in Argentina's nonagricultural sector, 1958–63

of payments on current account deteriorated sharply. This deterioration was hidden by the improvement on capital account. The later repayment of short-term external loans and of supplier credits, as well as a sudden collapse of confidence because of a domestic political crisis, reversed the movement of foreign capital in 1962, and a large outflow of capital took place. Foreign-exchange reserves deteriorated, and once again the government was forced into restrictive monetary, credit, and import policies. Industrial production was immediately affected, and 1962 and 1963 were severe recession years.

Table 7.2 and Figure 7.1 show the actual changes in prices,

Table 7.2. Actual and predicted changes in output, prices, and wages in Argentina's nonagricultural sector, 1958–65 (in percents).

Year	z_r Actual	z_r Predicted	P_r Actual	P_r Predicted	S_r Actual	S_r Predicted
1958	+6	+4	+39	+36	+4.4	+37
1959	−6	−5	+91	+79	+62	+63
1960	+7	+5	+23	+28	+31	+34
1961	+8	+7	+15	+23	+26	+25
1962	−4	0	+24	+27	+23	+27
1963	−6	−4	+28	+35	+30	+27
1964	+8	+4	+24	+35	+36	+31
1965[a]	+8	+6	+27	+31	+33	+35

Source: CONADE.

[a] Provisional.

wages, and output in the 1958–63 period. Note that the changes predicted by the equations are also revealed there. On the whole, the model gives a reasonably good explanation of prices, output, and actual money wages for the period. The decline in output is underestimated in the three recession years, 1959, 1962, and 1963, but seriously so only in 1962. The price increase is underestimated in 1959 and overestimated in 1962 and 1963, while the change in money wages is predicted with reasonable accuracy throughout.

There is, in fact, an explanation of why the output equation should underestimate the decline in output that occurred in the recession years. The term used to introduce the liquidity factor into the output equation $(B_r - \eta)$ probably fails to reflect adequately the liquidity squeeze on the private sector, since in those years the government built up substantial debts with its suppliers by means of postponing payment of its bills. Although the private sector probably replied in kind by postponing payment of its tax liabilities, the net result was almost certainly an intensification of the liquidity squeeze.

This made it desirable to rework our output equation so as to take account of the government's propensity to borrow from its suppliers. The annual increase in net debt to suppliers was subtracted from the annual increase in bank credit to arrive at our positive component of the liquidity term. The following result was obtained:

(4) $z_r = 2.40 + 0.13 \, (B_r^o - \eta) + 0.23 \, m_{o-\frac{1}{3}} + 0.14 \, z_a$ $R^2 = 0.87$

$d = 1.52$

where B_r^o is the percentage change in bank credits corrected for the increase in supplier credits to the public sector. The overall explanation is substantially improved (R^2 rising from 0.81 to 0.87), although the coefficients attached to the individual terms are almost unaffected. Application of this revised output equation to the recession periods produced a predicted fall of 6 percent in output in 1959, compared with an actual fall of 6 percent, and for 1962 a fall of 1 percent compared with an actual fall of 4 percent. The previous result for 1963 was left virtually unchanged. It thus seems clear that net public-sector debt owed to suppliers did have an important influence on the output of the private sector. We have preferred, however, not to make use of this revised output equation in what follows, for an increase in net government debt with suppliers was probably offset, in part at least, by an increase in the debt of the private sector with the government. Since we can not estimate the private sector debt, we feel it safer not to use the equation.

APPLICATION OF THE MODEL TO STABILIZATION POLICIES

The three original equations of the model show in a quantitative fashion what impact changes in money supply, bank credit to the private sector, and agreed money wages had on output and prices of the nonagricultural sector. If we substitute the output equation into the price equation, we get a reduced-form equation for the rate of inflation:

(5) $P_r = 0.35 \, M + 0.35 \, M_{-1} - 0.12 \, B_r + 0.42 \, \eta - 0.20 \, m_{o-\frac{1}{3}}$
$- 0.12 \, z_a - 1.82 \, \pi_c + 5.11$

The equation suggests that large increases in total money supply, and in agreed money wages *relative* to the expansion of bank credit, tend to accelerate the rate of price inflation. Money supply and money wages act *directly* on prices, whereas the relation between bank credit and agreed money wages act *indirectly* via the impact on output.

A further important implication of the price equation from the policy point of view is that because of the lagged influence of money supply, a substantial proportion of the rate of inflation of the current year is inherited from the previous year. For example, assuming that agricultural output grows by 2 percent and the current imports of the rest sector increase at the same rate as the output of that sector, the 25 percent increase in money supply which occurred in 1965 ensures a minimum price rise of 13 percent in 1966 even if money supply and agreed money wages of that year are frozen. Moreover, the freezing of agreed money wages would result in some fall in real wages, which would create political difficulties.[9] To avoid that outcome, a stabilization policy seems to be needed that, while gradually reducing the rate of inflation, maintains a reasonable growth of output and avoids a depression of real wages.

The model can be extended so as to explore the outcome of various stabilization strategies. Thus, if it is supposed that the government has an influence over wage agreements such that it can keep the rise in agreed money wages at some fraction of the rate of inflation of the previous year, the following equation can be added to the model:

$$(6) \qquad\qquad \eta = \alpha P_{t-1}$$

where α is a government policy parameter.

Further, since the government can influence the supply of bank credit to the rest sector by manipulation of commercial bank-reserve requirements and by the rediscount policy of the Central Bank, it can follow the strategy of increasing bank credits to the rest sector at a desirable rate relative to the increase of agreed money wages. We would then have:

$$(7) \qquad\qquad B_r = \lambda \eta$$

where λ is another government policy parameter.[10]

Finally, a policy decision has to be made regarding the expansion of total money supply. A crucial point is whether to allow total money supply to increase at a rate slower or faster than the growth rate of bank credits to the private sector. In general, because of difficulty in controlling the size of its budget deficit, the government

---

9. If agreed money wages rose by 30 percent in 1965, the wage function of Equation (3) indicates that actual money wages in 1966 would rise by about 11 percent.

10. It is assumed here that credit to the agricultural sector grows at the same rate as credit to the rest sector. The growth rate of bank credit to the whole private sector can then be represented by B_r.

is usually compelled to restrict credit to the private sector more severely than to the public sector.[11] However, for our present purposes we can write:

$$(8) \qquad\qquad M = \beta B_r$$

where β is a third policy parameter.

The three main equations and these policy parameters can now be used to trace the consequences of four possible stabilization strategies. Strategy 1 relies on a progressive stabilization of the money supply. The growth rate of money supply in 1965 was approximately 25 percent. Assume that the government decides to reduce the rate of expansion of money supply to 18 percent in 1966, 13 percent in 1967, 8 percent in 1968, and 4 percent in 1969. Assume also that the government aims at dividing the burden of adjustment equally between the public and private sectors ($\beta = 1$).[12] As a consequence, bank credits expand at the same rate as total money supply, without regard to what happens to agreed wages (λ is thus variable). It is assumed that no wage policy is in operation, and that the unions bargain for and obtain wage increases equal to the rate of inflation of the previous year (α is therefore equal to one). The stabilization path corresponding to this strategy is given in Table 7.3.

Table 7.3. Progressive stabilization of the money supply.[a]

Items	Percentage changes			
	1966	1967	1968	1969
Money supply	18	13	8	4
Bank credits	18	13	8	4
Agreed wages	30	30	27	23
Actual wages	33	32	30	26
Output	1	0	0	0
Prices	30	27	23	18

[a] Strategy: $\alpha = 1$; $\beta = 1$; λ = variable. Assumptions: $z_a = 2$; $m_{0-\frac{1}{3}} = z_r$. Data: $P_{r\ 1965} = 30$; $M_{1965} = 25$; $\eta_{1965} = 34$.

11. For instance, in 1959 total money supply expanded by 39 percent, while credit to the private sector rose by only 18 percent. In 1963 the increases were 21 percent and 13 percent, respectively.

12. The foreign sector is assumed here to have a neutral effect on money supply. By making the growth rate of current imports equal to the growth rate of rest sector output in all the strategies analyzed, we also assume that the foreign-trade sector is not limiting the growth of output.

The trouble with this stabilization strategy is that, although it reduces the rate of inflation from 30 to 18 percent within a four-year period (not in itself a great achievement), it leads to a complete stagnation in output, because the increase in bank credits does not match the continued rise in agreed money wages. Moreover, both real wages and the implied velocity of circulation of money are rising rapidly, which is likely to produce a breakdown in the policy before stabilization is successfully concluded.

Strategy 2 is based on progressive wage stabilization. It is now assumed that the government has some influence over the outcome of the annual wage agreements and keeps agreed wage rises to a fraction of the rate of inflation of the previous year. Since there are obvious limits to the power of any government to carry out such a policy, a lower limit of 0.4 for the value of the stabilization parameter α in Equation (6) is assumed. It is further assumed that bank credits are allowed to expand at the same rate as agreed wages ($\lambda = 1$) and that total money supply expands at the same rate as bank credits ($\beta = 1$). The effect of alternative wage policies can be followed in Table 7.4.

The introduction of a wage policy clearly improves the chances of success of the stabilization program. For example, in the case of $\alpha = .4$ the terminal growth rate of money supply is the same as in Table 7.2, but the rate of inflation is only half as high. Moreover, instead of being constant, output is growing at the basic rate of 3 percent throughout the whole period. However, after the first year real wages suffer a constant deterioration and will have worsened by more than 4 percent by the end of the fourth year. A larger α does not prevent the fall in real wages but reduces the speed with which the rate of inflation is lowered. If α exceeds .8, the rate of inflation is not reduced at all, and the situation becomes explosive.

Strategy 3 is a combined wage and monetary policy which avoids the fall in real wages associated with Strategy 2. Suppose, for instance, the government can enforce a particular wage policy in which $\alpha = 0.5$. As shown in Table 7.4, this policy is likely to stabilize the rate of inflation to about 13 percent by the end of 1969 without affecting the basic growth rate of output, but it will probably lead to a deterioration in real wages. In order to avoid this, the government can manipulate the relationship between total

Table 7.4. Alternative wage policies.[a]

Items		Percentage changes						
	$\alpha =$	.4	.5	.6	.7	.8	.9	1.0
1966								
Money supply		12	15	18	21	24	27	30
Bank credits		12	15	18	21	24	27	30
Agreed wages		12	15	18	21	24	27	30
Actual wages		21	23	25	27	29	31	33
Output		3	3	3	3	3	3	3
Prices		21	23	25	27	29	31	33
1967								
Money supply		8	12	15	19	23	28	33
Bank credits		8	12	15	19	23	28	33
Agreed wages		8	12	15	19	23	28	33
Actual wages		12	16	19	22	26	30	34
Output		3	3	3	3	3	3	3
Prices		14	18	21	24	28	32	36
1968								
Money supply		6	9	13	17	22	29	36
Bank credits		6	9	13	17	22	29	36
Agreed wages		6	9	13	17	22	29	36
Actual wages		10	13	17	20	25	31	37
Output		3	3	3	3	3	3	3
Prices		11	15	18	22	27	33	39
1969								
Money supply		4	8	11	15	22	30	39
Bank credits		4	8	11	15	22	30	39
Agreed wages		4	8	11	15	22	30	39
Actual wages		8	12	15	18	24	32	39
Output		3	3	3	3	3	3	3
Prices		9	13	16	20	26	34	42

[a] Strategy: α between .4 and 1.0; $\beta = 1$; $\lambda = 1$. Other assumptions and data as in Table 7.2.

money creation and the increase in credits to the private sector so as to limit even more the rate of increase in prices.

Table 7.5 sets out what happens under the wage strategy $\alpha = 0.5$ when the relationship β varies between 0.6 and 1.0. (The implications of varying β for budgetary policy are examined later.) It can be seen immediately that prices stabilize more rapidly under these conditions than when wage stabilization policy is used alone. If β is less than 0.8, real wages can even show a positive improvement

Table 7.5. A combined wage and monetary policy.[a]

			Percentage changes		
Items	β =	0.6	0.7	0.8	0.9	1.0

Items β =	0.6	0.7	0.8	0.9	1.0
			1966		
Money supply	9	11	12	14	15
Bank credits	15	15	15	15	15
Agreed wages	15	15	15	15	15
Actual wages	23	23	23	23	23
Output	3	3	3	3	3
Prices	21	22	22	23	23
			1967		
Money supply	7	8	9	11	12
Bank credits	11	11	11	12	12
Agreed wages	11	11	11	12	12
Actual wages	15	15	15	16	16
Output	3	3	3	3	3
Prices	13	14	15	17	18
			1968		
Money supply	4	5	6	8	9
Bank credits	7	7	8	9	9
Agreed wages	7	7	8	9	9
Actual wages	11	11	12	13	13
Output	3	3	3	3	3
Prices	10	11	12	14	15
			1969		
Money supply	3	4	5	6	8
Bank credits	5	6	6	7	8
Agreed wages	5	6	6	7	8
Actual wages	9	10	10	11	12
Output	3	3	3	3	3
Prices	8	9	10	11	13

[a] Strategy: $\alpha = 0.5$; $\lambda = 1$; β between 0.6 and 1.0. Assumptions and data as in Table 7.2.

in the course of the stabilization policy. In addition, as a result of equalizing the rate of increase of bank credit available to the private sector with the rate of increase of agreed money wages ($\lambda = 1$), the rate of increase of output remains at 3 percent per annum.

This result raises the question of whether, by raising the rate of increase of bank credit above that of agreed money wages (making $\lambda > 1$), the growth of output could be raised above 3 percent and the rate of inflation more quickly reduced. Real wages may also be more favorably affected. It would, however, be unrealistic to believe that the rate of growth of output could be raised without limit simply by increasing bank credit to the private sector: the availability of credit to producers is likely to have a greater effect on output when it is being restricted than when it is being expanded. Nevertheless, the restrictive credit policy that has been followed in Argentina over most of the period since 1959 has produced a tight liquidity position in the private sector, and there is reason to believe that output at present is very sensitive to credit availability.

Strategy 4 is, therefore, a combined wage, credit, and monetary policy. Table 7.6 examines theoretically the possibility of raising the rate of increase of bank credit above that of agreed money wages. The coefficients α and β are put at 0.5 and 0.8, and λ is

Table 7.6. A combined wage, credit, and monetary policy.[a]

	Percentage changes		
Items	$\lambda =$ 1.2	1.3	1.4
	1966		
Money supply	14	16	17
Bank credits	18	20	21
Agreed wages	15	15	15
Actual wages	23	23	23
Output	4	4	4
Prices	22	22	23
	1967		
Money supply	10	11	14
Bank credits	13	14	17
Agreed wages	11	11	12
Actual wages	15	12	13
Output	4	4	4
Prices	15	13	15
	1968		
Money supply	8	8	10
Bank credits	10	10	13
Agreed wages	8	8	9
Actual wages	12	12	13
Output	4	4	4
Prices	12	13	15
	1969		
Money supply	6	7	9
Bank credits	7	9	11
Agreed wages	6	7	8
Actual wages	10	11	12
Output	3	4	4
Prices	11	11	13

[a] Strategy: $\alpha = 0.5$; $\beta = 0.8$; $\lambda =$ variable. Assumptions and data as in Table 7.2.

allowed to vary only between 1.2 and 1.4, since it would be unrealistic to rely on values that lie outside the experience of the period on which our model is based. Although the rate of growth of output is by this strategy raised from 3 to 4 percent, the favorable effect expected on prices is offset by the larger annual increases in money supply. Nonetheless, this strategy is probably preferable to Strategy 3 because the gain in terms of a higher growth rate of output more than compensates for slightly less success in reducing inflation.

If the supply of bank credit to the private sector could be increased without bringing about a commensurate increase in the total money supply — that is, if, as compared with Strategy 3, λ could be made larger than 1.0 while β was lowered from 0.8 to 0.7 — the annual price increases would be less than under Strategy 3, and real wages could more easily rise over the course of stabilization. Lowering β while raising λ would, however, cause considerable difficulties in that it would involve a substantial shift of bank credit away from the public to the private sector, which would not be possible without a large reduction in the size of the government's budget deficit. The size of the budget deficit and its method of financing does in fact provide a crucial limitation on the freedom of monetary policy. In the remainder of this chapter, therefore, we shall examine the implied relationship between the budget deficit, on the one hand, and money and credit policy, on the other.

Summing up to this point, one can reasonably speculate that if the government can exercise some control over three crucial policy parameters, it can influence prices, output, and real wages in the nonagricultural sector. The three parameters are the relationships between (a) the increase of agreed money wages in the current period and of prices in the previous period (α), (b) the increase of bank credit to the private sector and of agreed money wages (λ), and (c) the increase of total money supply and of bank credit to the private sector (β). Examination of four possible stabilization strategies suggests that the best results, in terms of the speed with which inflation is slowed and the success with which output growth and real wages are maintained, would be produced by a policy which ensures that the values of both α and β are below unity, while that of λ is above unity — subject to a realistic limit. This policy would have two main features: a limitation of current wage increases below previous price increases, and a restriction of money supply that falls more heavily on the public sector than on the private. Obviously there are difficulties in the way of implementing such a policy, which are discussed below.

RELATION BETWEEN THE BUDGET DEFICIT AND MONETARY POLICY VARIABLES

Assuming that there is no change in the net foreign-asset position of the Central Bank — that is, the foreign sector remains neutral with respect to money creation — the part of the government deficit that can be financed through the banking system can not, by definition, be larger than the difference between the total increase in money supply and the increase in credit to the private sector.[13] This is expressed by the equation:

$$(9) \qquad\qquad a\overline{D} = \Delta\overline{M} - \Delta\overline{B}$$

where $\overline{D}$ is the size of the public-sector deficit, the amount by which the government fails to cover the whole of its expenditures lending by the banking system; $\Delta\overline{M}$ is the overall increase in money by current revenue; a is the fraction of the deficit financed by net supply; and $\Delta\overline{B}$ is the increase in bank credit to the private sector of the economy. Dividing both sides of Equation (9) by the money value of current GNP and translating the absolute changes of the right-hand side into growth rates, we obtain:

$$(9a) \qquad\qquad d = \frac{x(M - Bk)}{a(1 + Y)}$$

where

d = the ratio of the current budget deficit to the money value of current GNP;

x = the ratio of the stock of money at the end of the previous year to the money value of GNP during that year;

M = the rate of growth of money supply during the current year;

B = the rate of growth of bank credit to the private sector;

13. Although it would be easy to alter the formulae in this section to take account of the foreign sector, the relative importance of changes in the net foreign-asset position for changes in the total money supply is usually relatively small, so that no great error is made by neglecting them.

k = the ratio of outstanding credit to the total money stock at the end of the previous year;

Y = the growth rate of money GNP during the current year.

Finally, using Equation (8), which relates the overall change in money supply to the target growth rate of credit to the private sector, we obtain:

$$(9b) \qquad\qquad d = \frac{Bx(\beta - k)}{a(1 + Y)}$$

where, as before, β is the relation between the growth rate of total money supply and the growth rate of credit to the private sector.[14]

The budget deficit relative to GNP is now a function of: the target increase in bank credits to the private sector (presumably determined as a function of the wage agreements and/or the target growth rate of real GNP); the strategy pursued regarding the relative growth rates of total money supply and of credit to the private sector; and the growth rate of money GNP. The coefficients x and k are predetermined by the situation at the beginning of the period and may therefore be regarded as exogenous.

The equation reveals what size deficit relative to current GNP, and what manner of financing it, are consistent with the stabilization policy as defined by β and B and the initial values of x and k. The larger B and β are, the larger can the public-sector deficit, or that part of it financed by the banking sector, be as a fraction of GNP. The size of k — the initial ratio of outstanding credit to the total money stock — provides a lower limit to the value of β at which net bank lending to the public sector can still take place. If β were in fact smaller than k, either the public deficit would have to be negative, and the public sector thus have to run a surplus, or borrowing from sources outside the banking system would have to exceed the size of the deficit.

This equation can be used to show the effect of a strategy 4 stabilization policy if applied to the development of the Argentine economy in 1966. Suppose that the government's aim is to limit the increase in total money supply in 1966 to 18 percent, while allowing bank credit to rise in excess of the agreed increase in

14. Credit to the agricultural sector is assumed to increase at the same rate as overall credit and thus equally with credit to the rest sector. As a consequence, Equation (8) becomes $M = \beta B$.

money wages, which is put at 15 percent. Let λ be 1.4, so that $B_r(=B)$ is 21 percent. β would then be about 0.8. The 1965 values of x and k are about .2 and .66. Our equation then shows that the amount of the deficit that can be financed by the banking system can not exceed about one-half of 1 percent of 1966 GNP (which, given the rise in prices and output predicted by the main equations, would be about 28 percent above the 1965 level). If this type of stabilization policy continued through later years, the influence of a falling B_r and x combined with a rising k would soon reduce the critical amount of bank finance that could be made available for financing the government deficit — reduce it, in fact, to a negligible proportion of GNP.[15]

This requirement concerning the size and manner of financing of the government deficit should be compared with what has been customary in recent years. Table 7.7 sets out the facts. Over the ten years from 1955 through 1964 the budget deficit averaged about 25 percent of total government expenditure and over 3 percent of GNP; in some years it exceeded 40 percent of the former and 5 percent of the latter. Moreover, owing to the absence of a market for government debt, an average of almost half of it had to be financed through the banking system. Thus, for the period as a whole the contribution of the banking system to the financing of the deficit amounted to over 1½ percent of GNP.[16]

15. Enforced borrowing from the private sector via nonpayment of bills would be equally damaging to the government's money and credit policy. A problem that is not dealt with here is the possible effect of changes in public expenditure or taxation on the liquidity of the private sector. An important implication of the stabilization strategies discussed here is that the public sector must reduce its borrowing from the banking system in order to make greater bank lending to the private sector compatible with a given monetary program. But a reduction in government expenditure, or an increase in taxation or public-sector borrowing, would tend to reduce the liquidity of the private sector, which would in part offset the gain obtained from more liberal access to bank credit. Thus, in an actual application of the model it would be desirable to amend the equations to take account of this problem. However, there seems to be considerable room in Argentina at the present time for reducing public-sector expenditure, such as by reducing the labor force, or for increasing revenue, such as by raising public utility rates, which would not impinge directly on the liquidity of producers.

16. This estimate of the impact of government borrowing on money supply is intended to give the order of magnitude only. On the one hand, the public-sector deficit that must be financed is somewhat larger than indicated in Table 7.7, for it includes the deficits of the provincial governments as well as of the national government. On the other hand, *net* borrowing from the banking system may be overestimated, since no account is taken in the table of the rise in public-sector deposits in the banking system.

Table 7.7. Argentina's national government budget deficit, 1955–64.

Budget deficit	1955	1956	1957	1958	1959	1960	1961	1962	1963	1964	1955–64 average
Deficit (billions of pesos)	8.9	2.5	6.0	26.8	28.8	20.4	18.1	50.4	53.2	118.1	33.0
Percent of government expenditure	33.0	8.3	19.3	42.2	29.2	16.8	12.0	27.5	24.3	40.4	25.0
Percent of GNP	5.1	1.1	2.1	6.5	4.0	2.0	1.5	3.5	3.0	5.1	3.5
Government borrowing from banking system: Percent deficit	62.0	8.0	11.0	60.0	74.0	44.0	6.0	37.0	81.0	92.0	47.0
Percent GNP	3.1	0.09	0.23	3.9	3.0	0.88	0.09	1.29	2.4	4.6	1.5
GNP (billions of pesos)	172.5	217.0	280.9	395.4	750.7	973.0	1,118.3	1,451.0	1,765.0	(2,360.0)[a]	(947.4)

Source: CONADE.

[a] Provisional.

In these figures we can discern the real difficulty facing the government in formulating a satisfactory monetary policy. Inability to reduce the size of the deficit or to finance it through the normal private capital market has meant that a large part of monetary restriction has had to fall on the private sector, with an adverse effect on output. When monetary restriction has been combined with massive devaluation or restrictions on imports, the result has been a severe depression.

This is not the place to examine the causes of successive governments' inability to balance their budgets. These causes include such items as an ineffectual tax system, grossly inefficient public enterprises whose current as well as capital deficits have to be met by the treasury, and periodic overvaluation of the exchange rate. The most important factor is probably the de facto inelasticity of tax revenue with respect to money income, that is, the failure of tax revenue to grow as fast as GNP over the short or long run. In part this failure results from inefficient tax administration, and in part it stems from the fact that changes in tax rates and tax allowances have reduced the effective marginal rate of tax; but it is also partly the consequence of structural features of the tax system. The most important of these is the time lag between the earning of taxable money income and the receipt by the government of the corresponding tax revenue. In Argentina taxes payable on current income and on current sales of goods are generally estimated according to the previous year's tax base, and very often they are not collected, at least in their entirety, until the following year. Thus, for instance, when an increase in the rate of inflation causes the growth of aggregate money income to accelerate, with government expenditure roughly keeping pace, current tax revenue tends to lag well behind, which enlarges the current deficit. Also, when rapid inflation is taking place, the collection of revenue one to two years in arrears involves a severe fall in its real value, which, quite apart from the administration aspects, naturally encourages the taxpayer to delay payment as long as possible. In addition, a significant part of total revenue is raised by *specific* excise taxes on a wide range of goods, both necessities and luxuries. Failure to adjust these specific tax rates in accord with changes in the price level causes tax revenue to lag behind the value of sales. Finally, the government, wary of putting further pressure on the price level, is often reluctant to approve increases in the rates charged by public utilities, with the result that the increased losses of these enterprises have to be met by the treasury.

The budgetary problem is further complicated when the government imposes credit restrictions on the private sector. Very often the private sector, finding its liquidity position squeezed by the credit policy, retaliates by the non- or late payment of its taxes: indeed, many firms have found it less costly to incur fines for late payment of taxes than to go short of liquid funds or pay the market rate in order to borrow them. The government has therefore found its own revenue dropping off when it has attempted to reduce credit to the private sector. Anxious not to go to the banking system to finance its larger deficit, which would tend to undermine its credit policy, the government reacts by not paying the bills of its own suppliers of goods and services. It has also issued debt-cancellation certificates, which can be used by their recipients to pay taxes but which are often in the short run discounted in the market to provide finance instead. An impasse has thus been reached, in which by implicit mutual agreement government and private sector have failed to settle debts with each other. In the last resort, however, the government does have cash payments to meet and is forced to ease the overall monetary situation by borrowing more from the banking system. Attempts to offset the monetary impact of its borrowing by restricting private credit even more become self-defeating, for tax revenue once again falls off.

CONCLUSIONS

We have offered here a quantitative model for the type of stabilization policy that is required in Argentina to slow down the rate of inflation while maintaining the growth of output and the level of real wages. No pretense is made of providing a complete explanation of inflation in Argentina. Although we have been concerned solely with establishing a basis for monetary and wage policies, we do not believe that these are sufficient in themselves to stop inflation. Important structural bottlenecks exist, not least of which is the long stagnation of agricultural output, and these may explain why growth without some inflation can not be expected.[17] But the conversion of the rates of inflation associated with the relative price changes that may be required for bringing about structural changes in the Argentine economy into rates far exceeding 30 percent per annum implies the presence of a vicious wage-price spiral and an endemic process of monetary creation. Indeed, the point may have been reached in Argentina where rapid inflation is itself a major barrier to necessary structural changes. Thus, the desirable prior aim may well be to reduce the rate of inflation so that the important structural problems can be dealt with.

To this end a combination of at least three different policy instruments is necessary: control or at least influence over money-wage negotiations; control over bank credit to the private sector; and control over total money supply. In practice, the second of these is most easily achieved, since the government can enforce liquidity controls on the commercial banks and determine the rediscount policy of the Central Bank. But as experience has demonstrated, restriction of bank credit without restriction of money wages tends to have a depressive effect on output. Moreover, restriction of bank loans to the private sector does not necessarily imply restriction of total money supply, although such may certainly be the government's intention. Government has had much less success in restricting the increase in total money supply than

17. There were signs through early 1966 that agriculture had begun to make progress.

in restricting the growth of private-sector credit, with the frequent result that recession in output is accompanied by acceleration of inflation.

The main problems clearly lie in the fields of wage policy and public-sector deficits. Imposition of a wage policy is difficult in all countries, but it is particularly difficult in a country that has a long history of rapid inflation. Wage bargainers have come to base their price expectations on experiences of past inflation; they bargain for corresponding future wage increases. Businessmen, too, expect prices to go on rising at the same or even faster rates in the future as in the past, and they grant money-wage demands on the basis of these expectations. Whatever may have been at the root of inflation when it first started, the fact can hardly be disputed that expectations play a large role in the continuance of current inflation. Acceptance of a wage policy is further complicated by the fact that over the last ten years or so changes in money wages have tended to lag behind price changes in time: workers have constantly found themselves in a position of striving to catch up. In these circumstances it is difficult for them to accept the argument that by limiting their wage increases to something less than the previous year's price increases they will not be accepting a fall in real wages in the current period. By cooperating in this way, they would seem to be permanently accepting a deterioration in their relative position.

An important precondition for a reduction in the wage-price spiral is a much greater degree of exchange-rate stability than has been experienced in recent years. Frequent and large devaluations have been employed to improve agriculture's terms of trade and export performance, but the low short-run supply elasticity of agriculture, combined with the great importance of agricultural products as the principal wage goods, has given rise to strong pressures for increased money wages, which have proved impossible to restrain. Serious inflationary pressures have consequently been set up, and agriculture's early gains have soon been wiped out.

A reduction of inflationary pressure in the Argentine economy will be made much easier if large exchange-rate devaluations aimed at reducing imports and increasing agricultural exports are avoided. In turn, policy must aim at a realistic rate of industrial growth in the short or intermediate run so as to prevent the growth of imports from outstripping the growth of foreign-exchange earnings and capital inflows from abroad. In the long run the government must aim at eliminating or reducing the foreign-exchange bottleneck by raising output and lowering the cost profile of traditional agricultural exports, as well as by developing nontraditional ones.

The budgetary problem is essentially one of reducing the size of the deficit and establishing a market for government debt. Reducing the deficit requires substantial administrative changes in tax assessment and collection, which are, in fact, taking place. A more ticklish problem is the reduction and elimination of the deficits of the public enterprises, particularly the railroads. No Argentine government has yet succeeded in this area. As for creating a market in government debt, this depends primarily on the government's ability to stop inflation itself and therefore has probably a limited part to play in stabilization policy.

Despite the many difficulties involved, a progressive stabilization policy remains the best solution. The alternative is to produce a massive and prolonged depression in the Argentine economy in the hope of eventually destroying inflationary expectations and providing a basis for a more stable price level in the future. Politically and in good conscience, this approach is not feasible. A recession in output tends to put pressure on the government to relax its restrictive policy and to promote growth instead. Usually its promotion is taken to excess, at which point a balance-of-payments problem re-occurs, because the consequent growth of output implies a faster growth of imports than the growth rate of exports can sustain. Credit restriction and massive devaluation again become necessary.

The wise policy is to aim at a rate of growth of output that is sustainable in the long run. Such a rate will be determined by the long-run growth of exports and therefore by the long-run growth of agriculture.[18] Almost certainly output will have to grow more slowly than it did in the years preceding 1959 or in 1960 and 1961. Given a sustainable rate of growth, the task of government should be to produce a progressive decline in the annual rate of increase in money wages, while still providing sufficient credit to the private

18. An increase in the flow of foreign aid would help stabilization policy since, by allowing more imports, it would directly and indirectly reduce pressure on the price level.

sector to avoid a liquidity squeeze. Success in reducing the size of the budget deficit will then enable a progressive reduction in the rate of growth of the money supply, so that in time the price level will become reasonably stabilized.

We must conclude by reemphasizing an earlier point — namely, that the model of the Argentine economy presented here is essentially short-run and assumes that no shortages of capital or labor exist to hinder the growth of output. Consequently, the illustrative stabilization strategies considered here also assume that capital and labor will continue to be in excess supply during the periods of their operation. This may not be the case, particularly as far as capital is concerned. In that event, the economy would not behave in the way described by the equations of the model; nor would the stabilization strategies necessarily remain appropriate. A new model might become necessary. Even so, it seems likely that money, credit, and wage policies will remain essential ingredients of an overall stabilization policy, even if the economy approaches full employment of some resources.

Part III

FISCAL POLICY

Richard M. Bird

8

~~~~~~~~~~~~~~~~~~

Sales Taxation and Development Planning — Colombia

Colombia in late 1963 was in serious fiscal difficulty. Following a substantial devaluation in December 1962 and some unfortunate domestic policies in early 1963, inflation was proceeding at a faster rate than the country had ever experienced. The national public finances approached collapse as expenditures grew rapidly, owing chiefly to a substantial statutory wage increase that added 30 percent to labor costs in the public sector, while revenues lagged well behind, in part because about one-half of the current income of the national government came from income taxes based on the much lower money incomes of 1962. It seemed clear that something had to be done at once to close this fiscal gap, and a 20 percent surcharge on the income tax due to be paid in 1963 and 1964 was chosen as the best way to increase government revenues quickly. This surcharge, however, was considered only a temporary expedient — primarily because of the attitude of the powerful organized business community, which paid over one-half of the income tax and thus of the surcharge. A more permanent fiscal change seemed necessary to avoid another fiscal crisis as soon as the surcharge lapsed. The desired change was found in the introduction of a general sales tax, legislated in 1963 to go into effect in 1965 when the income-tax surcharge was to disappear. The immediate occasion for the intro-

NOTE: I am grateful to John Sheahan, David Felix, Oliver Oldman, William Rhoads, and Olaf Saetersdal, as well as other colleagues in both Colombia and the United States, for helpful criticisms of early drafts of this chapter.

duction of the sales tax in Colombia was thus the fiscal crisis of 1963 and the desire to avoid similar crises in the near future by widening the base of the national tax system.[1]

One object of this chapter is to appraise the adequacy of the Colombian sales tax in achieving its primary avowed purpose of transferring more resources from the private to the public sector. My major concern, however, is the structure of the tax — rates, exemptions, treatment of capital goods, imports, and exports — as well as the impact of this structure on the allocation of resources. Although the major immediate consequence of the sales tax was clearly a reduction in private consumption and investment, a similar effect on spending could have been achieved in other ways, such as by continued income-tax surcharge or a different kind of sales tax. With regard to its long-run effects on development, therefore, the sales tax introduced in Colombia must be appraised on the basis of its effect on income distribution, the balance of payments, and the production and consumption of various types of goods rather than on its aggregate impact alone. The analysis of the structure of the sales tax is preceded by a brief discussion of the background of the Colombian tax and of its actual operation in 1965.

BACKGROUND AND DEVELOPMENT OF THE SALES TAX

The first serious mention of a general sales tax in Colombia in recent years appears to have been made in the General Plan of Economic and Social Development issued by the government in 1962, which recommended almost precisely the form of general sales tax that was subsequently introduced: "It is suggested that the establishment of general taxes on the sales of industrial products and similar taxes on consumer goods imports, especially of non-essential goods, be considered as a way to discourage the growth of demand. These taxes can be established at the manufacturing level,

---

1. An essentially short-run focus of this sort is an almost inevitable accompaniment of major fiscal changes in developing countries, or even in any country. As John Due noted, "Perhaps more than any other tax, the sales tax has been introduced as a measure designed to raise large sums of money quickly, under the pressure of financial emergency." Due, *Sales Taxation* (Urbana: University of Illinois Press, 1957), p. 30. However, this fact of political life should not preclude better integration of new taxes with other economic policies than is now the case in most countries.

complemented with taxes on competitive imports, or at the whole-sale level." [2]

The first real attempt to implement this suggestion came in the fiscal crisis of 1963, when the President was given extraordinary power by the Congress "to establish national taxes on sales of finished goods effected by producers or importers." The tax rates were to range from 3 percent to 10 percent, with exemptions for food items *de consumo popular,* school texts, drugs, and exported products. In a speech supporting the request for the extraordinary powers, the Minister of Finance had stated that a general sales tax was the only means by which a lasting stability could be imparted to Colombia's precarious public finances. He alleged that Colombia's reliance on direct taxes was far too heavy for a country at her stage of economic development and that a sales tax would redress the balance between direct and indirect taxes. Furthermore, the needs of development required that pressure on the few payers of income tax and on industrial investment be lessened. "This tax," he said, "is designed to increase the number of taxpayers and to distribute among them in an equitable manner the support of the State, to which as a moral and civic duty all citizens must contribute." [3] Any regressive element was thought to have been removed by the exemption of food. Similar arguments were repeated many times by other supporters of the sales tax.

A brief digression is in order here to dispose of the argument about Colombia's undue reliance on direct taxes. This argument — always popular with politically articulate taxpayers in Colombia — is superficially strong, for the income tax accounts for about 50 percent of national government current revenues and about 30 percent of public-sector current revenues, excluding the important decentralized institutions. However, Colombia takes a relatively small proportion of the national income in taxes, even compared to other countries in Latin America, so that income taxes amount

2. Departamento Administrativo de Planeación, *Plan General de Desarrollo Económico y Social* (Cali, 1962), pt. I, p. 442. (All translations from Spanish in this chapter are mine.) Earlier attempts at "sales taxation" in 1914 and 1942 amounted only to excise taxes on selected commodities and apparently had no influence on the form of the 1965 tax. See Jonathan Levin, "The Effects of Economic Development upon the Feasibility of a General Sales Tax: A Case Study of Colombia," unpub. May 1966, pp. 1–6.

3. Carlos Sanz de Santamaria, *Memoria de Hacienda presentada al Congreso Nacional de 1963* (Bogotá: Imprenta Nacional, 1963), I, 140–44.

to only about 4 percent of national income, and personal income taxes to about 2 percent. These figures are by no means out of line for a country at Colombia's level of development. More important, the use of comparative data of this sort as evidence of the need for a change in any particular country is in general neither convincing nor helpful. There is no apparent reason, apart from the hortatory one, that the tax structure of the "average" or "representative" poor country should be taken as a model for other poor countries.

A manufacturer's sales tax with four rates of 3, 5, 8, and 10 percent was finally enacted by Decree 3288 in 1963. Compensating taxes at similar rates were levied on imported products. One important change from the government's original intentions was made in that the date at which the tax came into effect was postponed one year, until January 1965. This delay was the cause of considerable confusion and uncertainty both to the public and to the tax administrators themselves. Press criticism of the impending tax grew in volume and strength in the closing months of 1964, most of it focused on the disastrous impact expected on prices and the cost of living as a result of the sales tax. Surprisingly little was said at first about the probable regressive impact of the tax. Although the equity issue was later raised in connection with the general strike, especially by the Communists, it never received the prominence given to the alleged influence of the sales tax on prices.[4] Since the cost-of-living indices rose only about 1 percent from December 1964 to February 1965, the immediate impact of the tax on prices appears in fact to have been slight, as had been earlier calculated theoretically. It is impossible to discern the magnitude of the effects later in 1965 because of the deepening foreign-exchange crisis and of general inflationary pressure over the year.

Great efforts were made within the Congress to repeal the sales tax before it could come into effect: a repealing measure actually passed the lower house but was defeated in the Senate. Even within the Ministry of Finance it was generally believed until the last moment that the sales tax would never come into force. This belief, together with the lack of staff and funds and all the other ills com-

---

4. *Voz Proletario*, January 21, 1965, p. 16, carried a full-page advertisement in socialist-realistic style, headed "Down with the tax on consumption," a slogan that at this time appeared on walls all over Bogotá. A leaflet was circulated which brought in the Yankees by declaring that the sales tax was imposed only "to satisfy the Colombian exploiters and the gringo monopolists."

mon to tax administration in most underdeveloped countries, meant that administrative preparation by the ministry to issue the necessary regulatory decrees, to process sales-tax registrations, and to check that firms obliged to register did so in fact were no more advanced than public acceptance of the tax.

On January 1, 1965, however, sales taxation came to Colombia. Although the overall effect on prices appears to have been minor, no doubt there were some abuses in the form of speculative price rises, and considerable feeling developed against the tax because of its alleged impact on the cost of living. This feeling culminated in the two major trade unions' scheduling a general strike for the end of January, intended as "a collective demonstration against the sales tax, the high cost of living, and other governmental measures that have brought about confusion and general uneasiness." [5] Whereas the imposition of the sales tax was the occasion for the strike threat, it was hardly the principal cause, for an atmosphere of uncertainty and doubt had long been building up in the country.

At the last minute the general strike was called off because the government agreed to convene a high-level study commission, representing all major interest groups, to discuss its fiscal problems, including the new sales tax. While this commission was sitting, the tax was in fact revised somewhat, particularly by clarifying the scope of the exemptions, so that the commission's final report, presented in March 1965, recommended essentially the retention of the existing tax with further minor changes in exemptions and rates.[6] Although these proposals were embodied in a draft law presented to the Congress in 1965, interest in the sales tax had by then so much lessened that this draft was never discussed in Congress. By January 1966, when a new revenue-raising increase in certain sales-tax rates was proposed, the earlier controversy appeared forgotten by everybody. In essence, then, the basic structure of the sales tax remained unaltered from its first proposal in 1963 until the rates were increased and the base revised by executive decree in June 1966. The tax discussed in this chapter is the one in force throughout 1965.

On the administrative side, although the Director of National

5. Official statement of the two labor groups (the UTC and the CTC), reproduced in *El Tiempo,* January 9, 1965, p. 7.
6. Comisión de Estudios, *Asuntos Económicos y Fiscales 1965* (Bogotá: Talleres Gráficos del Banco de la República, 1965), p. 211.

Taxes stated in January 1965 that he expected about 40,000 manufacturers and importers to have to register for sales-tax purposes, by the end of the year only 5,137 firms had actually registered, and less than one-half of those registered were bothering to pay the tax when due.[7] Since the basic steps in the administration of any sales tax are, first, to get a full list of required taxpayers and, second, to make sure that those registered pay on time, the Colombian tax authorities obviously had some difficulty in getting the sales tax under control. Actual collections for 1965 appear to have been about half the potential yield (see Table 8.1). After over a year of relative

Table 8.1. Colombian sales tax collections, 1965.[a]

Rate	Amount (millions of pesos)	Percentage of total sales tax collected
10%	53.90	13.7
8%	12.52	3.2
5%	78.13	19.9
3%	246.62	62.8
Interest	1.45	0.4
Total	392.62	100.0

Source: Collection Subdivision, Division of National Taxes, Ministry of Finance.

[a] These figures include all collections recorded by the Tax Division up to the end of February 1966. Although some delinquent returns were received subsequently, the above total includes about 98 percent of the total sales tax collected on sales in the calendar year 1965. Since the potential yield for 1965 may be estimated as about 650 million pesos, the actual collection efficiency may be put at around 60 percent. If anything, this estimate is probably a little high, since the base estimate, details of which are not given here, is conservative.

inaction, however, many of these problems were tackled by a new Sales Tax Administrator, who was made directly responsible to the new Tax Director, and there is good reason to expect that sales tax administration can be made considerably more effective within two or three years. To the extent that administrative effectiveness improves, the structural difficulties with the tax are likely to become more important.

7. The director's statement is in *El Siglo,* January 21, 1965, p. 2. The Departamento Administrativo Nacional de Estadística estimated in 1964 that there were 11,674 manufacturers alone in Colombia, or double the number of manufacturers *and* importers registered for the sales tax in 1965. *Boletín Mensual de Estadística,* no. 180 (March 1965), 16. The evidence of the first year's collections indicates that mostly smaller firms had failed to register.

TRANSFER OF RESOURCES TO THE PUBLIC SECTOR

The passage from the Colombian General Plan quoted above justified a general sales tax by the need to restrain the growth of consumer demand in order to free for public investment and consumption an increasing share of the increase in output resulting from economic growth. The usual economic case for general sales taxation in a developing country is that the resources needed for the expanding public sector can not be obtained simply by increased direct taxation of the wealthy, since their share in aggregate consumption is too small. Mass-commodity taxation is therefore needed to check the *potential* increase of consumption even though the object of tax policy is not to curtail the *actual* consumption of the masses.[8] The need for additional restraint on consumption seemed obvious to many in Colombia in 1963. According to the General Plan, for instance, increased consumption, including government consumption, was supposed to absorb only 48 percent of the expected increase in final supply, production plus imports, in the 1959–64 period. In fact, the *absolute* increase in consumption had reached the planned 1964 figure by 1963, but final supply had increased so much less than expected that this absolute increase in consumption absorbed 87 percent rather than 48 percent of the total increase in available output over the 1959–63 period.[9] The result was that the investment figures and growth rates actually realized in this period were well below those planned.

A rough idea of the magnitude of the problem and the possible usefulness of the sales tax in solving it may be obtained from a simple illustrative calculation. Suppose the aim of tax policy in 1963 had been to divert the planned 52 percent of the expected increase in

8. See Raja J. Chelliah, *Fiscal Policy in Underdeveloped Countries, with Special Reference to India* (London: Allen & Unwin, 1960), pp. 85–90, for a good discussion of the role of mass-consumption taxation in development finance. Nicholas Kaldor in a famous study of Chile, reprinted in his *Essays in Economic Policy* (London: Duckworth, 1964), II, 242–67, concluded that the Chilean upper-income groups saved so little that heavy direct taxation of their incomes could in fact serve a useful role in suppressing "inessential" consumption. However, the scanty distributional data for Colombia cited later in this chapter do not appear to support the applicability of Kaldor's finding, so that the conventional (Chelliah) view is perhaps more applicable there.

9. Calculated from data (in 1958 prices) in *Plan General de Desarrollo*, pt. I, p. 135, and in Banco de la República, "Cuentas Nacionales" for 1950–61 and 1962–63 (mimeo, Bogotá, n.d.), tables 6–7.

total supply to the public sector from private spending. Additional taxation of about 440 million pesos (in 1958 prices) would have sufficed for this purpose. The sales tax, had it been imposed in 1963, would have yielded perhaps 200 million pesos, or about half the needed amount.[10] On this reckoning the effective rate of taxation on taxable items, which comprise only about one-fifth of total consumption, would have been about 5 percent — a figure slightly above the actual weighted average rate on taxed goods in 1965, apparently owing to greater evasion in the high-rate items. For the sales tax to have held private spending to the assumed target level, this effective rate would have had to be more than doubled — for example, by a combination of more effective administration and higher statutory rates. Nevertheless, if demand restraint were the aim of the sales tax, this crude calculation indicates the tax should play a useful role in future fiscal policy, particularly since many of the more income-elastic goods are included in the sales-tax base.

Two objections may be made to the above analysis. First, if the scarcity of foreign exchange is the dominant constraint holding back Colombia's development, a reduction in the investment-savings gap, whether achieved by a sales tax or by any other means, will not permit increased growth and therefore is not a useful aim for a growth-oriented policy. In fact, however, the sales tax, both by its general impact on the distribution of private income and through particular structural features, would tend to affect the balance of payments by altering the composition of final demand and the allocation of investment resources between import-substituting, export, and other activities. The transfer of resources to the public sector also constituted an important change in the composition of demand, probably resulting in a decreased demand for imports, since much public development spending has a low import component. In addition, whether or not there is a general "savings gap," the greater elasticity of public expenditures than of public revenues with respect to changes in national income ensures that there is a *public* savings gap that the sales tax will help close.

A second possible objection is to the assumption implicit in this argument that the government will in fact put the resources obtained

10. This figure is a very rough estimate based on detailed calculations made for 1964 in current prices and assuming collection efficiency of 60 percent (see note to Table 8.1).

through the new tax to good use from the point of view of economic development. I simply *assume,* as was in fact true in Colombia, that it was decided to raise a certain amount of new tax revenue through increased sales taxes and then explore how this in fact affects some of the complex of means and ends customarily called "economic development." In order to reduce the range of issues being considered, these effects of the sales tax are compared in a necessarily rough and qualitative way to those that might have resulted from a collection of excise taxes yielding the same revenue. Neither the alternatives of increased progressive income taxation, other nonconsumption taxes, or inflation, nor the problem of whether foreign-exchange shortage or savings shortage is the dominant constraint on growth, can be treated systematically within the scope of this chapter.

STRUCTURE AND INCIDENCE OF THE SALES TAX

The most obvious structural feature of the sales tax is its differential rate scale. The basic tax rate is 3 percent on the manufacturer's sales price. This rate applies to all products manufactured in Colombia or imported, except for items specifically exempted or taxed at one of the three higher rates.[11] Since imports are taxed at the time they are sold by the importer, they are in fact generally taxed on their wholesale price. Table 8.1 shows the yield of each rate in 1965 and illustrates the great revenue importance of the basic 3 percent rate.

The administrative argument for a uniform sales tax rate is very strong. For example, a uniform 4 percent rate on the same tax base would yield approximately the same revenue as the present system. Rate differentiation always increases the possibilities of evasion, as

11. The miscellaneous nature of the items selected for high taxation is clear from a partial listing: the 5 percent rate applied to cosmetics, pens, sporting goods, stoves, heaters, dishes, jeeps, small trucks, motorcycles, bicycles, silk fabrics, bracelets, umbrellas, domestically produced alcoholic beverages (later ceded in part to the departmental governments and consolidated with other excise taxes); the 8 percent rate to radio and television sets, records, tape recorders, cameras, and various electrical consumer durables; and the 10 percent rate to jewelry, automobiles, boats, safes, watches, hairdryers, tobacco products, chiclets, and imported dishes, imported glassware, imported olive oil, imported canned food, imported clothes, and imported liquors. The June 1966 reform increased the 5 percent rate to 8, and the 8 and 10 percent rates to 15, but made no significant changes in the classification of taxable items.

well as the incentive to evade, perhaps especially when the higher rates mainly affect imported goods that are already being smuggled in considerable quantities, as is true to some extent in Colombia. As a rule, however, the desire to encourage import-substitution industries prevailed in the setting of sales-tax rates. The result is that in several instances imported products are taxed at rates two or three times higher than similar goods produced in Colombia.

The differentiated rate structure of the sales tax may be advocated in terms of its probable effects on either resource allocation or income distribution. To take the allocative argument first, specific excise taxes or differential rates are often said to be inherently less desirable than more general sales taxes or uniform rates, because the less general a tax is, the more it "distorts" the allocation of resources from that determined by market forces. A general tax, whether on income or sales, which disturbs only the choice between leisure and consumption, is thus preferable to a partial tax, which also disturbs the choice between different commodities. One may argue equally well, however, that if the economy is not in an optimal position before the tax is levied, as was clearly true for Colombia, then a set of differential excise taxes with the "right" distorting effects, tending to shift the economy to a better position by correcting existing distortions in the price system, may be superior in its allocative effects to any general tax. For example, it may be argued that increased taxes on leisure activities, such as travel, or on leisure complements, such as cameras and alcoholic beverages, will induce consumers to work more and thus reduce the loss of "welfare" from the introduction of the sales tax. Much of the rate structure of the Colombian sales tax may in fact be justified on these rather esoteric grounds, although in Colombia as elsewhere, given the vast number of unknowns in any such formulation, there is much to be said for a general tax as providing less scope for worsening rather than offsetting existing distortions. The discriminatory treatment of imports provides a good instance of the distortions that may result when a selective tax is imposed without adequate consideration of the probable direction of its effects on resource allocation.

Much more important in the actual design of the rate structure in Colombia was the distributional argument for progressive rates of commodity taxation. Underdeveloped countries such as Colombia with sharply class-differentiated consumption patterns often conform closely to the assumption implicit in progressive indirect taxes that some goods are better indices of taxpaying ability than others.[12] In more advanced countries, where one man's "luxury" is almost always another man's "necessity," there is no such single-value scale on which goods can be ranked for tax purposes.

To some extent the items chosen to be taxed at higher rates (see note 11) can be explained by the desire to tax consumers progressively in relation to income. For the most part, however, given the unequal income distribution and the difficulties of enforcing progressive income taxes, really high taxes on domestic luxury goods appear never to have been seriously considered in Colombia. One reason for this neglect is perhaps that the government has never made a good case to its constituents — who are essentially those who buy luxury products — that such taxes are needed. Another reason might be the desire to foment domestic production, whether of luxury or other goods. In any event, well-off Colombians seem as much concerned as well-off people everywhere with how the anonymous poor spend their money, for increased liquor and tobacco taxes — which in terms of income are clearly regressive — figured prominently among the items on which higher rates were levied in the new sales tax. Probably over one-half of the 1965 yield of the 5 percent rate came from beer alone, and about 80 percent of the yield of the 10 percent rate was from tobacco products (see Table 8.1) — both items being already heavily taxed mass-consumption goods and "luxuries" only in the most moralistic sense.

Apart from the attempt to make the rate structure more progressive, the desire to reduce the regressivity of the sales tax as a whole, as well as its impact on the cost-of-living index and hence on the inflationary spiral, led to the unconditional exemption of a number of "basic necessities." The probable impact of these exemptions is indeed to reduce considerably the regressivity of the

12. See also Richard Goode, "Taxation of Savings and Consumption in Underdeveloped Countries," *National Tax Journal* (December 1961), reprinted in Richard Bird and Oliver Oldman, eds., *Readings on Taxation in Developing Countries* (Baltimore: Johns Hopkins Press, 1967), pp. 248–49. Any rate differentiation inevitably taxes people on the basis of their preferences rather than their ability to pay, for even when the consumption pattern of the well-off group is distinct, as is generally true in Colombia, the individuals within the group differ considerably in their tastes for taxed goods.

sales tax. In addition, however, the complete exemption of food, drugs, school materials, and all services had various effects on resource allocation, none of which were discussed in designing the tax and some of which are not particularly desirable in a developing country.

The major such effect, perhaps, was to shift still more of the demand of the low-income groups to the now relatively cheaper food items. If the supply of agricultural commodities is relatively inelastic in the short run, as has often been argued, food prices will tend to increase as a result of this shift in demand. Even if production is in fact increased in response to the increased demand, prices will rise if agriculture is an increasing-cost industry, as seems likely. Exemption of food is thus certain to put some upward pressure on food prices insofar as consumers are able to substitute untaxed food for taxed nonfood consumption. Unfortunately the available data do not permit the testing of this hypothesis. Since agricultural production is an activity that uses relatively few imported inputs, any minor demand shift induced by the change in relative prices would be useful in relieving a little of the pressure on the balance of payments.

The sales tax is also likely to shift more demand, and hence productive resources, to the products of small-scale, often inefficient industries — which are not actually exempted by law but are so difficult to control that they must enjoy considerable exemption in fact — and to the exempted luxury service industries. One might expect a particularly high elasticity of substitution between taxed luxury commodities and such untaxed luxury services as entertainment, travel, and servants, though there is no good evidence in Colombia of the elasticity of substitution in response to tax-induced changes in relative prices. One interesting exception is the apparent rapidity with which smuggling, especially of cigarettes, and illegal domestic production, especially of liquor, appears to expand in response to increases in domestic prices of these goods, although the data again are not adequate to permit a satisfactory analysis.[13]

13. The unsatisfactory evidence available for most countries usually indicates a relatively low elasticity of substitution, apart from the substantial geographical shifts sometimes found with local sales taxes. See, for example, on India and Britain, I. M. D. Little, "Tax Policy and the Third Plan," in P. N. Rosenstein-Rodan, ed., *Pricing and Fiscal Policy* (London: Allen & Unwin, 1964), pp. 560–61. One study of Pakistan, however, indicated a considerable shift in the compo-

The shift in demand induced by the tax once again is in general toward less import-intensive industries — except for such important luxury items as foreign travel, telephones, and smuggled goods — so that the net effect on the balance of payments is presumably favorable, though at the cost of giving a relative stimulus to some of the less efficient parts of the domestic economy. The exclusion from the base of the sales tax of the sorts of services consumed by

Table 8.2. Incidence of the sales tax on 1953 employee income brackets[a] (weighted average of seven cities).

Monthly income in pesos	Tax base as percent of total expenditures[b]	Average rate on taxable expenditures	Tax as percent of total expenditures	Tax as percent of average income[c]
100–199	25.0	2.88	0.72	0.91
200–299	24.7	3.20	0.79	0.96
300–399	24.7	3.21	0.77	0.79
400–499	24.0	3.33	0.81	0.81
500–599	24.3	3.38	0.74	0.69
600–699	21.9	3.33	0.79	0.78
700–799	23.7	3.46	0.82	0.77
800–899	23.7	3.59	0.85	0.75
900–999	22.7	3.48	0.79	0.67
1,000–1,499	23.4	3.55	0.83	0.60
1,500 and over	25.7	3.74	0.96	—

Source: Jonathan Levin, "The Effects of Economic Development upon the Feasibility of a General Sales Tax: A Case Study of Colombia" (unpublished, May 1966), p. 22. Levin based his calculations upon a 1953 consumer expenditure survey reported in Departmento Administrativo Nacional de Estadística, *Economia y Estadística* (November 1958), and upon the text of the 1965 sales-tax law.

[a] Excludes tax on liquor, which was never effectively collected by the national government in early 1965 and was later ceded to the departments.

[b] Percent of total expenditures not excluded by exemptions for food, drugs, and services.

[c] For each of the seven cities, the several hundred consumption items covered in the 1953 survey were first classified according to the sales-tax rate applicable. Since item detail was not available by income brackets, the average tax rate for each of the fifteen major expenditure categories was then calculated for each city and applied to the expenditures shown for each income bracket. Next, the resulting tax was calculated as a percentage of average total expenditures in each income bracket and as a percentage of income at the mid-point of the bracket, and the result for each city was then weighted appropriately to obtain the national averages given in the table.

sition of imports away from those products taxed at higher rates even within commodity groups such as consumer durables. Stephen R. Lewis, Jr., "Sources of Change in Revenue from Import Taxes, 1954–63" (Pakistan Institute of Development Economics, Research Report No. 25, mimeo, January 1965), pp. 20–22.

the well-to-do also considerably moderates the apparent income-group progressivity of the differential rate scale.

Table 8.2 contains a partial estimate of the incidence of the sales tax on the incomes of salaried urban workers in Colombia.[14] In general, these figures indicate that the tax base, which is determined by the exemptions, was probably more or less proportional with respect to expenditures and that the effective tax rate on taxable expenditures, which includes the effect of the differential rates, was therefore mildly progressive with respect to total expenditures, though still regressive with respect to income. The basic 1953 consumer budget data used in this table — the only such data available — almost certainly do not reflect adequately the current consumption patterns of either the politically articulate middle and upper classes or the large rural population living close to subsistence level. Even for urban employees, the sales-tax collection data in Table 8.1 indicate that less has been collected at the hightest rates than one would expect on the basis of the consumer budget data, so that the incidence of the tax was in fact more regressive than indicated in Table 8.2, where it is assumed that all taxes decreed in the law were collected.

Apart from these narrow criticisms of the results, most tax economists would now consider that this sort of analysis of the incidence of sales taxation is rather simple-minded. Recent studies in advanced countries indicate clearly the importance of allowing for factors such as variations in family size and age composition, as well as the great difference in results because of the transitory component of income in different cross-sectional income groups; but no more sophisticated analysis is possible on the basis of information available in Colombia.

The assumption of full forward-shifting, particularly of the differentiated rates, is also questionable. Since less than one-quarter of total consumption expenditure is covered by the sales tax, it is clearly a very partial tax and hence unlikely to be shifted forward fully even in the long run. The obvious frictional difficulties of supply adjustments in Colombia would also hinder forward-shifting, as might the import-licensing system if the effect of limiting supplies by quantitative restrictions is to make supply completely inelastic

14. In this paragraph I rely almost entirely on the exhaustive analysis in Levin, "Feasibility of a General Sales Tax," pp. 20–28.

both before and after taxation so that the imposition of the tax simply reduces the economic rent of the importer.[15] The part of the sales tax that is not shifted forward in higher prices will also alter the distribution of income on the sources side, though not in any readily apparent, systematic way that can be taken into account here.

Despite the deficiencies of the incidence analysis in Table 8.2, one may perhaps conclude safely that the Colombian sales tax is not too regressive as sales taxes go. A recent study of the incidence of taxes levied by all levels of government in Colombia in 1961 indicated a mild and uneven progression of the tax system with respect to income — the tax "burden" ranging from 10.9 percent for the lowest quartile of income recipients to 12.7 percent for the highest. The extremely unequal income distribution before taxes, with the upper 1 percent of the labor force receiving 12 percent of total income, while the lower 64 percent got only 26 percent, was thus more or less unchanged by the tax system before the introduction of the sales tax.[16] This outcome would not be altered much by the sales tax, except to make the extent of income redistribution through the tax system even less impressive than before. Whether this result is good or bad is in part a matter of personal value judgment and in part depends on one's view of the role played in development by the reduction of income inequalities.

ALTERNATIVE FORMS OF COMMODITY TAXATION

Since the sales tax was not severely regressive in its incidence, the intended object of the differential rates and exemptions was at least in part achieved. However, it would have been quite feasible to design an alternative system of commodity taxation that was easier to administer, whose incentive effects were more consciously

15. Ghulam Mohammad Radhu, "Relation of Indirect Tax Changes to Price Changes in Pakistan," *Pakistan Development Review* (spring 1965), p. 55.

16. The study, directed by Milton Taylor and sponsored by the Joint Tax Program of the Organization of American States and the Inter-American Development Bank, is *Fiscal Survey of Colombia* (Baltimore: Johns Hopkins Press, 1965); see pp. 221–28 on income distribution. Although the analysis of incidence in this report is not definitive — some assumptions used to distribute taxes by income quartiles appear weak, and no attempt was made to estimate the distribution of benefits from government expenditures — further refinements would probably not change the picture substantially.

designed to be beneficial, and which had a more progressive incidence. The alternative of a mixed set of luxury excise taxes — including taxes of various sorts on services such as foreign travel, telephones, and housing (through heavier property taxes), as well as taxes on income-elastic luxury consumer goods such as gasoline and consumer durables — could definitely have had a markedly greater effect in reducing income inequality, assuming this goal is desirable in Colombia on both sociopolitical and long-run economic grounds.

Insofar as there is already a substantial middle-class consuming group in Colombia, the sales tax as now established should sop up part of their increasing consumption, since it falls on some of the price-inelastic, income-elastic goods that they will try to buy with increased incomes, although not on the important services such as housing and entertainment. But this goal, too, could have been attained more effectively by a markedly progressive set of selective excises.[17] Partly because a major component of such a set of excises would be a much heavier gasoline tax — which would be progressive in incidence as well as helpful in rationalizing Colombia's transport structure by increasing the private cost of motor transport — the long-run yield of the suggested selective system may be estimated, at least for the next decade, as very similar to that of the more general sales tax in practice, given the administrative difficulties of the sales tax. Substantially heavier use of the traditional sumptuary taxes (tobacco, beer, liquor, gambling) can not be equally recommended, because of the proven relative income-inelasticity of most of the relevant tax base and the presumably undesirable regressive incidence. The increased use of taxes on luxury commodities should also work toward a more desirable long-run pattern of industrial development.

On balance, therefore, increased use of selective excise taxes,

17. Taylor, *Fiscal Survey of Colombia*, p. 217, makes a similar point. Estimates of the income-elasticity of demand for various consumer goods in Colombia in the early 1950's appear in United Nations Economic Commission for Latin America, *The Economic Development of Colombia. Analyses and Projections of Economic Development*, Vol. III [Geneva: Department of Economic and Social Affairs, 1957], pp. 67, 260, 424, 427. No mention is made here of the differential impact on savings of different degrees of progressivity, in part because of the complete lack of information and in part because of the probable constancy of the *marginal* propensity to consume over fairly broad income ranges in Colombia as elsewhere.

with heavy emphasis on luxury goods and services, would have been a more advisable policy for Colombia to adopt in 1963 than a general sales tax, particularly in view of the considerable administrative difficulties in effectively implementing the sales tax. The fact that few taxes require as high a degree of cooperation from taxpayers for effective administration as does a general sales tax was not fully realized; it is in fact surprising that even a moderate degree of success was achieved with such a major tax innovation in the conditions of Colombia in 1965.

The form of sales tax adopted — based in part on a similar tax in Chile and, more remotely, on an earlier one in France — was not adapted to the realities of Colombia's market structure, which is characterized by an abundance of the small firms and self-employed persons that are so hard to control in all countries. The sales-tax law, like the income-tax law, was couched in such sweeping and unenforceable terms that it inevitably became in large part yet another tax on "honesty" and bigness. These problems could have been alleviated by arbitrary administrative devices such as the exemption of small firms in certain lines of business or limited use of a *forfait* system of agreed taxes, as in France, but no consideration was given to such compromises. The relative success of the sales tax in its first year, in spite of its structural defects and the weakness of the administration, may well indicate that there is a larger reservoir of taxpayer honesty and willingness to cooperate in Colombia than is generally believed. If so, this discovery reinforces the importance of improving the degree of certainty with which taxpayers can confront the law, through, for instance, provision of much more information to taxpayers and clarification of the numerous obscure points that remain in the present law.[18] Unfortunately it is all too easy to forget such simple matters in the excitement of major tax reforms, with the result that the reforms often fail to live up to expectations.

18. Adam Smith's second canon of taxation would thus appear to be as applicable to Colombia in 1966 as to England in 1776: "The tax which each individual is bound to pay ought to be certain and not arbitrary. The time of payment, the manner of payment, the quantity to be paid, ought all to be clear and plain to the contributor, and to every other person. Where it is otherwise, every person subject to the tax is put more or less in the power of the tax-gatherer, who can either aggravate the tax upon any obnoxious contributor, or extort, by the terror of such aggravation, some present or perquisite to himself." Smith, *The Wealth of Nations* (New York: Modern Library, 1954), p. 778.

Even if a system of excise taxes had been imposed in 1965, of course, a move to a more uniform, general sales tax and a consolidation of the special excises would undoubtedly have become advisable for Colombia in time, as economic activity and consumption patterns became more diversified. Since it was in fact decided to impose a general tax instead of excises, a wholesale-level tax instead of a manufacturers' sales tax would clearly have been a better choice in Colombia. The three reasons for preferring a wholesale-level tax are the importance of imports in the tax base, the importance of small, artisan-type manufacture, and the apparent importance of the forward integration of manufacturers into wholesaling and retailing functions, especially since the sales-tax law defines as "manufacturers" those firms that have goods made to their specifications such as Sears, Roebuck.[19] Imports probably constituted over one-third of the potential sales-tax base in value terms in 1965, and the problem of achieving neutral or correctly biased taxation of imports and competing domestic production is considerably more difficult with a manufacturer's tax than with a wholesale tax, because the former will almost always tax imports on a higher price than competing domestic manufactures. Although artisan manufacture accounted for only 13 percent of manufacturing production in the early 1960's, almost two-thirds of the non-artisan manufacturing establishments had less than ten employees and proved almost equally difficult to deal with, as the sales-tax registration data cited earlier indicate. A tax collected at the wholesale level — that is, on sales to retail stores by both wholesalers and manufacturers — would have concentrated perhaps 90 percent of the tax base in the much smaller number of regular wholesale establishments — about one-half the number of nonfood manufacturers, not counting artisan-type establishments. The relative distortions introduced by pyramiding and by differences in the channels of distribution employed by competing firms would also be less with a wholesale tax simply because the tax is levied one stage later in the production-distribution process. Rather than scrap the potentially powerful fiscal instrument of a general sales tax and

19. Levin, "Feasibility of a General Sales Tax," pp. 29–44, discusses these points in detail and similarly concludes that a wholesale-level tax would be more suitable for Colombia. He would not, however, agree with the earlier proposal for a more selective excise tax system, in part because his analysis of this alternative focuses entirely on the shrinking tax base afforded by the traditional sumptuary items (p. 36).

start again with a more immediately optimal set of excises of the sort proposed here, it would now probably be better to work within this framework toward a wholesale-level tax.

SALES TAXATION AND THE BALANCE OF PAYMENTS

The introduction of the sales tax in Colombia in 1965 influenced in several ways the size and composition of the import flow needed to maintain any given growth rate. The change in the composition of final demand, a change owing to the transfer of resources to the public sector and to the allocative effects of the rate and exemption structure, should on balance have reduced the demand for imports and hence increased slightly the potential growth rate at any given capacity to import (assuming the capacity to import to be the dominant constraint on growth). The mild regressivity of the tax exerted some influence in the opposite direction. The most important impact of the sales tax on the balance of payments, however, at least potentially, is its more direct effect on the allocation of investment resources between domestic, import-substituting, and exporting industries.

The fact is now generally recognized that for allocative efficiency it is better to tax goods whose consumption is to be discouraged without regard to national origin than to levy discriminatory taxes on imported goods alone. If luxury consumer goods, for example, are taxed by high import duties, as in Colombia, the inefficient domestic production of these products is encouraged by the height of the tariff wall. An obvious remedy is to place compensating high luxury taxes on domestically produced luxury goods as well.[20] Once a country's industrial sector reaches the size of Colombia's, the

---

20. Taylor, *Fiscal Survey of Colombia*, p. 200, makes the same recommendation but continues (p. 217): "The introduction of a system of internal excises would facilitate this shift in emphasis (from import substitution to the development of exports) by increasing the prices of internally manufactured luxury and semi-luxury goods, which would, in turn, reduce their demand and channel investment funds to the production of more essential goods or exports." This argument may be vulnerable to criticism. For example, some excises will be demand-absorbing rather than demand-shifting, depending on price elasticities, and there is no guarantee that resources frustrated or deterred from investment in "undesirable" activities will be automatically invested in "desirable" activities — they may instead be consumed or sent abroad. Similar objections can be made to the related argument in Chelliah, *Fiscal Policy in Underdeveloped Countries*, p. 89. Here I assume that high duties on luxury imports can be enforced and that domestic production can, at least to some extent, provide adequate substitutes for imports.

allocative case for equal taxes on domestic and imported goods becomes strong.

At present the sales tax, by levying higher rates in some instances on imported consumer products than on competing domestic products, adds only marginally to the pressure for inefficient import substitution exerted through the tariff and licensing system. In the future, however, the government will almost certainly have to rely more heavily on the sales tax for revenues to replace the declining foreign-trade taxes, and the distortions of internal taxation will therefore become more important. Although the persistent public finance gap in Colombia still leads to the use of tariffs on consumer goods such as automobiles for revenue purposes alone, their importance is bound to disappear in the future as the goose (trade) that laid the golden egg (revenue) is finally killed by its own progeny, the protected import-substitution industries. Import duties fell from 32 percent of national government current revenues in 1951 to 17 percent in 1964, and a further fall can be confidently projected under present policies, in part as the result of a shift in the composition of imports toward the more favorably treated raw materials, spare parts, capital goods, and "cost-of-living" or wage goods. In the past, the resulting need for increased revenues has been partly satisfied by exchange-rate profits and by increased income taxes on the industrial sector. These two sources do not seem likely to grow as fast in importance in the future, so that increased personal income taxes and commodity taxes appear to be the most promising revenue sources for the next few decades.

Increased use of internal consumption taxation, however, poses a problem for industrialization policy. At present, most import-substitution industries are, on the one hand, protected by high tariffs applied to final output and, on the other hand, subsidized by low tariffs charged against their raw and intermediate materials and against capital goods, which puts domestic production of these less protected inputs at a relative disadvantage. If current trends continue and tariff revenues decline further in importance, does it seem reasonable to suppose these protected industries can support sales-tax rates of, say, 40 or 50 percent — tariffs on final products now range from about 40 to 300 percent — without great, and very likely successful, pressure for higher offsetting protective walls and hence more distortion of consumption and investment patterns?

Further, would even the captive Colombian market pay such high prices, given the existence of the substantial untaxed service sector and of competition from smuggled goods? At the present time it seems probable that the answer to such questions would be no and that there is not a *politically* feasible way in which the declining revenues from imports can be offset by increasing revenues from similar domestic consumption goods. The same pressures that maintain the distorted tariff structures, which in turn call for compensating luxury excises, thus tend to produce tax structures with the same distortions, for once artificial fostering has induced the creation of a relatively inefficient industry in world terms, its output can not easily be taxed at rates similar to the protecting tariffs themselves without killing off the industry — an outcome not likely to be politically acceptable. This very argument was discussed in the process of designing the present sales tax: the only reason that even heavier discriminating taxes were not levied on imports competing with domestic production was the fear of encouraging illegal imports still further. The emergence of politically powerful and protected domestic industries thus has placed the government on the horns of a small fiscal dilemma, as well as adding to the country's balance-of-payments problem by making imports more necessary to maintain employment and production levels and making exports more costly owing to the high cost of domestically produced inputs.

In short, since the same factors that shape tariff policy also shape tax policy, it is often not practical to propose tax policies to offset distortions introduced by bad tariff policies. The possibility of instituting a system of high luxury commodity taxes in Colombia in the near future is therefore small. The only feasible long-run solution remains the reduction of differential tariff protection with a corresponding increase in taxes on consumption goods regardless of national origin. In the interval the problem will be to prevent the internal taxes that must be imposed to keep government revenues up to the required level from accentuating present problems and making their eventual resolution more difficult. All elements in the present sales tax that tend to discriminate against imports — except perhaps for imported capital goods — should therefore be removed as soon as possible in order to exert a little pressure in the right direction.

This analysis must be qualified to take into account the fact that the way the sales tax is administered tends to offset certain bad effects of the sales-tax law. Like most sales taxes nowadays, the Colombian tax is levied on the "destination" basis, taxing only products consumed in Colombia and therefore exempting exports and taxing imports. The destination principle is not fully implemented in Colombia, however, in part because of the impossibility of fully compensating exporters for all sales taxes incurred — for instance, taxes on machinery used in export production — and the allied problem of controlling abuses of the exemption privilege. More important, a number of administrative difficulties on the import side at present lead to economic effects quite different from those implied by the formal structure of the sales tax.

Since the sales tax is levied on imports only when the importer resells the goods, direct imports for own use are actually *favored* relative to domestic production — not, as the above argument implied, discriminated against either by higher rates or by being taxed on a higher base price, including the distributor's margin. Machinery, for example, is commonly imported directly by the user, so that domestic capital goods are at a relative disadvantage. Such an obvious means of legal tax avoidance was not long neglected by astute Colombians, who quickly began to change normal trade channels — as in the importation of automobiles — into apparently direct imports to avoid sales tax. To curb this abuse, the government was recently empowered to impose the tax at the time of import rather than of sale. Administratively it would probably be advisable to tax all imports, including those for resale, at the time of import: this system would put the tax proceeds into the national treasury sooner and more certainly. However, this administratively desirable system would restore the relative disadvantage of imports compared to domestic production, especially if the final tax base for resold imports continued to be wholesale or even retail price rather than manufacturer's price. In this case the advance payment of tax at the time of import could be credited against the tax due on resale. For final consumer products at least, the economic results of this administrative improvement do not appear beneficial in view of the distortions of present tariff structures. Paradoxically, the existing loophole by which imports can easily avoid the sales tax may even provide a desirable incentive to the rationalization of

Colombia's production structure by, in effect, putting relatively higher taxes on competing domestic production. Whether this benefit offsets the loss of revenue is questionable. A rough guess is that on balance it would be preferable to tighten the administration of the tax on imports. In the case of imported capital goods, however, increased effective taxation is definitely to be recommended on incentive as well as revenue grounds.

THE TAXATION OF CAPITAL GOODS

The present Colombian sales tax applies to capital goods at the basic 3 percent rate. Although one may think the taxation of capital goods will affect resource allocation adversely from the point of view of development, there has been no discussion in Colombia of the allegedly evil effects of capital-goods taxation put forth in conventional public finance literature — effects such as distorting the choice of productive techniques, raising the price of final goods, and increasing the cost of investment. As Due put this traditional view in his treatise: "Taxation of such items as capital equipment is particularly objectionable because of its restrictive effect on investment. This result is most objectionable in periods of deflation, in undeveloped countries, and in others in which the modernization of industry is of particular importance." If the basic economic purpose of taxation in a developing country is to raise investment levels, as is often assumed, there appears to be little point in taxing investment and thus lessening the substitution effect in favor of saving that would otherwise result from consumption taxation. Conventional public-finance analysis would therefore lead to a recommendation for the unconditional exemption of machinery designed specifically for production use at least; exemption conditional upon use would be better but so difficult to administer effectively in Colombia that the unconditional approach has more merit.[21]

---

21. Due, *Sales Taxation*, pp. 42, 271–73. A third alternative exemption technique, which also has the considerable merit of clearing up the present murky situation on the tax treatment of intermediate products such as fuels and lubricants, is to permit the crediting of taxes paid on all products incorporated in a cost-accounting sense in the final product against tax due on the sale of the final product. A partial move in this direction was made in the 1966 tax reform. This sort of problem could be resolved in the same way with exporters and importers.

The actual reasons for taxing capital goods in Colombia were, as in other countries, both the need for revenue — the potential revenue from capital-goods taxation in 1965 was about 60 million pesos, or 10 percent of the total potential yield — and the increased administrative complexities that would arise from still more exemptions. These are valid reasons in the Colombian context. Moreover, even in the limited terms of conventional public-finance analysis, it may be argued that precisely because a tax on investment is in a sense equivalent to a tax on saving, the taxation of capital goods makes the final incidence of the sales tax with respect to income less regressive on balance.[22] This argument carries more weight if the sales tax is viewed not as a tax on consumption but as an indirect income tax — for example, a way of reaching income that would escape direct income taxes — as indeed appears to be the case in Colombia.

The taxation or nontaxation of capital goods should not really be decided on its own merits within the sales-tax framework alone. From the broader viewpoint of development policy, there is in fact a strong economic argument *for* the taxation of capital goods. A subsidy on the importation of machinery and equipment is in effect granted through the exchange-rate system. The combination of this subsidy with the relatively high cost of labor in organized industry, owing in part to Colombia's advanced labor and social-security legislation, means that there is already a considerable tendency to overmechanization in Colombian industry, as indicated by the frequency of considerable idle machine capacity.[23] If the actual price of labor is in fact above its equilibrium price, the resulting bias in the capital intensity of new investment will be redressed, if only in small part, by the taxation of capital goods. Since even after the 1965 devaluation the exchange rate at which equipment can be imported is almost certainly less than the shadow exchange rate, the small tax on capital goods should still work in the right direction. This appears to be a clear case in which an "unneutral" tax tends to alter the results of the price mechanism

22. This point is developed in Clara K. Sullivan, *The Tax on Value Added* (New York: Columbia University Press, 1965), chap. 1.

23. Cf. Lauchlin Currie, *Accelerating Development: The Necessity and the Means* (New York: McGraw-Hill, 1966), p. 34. Currie considers the availability of these idle capital and labor resources the key factor in the development strategy that Colombia should follow to escape at least temporarily from the foreign-exchange bottleneck and to achieve a breakthrough to sustained growth.

in a direction conducive to sounder long-run development. The tax on capital goods should therefore be retained as long as the exchange rate is overvalued.[24]

Actually, three groups of inputs are involved in this problem: imported capital goods, domestic capital goods, and other domestic inputs that may be substituted for capital. The distortion argument for taxing imported capital goods is clearly a strong one: it greatly strengthens the administrative case for rectifying the present easy evasion of the tax on imported machinery and equipment. Insofar as the market cost of labor is above its social cost, there is also reason to tax domestic capital goods. Yet there is also a case for levying a discriminatory tax on imported as opposed to domestic capital goods. If the scarcity of foreign resources is holding back Colombia's development, it does not appear sensible to have a price structure that encourages the adoption of import-intensive, capital-intensive methods of production. Although the potential role of the sales tax in alleviating this complex of problems is a minor one, the influence of the present system is exerted in the correct direction and should be maintained and strengthened.

The pattern of investment in Colombia was thus affected both directly and indirectly by the imposition of a general sales tax — directly by the increase in noninflationary public investment and by the taxation of capital goods, indirectly by the shift in the nature of final demand as a result of the effects of the tax on income distribution and of the differential taxation of different products. The effects of the sales tax were definitely not neutral, and on the whole, they were biased in the right direction, tending to shift resources to less import-intensive uses.

THE SALES TAX AND DEVELOPMENT POLICY

The probable relation of the sales tax to the pattern and rate of economic growth in Colombia, given the existing economic pol-

24. This argument was developed at more length in John Sheahan's chapter in this volume. The offsetting effect of the tax on capital goods is somewhat weakened by the fact that the additional cost of a depreciable asset due to sales tax can be written off against income tax, according to prevailing depreciation schedules. Although the treatment of contractors under the sales tax is obscure, it also appears that most building materials are taxed, while the labor of construction is not, so that construction, as compared to other forms of capital investment, is made relatively more attractive by the tax. Though biased correctly toward labor-intensive, import-intensive investment, this incentive is perhaps not needed in Colombia today.

icies and distortions, may be summed up in the following six propositions. First, the sales tax will clearly enable the government to finance more investment in a noninflationary way, assuming the proceeds are properly used. It will also tend to restrain aggregate private spending substantially. The more efficiently the tax is administered, the more striking will be these results. The same transfer of resources and demand restraint, however, could have been achieved equally well by other tax changes.

Second, the incidence of the sales tax on income distribution in the private sector is moderately regressive. This result does not seem desirable, given the present degree of income inequality and the small amount of redistribution through the pre-existing tax system. A more acceptable pattern of incidence could have been achieved by more selective taxation of certain commodities and services. More selectivity would also have been desirable on incentive grounds, particularly to offset the distorting effects of high tariffs on luxury imports. Structurally, the incidence of the present sales tax reflects its exemptions and rates: the incentive and distributional effects of exempting "necessities" seem beneficial, in general, but the results of exempting all services are less desirable.

Third, the present treatment in the sales tax of imported goods as compared to domestic production would in general, if effectively administered, add to the distortions imposed by the tariff and license systems on the pattern of investment in Colombia. The tax should therefore be altered to tax the consumption of specified goods without regard to their national origin. An exception should be made for imported capital goods against which some discrimination appears desirable at this stage of Colombia's industrial development, and administration should be tightened to achieve this end. The problem of correcting the distortions in consumer-goods production resulting from the past policy of fostering any and all import-substitution industries is a political, not a technical, one. Despite this bias in the present tax and its regressive incidence, which has a similar effect, the import bill needed to maintain any growth rate is probably less now than before the imposition of the sales tax because of the change in the composition of final demand toward less import-intensive public investment and toward the agricultural and service sectors.

Fourth, if the fiscal gap existing in the early 1960's *had* to be closed by increased commodity taxation — in itself a debatable proposition — a more selective system of excise taxes would have been preferable to a general sales tax on most counts, even at this stage of Colombia's development. The yield of a properly designed selective system would be comparable to that of the present tax. Since a general sales tax was in fact imposed in 1965, it would now be more advisable to improve it than to attempt a drastic revision. The base of the tax should be changed to make it a whole-sale-level tax in order to simplify administration, especially with regard to the treatment of imports, which are thus put on an equal footing with domestic production; and taxes on domestic production of luxury consumer goods should be increased as much as possible. The taxation of capital goods should be retained, and every attempt should be made to increase gasoline taxes and to put whatever special taxes are possible on such services as foreign travel and luxury residential housing.

Fifth, the declared goals in imposing a sales tax in Colombia in 1965 were to restrain private demand, to increase government revenues, to discourage luxury consumption, and to reach indirectly incomes now escaping taxation, which implied that the tax should have a progressive incidence. The first two goals were achieved in part by the present sales tax, as they could have been by a number of alternative taxes; the last two goals were not, though they could be if the changes proposed in the second and fourth propositions above were made.

And last, not everyone will consider the goals recommended here to be appropriate for Colombia at this time. Depending on one's view of the kind of development problem facing the country, other aims might be to relieve the pressure on the balance of payments, which would reduce the foreign-resources constraint on development, or to encourage the use of more labor-intensive methods of production, which would reduce the need for imports as well as increase the present low absorption rate of additions to the urban labor force. Both of these objectives will be approached a bit more closely as a result of the imposition of the sales tax.

All the effects mentioned here are undoubtedly small in quantitative terms; but the point is, given the relatively few and limited policy instruments available to the government in most underdeveloped countries, even these minor effects ought not to be neglected. At the very least, gross incompatibilities with the avowed objects of development policy ought to be avoided. Even if an optimal development strategy is too much to expect on the basis of existing knowledge in many countries, an internally consistent one should be possible, as indicated by this simple analysis of one particular tax policy. Since other Latin American countries, such as Argentina, Chile, and Brazil, have similar sales taxes and development policies, most of the above points are perhaps equally applicable to them, although the details of the analysis will be different for every country.

A final lesson for development taxation from the Colombian experience with the sales tax is that trying to resolve urgent short-run revenue problems before thinking about the long-run development implications of tax structure is not usually advisable. To a considerable extent, basic tax changes can be made only in times of acute fiscal crisis, so that there is a real danger that if tax reform is regarded merely as something incidental to be gotten out of the way before going on to the *important* task of long-range planning and spending, bad economic incentives may inadvertently be established. Once an economic policy is set up in a certain way, it generally becomes much more difficult to change than if it had been set up properly in the first place: tax policy, like tariff policy, should therefore be constructed so far as possible with an eye not only to the revenue it will produce but also to its probable effects on the structure of incentives in the economy and on the key variables affecting development possibilities and patterns — such as balance of payments, composition of final demand, size of the public sector, income distribution, and productive techniques. Since the initial cost of good design is generally no higher than that of bad design, and the potential long-run benefits are so much greater, more attention to the design of new taxes would be a worthwhile investment for most developing countries today.

Part IV

AGRICULTURAL DEVELOPMENT

Walter P. Falcon and Carl H. Gotsch

9

Lessons in Agricultural Development — Pakistan

In contrast to earlier writings on economic growth, which concentrated mainly on industrialization, recent works show an almost universal acceptance of the key role that agriculture must play in the development process.[1] Yet in spite of this emphasis, there are startlingly few agricultural success stories among the less developed countries. The agricultural bottleneck unfortunately remains one of the largest and most widespread development problems of the 1960's.

Compared with the general stagnation in the agricultural sector of most underdeveloped countries, the recent growth of rural Pakistan makes an extraordinary case study. In the first dozen years of her separate existence (1947–59) Pakistan was typical of much of the underdeveloped world. Many of her initial difficulties can be traced to the political and social upheavals accompanying partition. The rest, however, involved the familiar pattern of reliance on an age-old agricultural technology and of constraints on key agricultural inputs such as water and fertilizer. The result was that the agricultural sector, which comprised about 80 percent of the population and contributed about 55 percent of the GNP, grew at a rate less than the expansion of population.

During the Second Plan period of 1960/61 to 1964/65 the agricultural picture changed radically. (See Table 9.1.) The annual

1. See, for example, J. W. Mellor and B. F. Johnson, "The Role of Agriculture in Economic Development," *American Economic Review* (September 1961), pp. 556–593. W. H. Nicholls, "An Agricultural Surplus as a Factor in Economic Development," *Journal of Political Economy* (February 1963), pp. 1–29.

Table 9.1. Growth of agricultural value added in all Pakistan, 1947/48 to 1964/65 (1959/60 prices).

Items	Trend rates of growth per annum[a]	
	1949/50 to 1958/59	1959/60 to 1964/65
Total agriculture	1.1	3.2
Major crops	1.0	3.6
Minor crops	−1.1	3.6
Livestock	2.2	1.9
Forestry	2.3	3.2
Fishery	6.2	4.9

Source: Government of Pakistan Central Statistical Office, *Statistical Bulletin* (August 1965), pp. 932–33.

[a] Least-squares estimate of "*b*" in the equation $\log Y = a + b \cdot \text{time}$.

agricultural growth rate nearly tripled, rising from 1.2 percent to 3.2 percent, agricultural exports expanded rapidly, and there was a surge in rural private investment. A closer examination of Pakistan's rural transformation is therefore important, not only for an understanding of the past and prospective development of the world's fifth largest country, but also for the lessons it provides for other countries.

Following is a detailed analysis of the magnitude and sources of the recent rural growth. The analysis, which focuses on the Second Plan period, deals separately with each of the two provinces. The monsoon rice-jute agriculture of East Bengal is radically different from the irrigated wheat-cotton-rice culture of West Pakistan; in addition, the factors that accounted for most of the growth in the two regions appear to be quite dissimilar. In both regions, however, government policy played a key role, and particular attention is paid to the policy variables that made the rapid changes possible. The final portion of the chapter consolidates the lessons learned in Pakistan's two provinces during the First and Second Plan periods and indicates their implications for Pakistan's Third Plan as well as for the rest of the developing countries.

WEST PAKISTAN: MAGNITUDE AND SOURCES OF RECENT GROWTH

The general growth in West Pakistan agriculture has been an integral part of the two-period national agricultural performance.

During the years 1947/48 to 1958/59 there were considerable year-to-year fluctuations, but few of the major crops showed significant increases. "Stagnant" was the adjective most often used to describe the rural environment, and to predict a sudden upturn in production would have appeared rash.

But a sudden upturn did, in fact, take place in the 1959/60 to 1964/65 period. One indication of the surge is given by the trends in the national accounts data shown in Table 9.2. From these series

Table 9.2. Growth of value added in West Pakistan agriculture, 1959/60 to 1964/65 (1959/60 prices).

Items	Percent per year[a]
Total agriculture	3.8
Major crops	4.9
Minor crops	4.8
Livestock	1.9
Forestry	3.9
Fishery	9.7

Source: Computed from Government of Pakistan Central Statistical Office, *Interim Report of the National Income Commission* (September 1964), p. 106; 1964/65 data obtained directly from the Central Statistical Office.

[a] Least-squares estimate of "b" in the equation: $\log Y = a + b \cdot \text{time}$.

it is clear that the 4.9 percent annual expansion of "major crops" played the decisive role. Because of their growth and absolute level of importance, and also because the data are much more reliable, most of the West Pakistan analysis will focus on the major crops produced in the Indus Basin.[2]

A more disaggregated picture of the widespread improvements within the crop portion of GNP is given in Table 9.3. The computations show that virtually all commodities recorded a sizable

2. Data for the livestock sectors of both East and West Pakistan are particularly suspect. See mimeographed Pakistan Planning Commission papers by Walter P. Falcon and Carl H. Gotsch: "Growth of Livestock Products in East Pakistan during the Second Plan Period" (May 1965); "Recent Growth of the Livestock Sector of West Pakistan" (May 1965). The fact that livestock contribute as much to GNP as do combined large- and small-scale manufacturing underscores the importance of improving information about the animal-product sector. For discussion of data on the major crops, see Walter P. Falcon, "Reliability of Punjab Agricultural Data," *Statistical Papers* (Karachi: Institute of Development Economics, 1962), and "Farmer Response to Price in an Underdeveloped Area: A Case Study of West Pakistan," unpub. Ph.D. dissertation, Harvard University, 1962.

Table 9.3. Crop production in West Pakistan, 1959/60 to 1964/65.

Crop	Average production (thousands of tons)	Annual rate of growth[a] (percent)
Rice	1,127	7.8
Wheat	4,021	3.7
Bajra	375	6.9
Jowar	247	3.7
Maize	485	3.4
Barley	120	−6.2
Gram	614	—[b]
Other pulses	180	—[b]
Sugarcane	14,757	10.6
Rape, mustard	236	—[b]
Cotton seed	682	7.6
Potatoes	123	9.0
Onions	129	12.0
Other vegetables	730[c]	—[d]
Fruits	980[c]	—[d]
Cotton lint	1,934[e]	7.1
Tobacco	152[e]	6.7

Source: Computed from Government of Pakistan Planning Commission, *Handbook of Agricultural Statistics* (June 1964), pp. 70ff.; 1964/65 data supplied by West Pakistan Department of Agriculture.

[a] Least-squares estimate of "b" in the equation: $\log Y = a + b \cdot \text{time}$.
[b] No significant trend at the 5 percent level.
[c] For the years 1960/61 to 1963/64.
[d] Insufficient data for trend calculation.
[e] Production of cotton lint given in thousands of bales, production of tobacco in millions of pounds.

and consistent growth during the six-year period. Whereas these averages and trends are in themselves impressive, they serve mainly to pose the major question: was the 27 percent trend growth in crop output during the Second Plan period a weather phenomenon, or was there a more fundamental structural transformation accounting for most of the growth? In attempting to answer this question it is useful to examine first the increased use of improved inputs that might explain the growth — that is, to provide a rather crude but descriptive agricultural production function for West Pakistan.

Water. Any analysis of agriculture in West Pakistan must begin with a study of the irrigation system, for except in the relatively small rain-fed area in the northern portion of West Pakistan, the agriculture of the region directly depends on irrigation water from the world's largest irrigation network. This system, the northern portion of which was installed between 1880 and 1930, delivers about 59 million acre feet of irrigation water (m.a.f.) annually to a cultivated area of about 26 million acres. However, production in the Indus Basin area is hampered by water deliveries that are low relative to the area commanded and by the considerable variation in canal discharges. As a result, water is the key input in the basin region, which produces about 80 percent of the total provincial output.[3]

Prior to 1957/58 individual farmers could do little to supplement their meager water supplies. The public canal system was outside the purview of individual decisions, and traditional means of supplementing water supplies, such as the Persian wheel, were too inefficient for large-scale water development. Furthermore, there was relatively little increase in public water supplies at the field level between 1947/48 and 1957/58. To be sure, marginal improvements were effected in the existing canal system, several canals were run somewhat above their designed capacity, and a start was made on several major barrage areas in southern West Pakistan.[4] But these were in part offset by the vagaries in canal flows resulting from the Indus Basin dispute with India.

One irrigation program in the earlier period does, however, deserve special comment. For approximately thirty years the Department of Agriculture had been sinking a limited number of small mechanical tubewells for private farmers.[5] These wells were designed to tap the high-quality underground aquifer or reservoir filled by the leakage of water from canals and rivers. Although the water delivered by the wells was only marginally important — the Department drilled only six hundred wells between 1950/51 and 1954/55 — these installations helped to spread a new water tech-

3. For the importance of irrigation water as an input to production, see Walter P. Falcon and Carl H. Gotsch, "Relative Price Response, Economic Efficiency, and Technological Change: A Case Study of Punjab Agriculture" in Gustav F. Papanek, ed., *Government Policy and Private Enterprise in Pakistan* (Cambridge: Harvard University Press, 1967). Only about 25 percent of the wheat, 1 percent of the cotton, 7 percent of the rice, and 2 percent of the sugarcane are grown on a rain-fed basis in the former Punjab.

4. Although the Guddu and Ghulam Mohammed Barrage projects were begun earlier, little agricultural development was effected by them before the Second Plan period; most will not occur until the Third Plan period.

5. For history, see Ghulam Mohammed, "Private Tubewell Development and Cropping Patterns in West Pakistan," *Pakistan Development Review* (Spring 1965), pp. 1–53.

nology, which was to play a critical role in the Second Plan period.[6]

This description of irrigation in West Pakistan gives only the scantiest picture of a complicated system. Nevertheless, it suggests two important points: that irrigation water was an input with a very high marginal-value product, especially in certain critical periods, and that a tubewell technology, known for years on the subcontinent, had in the First Plan period begun to be disseminated in West Pakistan to farmers *and* to private firms in the business of sinking wells.

Both of these factors were probably necessary conditions for one of Pakistan's most amazing developments during the Second Plan period — the surge in private tubewell installations.[7] In 1959/60 about 1,350 tubewells were installed, of which approximately two-thirds were sunk by private drillers using a simple percussion technique. By 1963/64 the number of annual installations had accelerated to 6,600. (See Table 9.4.) As of July 1, 1965, it was estimated that a total of over 31,500 private tubewells had been installed, primarily in the cotton and rice regions of the former Punjab. Of this total, about three-fourths were powered by diesel engines, the remainder by electricity.[8]

The private tubewells installed were of various shapes and sizes. From a technical engineering point of view many were not very efficient, but they all had one point in common: they were extraordinarily profitable. Installation costs ranged between Rs.5,000 and Rs.12,000, with the shallower electric wells in the rice area at the lower end of the scale and the deeper diesel wells in the cotton area relatively more expensive. Most of these wells were installed

6. For an excellent nontechnical discussion of tubewells in West Pakistan, see R. Revelle, "Water," *Scientific American* (September 1963).

7. Another important factor was the liberalized import policy. Whereas most of the pumps and engines were manufactured locally, the freeing of basic commodities such as pig iron meant that the small shops producing the equipment could acquire the necessary inputs. See W. P. Falcon and S. R. Lewis, Jr., "Economic Policy and the 'Success' of Pakistan's Second Plan" (mimeo, Harvard Center for International Affairs, November 1966).

8. The rapid acceleration in installations was mostly unexpected and unnoticed. As a result, there was some initial controversy about the tubewell data cited here, which were acquired in a census undertaken by the Institute of Development Economics in conjunction with the Department of Agriculture. Later recounts in proposed public tubewell project areas and cross-checks with land revenue and electrical connection records generally verified the accuracy of the original I.D.E. survey.

Table 9.4. Location of private tubewells by district, summer 1964.

District	Total tubewells installed	Total electric tubewells	Total diesel tubewells	No. installed in 1963/64
Gujrat	719	299	420	274
Sargodha	352	181	171	109
Lyallpur[a]	1,063	291	772	301
Jhang	1,540	448	1,092	304
Mianwali	228	107	121	60
Sialkot	2,458	434	2,024	503
Gujranwala[b]	4,234	1,270	2,964	1,170
Lahore	1,607	856	751	504
Montgomery	4,055	1,175	2,880	1,049
Multan	5,148	624	4,524	1,345
Mozaffagarh	443	—	443	142
D. G. Khan	220	—	220	40
Bahawalpur	398	26	372	122
Bahawalnagar	273	3	270	87
Rahimyar Khan	443	9	434	177
Sheikhupura[c]	460	117	343	125
Subtotal	23,641	5,840	17,801	6,312
Former Northwest Frontier Province[d]	359	310	49	88
Southern Zone[d]	1,000	50	950	200
Total private tubewells	25,000	6,200	18,800	6,600

Source: Institute of Development Economics Survey, completed by Department of Agriculture field staff.

[a] Excludes Jaranwala Tehsil, an administrative subdivision of a district, which falls in SCARP I (the first Salinity Control and Reclamation Project).

[b] Excludes Hafizabad Tehsil, which falls in SCARP I, but includes Ferozwala Tehsil of Sheikhupura District.

[c] Estimated number of private tubewells in Sangla Hill and Sheikhupura Tehsils of Sheikhupura District, Hafizabad Tehsil of Gujranwala District, and Jaranwala Tehsil of Lyallpur District. The major parts of these tehsils are included in the SCARP I project area.

[d] Estimated.

by cultivators with 25 acres or more, but there were important exceptions. In the Gujranwala area, for example, perhaps 20 percent of the installations were made by town investors who had little or no land.[9] In addition, there was widespread selling of water as smaller farmers attempted to utilize more fully the capacity of their tubewells.

9. Tipton and Kalmbach Inc., *Salinity Control and Reclamation Program No. 4 Upper Rechna Doab, West Pakistan* (West Pakistan Water and Power Development Authority, June 1965), p. II-3.

By any standard the benefits produced by the tubewells were large, both to the individuals who installed them and to the entire economy. A typical well averaged about one *cusec* in delivery; that is, it could produce about 2 acre feet of water in a 24-hour day.[10] Annual utilization averaged about 2,400 hours, or about 200 acre feet per well. In total, therefore, the estimated 25,000 wells installed during the Second Plan period increased the annual rate of irrigation water available at the field level by about 5 million acre feet.

The 25,000 wells represented an initial investment on the order of Rs.250 million, a sum thought impossible in West Pakistan's traditional agriculture. This investment was an important stimulus to the small-scale machine industry. Whole streets in such cities as Multan, Lyallpur, Lahore, Gujranwala, Sialkot, and Daska are now lined with shops manufacturing pumps and engines, and the skill, ingenuity, and training demonstrated in these shops have been impressive.[11]

Measured in value terms, the returns from the wells were very large. Assuming Rs.1,100 per year as average depreciation charges, and approximately Rs.3,000 per year as operating expenses, the cost per acre foot of water averaged about Rs.20. In the case of cotton, where approximately 2.5 acre feet of water per acre were typically used, the total water cost approximated Rs.50 per acre. The gross return was on the order of Rs.240 per acre, clearly a profitable venture even if the other small costs of production were included.[12] In several more detailed sets of calculations Ghulam

10. Harza Engineering Co., *Reconaissance Survey of Private Tubewells* (West Pakistan Water and Power Development Authority, February 1965), appendix, table 1.

11. Daska is a particularly interesting town in this respect. A visit in 1961 revealed only a few machine shops. By mid-1965 Daska had become one of the main diesel-engine centers: over 120 shops were engaged in production, and output totaled about 250 engines per month.

12. The figure Rs.240 assumes 8 maunds of seed cotton per acre at Rs.30 per maund. (One maund = 82.2 pounds; one Rs. = $0.21.) An alternative calculation of the marginal revenue product of tubewell waters was made by Tipton and Kalmbach, Inc., *Salinity Control*, p. F–26. Using a linear programing framework, they estimated the value of an additional acre foot of water distributed October–May and November–April to be Rs.106 and Rs.97, respectively. The so-called Revelle Report (*Report on Land and Water Development in the Indus Plain* [Washington, D.C.: The White House 1964]), p. 428, also using a programing technique, estimated the value of water at Rs.66 per acre foot for Kharif (spring-planted) season. In their Tarbela Report for Priority Area 1, the Harza Co. obtained even higher estimates of value—188 rupees per acre foot at the

Mohammed estimated that the annual net income from tubewell installations ranged between Rs.3,000 and Rs.17,000, depending on the size of farm and the type of installation; he also reported that the investment payout period was generally less than two years.

General profitability was one major reason for the rapid spread of tubewells. Their acceleration in numbers in the 1960's was also aided by public policy. Rates of return, always considerable, were increased by relatively higher and more stable prices for agricultural products, by lower-cost power as a result of the government's electrification program, and by increased availability of pump materials under the import liberalization program. An acceleration in tubewell numbers might have been expected in any case if they followed the typical pattern of innovation in agriculture, but the increase in profitability speeded the process, as did the demonstration effect of the public tubewell development program.

The exact contribution of the private tubewells to the growth of aggregate agricultural GNP is difficult to measure. Primarily, the difficulty is one of sorting out from short series of aggregated data the three main effects of tubewells: increasing the intensity of cultivation by decreasing fallow, improving the yields per acre, and changing the composition of output, generally toward higher-valued products. Ideally, a measure for each component would be as follows. In the base year t for the ith crop:

$$\text{Production}_{ti} = I_{ti} \cdot C_{ti} \cdot Y_{ti} \cdot A_t$$

where

P = gross production of crop i
I = overall intensity of cultivation (in percent)
C = composition of the cropping pattern (in percent)
A = commanded area
Y = yield per acre

After the installation of the tubewells and assuming, say, year $t + 5$:

$$P + \Delta P = (I + \Delta I) \cdot (C + \Delta C) \cdot (Y + \Delta Y) \cdot A$$

$$\Delta P = (\Delta I \cdot C \cdot Y \cdot A) + (\Delta C \cdot I \cdot Y \cdot A) + (\Delta Y \cdot I \cdot C \cdot A)$$

| Intensity effect | Composition effect | Yield effect |

---

dam, or about 270 rupees at the head of the watercourses. Although there are some differences in assumptions behind these estimates, all the calculated benefits greatly exceed the capital and operating charges of pumping water.

In any case, at the start of the Second Plan period the revised Master Plan indicated that the total field availability of irrigation water (wells plus surface) in the Indus Basin was approximately 59 million acre feet — 34 m.a.f. in the Northern Zone and 25 m.a.f. in the Southern.[13] Therefore, private tubewells alone during the Second Plan accounted for about a 9 percent increase in irrigation water supplies. This increase in water supplies probably had an equally direct impact on irrigated crop production. It thus appears that private tubewells accounted for about one-fourth of the total 27 percent increase in the value of crop output.[14]

This last assumption implies a constant marginal productivity of water with increased supplies. Such a proposition appears reasonable over a 10 percent range, given the large amounts of uncultivated land and underemployed labor and bullocks available in both seasons, the low yields, the cropping pattern changes that this water allowed, and the increased flexibility in total water use that was possible with tubewells. For example, the application of water at certain critical stages because of a tubewell installation was likely to have a very high return. These factors should have been more than sufficient to offset any tendency toward diminishing returns that might have been expected if water supplies had been increased without changing the time distribution. Survey work now in progress in West Pakistan by the World Bank should provide more light on this subject, but pending its completion, the proportionality assumption appears reasonable.

In summary, private tubewells played a critical role in the increased agricultural performance of West Pakistan. During the Second Plan, besides their overall contribution to the gain in the value of major crops, their concentration in the cotton and rice area of the Northern Zone were major reasons for the spectacular recent growth of these commodities.[15] Moreover, the wells gave tangible

13. For the unrevised figure, see Harza Engineering Co., *Program for Water and Power Development in West Pakistan through 1975* (West Pakistan Water and Power Development Authority, January 1964), p. 41.
14. This calculation assumes that 80 percent of gross value of crop production comes from irrigated lands. Thus, .80 × .09 = .072, or about one-fourth of the 27 percent.
15. Multan Division, for example, produces about 40 percent of Pakistan's total cotton. The 10–15 percent annual rates of growth in cotton during the Second Plan were highly correlated with the installation of over 10,000 private tubewells in the region. The rapid growth of rice in the Gujranwala area can be

evidence of the rural resources that were available for high-return, nontraditional investments in agriculture.

Although the private tubewell development is especially interesting because of its large, unplanned nature, it was definitely not the only element in the water-improvement program of the Second Plan. Indeed, the combined *public* tubewell and surface water developments were of almost equal importance. The first Salinity Control and Reclamation Project, covering some 1.2 million acres (SCARP I), reached completion in 1961. It was the first of many contemplated projects in a widespread public program in the field of water development and salinity control that has attracted worldwide attention.[16]

SCARP I consisted of approximately 2,000 deep turbine tubewells, which averaged about 3 cusecs in delivery. In 1963/64 these wells supplied more than 2.5 m.a.f. of supplemental water. This water was pumped in part for the leaching of salts and in part for the consumptive use of plants. The increased acreage, the improved yields, and the changes in the composition of output that the public tubewells permitted were the main factors in approximately doubling output at constant prices (see Table 9.5).[17] These changes in output raised the incomes of cultivators, though the suddenness and concentration of the water input severely strained the marketing, storage, and transportation facilities of the area. In addition to SCARP I, approximately 0.5 m.a.f. of irrigation water was delivered in the last year of the Second Plan by public wells in Chaj Doab (SCARP II).

There were also a few public tubewells operative in the Southern Zone near Khaipur. In the former Sind, however, neither public nor private tubewells were significant factors. Several reasons account for this, the most prominent being the limited area (approxi-

accounted for similarly. W. P. Falcon and C. H. Gotsch, "Agriculture in West Pakistan: Past Progress and Future Prospects" (mimeo, Pakistan Planning Commission, December 1964), pp. 14–16 and Appendix D.

16. See, for example, Revelle, "Water"; the Revelle Report; A. V. Karpov and R. Nebolsine, "Indus Valley: Key to West Pakistan's Future," *Indus* (December 1960), pp. 2–10 (January 1961), pp. 4–13 (March 1961), pp. 4–10 (April 1961), pp. 9–18 (May 1961), pp. 4–20 (November 1961), pp. 4–32 (January 1963), pp. 7–14.

17. For a fuller discussion, particularly of the impact of extension activities in the project area, see U.S. Agency for International Development, "Progress and Evaluation, Salinity and Reclamation Project Number One (SCARP I), West Pakistan" (mimeo, April 1965).

Table 9.5. Increase in net value of production resulting from tubewell installations, SCARP I.[a]

Crops	Irrigated crops (thousands of acres)		Net value of production (thousands of Rs.)		Net change (percent)
	Before tubewells	1963/64	Before tubewells	1963/64	
Rabi[b] (*fall-planted*)					
Wheat, barley	179.2	381.3	8,958	24,787	+178
Pulses	13.4	9.3	323	327	+ 1
Oilseeds	25.4	14.5	330	305	− 8
Berseem	83.2	181.5	29,129	71,642	+146
Fruits, vegetables	5.0	11.3	3,250	7,359	+126
Miscellaneous	8.0	3.2	144	58	− 60
Subtotal	314.2	601.1	42,134	104,478	+148
Kharif (*spring-planted*)					
Rice	104.2	157.3	8,339	14,465	+ 74
Cotton	106.5	91.2	5,964	6,749	+ 13
Sugarcane	61.5	78.9	12,316	23,681	+ 92
Maize	9.3	57.1	547	5,312	+870
Kharif fodder	84.9	134.7	12,308	22,494	+ 82
Miscellaneous	6.6	35.5	117	639	−470
Subtotal	373.0	554.7	39,591	73,340	+ 85
Grand Total	687.2	1,155.8	81,725	177,818	+118

Source: Government of West Pakistan Directorate of Land Reclamation, "Progress of Reclamation in SCARP I (mimeo, November 1962); Government of West Pakistan Land and Water Development Board, "Progress Report for the Period October 1963 to September 1964, SCARP I" (mimeo, 1964); Ghulam Mohammed, "Private Tubewell Development and Cropping Patterns in West Pakistan," *Pakistan Development Review* (Spring 1965).

[a] This table implicitly assumes that weather and other factors were the same in the before-and-after calculations. Although the assumption is not strictly true, the differences do not appear to have been large.
[b] The proportionately large increase in winter crops results primarily from the fact that a substantial part of the area received only summer water prior to the installation of tubewells.

mately 15 percent) underlain with nonsaline ground water directly suitable for irrigation purposes. Also important was the fact that much of the former Sind suffers from regressive tenure arrangements, which tend to discourage investment by the individuals who actually cultivate the land.

The contribution of the public tubewells to agricultural growth, as in the case of the private wells, can not be determined precisely. However, the SCARP I data indicate that increases in output were somewhat less than proportional to improvements in water supplies. Several reasons may be adduced for this nonlinearity. First, the project was too limited, and tubewell capacity did not exist for the critical sowing periods to permit the planting of maximum acreages. This factor, coupled with the pricing of tubewell water on an acreage rather than volume basis, gave rise to extremely high seasonal applications of water per acre. Studies by the World Bank consultants indicated that irrigation deltas of as much as 100 inches per acre were being applied to rice, and 60–70 inches to berseem (Egyptian clover). With these high deltas, returns were bound to diminish sharply at the margin. Second, the SCARP I area was a severely waterlogged, saline area, and that portion of the water used primarily for reclamation purposes had a very low direct effect on production. Therefore, even though public tubewells increased total irrigation supplies in West Pakistan by about 5 percent, they increased output by only about 3 percent during the Second Plan period.

Between 1960 and 1965 progress was also made on a number of public surface-water projects. Included in this category are the Guddu, Ghulam Mohammed, and Taunsa Barrage developments and a number of smaller schemes outside the Indus Basin. Preliminary estimates indicate that approximately 0.8 million acres of new area were affected.[18] In addition, about 2 million cropped acres received increased irrigation deltas. In total, an increase of about 3 m.a.f. of water is estimated to have been utilized for crop production from these sources. However, a firm conclusion must await the final updating of irrigation data.

Although the figure 3 m.a.f. represents approximately 6 percent of the total irrigation supply of the Indus Basin, this water clearly had a less-than-proportionate effect on output. Unlike tubewell installations in settled areas, the development and settlement of new agricultural lands involve relatively long time periods. In the Ghulam Mohammed Barrage area the problems have been particularly difficult, and reported yields in that area are much lower than

18. Pakistan Planning Commission, "Targets of Crop Production for the Third Five Year Plan" (mimeo, January 1965), table 2.

yields in other irrigated areas of West Pakistan. In addition, increased canal supplies have the same time distribution as the existing canal water and thus lack the flexibility of tubewells in meeting critical water demand periods. Hence, the increase in agricultural production from surface-water development between 1960 and 1965 was probably on the order of 3 to 4 percent.

If this 3–4 percent is added to the 10 percent increase in output estimated to have resulted from ground-water development, additional irrigation water accounts for approximately half the increase in crop production during the Second Plan period. In addition, the larger and more flexible water supplies helped to "induce" the use of other improved inputs, especially fertilizer, and permitted a greater utilization of underemployed land, labor, and bullocks.

Fertilizer. Fertilizer ranks second only to water in accounting for the increased agricultural growth during the Second Plan, and performance with regard to this variable was also profoundly influenced by government policy. From a base of 31,000 nutrient tons in 1960/61, consumption more than doubled during the Second Plan period.[19] In 1964/65 it was estimated that about 75,000 nutrient tons were distributed, and the widespread black-marketing of fertilizer that existed throughout the countryside indicated that consumption would have been much greater had more adequate supplies been available.

A comparison of fertilizer distribution in 1965 and 1960 shows an increase of about 45,000 nutrient tons. This amount, although smaller than might have been hoped, made an important contribution to growth. A rough idea of the contribution of this quantity to crop production can be obtained by distributing the fertilizer over the major crops and multiplying by the estimated response factor of each crop. These calculations, given in Table 9.6, indicate that the 45,000 nutrient tons added approximately Rs.200 million of output. When compared with the estimated gross value of major crops in 1960/61 (Rs.4,290 million), these figures show that fertilizers contributed about 5 percent to the gross increase in crop production during the Second Plan.

Other Sources. These rough calculations indicate that about 14 percent and 5 percent of the 27 percent Second Plan growth in

19. Nutrient tons here mean the tons of N, K_2O, and P_2O_5 in the various fertilizers.

Table 9.6. Increase from fertilizer in the value of West Pakistan agricultural output during the Second Plan period.

Crops	Distribution among crops (percent)[a]	Increment in nutrient tons	Tons of output/ton of nutrient[b]	Value of output/ton of nutrient[c] (Rs.)	Total increase in value (millions of Rs.)
Wheat	35	15,750	9	3,700	58.3
Rice	8	3,600	8	4,300	15.5
Minor grains	2	900	10	3,360	3.0
Oilseeds	1	450	6	4,030	1.8
Sugarcane	22	9,900	150	6,720	66.5
Fruits, vegetables	4	1,800	20	6,500	11.7
Cotton (unginned)	28	12,600	4	3,580	45.1
Total	100	45,000	—	—	201.9

[a] Essentially the distribution provided by the Ministry of Agriculture.

[b] These estimates are based largely on Pakistan farm trials conducted by A. Wahhab and J. G. Vermatt. See A. Wahhab, *Fertilizer Trials in Farmer's Fields* (Lahore: West Pakistan Department of Agriculture, 1965). Results are also summarized in the Revelle Report, pp. 118–121.

[c] Subsidized costs of fertilizer to the farmers are about Rs. 900 per nutrient ton. Crop prices are those of the National Income Commission for 1959/60.

major crops can be attributed to water and fertilizer development, respectively. Several other categories of improved inputs remain — plant protection, improved seeds, improved cultural practices, and interaction effects — and their combined contributions are on the order of 7–8 percent for the years 1960–1965.

By the last year of the Second Plan approximately 6 million acres of crops were covered annually by preventive or curative plant-protection measures.[20] On this acreage the average increase in yield was estimated to be approximately 10–20 percent, with the exact contribution dependent on the particular crop, the intensity of infestation, and the number and timeliness of sprayings.[21] Thus, a small part of the 27 percent growth in Second Plan crop

20. Pakistan Planning Commission, *The Third Five Year Plan, 1965–70* (May 1965), p. 421.

21. At a "Third Plan" meeting held in Karachi, December 1964, a group of Pakistan agricultural experts suggested the following effects on yields from plant protection: rice, 15 percent; wheat, 10 percent; minor grains, 15 percent; pulses, 10 percent; sugarcane, 20 percent; oilseeds, 10 percent; fruits and vegetables, 20 percent; cotton, 20 percent; tobacco, 15 percent; other, 10 percent. More research is needed on this important topic. The drop in cotton production in 1964/65 was thought to be directly related to insect infestations.

production is due to the 4–5 million acre increase in the area treated with plant protection. When a 15 percent yield factor is applied to the approximately 15 percent additional cropland covered, over 2 percent of the growth in gross production becomes directly attributable to plant-protection measures. In addition, these measures helped to "save" increases obtained from the other factors.

Much has been written about the necessity for, and potential of, improved seed varieties that are fertilizer responsive.[22] Whereas the future looks very promising in West Pakistan, especially in the case of wheat, most observers agree that improved seeds have been only marginally important in explaining the recent growth performance.[23] That seed improvements did not progress farther may be explained by the lack of good foundation stock for many commodities, bureaucratic difficulties in multiplying good seeds, and several transfers of the responsibility for distribution among government agencies. As a result of all these difficulties, most of the seed improvements came from farmer-to-farmer transfers of relatively better *desi* (local) varieties.

Limited survey work indicates that about 3 million additional acres (1965 relative to 1960) were sown with locally improved seeds during the Second Plan. If a 10 percent yield factor is applied to the approximately 6 percent of the total area affected, it explains slightly less than 1 percent of the five-year growth. Since measuring increases from farm-to-farm seed sales is extraordinarily difficult, the data presented here are very rough and probably conservative. Nevertheless, even if the data are off by a factor of 200 percent, as seems unlikely, the conclusion must still remain that "improved" seeds were not a major element in West Pakistan during the Second Plan period.

22. See, for example, N. E. Borlaug, "Accelerated Wheat Improvement in West Pakistan and the Revolution in Agriculture" (mimeo, Ford Foundation, April 1965); A. C. McClung, "Accelerated Rice Research Program for East Pakistan in Cooperation with the International Rice Research Institute (IRRI)" (mimeo, Ford Foundation, May 1965); R. W. Herdt and J. W. Mellor, "The Contrasting Response of Rice to Nitrogen: India and the United States," *Journal of Farm Economics* (February 1964), pp. 150–160.

23. Experiments with Mexican varieties have indicated a possible tripling of wheat yields under farm conditions. Borlaug, "Wheat Improvement in West Pakistan." The past results were sufficiently impressive that about Rs.0.5 million was allocated in 1965 for the importation and disbursement of approved Mexican varieties to leading West Pakistan farmers.

Several other factors were potentially important in explaining the increase in output not directly attributable to "hard" inputs. Among the most important were the more than additive effects of using several inputs in combination and improved agricultural techniques, including more intensive use of traditional factors of production such as hand and bullock labor.

Both types of factors are, of course, difficult to quantify. However, with regard to interaction effects, experimental studies indicate that the increase in yield resulting from the simultaneous application of fertilizer and water is significantly more than additive. For example, the results of various trials throughout the subcontinent show approximately a 25 percent gain in fertilizer response as a result of an adequate water supply. Such evidence, coupled with Ghulam Mohammed's finding that private tubewell farmers used significantly more fertilizer than nontubewell farmers, leads to the conclusion that the interaction effects from these two inputs alone may have been substantial.

Given the low level of extension efforts during the period, it was unlikely that much of the residual output could be attributed to new methods of plowing, weeding, or harvesting. In most cases, improvement would have required the adoption of better and more expensive implements; the failure of all but the very large farmers to move in this direction is a matter of record. Except for the tubewell, therefore, the technology factor was probably overshadowed by production increases attributable to a more intensive use of hand and animal labor.

There were two reasons for expecting increases in output from a more intensive use of the traditional factors. The first is the effect of an increasing man-land ratio. Population growth for the Second Plan period has been estimated at about 2.5 percent per annum, well above the rate of increase in the availability of new cultivatable area. A second reason for expecting a greater commitment of hand and animal labor is the significant improvement in the prices received by farmers relative to prices paid. Economically motivated farmers would respond to the improved terms of trade by moving upward along their "traditional" production function and hence along the aggregate supply curve. Such an increase in output should be distinguished from increases that result from an upward shift in production functions stemming from an investment in inputs such as water or fertilizer. In summary, these factors seem capable of accounting for the residual growth of approximately one-half percent per year.

In addition to interaction effects and movement along the traditional production function, many other forces were at work. Some of them, such as soil conservation or improvements in livestock breeds, undoubtedly had a positive effect on production; others, such as the increase in waterlogging and salinity, acted negatively. But five years is not a very long period in which to expect significant changes in these variables; on balance they probably tended to cancel one another out.

Recently there has been a great deal of concern about the decline in output due to waterlogging and salinity. However, these problems have been building up for from 50 to 100 years, and a clear distinction must be made between the absolute levels that are a partial explanation of the present low yields in West Pakistan, and the changes in effect that are likely in a five-year period. It is commonly estimated, for example, that the equivalent of from 50,-000 to 100,000 acres are being lost through waterlogging and salinity each year.[24] Over a five-year period this loss would amount to at most 500,000 acres, which would in turn have the effect of reducing the gross value of crop production by a total of only about 3 percent. (See Table 9.7.) While we do not minimize the difficulty of waterlogging and salinity problems, in the short run their effect was small relative to the vast improvements in irrigation.

Summary of Growth Factors. It is possible to explain the 27 percent trend growth in major crop output during the Second Plan period in very broad quantitative terms. The public and private groundwater development increased irrigation water availability by over 8 million acre feet and also improved the time distribution of water to farmers. These qualitative and quantitative improvements helped to increase the utilization of underemployed land, labor, and bullocks and were directly responsible for more than one-third of the increase in crop output. Moreover, the groundwater-development program, and the control that it gave farmers over critical water supplies, helped to "induce" the use of other improved inputs, such as fertilizer. In addition to the 10 percent

24. Revelle Report, p. 63.

Table 9.7. Estimated effects of waterlogging and salinity in the Second Plan period.

Crops	Composition of cropping pattern (percent)[a]	Thousands of acres	Yield (maunds)	Decrease in production (thousands of tons)	Prices 1959/60 (Rs./ton)[b]	Decrease in gross production value (millions of Rs.)
Rice	4	20	10	7.3	545	4
Wheat	28	140	11	56.4	410	23
Minor grains	10	50	9	16.5	350	6
Pulses	15	75	8	22.0	390	9
Sugarcane	6	30	380	417.6	50	21
Oilseeds	9	45	6	9.9	670	7
Fruits, vegetables	9	45	70	115.4	325	38
Cotton	19	95	9	31.3	900	28
Total	100	500	—	—	—	136[c]

[a] Cropping patterns and yields are representative of average data for the Northern Zone. See study prepared by Harza Engineering Co. for West Pakistan Water and Development Authority, *Program for Water and Power Development in West Pakistan through 1975* (January 1964).

[b] Prices are those of the National Income Commission for 1959/60.

[c] The gross value of total production in 1960/61 was Rs. 4290 million.

growth from groundwater, approximately 4 percent of the growth came from surface-water development, 5 percent from fertilizer, and 8 percent from improved seed, plant protection, and other residual factors.

Table 9.8. Sources of increased crop output, West Pakistan.

Sources	Percent per year
Private tubewells[a]	1.4
Public tubewells	0.6
Surface water	0.7
Fertilizer	1.0
Plant protection	0.4
Seeds	0.2
Residual (interaction, improved practices, increased labor intensity, etc.)	0.6
Total growth	4.9

[a] Cropped area increased about 3 percent per year during the Second Plan period. This increase has been included under the water categories, since water, not land, is the binding resource in most parts of West Pakistan.

The sustained West Pakistan agricultural growth, summarized in Table 9.8, was clearly more than a weather phenomenon. The table, and the analysis that underlies it, are important for several reasons: first, it provides a picture of what has happened in rural areas of West Pakistan; second, it draws attention to the major inputs that have been the quick contributors to agricultural growth; and third, it suggests a general technique for projecting future growth. It should be added, however, that the investments directly responsible for growth under the Second Plan depended on the public policy toward agriculture, discussed in a later section.

EAST PAKISTAN: MAGNITUDE AND SOURCES OF RECENT GROWTH

Given the great differences between the irrigated Indus Basin and the monsoon rice agriculture of East Bengal, the close coincidence between the general performance of agriculture in the two regions is striking. After a stagnant period between Partition and the end of the First Plan, the rural sector in the East as well as the West grew remarkably during the Second Plan. In recent years East Pakistan has become almost self-sufficient in terms of rice. This accomplishment again raises the question: does it represent a climatic phenomenon or a structural change in agriculture?

Although the recent agricultural growth has been fairly widespread in East Pakistan (see Table 9.9), the major contributor to growth has been rice. Hence, we will concentrate primarily on

Table 9.9. Growth of value added in East Pakistan agriculture, 1959/60 to 1964/65 (1959/60 prices).

Items	Percent per year[a]
Total agriculture	3.0
Major crops	3.2
Minor crops	2.7
Livestock	2.0
Forestry	3.1
Fishery	2.9

Source: Computed from Central Statistical Office, *Interim Report of the National Income Commission*, Appendix XIV. Data for 1964/65 supplied directly by the Central Statistical Office.

[a] Least-squares estimate of "b" in the equation: $\log Y = a + B \cdot \text{time}$.

this commodity, which contributes nearly 70 percent of the crop value added.[25] Most of the analysis will also be made on the basis of trends, although analyzing the growth rate for agriculture in East Pakistan is far more difficult than in the western province. In East Pakistan general knowledge about agriculture is more limited, and the effect of weather is much more dominant. Floods, droughts, and hurricanes are common occurrences, and the different permutations and combinations of weather effects are almost infinite. As a result of the weather factors, fluctuations about trends in production are very large — as much as 20 percent in successive years. These large, weather-induced variations in production make it difficult to estimate with assurance the magnitude of growth in short periods, and the use of trends or averages over longer periods is also not without its difficulty. Given this caveat, however, what can be observed quantitatively about agricultural growth between plan periods, and about progress within the Second Plan period?

Table 9.10 provides information on rice for three periods. It

**Table 9.10. Five-year average of rice production
by season, East Pakistan.**

Season	Pre-Plan 1950/51 to 1954/55	First Plan 1955/56 to 1959/60 (thousands of tons)	Second Plan 1960/61 to 1964/65
Aus	1,829	1,939	2,437
Aman	5,345	5,231	6,765
Boro	335	344	500
Total	7,509	7,514	9,702

Source: Planning Commission, *Handbook of Agricultural Statistics*, pp. 72ff.

indicates the stagnant nature of rice production during the 1950's, when the decline in production in the Aman season offset the gains in the Aus and Boro seasons.[26] To be sure, Aman production during the First Plan period was marked by floods of record proportions, but the net impression for the period 1950/51 to 1959/60

25. W. P. Falcon and C. H. Gotsch, "An Analysis of East Pakistan Agriculture during the Second and Third Plan Periods" (mimeo, Pakistan Planning Commission, May 1965), p. 52.

26. Aus, Aman, and Boro refer to the different seasonal types of rice, harvested in July, December, and March, respectively.

is one of large fluctuations about a rather steady level.[27] The Second Plan period registered a marked difference, with average production approximately 30 percent greater than under the First Plan and with gains in production for all types of rice.

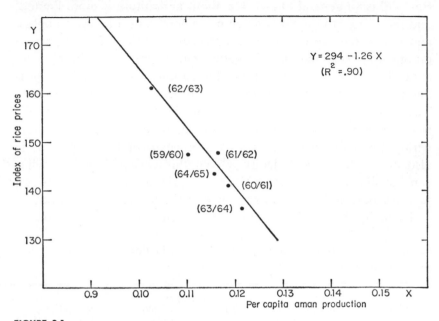

FIGURE 9.1

Relationship between per capita Aman rice production and average February to March rice prices, East Pakistan

It has sometimes been implied, usually without supporting evidence, that the reported growth in East Pakistan rice production during recent years represents nothing more than statistical manipulation.[28] Although the agricultural data do have definite limitations, such a charge does not appear warranted. In the first place, significant improvements have been made in data collection. The start of cluster-sampling for the area data and the beginning of crop-cutting experiments for yield calculations have provided important cross-checks on judgment methods and have generally ver-

27. The year 1955 is one of the "maximum flood" bases used by the East Pakistan Water and Power Development Authority in calculations for flood and drainage projects.

28. See, for example, K. B. Griffen and B. Glassburner, "Financing Development Plans in Pakistan," *Pakistan Development Review* (Autumn 1965), p. 3.

ified their relative accuracy.[29] In addition, the production data are consistent with the price performance of the Second Plan years. This consistency is substantiated by the simple yet revealing price-quantity models for rice shown in Figures 9.1 and 9.2. Figure 9.1

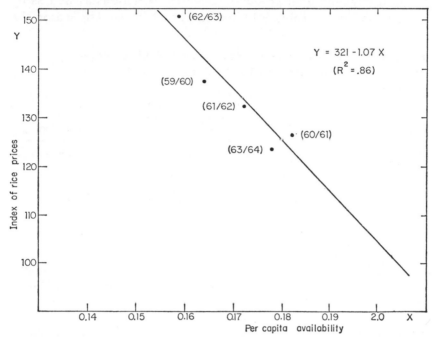

FIGURE 9.2

Relationship between per capita rice availability and annual rice price

indicates the relationship between Aman rice production per capita (the major type of rice and the major contributor to production fluctuations) and the rice price prevailing in forty retail markets between December and February. There is a strong relationship between the variables ($R^2 = .90$), and if the production data had been artificially adjusted to any substantial degree, there would have been little reason to expect this close correlation and the reasonable price relationship it implies.[30] Figure 9.2 shows a similar strong

29. East Pakistan Directorate of Agriculture, "Sample-Survey Operations and Crop-Cutting Experiments Conducted by the Bureau of Agricultural Statistics, 1962/63" (Dacca, 1963).

30. Neglecting certain problems of specification and statistical identification, Figure 9.2 indicates a mean price elasticity of demand for rice in East Pakistan of about −0.75 for the period 1959/60 to 1964/65.

relationship for average annual prices and total rice availability per capita. These models, although very crude, help confirm the fact that a 3.4 percent annual growth in production did occur.

Further insight into the growth in rice production is obtained by disaggregating total production figures by seasons as well as by acreage and yield. Table 9.11 indicates that in the Aus season the

Table 9.11. Annual growth rates of rice yield, acreage, and production by season, 1959/60 to 1964/65.

Season	Percent per annum[a]		
	Yield	Acreage	Production
Aus	0.8[b]	2.1	2.9
Aman	2.5	0.8	3.3
Boro	3.6	2.6	6.2
Total	2.1	1.3	3.4[c]

Source: Computed from Planning Commission, *Handbook of Agricultural Statistics*, pp. 72ff.

[a] Least-squares estimate of "b" in the equation: $\log Y = a + b \cdot \text{time}$.

[b] No trend at the 5 percent level of significance.

[c] In terms of total contribution, Aus rice accounted for about 20 percent of the growth, Aman rice for 70 percent, and Boro rice for about 10 percent.

gain was primarily from acreage increases; in Aman, the season when the acreage sown is already near the physical maximum, the gains came almost entirely from increased yield; and in Boro about 40 percent of the increase arose from additional area and 60 percent from higher yields. Overall, approximately two-thirds of the increase in rice production came from increased yield and about one-third from additional area. Moreover, even though the rate of growth in Boro rice was the most rapid, its contribution to the total growth in rice production was limited (10 percent) because of the relatively smaller size of the Boro harvest. In fact, over 50 percent of the total increase in rice production between 1960/61 and 1964/65 can be explained by improved Aman yields.

Acreage Effects. Boro acreage grew about 2.5 percent per year, or about 25,000 to 30,000 acres annually, during the Second Plan period. One important factor in this growth was the increased irrigation capacity for the winter season. For the seven years ending in 1964/65 the East Pakistan Agricultural Development Corporation (EPADC) supplied approximately 1,500 more power pumps, which irrigated nearly 100,000 additional acres (see Table 9.12).

Table 9.12. Low-lift pump irrigation in East Pakistan.

Year	Number of pumps	Area irrigated
1958/59	772	30,000
1959/60	1,130	49,000
1960/61	1,267	65,000
1961/62	1,543	98,000
1962/63	2,024	133,000
1963/64	2,456	156,000
1964/65	2,238	131,000

Source: J. Hendry and U. Hpu, "East Pakistan Agriculture during the Third Five Year Plan" (mimeo, East Pakistan Planning Department, July 1964), p. 15; 1964/65 data supplied by the East Pakistan Planning Department.

Since it is estimated that from 80 to 85 percent of the area affected by power pumps went into rice production, the EPADC power-pump program alone explains nearly 15,000 acres out of the annual increase of 25,000 acres in Boro rice. Moreover, the assured water supply on the additional acreage was undoubtedly a cause of the increase in average Boro yields.

The remaining increase in area may be attributed primarily to two factors. East Pakistan Water and Power Development Authority (EPWAPDA) schemes accounted for perhaps 3,000 additional acres on an average annual basis. The residual, about 10,000 acres per annum, probably resulted from a continuation of a long, upward trend in Boro acreage from indigenous irrigation methods. This increase, which is more easily measured in the eight years immediately following Partition, when there were few mechanical pumps, seems to have continued throughout the Second Plan period.

Since 1947/48 there has been a steady long-run increase of around 1 percent per year in the Aus area, or about 120,000 acres annually. One reason for this improvement in output was the continued development of indigenous irrigation facilities that permitted cropping in the Aus season. A second reason was the pressure of population and the resulting expansion into marginal lands — marginal in terms of flooding, rainfall, or soil characteristics. Finally, part of the increase in acreage stemmed from the reclamation of land along the coastal areas of southern East Pakistan. For example, some of the large increase in the Barisal District derived from improvements in the coastal embankments. Many of the structures had seriously deteriorated following Partition and the departure of a large number of Hindu *Zamindars* (landowners), who were instrumental in maintaining them. These dikes are gradually being replaced through large, public-investment programs, and they should be an even more important contributor to increased production in the future.

There was very little growth in Aman acreage between 1959/60 and 1964/65. It is clear that land use in that season was already "tight" in a physical sense.[31] Aman rice was harvested from nearly 15 million acres each year, which compares with a provincial total of only about 22 million acres of cultivated area. When crop rotations are considered, and when other Aman crops are deducted, there appears to have been little scope for extension of Aman area during the Second Plan period. To the extent that there was an increase, it was probably a result of labor pressure and, to a limited degree, improvement in coastal embankments.

In total, slightly more than one-third of the growth in rice during the Second Plan came from bringing increased area under rice cultivation. The major causal factors for this acreage increase were the extension of irrigation facilities, the push into marginal lands because of population pressure, limited reconstruction of coastal embankments, and some change in rice culture from a one-crop to a two-crop system of Aus and transplanted Aman.[32]

Yield Effects. Approximately 2.1 percent out of the total 3.4 percent increase in rice production during the Second Plan resulted from yield improvements. Unfortunately it is impossible to distinguish by season the various inputs that were used to improve rice yields, so it is necessary to take up the various causal factors one at a time without regard to season.

Fertilizer was one of the major inputs that raised rice yields during the Second Plan period. In 1958/59 only 7,400 nutrient tons were distributed; by 1964/65 this figure had risen nearly sixfold.

31. J. Hendry and U. Hpu, "East Pakistan Agriculture during the Third Five Year Plan" (mimeo, East Pakistan Planning Department, July 1964), pp. 1–75.

32. The acreage under other major crops, such as sugarcane, jute, and oilseeds, also increased during the Second Plan period. Hence, the increase in the area under rice can not be ascribed to a "substitution effect."

Table 9.13. Fertilizer use in East Pakistan, 1958/59 to 1964/65 (in tons).

Year	N	P_2O_5	K_2O	Total
1958/59	7,141	244	0	7,385
1959/60	12,057	1,036	792	13,093
1960/61	19,423	3,122	492	23,337
1961/62	19,202	3,174	945	22,868
1962/63	23,657	1,936	1,979	26,537
1963/64	35,350	11,397	2,880	48,726
1964/65	33,740	8,610	1,965	44,315

Source: L. Mears and U. Hpu, "The Role of Fertilizer in Increasing the Growth Rate of Production of Major Crops during the Third Plan in East Pakistan" (mimeo, East Pakistan Planning Department, December 1964), Table 5.

(See Table 9.13.) It is estimated that approximately 75 percent of the total fertilizer was applied to rice and that on the average each pound of fertilizer nutrient increased cleaned rice production by about seven pounds.[33] Thus, the 37,000-ton increase in the annual use of fertilizer on rice probably accounted for an increase of about 260,000 tons of rice. On an annual basis, therefore, fertilizer alone accounted for an almost 0.5 percent increase per year in rice yields during the Second Plan period.

Increased plant protection activities were another cause for the improved yield performance. As shown in Table 9.14, the area treated with preventive or curative plant-protection measures increased from 427,000 acres in 1959/60 to 4.8 million acres in 1964/65. Since about 75 percent of the pesticides were applied to rice, approximately 3.3 million additional rice acres were protected during the Second Plan period. When a 10 percent yield factor is applied to the 8 percent of the area covered, pesticides appear to have accounted for about a 0.3 percent per year increase in rice production.

The development of new and improved seeds is potentially one of the most important means for increasing rice yields per acre. Although major improvements are yet to come in East Pakistan, the

33. H. Rashid, "Outline of a Proposed Strategy for Increased Agricultural Growth during the Third Plan Period" (mimeo, East Pakistan Planning Department, November 1964), p. 30; L. Mears and U. Hpu, "The Role of Fertilizer in Increasing the Growth Rate of Production of Major Crops during the Third Plan in East Pakistan" (mimeo, East Pakistan Planning Department, December 1964), appendix I.

Table 9.14. Field crops treated with plant-protection measures, 1959/60 to 1964/65.[a]

Year	Acreage (in thousands)
1959/60	427
1960/61	716
1961/62	919
1962/63	2,115
1963/64	2,811
1964/65	4,781

Source: Government of East Pakistan, Department of Plant Protection, "Progress Report" (mimeo, various monthly issues).

[a] Excludes aerial spraying.

spread of relatively improved local varieties was an important contributor to growth during the Second Plan period. The seed program was initiated in 1952, with a major emphasis at the beginning on seed selection by the specific-gravity method and on seed treatment for fungus.[34] The Department of Agriculture also released a number of improved varieties of rice. By 1964/65 it is estimated that farmer-to-farmer sales, plus very limited distribution by government agencies, permitted about 20 percent of the rice area to be covered by the better-quality rice seed.[35] Apparently these improved seeds produced yields about 15 percent greater than yields from the usual local varieties. A combination of these yield and acreage factors suggests that, between 1959/60 and 1964/65, seeds accounted for an annual increase in rice production on the order of 0.5 percent per year. This calculation may in fact be conservative. Certainly, the potential for seed development was large. As Rashid stated: "No less than sixty improved varieties have been successfully introduced by the Directorate of Agriculture in the last 15 years . . . The improved Aus and Shail transplanted Aman varieties yield about 20 percent more than the majority of local varieties. In 1957/58, the improved varieties really caught on . . . and very soon covered big areas . . . By 1961/62, there was a definite increase in production, at least half of which is attributable to seeds."[36]

34. A. Alim, *Rice Cultivation in East Pakistan* (Dacca: Food and Agricultural Council, 1956), pp. 42ff.
35. By 1964/65 over 3.2 million maunds of rice seed were being treated annually by the Department of Agriculture.
36. Rashid, "Proposed Strategy for Increased Agricultural Growth," p. 26.

Labor, Technology, and Rural Works. The combined effects of fertilizer, plant protection, and improved seeds have been estimated to account for about 1.3 percent out of the total 2.1 percent yield increase per year. If another 0.1 percent yield effect is added as a result of more controlled water supplies from irrigation and drainage facilities, about 0.7 percent per year still remains to be explained by other factors.

One explanation for this residual growth centers around the expanding population and the increased ratio of agricultural labor force to cultivated acreage. Between 1950 and 1965 average farm size showed a significant decline. The 1960 Census of Agriculture indicated that over 50 percent of the farm holdings then consisted of less than 2.5 acres each. When coupled with a larger number of workers per farm, this decline in acreage per farm significantly increased the labor intensity per acre. The general increase in labor intensity in turn affected crop production in several ways. First, it encouraged higher cropping intensities on the smaller farm. Such a tendency is illustrated in Table 9.15, which shows that farms in

Table 9.15. Farm size in East Pakistan, 1960.

Size of farm	Number of farms (percent)	Cropping intensity (percent)[a]	Cultivated area (percent)	Family working members per cultivated acre
Less than 0.5 acre	13	165	1	11.8
0.5 to 1.0	11	170	2	3.7
1.0 to 2.5	27	165	13	1.6
2.5 to 5.0	26	156	27	0.9
5.0 to 7.5	7	148	20	0.6
7.5 to 12.5	7	141	19	0.5
12.5 to 25.0	3	134	14	0.3
25.0 to 40.0	—[b]	128	3	0.2
Greater than 40.0	—[b]	115	1	0.1

Source: Government of Pakistan Ministry of Food and Agriculture, *1960 Pakistan Census of Agriculture* (October 1962), p. 39.

[a] Complete double cropping would give a 200 percent intensity. Total number of farms was 6,139,480; total cultivated area was 19,138,109 acres.
[b] Less than 0.5 percent.

the 1 to 2.5-acre category generally had about a 15 percent higher cropping intensity than those of 5 to 7.5 acres.[37] Second, the increased pressure of population probably meant larger quantities

37. The intensity effect, earlier included in the area expansion, is presented here only to give a more complete picture of the labor-pressure effect.

of traditional labor per cropped acre and consequently higher yields.[38] This relationship has been emphasized in several reports. For example, A. K. M. G. Rabbani in his definitive study on jute stated: "In the major jute-producing areas . . . the coefficient of labor was found to be highly significant . . . The input of labor was found to account for nearly 50 percent of the total variation in the yield of jute fibre . . . The elasticity of labor production . . . was found to be 0.88 and was not statistically different from unity. This suggested that a 10% variation of labor input per acre accounted for nearly 10% variation of yield rate of jute fibre." [39]

Similarly, Nurul Islam presented data that showed greater yields per acre for smaller farms.[40] M. Habibullah stated: "Labor plays an inseparable role in agricultural production. The volume, variety, and efficiency of labor is an important determinant of output." [41] Finally, the importance of increased traditional labor was emphasized by Alim.[42] He presented empirical data showing that the difference in yield as a result of one versus three weedings of Aus rice may be as much as 7.5 percent and that line sowing and other related operations versus broadcasting of Aman rice can improve yields from 8 to 18 percent.

A third factor, which is related yet distinct, involved changes in technology and corresponding increases in labor per acre. For example, the shift to the "Japanese Method" of rice culture involves a series of labor-intensive operations that increase yield per acre substantially. Alim reported experiments showing that the Japanese Method gives 38 percent greater output per acre. Similarly, the Japanese team at Comilla indicated 94 percent greater Aman yields, involving about 19 percent more labor, from improved methods of cultivation, including fertilizer.[43]

38. "Traditional" here means an increase in common cultural practices requiring additional labor, such as more weeding. The term does not imply a radical change in technology that may also require more labor, such as a shift to the "Japanese Method," which involves a package of activities such as transplantation, fertilization, or water control.

39. A. K. M. G. Rabbani, "Jute in the World Economy: A Statistical Study," unpub. Ph.D. dissertation, University of London, 1964, p. 346.

40. Nurul Islam, "Concepts and Measurement of Unemployment and Employment in Developing Economies," *International Labour Review* (March 1964), p. 254.

41. M. Habibullah, *The Pattern of Agricultural Unemployment* (Dacca University: Bureau of Economic Research, 1962), p. 38.

42. Alim, *Rice Cultivation in East Pakistan*, pp. 27, 45.

43. Japanese Agricultural Mission to Pakistan under the Colombo Plan, "Seventh Annual Report" (mimeo, August 1963).

Undoubtedly the most important cause of increased labor intensity was the decline in the land-man ratio. Not to be overlooked, however, is the effect on traditional labor inputs of radically altered "terms of trade" for agriculture. S. R. Lewis' calculations showed that prices received by farmers in East Pakistan between 1951–54 and 1961–64 rose 30 percent while the index of prices paid fell nearly 20 percent.[44] Although the quantitative effects of such a change in relative prices on agricultural output is difficult to establish, the notion that some upward movement along the "traditional" production function has taken place is entirely consistent with the observed increase in labor intensity.

A final group of production effects that are included in the "residual" are associated with the Rural Works Program.[45] The most important direct effects from this labor-intensive program resulted from improved drainage as over 5,000 miles of drainage canals were renovated in both 1963/64 and 1964/65. These improvements helped in reducing flood losses, although some of the roads constructed under the program probably deterred drainage in several regions.

Thus, there is little question that increased labor intensity, brought about by population pressure, changed technology, changes in agricultural terms of trade, and the Rural Works Program, was an important element in the improved yields. Whether it accounted for 0.7 percent of the 2.1 percent growth in rice yields during the Second Plan period can be questioned; nevertheless, that figure is certainly within the range of possibility in view of the fact that the rural population was growing at over 2.5 percent per year.

Summary of Growth Factors. Progress in East Pakistan agriculture during the Second Plan period was encouraging. Unlike the stagnant era of the previous ten years, rice production in this period grew on a trend basis at about 3.4 percent per year. This measured growth was a definite reality, not a mere statistical manipulation. Approximately one-third of the growth resulted from extension of area, the remainder from increased yields, especially during the Aman season. Important factors in the area expansion

44. S. R. Lewis, Jr., and S. M. Husain, "Relative Price Changes and Industrialization in Pakistan, 1951–1964," *Pakistan Development Review* (Autumn 1966), pp. 408–431.

45. For the Rural Public Works Program, see R. V. Gilbert, "The Works Programme in East Pakistan," *International Labour Review* (March 1964), pp. 213–226.

included the shift into marginal areas as a result of population pressure, the extension of low-lift irrigation facilities, some improvement in coastal embankments, better drainage and hence less loss from flooding, and increased indigenous irrigation facilities. Major elements in the improved yields were expanded fertilizer use, better plant protection, improved seeds, and more extensive irrigation and drainage facilities. Quantitative estimates of these contributions are summarized in Table 9.16.

Table 9.16. Sources of increased crop output, East Pakistan.

Sources	Percent per year
Area expansion (including effects of low-lift pumps, WAPDA projects, population pressure)	1.3
Yield improvement	
Fertilizer	0.5
Plant protection	0.3
Seeds	0.5
Irrigation, drainage	0.1
Residual: increased labor intensity, improved technology, rural works	0.7
Total growth	3.4

IMPACT OF AGRICULTURAL POLICY UNDER THE SECOND PLAN

So far we have dealt at length with the physical aspects of the increase in agricultural production under the Second Plan. But physical analysis is only a part of the story, and probably the lesser part in terms of the lessons it provides to other countries. Of greater importance are the rural institutions and agricultural policies that evolved after the late 1950's, for they created the economic climate that permitted or induced the use of improved physical inputs.

"Pragmatic" is a word heard often in discussions concerning Pakistan's economic policy of this period, and indeed it probably best conveys the attitude of the Pakistan government on a broad range of issues. From the late 1950's onward, there were a number of bold government policy actions in agriculture, most of which were aimed directly or indirectly at improving the price and income incentives to farmers. Although it is not possible to go into the history and complete details of all these actions, three examples covering the major steps will indicate the general direction of policy during this period. These examples also show the extent to which farmers responded to the improved economic climate.

Export Duties and Bonuses. The reduction of export duties on cotton and jute and the provision of export-bonuses on fine-quality rice were relatively simple measures for improving prices to farmers on three of the most important export crops. The duty system of taxation, which was really a revenue measure, had long had the adverse effect of altering internal price ratios *against* export commodities in which Pakistan appeared to have a comparative advantage. These duties were sizable, and because of the relatively large price responses that farmers had historically demonstrated in the cases of cotton and jute, their effects on production were substantial.[46] In short, these duties produced rupee revenue at a considerable cost in terms of lost production *and* lost foreign exchange.

In the case of cotton, for example, the export duty on American varieties was Rs.115 per bale in 1958. The negative effect of this duty on the cotton prices that farmers received was on the order of 25 percent.[47] In the post-1958 era there were several duty reductions, and by 1964/65 the cotton duty had been lowered to a nominal Rs.25 per bale.[48] The farmer-incentive argument played an important role in these reductions, and certainly harvest cotton prices were much stronger than they would have been in the absence of the policy of lowering duties.[49] The reductions were clear cases, therefore, of government policy raising the absolute and relative price of cotton and thus contributing to the rather spectacular growth in cotton production.

In the case of jute, the duty-reduction policy was initiated only late in the Second Plan period. In December 1964 export taxes

46. See Falcon and Gotsch, "Price Response, Economic Efficiency, and Technological Change." The price elasticity of supply for cotton and jute have been estimated at 0.4 and 0.7, respectively.

47. This calculation assumes that 15 maunds of seed cotton produce one bale of 392 pounds, that the export demand was elastic, and that the harvest price was Rs.30 per maund of seed cotton.

48. In one sense, the drop in duty after 1958 continued an earlier policy. However, the early changes were the result more of an attempt at internal trade stabilization during and after the Korean War than of a concern with farmer incentives.

49. Despite many outcries to the contrary, it appears that most of the reductions in duty were passed back to producers. In any event, cotton harvest prices to farmers remained an almost constant ratio of the Liverpool price minus the duty.

were halved from Rs.20 to Rs.10 per bale. Because of the nature of export demand for raw jute, and because of the lack of information on jute prices received by farmers in East Pakistan, much less can be observed about the specific effects of the duty reduction. It is clear, however, that internal wholesale jute prices were much stronger in 1964/65 than they had been in the two previous years. Moreover, the change in jute prices altered *relative* price ratios in favor of jute. In 1964/65, for example, the average wholesale jute-to-rice price ratios were about 25 percent and 40 percent greater than they had been in 1963/64 and 1962/63, respectively. Since there is a strong relationship between this price ratio and jute production the following year, the downward trend in jute production was reversed in 1965/66.[50] Hence, even though the price policy on jute was too little and too late, given the normal lagged response, to affect the Second Plan production of jute, government policy in the final year was one of the factors that set the stage for a large expansion during the first year of the Third Plan period.

Decontrol, PL 480, and the Works Program. A second policy lesson centers around the general decontrol of agriculture that took place after 1958. This decontrol is particularly interesting because of the way in which the government of Pakistan used surplus agricultural commodities provided under U.S. Public Law 480 as an effective instrument of agricultural policy.

The bureaucratic controls that existed in Pakistan in 1958 can only be described as extensive and cumbersome. Many of the regulations, such as the restrictive zoning of surplus areas and the compulsory sale of foodgrains to the government at less than market prices in those regions, were introduced during World War II. They had continued through partition and were still in effect to varying degrees at the start of the Ayub regime. There was also strict acreage zoning of cotton varieties in West Pakistan to prevent the mixing of staple lengths, and jute acreage was licensed in East Pakistan in an attempt to restrict output and to take advantage of the presumed inelastic export demand for jute and jute products.

Even more controls were added under Martial Law Regulations.

50. We take for granted a desire by the government to expand jute production. Whether expansion is the proper policy, given the duopoly position of Pakistan in the world jute trade and the competitiveness of jute with local rice production, is a subject for separate study.

As M. Haq stated: "Price and profit controls imposed by the Martial Law regime seem to have sprung from the belief that [the] free market invariably tries to "exploit" and there is some unique level of price and profits which is "fair" both for producers and consumers. This showed a fundamental lack of understanding of [the] market mechanism coupled with an excessive faith in administrative efficiency and benevolence. These medieval ideas of a "just" price naturally led to several absurdities." [51] By November 1958, fourteen "essential" commodities were under price regulation, and eighty-seven other items were regulated through various profit laws.[52] Even though many of the regulations were not totally enforced, they had a net negative influence on agriculture. One glaring absurdity was that the prices of foodgrains were held down in the surplus regions. In addition, the government, always an object of concern and suspicion among villagers, contributed to uncertainty about prices and deliveries through its forced procurement system.

The first effect of these regulations was to lower prices and to provide strong disincentives in the most productive agricultural regions. Second, because of the inadequacy of the rationing procedure, prices were inordinately high and wildly fluctuating in urban and deficit areas. The contrast in the case of wheat in West Pakistan can be seen vividly in Figure 9.3. Prices in Lyallpur, a surplus area, and Peshawar, a deficit region, show a close correspondence *prior* to the Martial Law regulations in 1958. This close correlation was to be expected in the absence of effective controls because of the good rail connection between these two cities. However, with the militarily enforced controls in late 1958, Lyallpur prices were depressed, Peshawar prices quickly rose, and the seasonal pattern of price movement was aggravated. Thus, the country had the worst of both worlds.

Much to the credit of President Ayub, the control system in the economy did not last long. In February 1959 a start was made on relaxing distribution and export controls, and controls on profit margins were drastically reduced. In January 1960 rice rationing was virtually abolished in East Pakistan, and the sale of rice, except

51. M. Haq, "Rationale of Government Controls and Policies in Pakistan," *Pakistan Economic Journal* (March 1963), p. 9.
52. Much of our historical discussion of controls is based on A. F. A. Husain, "Price Distribution and Controls in Pakistan," *Pakistan Economic Journal* (June 1961), pp. 17–25.

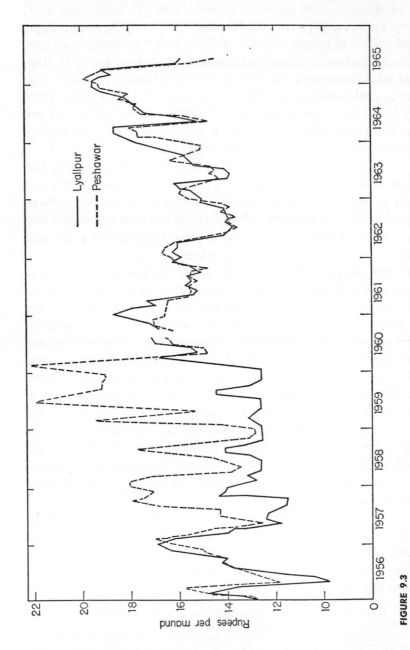

FIGURE 9.3
Monthly wholesale wheat prices at Lyallpur and Peshawar, West Pakistan, January 1956–December 1963. *Source:* Government of Pakistan Central Statistical Office, *Statistical Bulletin* (monthly issues).

in a five-mile border belt, was placed on a voluntary basis. At that time arrangements were also made with Burma for the import of up to 300,000 tons of rice annually to serve as a buffer in the event of short crops and rising prices.

An even larger decontrol action took place in April 1960. In spite of many dire predictions, the direct controls on wheat movements, wheat prices, and wheat rationing were abolished in West Pakistan.[53] Distribution was left instead to the private trade without any of the previous licensing restrictions and buffer-stock system was initiated. Under this system the government guaranteed farmers a minimum price of Rs.13.50 per maund of wheat. Sales to the government were voluntary, and the government entered usual market channels only when prices dipped below the statutory minimum. A ceiling was placed on wheat-price movements by establishing a release price of Rs.16 per maund, raised to Rs.17.25 in the summer of 1966. When prices rose above that level, the government released wheat into the market. In part these stocks came from government wheat procured from the support operation, but since the government was never especially vigorous in implementing its support activities, the bulk of this wheat came from wheat supplied under the expanded PL 480 program.

Because PL 480 was so critical to the entire decontrol policy, and because it has always been a source of considerable controversy, a few additional observations on the program are warranted.[54] There can be no doubt about the importance of PL 480 to the development of Pakistan's *total* economy during the Second Plan period. In the first place, approximately 15 percent of West Pakistan's wheat was supplied under Title I auspices, that is, through

53. To a considerable extent, the decontrol throughout West Pakistan was made possible by the one-unit rule passed in October 1955. Under this provision the former states and provinces of West Pakistan were consolidated into one large province. This unity contrasts markedly with the particularism of India, where individual states still exercise considerable control over foodgrain movements and prices.

54. For PL 480 in Pakistan, see C. Beringer, *The Use of Agricultural Surplus Commodities for Economic Development in Pakistan* (Institute of Development Economics Monograph No. 12, January 1964); R. V. Gilbert, "The P.L. 480 Programme for the Third Plan" (mimeo, Pakistan Planning Commission, March 9, 1964); W. P. Falcon, "Consistency of U.S. Policy towards P.L. 480, with Special Reference to Pakistan" (mimeo, Pakistan Planning Commission, March 1965); Ghulam Mohammed, "P.L. 480 and Agricultural Development during the Third Plan Period" (typescript, Institute of Development Economics, January 1966).

sale of U.S. surplus commodities for nonconvertible currencies. Its import permitted a stabilization of wheat prices in the Rs.14 to 18 per maund range, which in turn provided industry with the key wage good at stable prices. Price stability along with import liberalization were two important factors in permitting West Pakistan industry to grow at about 15 percent per annum in the 1959/60 to 1964/65 period.

In several other respects PL 480 commodities were so important as to be almost indistinguishable from hard-currency assistance. If it is assumed that the PL 480 assistance was an addition to total foreign assistance and that in its absence other types of aid would not have substantially increased, PL 480 transfers certainly helped relieve the critical foreign-exchange bottleneck. Without them, either foreign exchange would have been required for food imports, thereby decreasing the availability of producer imports in both provinces, or the threat of inflation would have required a drastic reduction in the size of the development plan. Either alternative could have seriously impaired the development of the general economy.

The effect of PL 480 on the agricultural sector per se was less clear but probably as positive in the long run. First, substantial investments within the agricultural sector were offset against PL 480 imports. Top priority was assigned to the Indus Basin program for the necessary irrigation replacement works on which the future of much of the rural economy of West Pakistan depends. Second, the PL 480 program was a critical element in the decontrol movement. Without the expanded program, the relaxation of controls might never have occurred, or at least decontrol might not have survived. It is only possible to speculate about such a consequence, but the disincentive and uncertainty aspects of a continued control system could have been disastrous.

The disincentive aspects of the prior control system highlight another aspect of PL 480 assistance. Much has been written about the negative price effects and hence the disincentives to agricultural production of PL 480 shipments. These arguments generally start with a basic assumption that perfect competition, in terms of product flows, prevailed initially. But in West Pakistan the shift from a very low controlled price in surplus areas to a PL 480 buffer-stock system did not lower and perhaps even increased prices and incentives for wheat production in "surplus" regions. (See Figure 9.3.)

The program also aided agricultural development in West Pakistan in a more subtle way. Many observers have rightfully argued that farmers could increase incomes from shifting from lower-valued subsistence crops, such as wheat and sorghums, to cash crops. However, because of uncertainty in prices and yields, farmers in Pakistan had long known that it made better sense to grow sufficient food for home consumption rather than to specialize and depend on the government's market for foodgrains. Since PL 480 wheat added an important element of stability to the foodgrain market, farmers soon learned that they could purchase foodgrains at reasonable prices in the market. PL 480 thus added an impetus for farmers to move into the higher-valued cash crops. Although this shift did not make the foodgrain self-sufficiency proponents in either Pakistan or the United States particularly happy, it was desirable from a broader economic point of view and no doubt contributed to the higher relative rates of growth in cash crops shown in Table 9.3.

In East Pakistan the net effect of PL 480 on the rural sector was also positive, though the mechanism was quite different. PL 480 commodities were used primarily in support of the Rural Works Program, which had several remarkable features.[55] First, it represented one of the initial attempts by government to reduce the severe seasonal unemployment and underemployment that existed in the rural areas of East Pakistan. This problem was of major consequence, since over half of the 7.5 million man-year equivalents of unemployment estimated for 1964/65 were in East Bengal.[56] Second, the program relied heavily on local initiative and organization. Plans of surprising complexity were developed and implemented by farmers and officials at the lowest levels of government. Finally, the financial support of the program came from the sale of a number of PL 480 commodities, primarily wheat. The financing of the program was particularly revolutionary, for many in government firmly believed that the rice eaters of East Bengal would never eat wheat.

The Works Program was tested on a pilot basis in 1962/63 in Comilla Kotwali Thana, an administrative subsection of one dis-

55. Much of this discussion is based on Gilbert, "The Works Programme in East Pakistan."
56. Planning Commission, *Third Five Year Plan*, p. 153.

trict, and expanded to the entire province in succeeding years. The program's primary emphasis was on drainage, and in 1963/64 and 1964/65 a combined total of over 10,000 miles of drains were excavated. Although insufficient research has been conducted on the effects of the program, the net result seems to have been beneficial. The drains did not prevent flooding per se, but they increased the velocity of the flood runoff and thus helped to reduce flood losses. Rice plants, for example, can withstand total submersion for about forty-eight hours, so that reducing the time of flooding from three to two days can have a significant effect on production.

In addition to drainage, farm-to-market roads were emphasized. Over 25,000 miles of *kutcha* (secondary) roads were constructed in both 1963/64 and 1964/65. These connected many heretofore isolated villages, which in turn reduced factor costs and increased product prices. Finally, the Works Program helped to put increased purchasing power into the hands of villagers. The combined inflow of some Rs.450 million into rural areas between 1962/63 and 1964/65 — particularly to part-time farmers — made sizable funds available for further agricultural investments. In many respects these funds helped to substitute for the very inadequate system of organized rural credit.

To the surprise of many, the financing of the Works Program proved successful. After considerable debate, the decision had been to pay Works Program laborers in cash rather than in wheat. The great fear at the time was that this procedure would prove inflationary: rupees would be put into circulation; there would be no effective demand for wheat, because the East Pakistanis were rice eaters; hence, excess demand would be generated for rice and other commodities not supplied under PL 480. Documents going back to the Bengal Famine Report of 1943 were cited as grounds for this expectation.

The Works Program proved, however, that rice eaters would eat wheat *if the price were right*. With an internal subsidy of approximately one-third the value, considerable wheat was sold in the open market, and more than sufficient rupees were generated to finance the Works Program. Though East Pakistan consumers had shown no willingness to substitute wheat for rice when wheat was non-subsidized, they were quite responsive to the favorable change in the relative price of subsidized wheat. One crude piece of empirical research estimated the marginal elasticity of substitution between rice and wheat to be greater than two when the ratio of wheat to rice prices was about one-half.[57]

Thus, for the first time a government policy was designed to attack seasonal underemployment. The Works Program created about fifty million man-days of employment in both 1963/64 and 1964/65. It created productive investments, which directly and indirectly aided agriculture. It was planned and implemented principally at the local level, where it had been claimed that no administrative capability existed. And it was paid for by a commodity that had been thought unacceptable in the East Pakistan context.

At the same time, PL 480 was not perfectly administered in either province, and it caused certain problems. On the administrative side, some of the early regulations for flour mills concerning the proportion of PL 480 wheat purchased to total wheat milled were superfluous. Since for historic reasons many mills were in wheat-surplus areas of West Pakistan, these restrictions had the effect of impairing the market for locally produced wheat; they were later changed. At other times the government was reluctant to support the minimum price or to release adequate PL 480 stocks to prevent prices from rising above the established ceiling. In East Pakistan there were difficult problems of storing wheat in a monsoon climate. Moreover, the "like commodity" clause of the PL 480 agreement caused Pakistan considerable difficulties for several years. The basic problem was that although Pakistan was deficient in wheat and had a surplus in rice, her coarse-rice exports were not permitted by the United States under the PL 480 re-export restriction because they were deemed to be "like" commodities.[58] Nevertheless, the expanded PL 480 program played a positive role in Pakistan's Second Plan performance. It was a critical ingredient in both the decontrol movement and the Rural Works Program, which are considered by most as among the highlights of the improved agricultural performance.

Input Subsidies and Input Distribution. Government policy generated incentives in yet a third way, through the pricing of improved agricultural inputs. Major subsidies were provided on such items as

57. W. P. Falcon and C. H. Gotsch, "A Note on the Foodgrain Situation in East Pakistan" (mimeo, Pakistan Planning Commission, June 1964).
58. See Falcon, "Consistency of U.S. Policy towards P.L. 480."

fertilizer, plant protection, and irrigation water by the central and provincial governments. The net result was to make the price of these inputs very low by world-price standards.

In the case of plant-protection activities, the government provided the service at no charge to farmers, and the extension staff of the Department of Agriculture spent a large portion of its time — perhaps 60 percent — on plant-protection activities. Even though there were obvious limits on the extent to which the extension personnel could directly cope with the problems of pest control and a large opportunity cost in using the staff in this manner, the program did spread pesticide technology throughout large portions of both East and West Pakistan.

The subsidy on fertilizer, another key input, averaged about 50 percent during the Second Plan period. In part, this subsidy compensated for the relatively high production costs of government-operated factories; nevertheless, its net result was to set an internal fertilizer price that was about 30 percent less than the world price at the official exchange rate.[59] With these subsidies the average return on fertilizer for the farmer was generally greater than four to one — a very appealing investment. (See Table 9.6.) These subsidies were borne on an equal basis by the central and provincial governments and were a major financial item in the Development Program. For example, in 1962/63, the middle year of the Second Plan, fertilizer subsidies amounted to about 15 percent of the entire development allocations for agriculture.[60]

During the early years of the Second Plan the subsidy features of the fertilizer program, though important, were not sufficient to induce rapid utilization because of severe difficulties in distribution. In West Pakistan fertilizer movement was the exclusive responsibility of the rural cooperatives, except in a few project areas under Agricultural Development Corporation (ADC) jurisdiction. In East Pakistan distribution to the farmer was at first generally handled by the Department of Agriculture and later by the East Pakistan ADC. There were a variety of reasons that fertilizer distribu-

59. From the beginning of the fertilizer program in Pakistan, fertilizer was heavily subsidized, but only after 1957/58 was sufficient fertilizer available to make any real difference to either the national budget or the development of agriculture.

60. *Handbook of Agricultural Statistics,* Pakistan Planning Commission, June 1969, p. 31.

tion was inefficient. In West Pakistan many cooperatives purchased fertilizer from government factories on credit, and often they also sold to farmers on a credit basis. Collections at the farm level were not always easy, and at times attempts at collection were not even vigorous. Indeed, many cooperatives found it convenient for accounting purposes to carry fertilizer that had already been distributed as stocks on hand rather than as accounts receivable. Since there were limits on the amount that cooperatives themselves could purchase from the factories without payment of earlier orders, a curious anomaly arose. The *reported* stock position rose at the same time that a strong fertilizer black market was springing up in the countryside.

On January 1, 1964, fertilizer distribution in West Pakistan was changed. In an act that took considerable courage, and which indicates both the government's pragmatism and its reliance on incentives, distribution was turned over to the private trade. Approximately five hundred "stockists" were appointed by the West Pakistan Industrial Development Corporation to serve as dealers at the local level. An attempt was made to keep some controls on pricing and markups, although many of the restrictions were not in fact enforceable, given the supply-demand situation in the rural areas. But the government went most of the way in accepting implicitly the advice of a former agricultural advisor: "The Government must learn to govern in areas in which it has competence — and to stand by in a fatherly posture where it is less efficient than the private citizen in hot pursuit of a rupee!" [61]

The results of this shift to private trade were remarkable. Within eight months the stock position went from a reported surplus of 250,000 tons in terms of ammonium-sulphate to a deficit (unfilled orders) of 125,000 tons. Although the reported surplus was probably greater than the actual supplies, the change was nonetheless spectacular. It was so rapid, in fact, that a lag in the placement of government import orders, coupled with a seasonally tight world fertilizer market, resulted in serious shortages in West Pakistan during much of 1964 and 1965.[62]

61. J. R. Motheral, "The Effect of Government Policy and Programs on Agricultural Production in Pakistan" (mimeo, Harvard Center for International Affairs, 1960).

62. In late summer of 1965, after the period covered by this chapter, first-priority fertilizer distribution was again given to the cooperatives — although now

In East Pakistan fertilizer distribution at the farm level was also opened to private trade in the early 1960's. This change was an important element in the large spurt in East Pakistan fertilizer consumption. But in the East no less than the West rapid private sales coupled with a lag in government procurement from abroad meant that fertilizer supplies were extremely tight in the last year of the Second Plan. In such situations the continued subsidy on fertilizer could be questioned, although the import policy rather than the subsidy should probably be faulted.

The incentive policy of the central and provincial governments led to other measures. Subsidies were provided for example, for tractor rentals, the digging of tubewells, and irrigation water — some of which were very controversial. Another controversial policy area was land reform. In neither province were any effective changes made in holding size or tenure conditions during the Second Plan period. However, insofar as it was the large farmers who spearheaded efforts to increase production, the failure to carry out drastic land reform may have even had a positive effect on agricultural growth. This aspect of government policy still awaits a detailed and critical appraisal.

CONCLUSIONS

The agricultural policy aspects of Pakistan's Second Plan must be considered a bright spot in the government's program. Designed to stimulate output by providing incentives for the use of improved inputs, they were a great success. Their performance had a profound influence on the entire economy of Pakistan. The near tripling of the agricultural growth rate was a major factor in permitting the total economy to grow at over 5 percent annually, in allowing exports to expand at 7 percent annually, and in providing

on a cash basis. This about-face was caused in part by aid difficulties, severe foreign-exchange pressures, and a tight world market for fertilizer. The government's view, seriously questioned by many, was that control of black marketing and the rationing of fertilizer could be handled more easily through the cooperatives. Many of the cooperative chairmen were politically strong at the grass-roots level, which undoubtedly was another factor in the switch. Given the demand situation existing in 1965, the cooperatives were probably capable of distributing the limited supplies. However, whether they can manage the expanded program called for in the Third Plan seems doubtful. This step backward in fertilizer distribution in West Pakistan may prove to be very costly.

sufficient jobs to prevent a rise in unemployment. Two questions immediately arise from this success story. What are the lessons that other countries should draw from the Pakistan experience? And is the Second Plan performance likely to be accelerated, or at least sustained, under the Third Plan?

To some, the Pakistan case shows only that a relatively large number of commercially-minded farmers with access to fair-sized holdings and thirty million acre-feet of inexpensive ground water can make agricultural development easy. Such a statement is only a half-truth. It overlooks the two basic lessons of Pakistan's Second Plan: the importance of achieving the right division in the agricultural development program between the public and private sectors, and the importance of incentives as a tool for inducing development activity in the agricultural sector.

All too often in the past, discussions about agricultural development have focused only on specific investment projects in the public sector. Whereas these schemes may be very important in particular geographic areas — such as the SCARP I region — direct public investments in agriculture are likely to suffer severe limitations in increasing output. This handicap is particularly serious when, as in the case of Pakistan, agriculture consists of millions of small decision-units. Thus, the agricultural sector is vastly different from the manufacturing sector, where a decision to double or triple domestic output in the public sector can be made almost overnight, though it may be very costly. Such a decision is not technically possible in the agricultural sector.

The limitations on increasing agricultural production via direct investment underscore the importance of incentives for farmers who are not directly affected by public investments. One lesson of the Second Plan was that the government of Pakistan did recognize the importance of these incentives. It used a variety of instruments — export-tax policy, input subsidies, price support-stabilization policy, and PL 480 policy — to create a favorable economic atmosphere. And to the surprise of a great many, the supposedly unresponsive farmers of Pakistan reacted to price and income opportunities.

The second important lesson of the Second Plan concerns the relative roles of the public and private sectors in agriculture. The private sector responded to the favorable economic climate, especially in developing and using fertilizer and water. But the public

sector was also vital, both for what it did and for what it had the
sense not to do. Public investments in ground-water development,
for example, had a high payoff, particularly with regard to the
spread of private tubewell technology. A similar effect can be expected from the public importation and distribution of new Mexican wheat varieties undertaken during the last year of the Second
Plan. The Rural Public Works Program showed that something
productive could also be done with seasonally unemployed agricultural labor.

These positive contributions of the government were important
and impressive. Equally impressive was the government's ability to
resist the temptation to do things that it probably could not have
done as well as the admittedly imperfect market. Foremost in this
category was the grain trade, where quick and decentralized decisions were vital. The focus of the government during the Second
Plan period was in helping to improve the working of the market
rather than in taking over the extremely difficult marketing function. The move after 1964 to return the distribution of some improved inputs to the private trade was another case where the advantages of decentralization and the profit motive were recognized.
Although there were probably other fields, such as pesticide distribution, where scope still existed for a change in the public-
private role, the Second Plan period showed that the public and
private sectors' contributions in agriculture could be complementary rather than competitive.

A third insight gained from the Pakistan experience involves the
"package" of inputs required for an effective agricultural development effort. To be sure, improved inputs yield a higher return when
used simultaneously than when used singly or even in pairs. But the
difficulties of carrying out an integrated program involving all inputs are much greater than if efforts can be directed toward identifying and breaking a single major constraint. In the case of the
former Punjab, water was the main bottleneck, and the large private and public investments made in irrigation were very profitable
irrespective of the availability of fertilizer, plant protection, or improved seeds. While a package approach has much to recommend
it, a growth-oriented agricultural policy must also consider the
trade-off between technical efficiency and ease of focus and administration. The successful concentration on irrigation water and to

some extent on fertilizer in the former Punjab highlights the necessity for evaluating this trade-off before embarking on a complex multifactor program.

Finally, the Pakistan experience showed that it was possible to have a major PL 480 program without creating serious inflationary or disincentive problems. In West Pakistan through foodgrain decontrol and cropping-pattern adjustments it was possible to accommodate without negative effects a program that provided about 15 percent of foodgrain supplies. In East Pakistan it was possible at appropriate prices to offset labor-intensive development investments with PL 480 wheat in a once strictly rice-eating society.

These are obviously not the only conclusions that might be drawn, nor is it likely that the lessons can be applied to all countries at all times. Nevertheless, they were major factors in Pakistan's ability to exceed most of the Second Plan targets. Moreover, if Pakistan continues to emphasize the quick-response inputs for agriculture and to follow the same sensible economic policies, the future appears very bright.

Part V

EDUCATION, MANPOWER, LABOR,
AND WAGES

R. S. Weckstein

10

Wages and Labor Scarcity — Liberia

Modern-day preoccupation with the economic development problems of labor-surplus economies has directed attention away from the characteristic problems of labor-scarce economies.[1] The presence of a labor surplus and a rapid rate of population growth has tended to focus attention either on the critical minimum level of investment necessary to raise the proportion of capital to labor or, if a two-sector model of development is employed, on the accumulation of capital in the industrial sector in order to absorb labor from the agricultural sector fast enough to change the employment structure in favor of industry. Little attention has been given to the circumstances that arise with the success of this program, when the part of labor in the traditional or agriculture sector has been reduced significantly and wage rates for the newly recruited labor must be raised. This transformation is sometimes regarded as the mark of successful achievement of the development objective, after which the incomes of all sectors will rise with the further accumulation of capital.

But this preliminary achievement does not necessarily make subsequent development any easier. An economy that is capable of achieving this turning point can not be certain thereafter of successfully continuing its development. The opposite appears to be the case, for so long as the wage paid to workers in the newly develop-

1. Current concern with problems of labor surplus is reflected in such works as J. C. H. Fei and G. Ranis, *Development of the Labor Surplus Economy* (New Haven: Yale University Press, 1964); W. A. Lewis, "Development with Unlimited Supplies of Labor," *The Manchester School* (May 1954).

ing industries is held down by the availability of labor coming from the traditional economy, profits are higher, and there is an opportunity for higher saving ratios than will exist once wages have risen. The favorable conditions for development associated with constant wages may pass and leave an economy, still very much underdeveloped, with greatly diminished growth power. Furthermore, some underdeveloped economies may never have had a labor pool that can be absorbed at a constant wage. Such an economy will manifest the characteristics of a labor-scarce economy as soon as the process of development begins. A number of African countries may be described in this way, one of which is Liberia.

Liberian development since the mid-1950's has been accompanied by a great increase in real wages in spite of the continuing location of the bulk of the country's manpower within the traditional economy, where workers produce much less for the inputs committed than would be possible in the new market economy. It is important to understand why this is the case in Liberia — important both for the sake of development policy there and for the lessons that might be applicable in other countries with a similar economic structure.

Liberia is a small country, but absolute size is a hindrance mainly to production for her own market; for other purposes only the relative magnitudes matter. Liberia's economically important natural resources are a warm climate, heavy rainfall, and large iron deposits. Surveys currently under way have not yet established the presence of economically significant quantities of other resources, but the known resources are still far from being fully exploited. The labor force engaged in the market sector in 1965 numbered between 80,000 and 100,000 and is mainly composed of unskilled workers. The jobs requiring higher levels of skills were filled by about 5,000 to 7,000 expatriates.

The total population of the country is, according to the 1963 census, only about one million people. The available summary of the census reports that total manpower is 583,000.[2] Thus, with approximately 100,000 employed in the market economy, a good fraction of the manpower has already been shifted from activities within the traditional economy. If the population were growing

2. M. M. El-Immam, *The Structure of the Liberian Population* (National Accounting Series, No. 3 [Monrovia: National Planning Agency, n.d.]).

rapidly, it would be important to include its natural increase in the estimation of the population able to participate in modernizing growth. However, public health officers serving in the World Health Organization in Liberia believe that child mortality is very high and the birth rate low, so that there may well be no natural population growth at all. This conjecture can not be checked against census results because there is only one census, for 1963.

Possibly population, and thus labor force, do increase by immigration. Labor migrations are said to be common in Africa, in particular of workers from the interior regions, Mali and Upper Volta, who leave their homes to work in the coastal countries. But there is no measurement of these movements into Liberia, and I am unable to find evidence of any significant numbers of such immigrants in the work forces of the major employers.

The capital of the country is concentrated in the major mining installations, associated transportation facilities, and the rubber plantations. The bulk of the capital owned by foreigners is engaged in production for export, which provides for repatriation without risk of currency value loss. The capital that produces for the Liberian market — and a growing stock of capital is in this form — generates its income in American dollars without state restrictions on its disposition. As a consequence of both the export opportunities and the use of the dollar as local currency, foreign capital is available without serious discrimination against Liberian projects in comparison with projects in the rest of the world. Even short-term working capital is available through American banks that maintain branches in Liberia.

The Liberian economy may then be characterized as one with incompletely exploited resource-based opportunities, a limited supply of labor, and an unlimited supply of foreign capital on terms that may require a small but constant premium over the cost of such capital used in the United States and Europe. There is nothing paradoxical about an underdeveloped country with a limited labor supply and an unlimited supply of capital, so long as these descriptions are understood to refer to the flow of factors and not to the present stocks. The present capital-labor-stock ratio for the entire country is low, as would be expected in a poor country. The ratio in the market sector of the economy is in fact rather high, because it includes mining, which tends to be highly capital intensive. But a major fraction of the labor force remains in the traditional sector, accompanied by very little capital, which keeps the overall ratio down. The accumulation of capital has proceeded far more rapidly than has labor transformation. The effective limitation on the supply of labor appears to be reflected in the rapid wage-rate increase.

Data for three different observations of total market-sector employment are available from which to derive the values for two periods of growth in market-sector employment. The increase in employment and the changes in wage rates are recorded in Table 10.1. For none of the three observation dates is there an adequate

Table 10.1. Liberian wages and employment (annual changes).

Items	1954/55–1958	1958–1960/61
Δ employment	3200	8000
% Δ employment	5%	10%
% Δ wages	5%	26%
Elasticity of labor supply	1.0	0.4

Source: R. Clower, Summary Report, in "Economic Survey of Liberia" (mimeo, Northwestern University, 1962), p. 4-A; Clower *et al., Growth Without Development* (Evanston, Ill.: Northwestern University Press, 1966), p. 6-A.

base figure for the absolute size of market-sector employment; consequently, only crude measures of elasticity are possible on the basis of order-of-magnitude estimates. The elasticity results shown in Table 10.1 are based on total employment of 60,000 workers in the market sector in the middle of the first period and of 80,000 workers in the middle of the second period. The results are not very sensitive to possible errors in the assumptions of labor-force size. Wages rose much more rapidly in relation to employment increases during the second period than during the first.[3]

Although there are no consumer price indexes covering the period of the 1950's, it is most likely that prices were stable; that

3. This estimate of a labor-supply function is based on assumed constant work-leisure preferences. Past development may have altered these preferences. If so, the observed supply function is a statistical fiction, a montage of more than one true supply, and future development may shift the true supply further. It is plausible to suppose that development *increases* workers' willingness to work for wages and that true static labor-supply functions have shifted to the right, producing an overestimate of their elasticity. The results should therefore be regarded as upper estimates of the elasticity of supply. Future expansion of the market-sector labor force will manifest a greater observed elasticity of supply only if future shifts of the true supply exceed past shifts.

is, the rise in money wages was not matched by a rise in prices. Rice, the basic food, is imported in large quantity. Imported rice has come to represent a major fraction of total rice consumption in urban areas. Priced only slightly higher than Liberian rice, it is of a higher quality. As imports replaced part of the domestic share during the late fifties and early sixties, some rise in the average price may have occurred, but the price differential was too small for the price rise to approach the order of magnitude of the wage increase.

What is true for rice is more certainly true for other goods bought by workers. Urban workers had probably for some time been dependent on imports for most commodities that they buy. Clothing, meat, household equipment, and housebuilding materials are all imported. The value of the currency remained unchanged, and changes in customs duties had been slight, especially on low-income consumer goods. The IMF *Financial Statistics* index of imports to underdeveloped countries declined slightly from 1959 (103) to 1965 (98). Furthermore, Liberian importers are free to substitute low-priced imports for high-priced ones, which permitted Liberia's own import prices to remain below world levels. It is clear, therefore, that there was a remarkable increase in real wages, at least until 1961 or a year later, while the investment boom continued. Such a wage increase is a surprising phenomenon in view of the large pool of low-productivity workers still in the traditional sector who presumably should have been available at a constant wage rate.

The paradox of a wage inflation with a labor surplus demands clarification, especially given the importance of wages for a continuation of the development process. The immediate temptation is to explain the anomaly as an aberrant signal, which may then be justifiably ignored or for which compensating transfers may be arranged to offset any incentive to uneconomic decisions in the use of labor. Are such explanations acceptable?

MARKET WAGE ABERRATIONS

Perhaps the modification that requires the least re-examination of our economic notions would be to assume that the wage policies of government are responsible for the great increases of Liberian wage rates in recent years. Since a minimum-wage law applies to both industrial and agricultural labor, this would be a plausible explanation. Furthermore, the wage rates set by the law have been raised a number of times during the period when market wages rose, which provides a continuous association between the market wage and the minimum wage.

Available evidence, however, casts doubt on a belief that the direction of causation runs from law to market. An interesting set of data, which is unavailable for reproduction, is the employment and wage records of the Firestone Company plantation in Harbel, Liberia. The company computes what it regards as its labor deficit or surplus for each year. Raising the wage rate by law above its equilibrium value would be expected to be associated with a labor *surplus*. Yet in every year in the period for which wage rises were reported, Firestone had a *deficit* in its labor force, which it was unable to remove at its current wage.

Furthermore, it would be remarkable if there were so great a legislative will in the government of Liberia. Whatever hope one may have that Liberia is advancing socially, it is not a workers' state. Most of the individuals of influence in or near the government are either themselves employers of labor or receive much of their income from others who are employers. If wages rise in spite of a labor surplus, it is not because government has arbitrarily raised wages.

Nor is it possible to attribute the increase in wages to the influence of powerful unions. There are unions, and in recent years they have conducted more than one strike; they provoked a government investigation, and concessions were obtained. Yet such events are highly sporadic, and the effect must be understood as something other than the exercise of power over wages by the unions. The closest that unions have been able to come to exercising power is that union bargaining has countervailed against a tendency of Liberian employers to act as a group to resist wage increases.

It would be more plausible to attempt to account for increases in wages by a rapid upgrading of labor after it had entered employment within the market sector. One would then expect to find increasing differentials between the wages of new recruits into such employment and the average wage. Unhappily, the structure of Liberian occupations does not support this view. The vast bulk of jobs held by indigenous Liberians recruited into wage employment require unskilled or low-skilled workers, such as rubber tappers and construction labor. In addition, the wage rates that are recorded in the statistical records are not really averages reflecting the weighted distribution of wage rates but are instead the basic wages paid for unskilled workers, which ignore the superstructure of wages paid to the more highly skilled.

Still another way of accounting for the wage rise would be to reconsider our information about the population. Perhaps a much greater proportion of the total manpower pool has already been shifted into market-sector employment and the wage rise is correctly indicating a physical scarcity of labor. This possibility is flatly contradicted by the 1963 census. Even if the census were regarded as unreliable, the accounting logic of food supply is inconsistent with a lower population estimate. Rice imports in particular are totally insufficient to support the known urban population. In 1964 approximately $3 million worth of rice was imported into the country. This is only $12 per capita for the quarter-million people in the urban population. Annual rice consumption of Liberians is at least double that amount, and the difference must be supplied by home production. Yet the farming population, which is almost entirely traditional and employs primitive rice-growing technology, would surely be incapable of producing the required marketable surplus unless the size of the rural population were on the order of magnitude reported in the census. There is little doubt that the population is comparatively large; yet there is a scarcity of labor.

West African migrations are a fourth possible way to explain the observed wage movements in a manner consistent with the presence of surplus labor. It has been reported by reliable observers that in the early 1950's labor moved into Liberia, driven by poor conditions in neighboring countries, but that the movement reversed itself in the late 1950's and early 1960's because of the more recent economic expansion in the neighboring countries, especially the French-speaking countries. Thus, the wage change observed in Liberia might be explained as the result of a shift in the supply of labor in Liberia. Yet migrations would have had to be of great magnitude relative to the labor force, and timed out of phase with the employment pressures in Liberia, to draw off so much surplus labor as to cause the rise in wages. If in fact migration did take place on such a large scale, one would conclude not only that Liberian labor was in surplus relative to those *internal* shifts in demand which have occurred or are likely to occur but also that, because shifts in the *foreign* demand for Liberian labor were so much greater, the surplus was eliminated, and the labor supply in Liberia became inelastic.

If, alternatively, there is supposed to have been an unlimited supply of labor even after the exodus of part of the labor force in the late 1950's, when wages had begun to rise rapidly, then wages in Liberia must be determined by labor-market conditions outside the country; wages in Liberia must be responding to increased wages available to Liberian workers outside the country. Furthermore, if wages outside Liberia rose in response to a flush of economic development in some of the neighboring countries, then there would appear to be a labor-scarcity economy in the entire geographic region of which Liberia is a part.

Although this version of the Liberian events is plausible, evidence exists that too little migration occurred for the hypothesis to be regarded as more probable than the simpler alternative: that there is a single Liberian labor-supply schedule of positive slope, which has been revealed by movements of the demand for labor in Liberia. The evidence is, first, that few non-Liberian workers are employed in the large firms.[4] Even in the past the attraction for most immigrant workers appears to have been diamond mining, as was true during the middle and late 1950's. It is even possible that the recorded employment data excludes these workers, for they were either self-employed or casual. Second, if there was a significant out-migration in response to wage differentials, wages in the neighboring countries would have fallen relative to Liberian wages during the early period and then risen in the later period. The available wage information for Ghana, Ivory Coast, and Nigeria indicates that during the 1954–58 period real wages in the three countries rose by the same order of magnitude — about 5 percent per annum — as Liberian wages.[5] During the second period, however, Libe-

4. R. Clower *et al., Growth Without Development* (Evanston, Ill.: Northwestern University Press, 1966), pp. 306–8.

5. See Elliot Berg, "Real Income Trends in West Africa," in M. J. Herskovits and M. Harwitz, eds., *Economic Transition in Africa* (Evanston, Ill.: Northwestern University Press, 1964), pp. 199–229. Ghana's real wages rose 4 percent per annum, and the import-price deflated wages rose 6.5 percent per annum. In

rian real wages rose much more rapidly than did wages in the neighboring countries.[6] Hence, if labor migrations were induced by wage-rate differentials, the migrations would have tended to moderate the Liberian wage inflation rather than to cause it.

There is one final intriguing possibility by which to account for the history of wage increases. Liberia has often been accused of the practice of "forced recruitment." This is said to be a system of obtaining labor by the imposition of a legal obligation to work for a wage determined arbitrarily. The obligation or coercion is imposed by the village authority or tribal chief. The chief receives a gift, which is presumably less than the sum of wages that would have been required to obtain a comparable work force voluntarily. If this practice had still been widespread by the early 1950's, and further, if it had been gradually replaced by a system of wage inducements, the average wage rate in Liberia would have risen as it did.

The assertion that labor recruitment by coercion is so widespread as to account for the level of wages is difficult to evaluate directly.[7] In some respects it is inconsistent with well-known characteristics of the labor force. "Recruitment" obligations are conceded to be limited to short periods — two months at a time. Yet plantation work is continuous throughout the year with only marginal seasonality. Recruitment rights are also said to be limited to government officials and to favored plantation employers. Hence, the practice applies at most to a fraction of total employed labor. But the wage rate is not determined by that fraction of the labor force which is in some way forced into employment. Rather, the least willing or least available part of the labor force is at any time most significant in the determination of the wage rate. The wage required to attract this most reluctant free labor is the wage that rules in the market. If there are workers who have been coerced into their jobs and are paid less than the market wage, their employers receive a surplus equal to the difference, if any, between the market wage and the lower wage paid to forcibly recruited workers.

Abidjan, Ivory Coast, real wages rose at a rate of 3.2 percent. In Lagos, Nigeria, real wages rose 2.2 percent, import-price deflated wages rose 5 percent per annum.

6. According to Berg, "Real Income Trends in West Africa," Ghana's real wage rate declined at one percent per annum, and the import-price deflated wage declined at 1.5 percent. Real wages in the Ivory Coast rose at 3.5 percent per annum. Nigerian real wages rose at 7.5 percent per annum, and the increase for import-price deflated wages was 10 percent per annum.

7. Clower *et al., Growth Without Development,* pp. 296–98, 326.

Nor is the trend of wages through the 1950's and early 1960's to be accounted for by reference to a relative decline in the employment of forcibly recruited labor. The wage-determining free part of the labor force must have been important in the labor market throughout that period, for it was a time of expansion of mining, construction, trade, and services which do not use conscripted labor. If there had been a two-wage system, comprising a low wage to recruited labor and a high wage to free labor, a weighted-average wage might have risen even without a change in the level of both the wages. But reported wages in this study are not a weighted average. The wage data show the level of the basic wage rate for unskilled labor in general. Apparently the wage rise is not a statistical illusion.

Thus, explanations of Liberian wage history that depend on the power of nonmarket intervention by unions or government, the labor-force skill structure, changes in recruitment institutions, population movements, or a denial of even the crude correctness of the census all appear to be unsatisfactory. In contrast, the following four explanations, each of which interprets the wage increase as a particular form of economic scarcity, are consistent not only with the wage facts but with other characteristics of the West African economy as well.

A WAGE-REMISSION MODEL

Consider an economy with a traditional sector and a market sector. The accumulation of new capital is concentrated in the market sector, and complementary labor requirements are met by transfers of labor from the traditional sector.[8] Although the opportunity cost of an additional worker in the market sector is equal to the marginal product of a worker in the traditional sector, the wage that it is necessary to pay is the higher average product actually received as income by workers in the nonmarket (non-wage) sector. In addition to this income, it is assumed in this model

8. The technology of the traditional sector affords limited opportunity for additions to its capital stock before declining productivity removes any motive for further accumulation. See T. W. Schultz, *Transforming Traditional Agriculture* (New Haven: Yale University Press, 1964), pp. 28ff. Hence, new capital is not invested in the traditional sector, and new employment opportunities there do not compete for labor with the expanding market sector.

that a component of income is received as a remittance from workers who have taken jobs in the market sector.

In some cases the remission of a part of the wages income is simply an amount of cash sent back. In other cases the workers themselves temporarily leave their market-sector employment to go home for a time, carrying with them money and goods.[9] The variation in practice is no doubt quite wide and depends on the opportunities provided by conditions of employment in the market sector.[10] The significant and stable element for a wide range of types of remission practice is that the average income in the traditional society is thus increased above what it would be on its own. The further consequence of the practice is an increase in the wage rate that the market sector is obliged to pay to induce workers to accept wage employment. Without discrimination between new and old workers, the wage for all workers rises. The essentials of these relations are more clearly displayed in the following equations.

The division of the labor force between the two sectors is

$$(1) \qquad\qquad n_T + n_M = n$$

where n is employment, the subscript T refers to the traditional sector, and M refers to the modern sector. On the assumption that expansion of production in the traditional sector is not affected by the scarcity of land available in undeveloped form in interior areas, and that very little durable capital is used, output can be written

$$(2) \qquad\qquad o_T = \alpha n_T$$

where α is a proportionality factor. Income in the traditional sector for the average worker is

$$(3) \qquad\qquad y_T = \frac{1}{n_T}(o_T + R)$$

where R is the amount paid as a remittance or transfer by those who receive income from work in the market sector. Remittances are written

$$(4) \qquad\qquad R = \beta w_M n_M$$

9. Elliot Berg, "The Economics of the Migrant Labor System," in Hilda Kuper, ed., *Urbanization and Migration in West Africa* (Berkeley: University of California Press, 1965), pp. 160–81.

10. It has been estimated that in 1960 $4.7 million was remitted to the traditional sector in Liberia. Clower *et al.*, *Growth Without Development*, p. 52.

where β is the average proportion of wages received in the market sector transferred to home villages. Finally, the wage that must be paid in the market sector is

(5) $$w_M = y_T$$

If in this model the proportion of total employment located in the market sector is increased, the resulting wage rate that must be paid in the market sector is obtained from an equation for y_T by substituting the values of Equations (1), (2), (4), and (5) in Equation (3). Thus,

(6) $$y_T = \alpha \Big/ \left(1 - \beta \frac{n_M}{n_T}\right)$$

Depending on the values assumed for α and β, the market-sector wage rises more or less rapidly. There is a tendency for wages to rise quite rapidly relative to traditional-sector wages if the remittance rate is at all large. However, for a value of $\beta > 1$, the wage to be paid in the modern sector rises without limit as employment is concentrated entirely within the market sector.

The model is too simple to apply outside the range of still very underdeveloped economies where remittances are important. It would be absurd to expect a larger and larger proportion of market-sector workers to go on paying a fixed proportion of their earnings to fewer and fewer relatives who remain in the village. Yet in the early stages of transforming the labor force, this model gives one rationale for a rising supply price of labor in a labor-"surplus" economy without resorting to arbitrary, extra-market forces to account for the observed facts.

A SPATIAL MODEL

A second, alternative explanation for the Liberian wage rise, and one with distinctive implications for development planning, is based on the geographical characteristics of the country. Simply, and somewhat abstractly, the country's market-sector economy may be regarded as a set of activity centers that are arrayed along a line, while the traditional economy employs its labor force in activities that are spread out over a plane. The density of population and thus of the labor force over the plane declines as the distance from the line of the market economy increases. Transportation cost of both people and goods is proportional to the distance from the line, and it is assumed that frequent trips are made to their home villages by workers who have accepted employment in the modern sector.

Each of these assumptions is in fact characteristic of the Liberian economy. The location of market-sector activity is mainly in a series of cities found along the coastal plain or along the single major road, which extends from Monrovia on the coast to the Nimba Mountains in the interior of the country, which may be regarded as an extension of the line of coastal towns. The indigenous population does in fact extend away from the coast and on either side of the major road, thinning out in a general way the farther it goes into the interior from the coast or the road. Finally, there is no doubt that transportation is important for workers who work in the modern sector and make the trip back and forth frequently. The assumption that activity is stretched along a line is somewhat troublesome. It is most convenient to assume that activity is found with uniform intensity along the line, but such is not quite the case. Activity tends to concentrate in towns and cities with significant separations between them. Yet the actual pattern is not necessarily better characterized by points in a plane.

These spatial patterns are the geographic correlates of deeper aspects of economic dualism. It is therefore useful to describe these economic characteristics further in order to make the assumptions appear less arbitrary. The economy of a traditional society that practices slash-and-burn agriculture is bound to be spread out over a plane because its land requirements are so extensive. Not only is it a subsistence economy in the sense that the total per capita income is low, but it is capable of producing most of the components of its total consumption at home and is not greatly dependent on transportation. But self-sufficiency does not mean at all that it will reject an opportunity to trade for new goods.

For obvious reasons, trade and transportation are so important to the modern-sector economy that it chooses a location with access to the rest of the world. This requirement favors coastlines. When an inland center is opened to take advantage of a mineral deposit or other attraction, the road itself becomes a focus for additional market-centered activity.

The most compelling reason for the population being densest

near the line of market-centered activity is that market-centered activities require labor, and their location is chosen to take advantage of higher labor density. The location of plantations is decidedly affected, *inter alia,* by population density. So are roads, where there is a choice. Sometimes a combination of geological and climate factors also makes for a greater density of indigenous populations near the coast, as is the case in Liberia.

Under these circumstances of uneven geographical distribution of population, one would expect that, even with a large remaining pool of labor in the traditional economy, the supply price of labor would rise, because the workers most easily induced to accept employment in the market economy are those who live nearby and for whom the cost of transportation is small. As the demand for labor expands, wages have to rise sufficiently to induce workers who must travel farther to reach the line. Although the transportation cost is an increasing linear function of distance, the thinning of the population implies that equal marginal increases in wages will be associated with diminishing increments to the labor force. Thus, on these assumptions, an increasingly inelastic labor supply may be predicted, such as the data for wages suggest in fact exists in Liberia.

Four cases may be considered if two assumptions are exchanged for their alternatives. Let transportation cost per worker be:

$$T/n = f(A^\alpha, D^\beta)$$

where A is the area swept by a constant transportation outlay, and D is the population density on the land. The first assumption is that market activity is located along a line so that each point competes for labor with neighboring points. Therefore, increments in transport expenditure per worker cover *proportional* increments in land area served, which is expressed by setting $\alpha = 1$. Its alternative assumption is that market activity is centered at a point so that an increment of transport expenditure per worker serves a land area increment proportional to the *square* of the distance from the point, which is expressed by setting $\alpha = 2$. The second assumption is that population grows geometrically thinner as its distance from market activity increases, which is expressed by setting $\beta = \frac{1}{2}$. The alternative assumption is that population density is homogeneous over the plain, in which case $\beta = 1$.

In the first case, if $\alpha = 1$ and $\beta = 1$, T/n increases linearly. In the second, if $\beta = \frac{1}{2}$ while $\alpha = 1$, T/n rises asymptotically to an upper bound. Third, if $\alpha = 2$ and $\beta = 1$, T/n rises geometrically, which seems most consistent with the characteristics in Liberia and with the observed wage rise. Fourth if $\alpha = 2$ and $\beta = \frac{1}{2}$, T/n rises linearly, as in the first case.

The plausibility of this explanation for the observed wage increase must be judged in light of the high cost of transportation, over rather long distances and poor roads, of people who do not readily sever their connections with their homes after taking jobs in the market economy. For such people the budgetary importance of these transportation expenses must be very great, and I believe careful budget studies will show that the wage increases required to cover these costs are of the correct order of magnitude to explain the wage increases that have occurred.

TRIBAL-PREFERENCE MODEL

Heretofore it has been assumed that all workers have similar attitudes about working in market-centered enterprises, so that wages paid for such work need equal only the average income of a worker in traditional-sector employment plus transportation costs in accordance with the previous model. Now recognition is given to the fact that the population of Liberia, in common with other West African countries, is composed of a large number of different tribes, and one of the distinguishing attributes of such tribes is that they have different work preferences. These preferences are reinforced by other tribal characteristics affecting the success with which individuals manage the cultural transition required to give up the security of life in a tribal village for the more regimented life of industry or plantation.

Differences in job preference permit an ordering of tribes according to their degree of availability for work within the money sector. Assuming no significant differences based on tribe in the productivity of individuals, the earliest recruits into the market-sector labor force would be expected to come from the most available tribes. If intertribal differences in preference are greater than intratribal differences, it is possible for very large proportions of the workers of one or a few tribes to be absorbed into the market sector before many workers appear from less available tribes. As a larger labor force is required by market-sector expansion, however, it would be necessary to raise wages, and for all workers since tribal discrimination is not practiced. The elasticity of labor supply would then depend on the specific structure of tribal size and preference.

The differences that would be required for this hypothesis to explain a rising supply price of labor do in fact exist in Liberia. The tribes most available, the Bassa and the Kru, are also large and in the early expansion probably provided a high proportion of the new labor force. The tribes providing the more recent supplies of labor are smaller, which would suggest that the "treads" of the higher steps are shorter. But one can only judge the height of the "risers" between the steps by the increasing wages; there is no way of measuring the disutility of wage labor for successively less available tribes for which wages must compensate. Nevertheless, the shortening treads resulting merely from the smaller size of less available tribes in part account for the increasing inelasticity of the supply of labor. It would be simple to establish whether the history of the tribal composition of the market-sector labor force is consistent with this hypothesis. Firestone keeps a record of the tribe of its employees, and probably other major employers do as well.

A FRICTIONAL MODEL

A final means of accounting for the rise of wage rates that has occurred with development is based on certain characteristics of West African life which introduce a lag in the labor supply response. The slowness of communications is one reason for a lag of greater length than would be found in more advanced countries and even in many more densely populated, underdeveloped countries. Communications with respect to employment opportunities are not solely a matter of radios and telephones. Transmission of job information is required in sufficient detail to induce potential workers to make the trip despite the risk of disappointment. Labor-market institutions in West Africa provide only crude channels through which such information can move, and there have been many past unhappy experiences in market-sector employment, which may have increased the subjective risk of further disappointments.

Another reason for a marked lag in labor supply response is the cyclical planting pattern, in which land is left fallow for long intervals. Urban employment for male workers must normally be timed between the periods of heavy labor required for cutting and burning of forest. To retain an urban labor force through these periods is bound to require higher compensation, even though only a part of the area in production must be cut down in one season, for the decision to work for wages instead of preparing the land for the next few crops comes close to a commitment to make a permanent shift to dependence on income from wages received for market-sector employment.

Thus, although there may be a large pool of workers in traditional employment, they are not in equally close contact with sources of job information, nor are they equally available in the same season. The greater the demand for labor in the market sector, the higher must the wage rise against these frictional supply limitations.

WAGE RATES AND LABOR SCARCITY

It is apparent that wages are not under all circumstances an equally satisfactory measure of labor scarcity; nor are increasing wage rates an infallible guide to the increasing scarcity of labor. Of the four explanations that are not obviously inconsistent with the evidence, one seems to account for wage rises that are not related to labor scarcity, while in different ways the other three do reflect some particular element of scarcity. I shall refer to wage increases that are effectively explained by a model which implies no increase in labor scarcity as Class I wage increases. Wage increases explained by a model that does imply increasing labor scarcity are Class II wage increases.

The Lewis-Nurkse model, in which wages are constant while a "surplus" labor force remains in the traditional society, implies an opportunity cost of labor equal to zero, for there is no loss of output within the traditional sector as a consequence of the transfer of labor to the market sector.[11] In an adaptation of the Nurkse model to an economy like Liberia's, in which land is not so scarce as to

11. W. Arthur Lewis, "Development with Unlimited Supplies of Labor"; Ragnar Nurkse, *Problems of Capital Formation in Underdeveloped Countries* (Oxford: Blackwell, 1953).

make labor superabundant in relation to it, the opportunity cost of labor would be equal to average labor income in the traditional sector. This is so because, with plentiful land and virtually no capital used in traditional agriculture, the reduction or change in the number of workers would change output proportionally. Hence, the average value product, the marginal value product, and the market-sector wage would all be equal. How should wage increases above this base labor cost be interpreted? Four explanations have been proposed, and it is impossible to choose among them on the basis of currently available information. Tests could easily be devised for each to narrow the range of possibilities, but there is a good chance that more than one, and possibly all four, would continue to be regarded as justified in the light of deeper knowledge. They are not themselves mutually inconsistent, and there is no forced option unless the policy choices to which they lead are inconsistent.

Consider the Class I wage rise. If Liberian wages rose, at least in part, because of the payment of remittances, then the rise of wage rates in Liberia can not be regarded as measuring increasing labor scarcity. The wage rise is the result of a redistribution of market-sector income in a manner that systematically increases the wage incentive required to recruit labor to new employment. Nevertheless, higher increasing wages will reduce the volume of investment by raising the cost of labor in market-sector employment and by reducing the share of income received as profits by entrepreneurs whose propensities to save and invest are of course higher than are such propensities of other traditional-sector recipients or market-sector workers.

If nothing offsets the process, the fact of higher wages will permit the development of only those activities, such as iron mining, which would continue to be profitable even with a much larger wage bill. The spread effects from these strong centers of economic development will decline, and general economic development will become less and less likely.

Policies to offset the effects of remittance payments can be devised. One such policy is the imposition of a tax on the tribal recipients of remittances and a subsidy, equal to the revenue so obtained, on the employment of labor in the market sector in proportion to wages paid. But would such a policy serve? The difficulties in identifying remittance recipients are probably insuperable, and the inequity in errors is considerable at the low level of village income. Furthermore, even if identification were possible, the tax would appear unreasonably discriminatory. Finally, since workers take employment in part in order to be able to support their villages, they would surely be less willing to work for wages if remittances were in effect taxed away. The alternative of sub- sidizing employment to offset the wage increase out of general taxes might be expected not to generate any net stimulation to economic development. These difficulties suggest that there is little practical difference between Class I and Class II wage increases. Both are the result of an effective labor scarcity.

Consider the other three explanations of the wage increase, which clearly fall into Class II. If wages rise because of the increasing im- portance at the margin of the transportation component of labor cost, the increasing cost reflects the necessity of using economic resources in order to increase the supply of labor. The scarcity may be regarded as a scarcity of transportation services. Accordingly, it may be feasible to remove the bottleneck by improving the transportation system. But such improvements require the alloca- tion of investable resources. It is then a matter of choosing between paying the transportation cost of the existing transportation system in the form of high wages or paying for a more capital-intensive form of transportation directly. If the capital-intensive system were sufficiently low cost at the prospective volume of traffic, the in- vestment might be justified. In the circumstances in Liberia, where population is spread out over wide areas of difficult terrain, invest- ment in improved transportation can not be expected to reduce the cost of transportation for many such projects. Unless part of the costs can be charged to other benefits, therefore, such transpor- tation investments are unlikely to improve the terms on which the market sector recruits its labor.

To the extent that the transport component does account for the wage rise, it is advisable to accommodate development to real labor scarcity. Such accommodation might mean some investment in transportation facilities for labor. It might mean the proliferation of market-sector centers of activity closer to concentrations of popula- tion wherever such choices satisfy general location criteria. In the end, accommodation means that wage costs in the market should be permitted to have their effect on the choice of goods and services produced and the capital-labor intensity of the techniques used to produce them. The effects of high wages should not be interpreted in a way that encourages a profligate, low-productivity use of labor, as though the high market wage were a false signal.

Next, consider the possibility that the cause of the wage rise is the structure of tribal preferences. A wage increase of this kind is a reflection of labor scarcity. Unless one thinks in purely physical terms, there is little difference between a scarcity that results from the preference of workers not to work for wages and one that results from the literal absence of more workers, except that in the first case there is some degree of elasticity in the supply of labor. However, once wages rise so high that continued employment expansion can not profitably pay the higher wage, the difference becomes meaningless.

Where labor scarcity is the result of the workers' preference to remain outside of market employment, changes in attitudes could significantly affect the supply of labor. Whether or not they will change as workers experience the blessings of a new life is a speculative matter. There is the possibility of inducing preference change by schooling and even more directly by "advertising" efforts. But it seems doubtful that such policies could be justified by the usual investment criteria. Even if they were, it is doubtful that they could be justified on welfare grounds. Raising the income aspirations of a class of workers who are then satisfied by finding new jobs for wages may in the end leave them no better off than they were to begin with.[12] In many circumstances there is even a risk that their ability to satisfy their new aspiration level may be less than their previous ability to satisfy their old level of aspiration. Situations of this kind may contain the makings of economic development, but they may also lead to a good deal of frustration and even pathological forms of extreme behavior. The organization of a labor force by the planned use of aspiration-raising efforts ought therefore to be coordinated with other actions that will control these risks of frustration.

Finally, consider the wage rise to the extent that it is a consequence of economic friction which produces a supply response lag. The scarcity of labor is validly reflected in the wage rise, and again,

12. R. S. Weckstein, "Welfare Criteria and Changing Tastes," *American Economic Review*, LVII (March 1962), 133–53.

as in the transportation case, the scarcity may be attributed to the lack of development of backward tribes of people. Improvements in labor-market recruitment facilities do not constitute a highly productive investment in a banker's sense, for the yield on the resources, in the form of a lower-cost labor force, is small. Yet this sort of investment, like the others, may be desirable from a political and philosophical viewpoint, because it is a way to unite such tribal people into a modern nation. Where political benefits are insufficient to justify investments in reducing labor-recruitment friction, such efforts should be subjected to the same criteria applied to other investments within the country

THE PLANNING CONSEQUENCES OF LABOR SCARCITY

In Liberia the rise of wages does reflect labor scarcity, as here defined, and this should affect economic policies if resources are to be used efficiently. Following are four illustrations of the policy implications of increasing labor scarcity. First, a further rapid expansion of activities that make claims upon labor resources may be expected to lead to a contraction of output of some of the country's established industries. As they contract, they give up their labor force, making it available for use elsewhere. This transfer of labor is similar to the original transfer of labor out of the traditional sector, only at a higher productivity level. It is a desirable shift in response to a growing stock of capital, and it permits labor to be withdrawn from activities with low yield to new, higher yielding activities.

Such transfers of labor already appear to have taken place out of the rubber plantations. A large number of trees capable of producing rubber are not being tapped for want of available tappers at their present wages. In some of the less well-managed plantations, the high wage has so depressed the returns to plantations that they have ceased to produce entirely. Thus, the rubber industry is adjusting to the scarcity of labor by eliminating the least efficient employers of labor. This constructive reaction should not be resisted on the spurious ground that the trees are being wasted or that Liberia's national needs require this output. It is evident that, under given technological circumstances, the cost of producing some rubber is greater than the gain.

A similar contraction of output has been occurring for essentially the same reason in the production of food in the village areas. The government has been conducting a food-growing campaign to reverse the trend. Liberian labor is apparently not well used in growing food, and with more attractive opportunities for work in other lines, food production has suffered. This adjustment, too, is desirable. Perhaps a new technology for food growing that makes more efficient use of labor will be found suitable and enable food growers to compete for labor. But programs which attempt merely to cajole growers into greater effort are misguided. A development plan must anticipate the economic activities that are likely to contract. Plans should not commit the naïve error of anticipating an expansion in all lines. If it is inefficient for food output to increase as food demand rises, technological change must be successfully introduced or else import increases should be planned.[13]

A second illustration of the policy implications of growing labor scarcity involves the choice among alternative techniques of production, which in a number of cases means a choice among more or less labor-intensive methods. Rubber production is now carried on by highly labor-intensive techniques. Tapping the trees, collecting the latex, and weeding use great labor gangs. But under increasing wage pressure Firestone has been reorganizing the production processes in such a way as to economize on labor, even though the company is obliged to invest more capital in new equipment and in other ways to change the layout for greater mechanization. In recent years a new high-yielding plant has also been introduced into Liberian plantations. By greatly increasing the output of latex per acre, it reduces the length of forest walks and the cost of collection. But the introduction of the new material requires the slaughter of producing trees and a wait of five to six years for the new trees to produce. These measures are evidently justified economically under the present conditions of wages and capital cost that Firestone faces. They ought to be regarded as justified for Liberian small producers as well. Thus, it is probably necessary for the government to support the spread of the new technology to Liberian small producers by means of technical as-

13. For a formal proof of the theorem that as one factor expands and the other remains constant, there is a reduction in the output of that good, which intensively requires for its production the nonexpanding factor, see T. M. Rybczynski, "Factor Endowment and Relative Commodity Prices," *Economica*, XXII (November 1955), 336–41.

sistance and agricultural credit. Yet such a labor-saving development may be regarded without enthusiasm unless the wage costs that justify the investment are accepted as a reflection of true labor scarcity.

Third, a broad policy issue is involved in the wage rate sometimes used for project evaluation. Opinions at one extreme go so far as completely to discount the market wage as a measure of the social cost of labor and to assume that, as long as the bulk of the population remains within tribal areas, there is a surplus of labor and hence its value is zero. Given this assumption, many projects that would otherwise be rejected are regarded as economically worthy. Subsidies or tariff protection are then recommended to compensate for the wages actually paid, to assure that such projects are profitable to their private owners. An evaluation of projects introduced under this policy during recent years would very likely show that a number of them have diminished national output.

Fourth, an economy in which labor is a scarce factor must avoid uneconomic expansion of labor-using social capital. Expansion of employment in the construction and operation of social capital uses the labor that would otherwise be available for directly productive activity. Ideally, the employment of labor in social-capital projects should be carried to the point where its marginal product there is equal to its marginal product in private employment. To disregard labor costs in social-capital project evaluation because of a large residual pool of unemployed, while private employers generally govern their own employment policies in accordance with the market wage, will lead to the wasteful overbuilding of public capital at the cost of directly productive private capital.

The planning of future public expenditures in these circumstances should be responsive to estimates of the prospective growth of the labor force and of demands upon that labor force. Total demands in a country like Liberia are likely to grow more rapidly than the supply of labor, and wage increases must be expected. The larger the public-sector demands for labor, the higher will wages rise in a given period and the more productive must private projects be to commence and to survive. In the past, development plans have been drafted for Liberia in which the entire increment to the labor force would probably have been pre-empted for public work. Even though this kind of plan is unlikely to materialize, it can be destructive to the degree that it encourages an unbalanced expansion of the public sector.

The example of Liberia is a warning that not all underdeveloped countries have labor-surplus economies. In the labor-scarcity case the process of development couples a large flow of capital to the small flow of new labor in the growing economy. If in the management of this growth an unwarranted assumption of surplus is made, it may cause a painful waste of labor and capital. Therefore, to associate underdevelopment automatically with labor surplus would be unfortunate. In the Liberian case, the scarcity of labor results from a small population that grows slowly and does not rush to leave its traditional condition as investment opens new opportunities for employment. In addition to countries like Liberia, still others may be expected to grow into a condition of labor scarcity as development proceeds successfully. The labor-scarce type of economy may thus become increasingly common.

Part VI

EVALUATION

11

Development Theory and DAS Experience

It is logical and probably inevitable that economists oriented to economics as a discipline and those primarily concerned with the solution of immediate problems differ significantly in their approach and in the priorities they assign to various issues. On the one hand, since the essence of contributing to the discipline is generalization, the economist primarily oriented to the discipline looks for patterns, for universal or at least widespread phenomena. He therefore tends to abstract, to simplify, to seek central tendencies and discard exceptions. On the other hand, the problem-solver is concerned with a particular issue in a specific environment. He therefore wants to know all he can about the issue that confronts him and to find solutions that work in a given situation, whether they can be generalized or not.

To say that there is no pure case of either the discipline- or problem-oriented economist is to state the obvious. But in a rough sense the two types do exist. Furthermore, the discipline-oriented economist is more often found in the universities, engaged in research and concerned with theory; the other is generally found in government or business, engaged in practice and concerned with policy. Common sense suggests that both the discipline and the solution of problems may be advanced most effectively when one person or a group of close collaborators combines a discipline-

NOTE: This concluding chapter has benefited greatly from the careful comments of Walter P. Falcon, Lester E. Gordon, and Raymond Vernon. In addition, Raymond Vernon was most generous in making available for plagiarism a summary of his comments on the Bellagio Conference papers.

oriented ability to generalize with the problem-oriented experience that provides a basis for generalization.

For a variety of reasons the distance between the discipline-oriented and the problem-oriented has been especially great in the field of economic development. Here distance in every sense — physical, psychological, and intellectual — separates the two groups of economists. When "development" became an object of study, discipline-oriented economists were often academicians engaged in research in the developed world. Those concerned with the problems of economic development were principally government officials, swamped by immediate difficulties in the less developed countries. In most other fields, economists with differing orientations are in frequent contact, and some of them occasionally shift their focus — for instance, as they move back and forth between universities and government. In the development field, however, most research workers in the universities of the rich countries have been separated, psychologically as well as physically, from the practitioners in the underdeveloped countries by a gap far greater than the one separating Robert Triffin *et al.* from the Group of Ten.

The tools on hand in the early 1950's were inadequate for spanning the distance. In part, discipline-oriented research on economic development problems tended toward the abstract because of inadequate data. Basic information on underdeveloped countries still is not often published. Much remains in confidential government documents, typescripts, or memoranda that never reach those outside government. Field studies by outside economists are hampered by high costs, political uncertainty, language barriers, and other difficulties of work in a foreign culture. In sheer frustration research has often been concentrated on narrow technical exercises on which economists could work without much data. During the early period practitioners in turn lacked computers, advanced knowledge of theory and mathematics, or the time required to generalize. They could not make use of most research results.

Today the gap is beginning to narrow. Not only are economists from the developed world showered with funds if they work in an underdeveloped country, but the supply of well-trained economists is increasing in the underdeveloped areas themselves. Computers have become widely available. Data accumulate.

Earlier, a few development economists pioneered in bridging the gap. They were under pressure to face in both directions, to focus in turn on the immediate problems of governments and on the generalizations to be made for the discipline. This volume reflects one attempt to generalize from experience — the experience of the Harvard Development Advisory Service. The book offers an opportunity to compare the concerns of involved economists with the general sweep of economic development literature. It throws some interesting light on economic development as a field. There emerge a number of differences between the perspectives of the practitioners and of the majority of discipline-oriented economists, even when the practitioners are unusually concerned with drawing generalizations from their experience.

INVESTMENT CRITERIA

The most startling discrepancy between the two groups lies in the attitude of each toward the economic basis for investment decisions. No subject has received more attention in the literature of economic development than sophisticated techniques for allocating resources. Yet the studies in this volume correctly reflect the almost complete neglect of such techniques in the actual work of planning agencies. There is no discussion at all of investment criteria, of social as against private returns and costs, of accounting prices or investment strategy.

The topic of investment criteria preoccupies the discipline-oriented in part because of the ease with which the subject lends itself to the techniques of economic analysis. The appraisal of investment decisions that is set forth in the literature involves little consideration of institutional, political, or social factors, which are intrusive with respect to many other issues in economic development.

Practitioners, by contrast, are frustrated by the absence of the data that the sophisticated techniques require. Promoters of projects do not want to see them rejected for failure to meet economic criteria, and usually they have enough wit to adjust the "facts" to assure that they pass scrutiny. Data on proposed investments therefore tend to be unreliable. Worse yet, even such accurate information as comes to hand is usually inadequate. Investment criteria are wielded by governments, but much investment is in private hands, and little information is provided to the government. Finally, many potential investment alternatives are never investigated by anyone. It is difficult for a planning agency to develop investment criteria and accounting prices if data cover only a fraction of alternative investment possibilities. That fraction may in itself be highly biased, as, for example, when estimates are limited to public utilities.

A related reason for the neglect of sophisticated investment analysis by problem-oriented practitioners is that many decisions are more or less obvious. Since most decisions have been taken in the context of short- or medium-term plans, only a few problem areas are crucial to the economy and worth an investment of scarce manpower in intensive analysis. Of these crucial decisions, many require exercise of economic common sense alone, not elaborate analysis — although elaborate analysis may enhance the political salability of the common-sense conclusions. Within the limits of administrative capacity, available data, and financial constraints, some proposals make obvious economic sense, while others seem justifiable only on prestige or political grounds. To use an actual example, Pakistan has ample natural gas and limestone but no iron ore, coking coal, or steelmaking experience. During the early stages of development, therefore, cement production was more likely to make economic sense than steel production.

In any case, many countries formerly suffered from a shortage of investment proposals, not a surfeit, at least in the public sector. When there are no alternatives, the real or opportunity cost of capital may be close to zero. Under these circumstances only proposals with practically no expected returns might be rejected, and they are usually spotted without requiring careful analysis.

Inadequate data, inadequate control over investment, and the common-sense nature of many investment decisions raise the cost and reduce the benefits of improving the analysis of investment decisions. Economic competence is a universally scarce resource. Like all scarce resources, it should be allocated to its most productive use. In the past, improving the choice of investment by the use of careful, quantitative techniques would have yielded only a moderate improvement in the functioning of the economy. Using scarce economic talent on other problems could often yield far higher returns. In Latin America stabilization was often the most important policy issue. In Asia, improvement in the functioning of a country's economy as a whole, clearing away inappropriate price incentives and inefficient direct controls, was probably the prime task. In many countries better preparation of requests for foreign aid could, at a moderate cost in technical manpower, sharply increase available resources. Nearly everywhere, improvements in fiscal policy were often important to the functioning of the economy. These issues, crucial to growth rate and economic efficiency, quite naturally have been given higher priority than the improvement of investment decisions by practicing government economists.

As a general phenomenon, this neglect of investment decisions has already begun to change. More economists and other technicians are on hand to prepare and evaluate projects. The cost of improving investment decisions is therefore declining. In some countries work on more urgent questions is well under way, and attention can turn to investment decisions at a lower opportunity cost. Often the chief constraint now is lack of capital rather than lack of investment proposals. "Perspective planning," calling for decisions on development strategy over fifteen to twenty-five years, is being seriously attempted. With a longer time horizon and a concomitant increase in the flexibility of resource allocation, economic common sense becomes an increasingly fragile basis for investment decisions. Problem-oriented economists are likely to turn to more sophisticated investment criteria a decade or so after they became a favorite of their discipline-oriented colleagues.

They will find that the state of the art leaves much to be desired for those concerned with policy problems, despite the attention paid to the subject in the economic literature. Although investment criteria are well worked out in theory and guidelines exist for calculating appropriate prices to measure costs and benefits, serious difficulties arise in applying principles that were not designed primarily for problem-solving. More serious, there has been little useful work on the important but complex issues of time, risk and uncertainty, location and external effects. These issues are related, and they share one unfortunate property — they do not readily lend themselves to analysis by the sharper tools of economics that are available.

An extensive literature deals with the time dimension and the factors that have a bearing on the interest and discount rate in the abstract. Unfortunately, however, the inescapable conclusion seems to be that there is no usable basis for calculating the appropriate interest rate for actual investment decisions. This failing is doubly unfortunate in that the choice of investment projects often depends on the interest rate. The choice of transport modes usually hinges on the interest rate, as do methods for power production and decisions on whether to build large dams or simple irrigation structures. The use of long-term planning increases the relevance of sophisticated investment criteria but also deepens the impact of the discount rate on investment decisions.

A longer time horizon for planning also increases the importance of risk and uncertainty. Here the planner finds himself in almost completely uncharted terrain. Existing analyses deal largely with the problems of the private firm and have only limited usefulness to decision-makers concerned with the whole economy. Unlike the businessman, the government economist does not face the possibility that his business will be wiped out. His attitude toward possible loss on a particular investment is therefore more relaxed. On the other hand, his problems in dealing with uncertainty and risk are compounded by his concern with the economy as a whole. Available techniques are nearly useless. Most investment criteria in fact simply ignore risk and uncertainty, at best taking account of trends only, with no estimate of likely variations.

Some uncertainties can be reduced by the physical proximity of investments. When the output of one enterprise is the input of another, it is often easier to assure quality and delivery schedules if the enterprises are located near each other. Proximity can also reduce the risk and cost of deviations from plans. Decisions on the location of new enterprises should therefore take account of the benefits of proximity: more effective communications, lower costs in sharing standby and repair facilities, and reduced transportation costs. The offsetting costs of concentration must be allowed for as well. The literature on regional economics and locational questions is vast. So is the literature on external economies and diseconomies, which are closely related to locational effects. Emphatic discussions of the effect of one investment on another boast a ripe old age, as the writing on development goes. However, there are practically no quantitative data on the importance of external effects and no usable guidelines for decision-makers interested in estimating locational or external economies. As a result, investment programs or plans are almost "spaceless," even though their execution is far from this ethereal state, and the location of investments is the hardest-fought political issue in many countries. External economies are often the last refuge of the scoundrel — cited, but not measured, to justify otherwise anemic projects.

The discussion may again be illustrated with the experience of Pakistan. Work on the First Five Year Plan in the middle 1950's involved a good deal of attention to investment decisions. Costs and benefits were calculated with some precision. Accounting prices were applied. Because the planning agency was not intimately involved in government policy, the staff could indulge its propensities for sophisticated analysis. For the Second and Third Plans, however, no accounting prices were calculated, and little effort was devoted to systematic cost-benefit calculations. By then the planning agencies were heavily involved in work on foreign aid, fiscal policy, price policies, and a shift to indirect controls. Little time was left for work on investment decisions, which were regarded as yielding lower benefits. In addition, as the planning agencies became influential and were therefore kept well informed on investment decisions, it became obvious that certain issues were reasonably clear-cut without careful quantitative analysis. Now, in 1966, still another reversal is in process, because of the longer time perspective for planning, the availability of more professional manpower, and progress on more urgent work. In the execution of the Third and preparation of the Fourth Plans investment decisions are again receiving some attention. The stage has been reached, a dozen or so years after systematic planning began, where the cost-benefit ratio for a systematic analysis of investment alternatives is quite favorable.

So much for the most obvious instance in which the concerns of the discipline-oriented economists preceded and exceeded the concern of problem-oriented practitioners. The studies in this volume also suggest an opposite case. Fiscal policies are an important problem but have been relatively neglected by the discipline-minded.

FISCAL POLICY

Most of the analyses in this book have mentioned the importance of fiscal policy, and their emphasis reflects its importance in the work of planning units and economic staff agencies. Government deficits, compounded of poor tax policies and inadequate expenditure controls, have been crucial in the inflation plaguing Argentina and Colombia. Taxes and tariffs, by pointing import-substituting industrialization in certain directions, have given rise to structural problems in those two countries. In both respects the situation in Argentina and Colombia is typical of many South American and other countries. Fiscal policy plays a central role in past problems and in programs for their solution.

Liberia provides another example. Foreign resources are available to finance most investments if Liberia can cover the local costs. Any increase in taxes or improvement in tax collection would therefore have an important effect on development. At the same time, the serious Liberian debt problem resulted from inadequate control over government expenditures. Liberia's urgent need to improve tax collection and expenditure control is shared by many underdeveloped countries.

Finally, fiscal policy, particularly the differential incidence of taxes, is one of the most powerful and widely used government tools for influencing private savings, investment, and production decisions. When a discrepancy appears between the savings-investment and balance-of-payments gaps in a two-gap model, the prescription relied upon usually involves a heavy use of taxes and tariffs.

Given the importance of fiscal policy, the extent of investigation with respect to underdeveloped countries has been risible. True enough, there are some books on the subject, and textbooks on development devote attention to it, but both generally report conventional wisdom, not new research. Government agencies do make a considerable effort to investigate aspects of fiscal policy, but they usually focus on specific aspects of particular taxes on an ad hoc, emergency basis. Richard Bird has here described a typical case, with many decisions taken on ad hoc administrative and legal, not economic, grounds.

The neglect of fiscal policy by discipline-oriented development economists may result primarily from the difficulty of generalizing in this field. Conclusions on fiscal policy require a great deal of knowledge about a specific country at a specific time. For instance, the effect of commodity taxes depends on price structure and distribution systems, on elasticities of supply and demand, on income distribution, and on attitudes toward consumption, saving, and work. Concern with fiscal policy therefore implies consistent work on a particular country, access to data not readily available to the outsider, and a considerable period of time in the country. The quantitative tools that can be used are limited. Generalization requires knowledge of a number of countries, and even then it may be difficult or impossible because of differences in causal factors. No wonder discipline-oriented economists shy away from research on fiscal policy — especially since the description most likely to be applied to such work, "institutional," has acquired a faintly pejorative connotation in the profession. For many, the word suggests fuzzy descriptive work, neither rigorous nor based on quantitative analysis, concerned with such supposedly noneconomic matters as motives and incentives.

MACRO-MODELS

The building of macro-models, expressing complex quantitative relationships between variables, is close to the opposite end from fiscal policy in the prestige scale of the discipline. A great deal of effort has been invested in model design over the last decade, because complex models were widely regarded in the discipline as a major tool to guide government intervention in any economy. Until recently, however, most model builders correctly referred to their efforts as heuristic, or illustrative, or theoretical. The tendency was toward the ever more complex model.

Many practitioners for a time believed that models would remain time-consuming exercises, quite irrelevant to their problems. The costs of obtaining and manipulating the data required even by simple models were high. Moreover, such data as could be gathered at any cost were generally unreliable. Therefore, a model could only project consequences on assumptions which were so poorly based that it was as justifiable to change the assumptions as the conclusions. Policy-makers recognized that data problems inevitably affected their work, but they feared that models would obscure the data problem. When the policy-maker based his recommendations on simple, back-of-the-envelope calculations, he felt reasonably sure he understood the implicit assumptions he had been forced to make in the absence of reliable data, and he thought he knew the value judgments implied in his conclusions. But when he used a model, built by others, whose complexities he might not fully grasp, he always had the sneaking suspicion that implicit assumptions had been incorporated which he might not fully understand or discover but which he would have disagreed with had they been explicit. For instance, any model usually identifies certain kinds of scarcities as having higher priority than others; the size of the savings-investment gap or the foreign-exchange gap, for instance, may be chosen by the model builder for prime attention, while other issues may be disregarded or treated as unyielding constraints. A model also states explicitly how the causal relations flow. In short, in the process of devising the model, the model builder is offered a wide-open opportunity to shape, consciously or unconsciously, the ultimate selection of strategies.

For a while the discussion between model builders, who were discipline-oriented almost without exception, and problem-oriented planners threatened to become sterile. The former tended to attribute the failure to use models to ignorance and incompetence; the latter suggested that the models were unusable or useless exercises. Yet the studies in this volume reflect the increased use that has been made of models in the last few years. In part this increase came about because a major effort was put forth recently to develop usable models and to use developed models. Model builders and model users became more experienced and learned from their mistakes. A familiar phenomenon of monopolistic competition may have played some role on the supplier's side. As the number of model builders proliferated, the attempt to differentiate their product would provide an added incentive to produce usable models. On the user's side, many planners were given thorough training in quantitative economics. Because of the effort it had cost them, they were under psychological pressure to apply what they learned. Data-gathering improved, in part in response to the needs of model builders. Other factors were even more important in the increased use of models in the work of governments in underdeveloped areas. As planners and economists began to be taken seriously by governments and faced the incredible complexity of the economies they were asked to understand, they were forced to look for efficient means to project possible consequences of a wide variety of alternative actions. They were therefore eager to use the tools developed earlier by the model builders to handle a wide variety of alternatives.

The writings collected here suggest two additional and probably crucial reasons for the effective use of models, which may have relevance for other areas of cooperation between discipline- and problem-oriented economists. In the first place, the models were not overloaded; they were not pushed beyond their capacity. Models were used to assist in finding solutions, not to provide solutions. They were expected to trace out the implications of a given set of alternative policies or events, to indicate whether several decisions were consistent with each other under various assumptions. But even as consistency models, those described in this volume were modest in scope and design. They were not designed to guide development strategy by indicating the optimum allocation of resources to fields or industries. Wouter Tims's Pakistan model, the most elaborate one presented here, is a standard two-gap model, with essentially only two scarce resources. All models are spaceless. In Pakistan, with two regions separated by twelve hundred miles and differences even more important than this physical distance, a spaceless model clearly leaves some vital issues to outside determination.

A second and related fact is that model building and model using went on as part of a continuing dialogue with others engaged in the planning and policy enterprise. The models were the result of successive approximations, that is, frequent changes to bring them in line with knowledge, decisions, or analyses derived from outside the model-building groups. This process was effective only because those working with the models could be in daily contact with conversational economists, technicians, and administrators. They could draw on the whole range of data, analyses, and decisions provided by others in the planning agency and by other government bodies. Model builders derived assurance from checking their assumptions with specialists in every field. The model's results in turn influenced judgments and decisions made by those outside the model-building groups. Policy-makers had a reasonable assurance that in the overlooked and not fully understood recesses of the model there was no assumption or relationship which was important to the conclusions derived from the model but which they would challenge if it had been baldly stated.

As a result of the continuous dialogue between model builders and other planners, models were elaborated that could actually be used in the planning process. The models employed so far have been primitive, but once builders and users have gained confidence in each other's judgments and techniques, elaboration and sophistication will be likely in the future. Even five years ago these statements could not have been made.

IDEOLOGY AND POLICY

Many of the economic policy issues now exercising government economists have been debated by their more discipline-oriented colleagues for some time. The discussions have involved strong ideological overtones in certain cases, but the studies in this volume suggest that an operational consensus is now emerging on some of these issues.

First, in the Latin American context there has been a longstanding debate between those who placed development first and those who regarded stability as paramount. The contributors to this book show a serious concern with stability. The consensus is that development is unlikely to be rapid unless inflation is brought under control and recurring balance-of-payments crises are avoided. But their studies do not lend support to advocates of measures that would produce stability no matter what the cost to development. The measures usually proposed in the past by supporters of monetary orthodoxy are given short shrift. It is argued that monetary stringency, the prime tool of the orthodox, has reduced the supply of goods more than demand, actually adding to inflation in some cases; that devaluation has at times contributed primarily to price increases which negated the desired effect on trade; and that the rigidity of international organizations can be as disastrous to a stabilization program as can the political weakness of indigenous governments.

The argument between the development-first and the stabilization-first schools parallels that between the structuralists and the monetarists of Latin America, and the personnel in the respective camps were for a time generally identical. Once again, the authors here give little comfort to either side. Monetary policy is considered inadequate, and import-substituting industrialization, which was once the favorite of the structuralists, is thought to have been the wrong policy to rely on for some time. By stressing exports and the problem of limited internal markets, most of the authors hint at the need for trade or common-market agreements.

The most striking consensus to emerge from these studies by committed planners is the reliance on a combination of the price mechanism *and* planning. The older orthodoxies consider the two tendencies antagonistic. The argument between those advocating reliance on the market and those opting for government intervention has been long, heated, and not always productive. But the argument presented here is in general for combining reliance on prices with substantial government intervention, e.g., flexible exchange rates, but with government subsidizing exports and intervening to stabilize the rate; heavy reliance on price incentives to farmers, but coordinated with government investment, government subsidies on inputs, and government stabilization of prices. Even Liberian laborers, drawn from tribal villages, are believed to respond to price incentives in a highly rational way, with important consequences for government plans.

THE OTHER SOCIAL SCIENCES

So far the discussion has dwelt upon economics. A good deal of the effort in development, however, has been concerned more broadly with change and thus has drawn on social sciences other than economics. Even more than economics, other social sciences have been dominated by the discipline-oriented. Their conclusions have often been thoroughly discouraging. They stress the complexity of human behavior and institutions and are ever conscious of how seemingly simple policies may produce unpredictable change elsewhere in a complex fabric. Frequently they conclude that, because economic policies are framed for political reasons, so-called Western economics is not only inadequate but close to useless in devising a strategy to initiate or step up economic development. Alternatively, they argue that human behavior determines the effects of economic policies, and the roots of human behavior are to be found in the values of a society, or the upbringing of its children, or its religion or ideology. In their opinion, therefore, research on development should concentrate on ways of affecting human behavior, not on improving economic policies or plans. The solution of pressing problems is generally ignored in these formulations.

Undoubtedly in some ultimate sense the emphasis on political and social factors is the correct one. But if one is willing to neglect the search for ultimate causes of change, if one is content with the proximate causes, the evidence in this book that economic policies influence economic development is rather strong, and rather encouraging for an economist. Ultimately the question of why Argentina did not develop as rapidly as Australia or the United States may lie in the realm of political science, sociology, and social psychology, and it will not be easy to answer. However, clearly discernible mistakes in economic policies and programs are important proximate causes, and changes in economic policies and programs could provide an important remedy. Little is known about the values and motivations of Pakistan's peasants; little about their rural institutions. But sensible economic policies will cause some peasants to increase their output significantly, even if the basic reasons for their behavior have not been clearly discerned. Why Latin America is particularly inflation prone is a question economists can not answer adequately, but this ignorance does not mean that economists lack the knowledge to prescribe policies to slow down the rate of price increase.

To sum up, there has been a considerable gap between the interests of discipline- and problem-oriented economists concerned with development. It should be possible as well as fruitful to continue narrowing that gap in the future. The discipline-oriented need not concentrate either on the description of institutional and other noneconomic obstacles to growth or on ever more refined and abstract approaches. In the past, problem-oriented officials, charged with the formulation of economic policies and plans, were often unwilling or unable to generalize or to apply the work of those who did generalize to their specific problems. Planners were often drawn from the civil service, where they had acquired the administrator's contempt for those they regarded as unrealistic academicians. Other planners arrived directly from the graduate schools in developed countries, aglow with the naïve faith in oversimplified formulations characteristic of newly minted advanced-degree holders. In the last decade, however, a rapidly growing corps of professional government economists has formed, able to understand, apply, and adapt generalizations, and in turn to generalize from their experience. The further the transformation goes, the better for economists and countries alike.

INDEX

Index

Accounting prices, 347, 351
Adelman, Irma, 37
Agricultural Development Corporation (ADC) (Pakistan), 310
Agriculture: Argentina, 59, 209; Chile, 59; controls on, 303; exportable products of, 88, 89; export surplus, 11; exports (*see* Exports); growth factors in, 286–288, 299–306; growth of output, 6, 9, 10, 11, 13, 89, 213, 219, 234, 270; incentives, 309; labor, 297; "package" of inputs for, 314; policy for, 13, 300, 312; "slash and burn," 331; subsidies, 309; supply and demand for products of, 11; terms of trade, 13, 232, 299; uncertainty in, 307; zoning regulations, 14
Alejandro, Carlos F. Diaz. *See* Diaz-Alejandro
Alliance for Progress, 119
Alta Comision, 135
Argentina, 55, 68, 70, 352, 358; agricultural production, 59; growth rate of GNP, 207; industrial promotion, 56; input-output tables, 70; ISI pattern, 87; model of, 46; stabilization model, 48; tariff structure, 65
Asia, 349

Backward linkages, 63, 66, 69. *See also* Investment
Balance of payments, 117, 122, 129; Argentine, 90; crises, 356; gap, 6, 8, 9, 36, 50, 246, 257, 265
Balassa, Bela, 76
Banking system, 231
Banks, commercial, 210, 232
Berg, Elliot, 329
Bird, Richard, 353
Boundary conditions, 11
Brazil, 55, 68

Bruno, Michael, 37, 41, 57
Bruton, Henry, 98
Budget: deficit, 220, 226; policies, 216; revenues, 150. *See also* Taxes
Burns, Arthur, 74, 77

Capital: coefficients, 10; exports, 57; flight, 65, 123, 127, 130; foreign, 164, 211, 216, 321; formation, 144; productivity of, 103; transfers, 50, 187
Capital goods: imports of, 62, 263; taxes on, 262–264
Capital intensity, 64–65, 262
Capital-output ratios, 62, 64
Capital stock, 64
Central American Common Market, 55
Certainty-equivalence, 47
Chenery, Hollis B., 37, 41, 57
Chile, 55, 68; agricultural output, 59
Clower, Robert W., 326, 327
Coastal embankments, 294
Coffee: exports, 165; price, 123; smuggling, 123
Coffee Federation, 128, 132, 141
Colombia, 55, 68, 352; constitution of 1958, 120; general plan, 240; sales tax, 239
Comilla, 307
Consejo Nacional de Desarrollo (CONADE), 77
Constitution of Colombia, 120
Constraints, 6; fixed target, 36
Consultative Group (Colombia), 124, 127
Consumer goods, substitution of, 63, 68, 82
Controls: direct, 349; profit, 303
Cooperatives, 311
Coordinating points, 4
Cost of living, 176; of Buenos Aires, 185
Credit: bank, 208, 209; ceilings, 139,